Adrian Gilbert is the bestselling author of *Magi: The Quest for a Secret Tradition* and co-author of *The Orion Mystery*, *The Mayan Prophecies* and *The Holy Kingdom*.

www.**books**at**transworld**.co.uk

Also by Adrian Gilbert

THE ORION MYSTERY
(with Robert Bauval)

THE MAYAN PROPHECIES
(with Maurice Cotterell)

MAGI: THE QUEST FOR A SECRET TRADITION

THE HOLY KINGDOM
(with Alan Wilson and Baram Blackett)

THE COSMIC WISDOM BEYOND ASTROLOGY

SIGNS IN THE SKY

Adrian Gilbert

CORGI BOOKS

SIGNS IN THE SKY
A CORGI BOOK: 0 552 14710 9

Originally published in Great Britain by Bantam Press,
a division of Transworld Publishers

PRINTING HISTORY
Bantam Press edition published 2000
Corgi edition published 2001

1 3 5 7 9 10 8 6 4 2

Set in 10/11pt Sabon by
Falcon Oast Graphic Art.

Corgi Books are published by Transworld Publishers,
61–63 Uxbridge Road, London W5 5SA,
a division of The Random House Group Ltd,
in Australia by Random House Australia (Pty) Ltd,
20 Alfred Street, Milsons Point, Sydney, NSW 2061, Australia,
in New Zealand by Random House New Zealand Ltd,
18 Poland Road, Glenfield, Auckland 10, New Zealand
and in South Africa by Random House (Pty) Ltd,
Endulini, 5a Jubilee Road, Parktown 2193, South Africa.

Printed and bound in Great Britain by
Cox & Wyman Ltd, Reading, Berkshire.

For all those, eminent or humble, who are following
the Way that leads beyond the stars.

CONTENTS

LIST OF PLATES

LIST OF ILLUSTRATIONS

ACKNOWLEDGEMENTS

My heartfelt thanks first to my wife, Dee, who has had to put up with much while this book was taking shape. Sincere thanks also to Bill Hamilton, Sara Fisher and the rest of the staff at my agents, A. M. Heath; to Ann Walker and to my friend, the Belgian archaeo-astronomer Gino Ratinckx, for their helpful advice; and to Joe Schor, Elizabeth Joyce and other associates on the 'Egypt' team. I hope we soon find the Hall of Records. Thanks are due to David Lewis, who drew the 'cartouche' illustrations in the colour sections as well as some of the other diagrams; also to Bengt Alfredson, who, in 'Opening the Stargate', has once again produced a painting that is star-correct and also encapsulates in visual form the philosophy behind my work. A big thank-you to Uri Geller for his encouragement and to my friend Noel Tyl, tallest astrologer in the world and a master of his subject. Many thanks, too, to all those others, too many to mention by name, in Israel, Egypt, Turkey, the USA, Britain and elsewhere, whose paths I have crossed while making this journey. My thanks to the following publishers: Penguin Books; Thames & Hudson; Aris & Phillips; Oxford at the Clarendon Press and many others whose published works have either been quoted from or have given inspiration. A final word of thanks to Sally Gaminara, Katrina Whone, Simon Thorogood, Prue Jeffries and the rest of the staff at Transworld who have worked so hard to make this book a success.

PREFACE

In October 1995, on a visit to Washington DC, I was interviewed on Voice of America, the US radio station that broadcasts around the world. It was a curious time to be in the US capital, for in the wake of a budgetary debacle and the ensuing stand-off between the President and the Congress, thousands of civil servants had been suspended, and as a result the major offices of state were closed and the streets almost deserted. The interview itself was an equally curious experience: for an hour I, a Briton, was quite literally the voice of America, the most powerful country in the world, as heard by millions of people around the globe. What made the experience all the more awesome was that the subject under discussion was not football, trade, finance or any of the usual pan-global concerns that fill the airwaves but a prophecy made thousands of years ago by the Mayan Indians that the world – or rather, this present age of the world – would come to an end on 21 December 2012: a date well within the expected life-span of myself and also of the majority of the listeners.

I spoke for a few minutes, outlining the thesis that world ages are linked to sun-spot cycles, and explaining the theory that the changes we are now experiencing in the climate of our planet have more to do with fluctuating solar emissions than with the 'greenhouse effect'; then the producers opened the lines for a live phone-in. Soon

I was fielding questions from right around the world: from callers in China and Saudi Arabia, Nigeria and the West Indies. The debate spread rapidly from the narrow confines of the Mayan calendar to the wider question of the Christian millennium. Was there any evidence, astronomical or otherwise, my callers wanted to know, that the prophecies in the Bible were coming true? Were we approaching the end of days spoken of in Matthew's Gospel and in the Apocalypse of St John?

I replied that I believed this was indeed so. For one thing, we had seen the return of the Jews to Palestine after nearly 2,000 years, an event of huge political and religious moment that was predicted by Jesus himself. Secondly, there was a 'sign in the sky', again prophesied by Jesus, that had not occurred for nearly 26,000 years. This sign was the group of stars called the Belt of Orion, which for the past 12,500 years or so had been drifting further and further north. At present, I said, it is situated with its most northerly star, Mintaka, just below the celestial equator. However, it would never actually cross the equator before it began its return journey back to its most southerly position. In other words, it was just reaching its turning point. 'The constellation Orion', I explained, 'is the symbol of the Son of man in heaven and the star Mintaka of his belt can now be seen throughout the entire world, from the North to the South pole. It is one of the signs we have been told to look out for in the Bible and is the Christian equivalent of a Mayan prophecy for the end of time.'

As I uttered these words I was extremely nervous. Here I was on Voice of America, telling the people of the world that there were signs in the sky indicating the end of the current age. It was no trivial matter, and I was aware that I could be cut off at any time should what I say be deemed at variance with US policy on these matters. Yet nobody at the station seemed to mind, and so I was able to carry on discussing these ideas with the listeners. It was not possible, however, in the short time available, to go into any great detail or to present all the evidence, both astronomical and archaeological, that I had to hand. Without this supporting evidence, gleaned over more than a quarter of a century, what I had to say that day may have seemed like the ravings of a street preacher. But I am not one of those; nor am I a psychic channel, clairvoyant or any sort of New Age prophet of doom. What I was talking about then and have since elaborated into the present book is based on fact and the logical evaluation of evidence. These facts are presented here in print for the first time.

I am able to say with certainty that an alarm bell predicted by the ancients is about to ring. Yet I do not promise fire and brimstone on the heads of those who choose to ignore what I say. It may be that though the bell rings, we are able to turn over in our beds and go back to sleep. On the other hand, it may not be an alarm bell at all that is going to ring but the timing clock on some other form of device that is going to shock us beyond our wildest imaginings. Which it is, I cannot be sure, though as a matter of faith I tend towards the latter view. Those reading this book must make up their own minds; my work will have been done in presenting the facts.

Adrian G. Gilbert
2000

For up-to-date information on this book and related issues, Adrian Gilbert can be contacted through his website at www.AdrianGilbert.co.uk

PROLOGUE

We have reached the millennium year 2000; a short moment in time that humankind has both longed for and dreaded. What is its real significance – if any? Is it simply, as the sceptical will surely assert, no more than the turning of a page in a calendar whose start was arbitrary and therefore whose 2,000th year is equally without meaning? Or is there, as many Christians believe, something more to it than that: the ending of one epoch and the start of another?

These are ideas and questions with which I, like many others, have wrestled throughout my adult life. Having lived through the halcyon days of the 1960s with their atmosphere of pregnant possibility, of hope for a better, more enlightened world, I am aware of the dangers of prophesying a new era that may never arrive. I have lived through the hangover of the seventies which followed the sixties party. I have witnessed the selfish greed of the eighties and the political uncertainty of the nineties that followed the defeat of communism and the falling of the Berlin Wall. Yet none of these decades has, I believe, prepared us for what is to come in the very near future.

In ancient Egypt, around 3100 BC, a king from the south named Narmer or Menes invaded the northern delta region and united Upper with Lower Egypt. He built a new capital at Memphis, close to where the apex of the Nile delta meets the slender valley of the river, and founded what was to become the First Dynasty. Near here, some four or five hundred years later, the first pyramids would be built.

At the time that Menes was consolidating his power in Memphis, on the other side of the Atlantic the Mayan Indians were beginning their own 'Age of the Jaguar'; here in Britain, meanwhile, our own New Stone Age ancestors were also building temples. The first phase of what was to become the most mysterious of these, Stonehenge, we now know from radiocarbon dating to have been begun around 3100 BC. Even then, perhaps a millennium before the famous trilithons were raised, Stonehenge I featured the alignment with sunrise at the summer solstice that is still celebrated to this day. The building of astronomically aligned stone circles in Britain was a radical departure from the past, and while the causes for this change are the subject of debate, there is no disputing that *c*.3100 BC marks the start of the New Stone Age (Neolithic) period not just in Britain but also in other countries of the Atlantic seaboard such as France and Portugal. Thus a new age began in America, Africa and Europe – on each continent at around the same time.

To identify the start of an 'age' is immediately to raise the question of its end; and when the age is our own, we naturally want to know how and when this is likely to come about. Inscriptions in a temple at Palenque in Mexico tell us that the Mayans believed that their previous age ended in a cataclysm after it had run for a period of thirteen *baktuns* (a *baktun* is a period of time equal to 400 *tuns*, each of which consists of 360 days). By their reckoning, the thirteenth *baktun* of our own age will come to an end on a date which, measured on our own Gregorian calendar, turns out to be 21 December AD 2012. As this is only (nearly) thirteen years after our own millennium, the date should perhaps give us pause for thought: if we follow the Mayan calendar and accept that each age is thirteen *baktuns* long, then we are fast approaching the end of what they called the Age of the Jaguar.

There are, of course, other reasons for concern, for we have only to look around us to see that things cannot go on as they are. Moment by moment we are depleting the earth's reserves of oil, gas and other minerals. Though we may be more technologically advanced than our fore-bears, we appear unable to halt the growing desertification of large swathes of the planet's land mass. Our record (and still growing) population of 6 billion or more is putting increasing pressure on the biosphere, which cannot support all our wants as well as maintain the level of biodiversity that we all agree is not just desir-able but essential. Human-induced global warming has exacerbated changes in our weather patterns, which are becoming more extreme and more unpredictable, threat-ening large-scale disruption to humanity and the natural world. We have polluted the land, the air and the seas with a cocktail of poisons that include not only such deadly chemicals as the dioxins but even plutonium, the radioactive element at the heart of nuclear weapons. If ever a species fouled its own nest, it is ours; and you don't have to be a supporter of Greenpeace to know that we cannot carry on in this way indefinitely. Sooner or later we must take responsibility for our actions and seek to put right the damage we have done to the earth. If we don't, there will be no earth – or at least, not one capable of supporting life as we know it.

To add to our confusion, we also find ourselves in a moral maze, as the religious certainties of yesterday have dissolved into a confused mass of contradictory philo-sophies and belief-systems. In the affluent countries of the West, Christian morality has been replaced by cultural relativism. It is no longer held possible to say with certainty what is right or wrong, only what is politically correct. Ours is a time of *fin de siècle* anxiety and decadence; and the feeling we have of being at sea without a compass is, I believe, at the heart of much of our millenarian angst. Yet there are signposts if we know where to look for them: astronomical 'signs in the sky',

21

which indicate that we are in for a time of change. It is my contention that certain wise men in ancient times knew this. They foresaw what was going to happen in our time and coded this knowledge in their monuments, most especially the pyramids of Giza.

In our book *The Mayan Prophecies*, Maurice Cotterell and I drew attention to an uncanny correlation between long-period sun-spot cycles and the Mayan calendar. This calendar, which is not Judeo-Christian in its origins, numbers the days of the great Age of the Jaguar that began in 3114 BC. We don't know what exactly happened in Mexico and its surrounding area at that time, but it must have been something remarkable to cause the Central American Mayans to take it as year zero of their calendar. The expectation that there would be a time of crisis at the end of the current age also seems to have been well known to the prophets who wrote the texts we now know as the Bible. Foremost among these prophets we must count Jesus Christ, whom millions of people, not all of them Christians, expect to return to earth at the 'end of time'. In the Gospel according to St Matthew he left clear instructions to his disciples as to what they should look out for as signs indicating that that time was near. These signs, when interpreted astrologically, repeat the message of the pyramids and indicate that that time is now.

Matthew's Gospel is the first book of our New Testament; the last is the Apocalypse or Revelation of St John the Divine, a curiously abstract work, filled with dream-like sequences that symbolize what will come about at the end of the present age. Over the centuries many people, with varying success, have tried to break its code; yet it has in essence remained a mystery. What is clear, though, to anyone making even a partial study of its content, is that astrology is one of the most important keys for unlocking the prophecies it contains. To take just one example, we might consider the description of the throne of God given in chapter 4, verses 6–8:

And before the throne was a sea of glass like unto crystal: and in the midst of the throne, and round about the throne, were four beasts full of eyes before and behind.

And the first beast was like a lion, and the second beast like a calf, and the third beast had the face of a man, and the fourth beast was like a flying eagle.

And the four beasts had each of them six wings about him, and they were full of eyes within: and they rest not day and night, saying, Holy, Holy, Holy, Lord God Almighty, which was and is, and is to come.

It is clear from this short extract that the four beasts are analogues of the four fixed signs of the zodiac: Leo, Taurus, Aquarius and Scorpio (which is commonly represented by an eagle or phoenix in Christian iconography, this being considered the 'higher aspect' of the sign). The 'eyes' are stars and the six times four wings, twenty-four in all, rotate the celestial or highest 'crystal' sphere through a constantly repeating cycle every twenty-four hours. Thus the entire universe is said to be constantly uttering a prayer to God, throughout the day and night and all through time.

This passage is but one illustration of the astrological underpinnings of Revelation. Throughout the entire book there are references to the seven planets of the ancients, which are described obliquely as candles or lamps. The two luminaries, the sun and moon, are included among the seven along with the visible planets: Mercury, Venus, Mars, Jupiter and Saturn. These were the only planets, or 'wandering stars', known to the ancients, and it was generally believed not only that they were moved in their spheres by guiding intelligences but that they ruled over the 'lower heavens' as lesser manifestations of the invisible spirit of God.

The Book of Genesis, at the very start of the Bible, tells us that the stars were put in the heavens for 'signs and for seasons'. Without doubt the ancients were more familiar with these than we are today, when most people live in or near towns and cities and rarely get a chance to see the sky without the glare of street lights. It is my contention that if we want to understand the Bible then we need to have a grasp of at least the rudiments of astrology, to be able to recognize the signs in the sky which we have been warned to look out for. Unfortunately the church, out of what I believe to be a misguided attempt to protect believers from falsehood, has completely turned its back on astrology, and many Christians today, so far from realizing that it is one of the keys to a correct inter-pretation of biblical prophecy, fear that astrology is a black art that will lead to damnation. It is certainly true that astrology has in the past been practised in a negative way by satanists and others with evil motives, who have tainted by association what was once considered the highest of sciences. However, the astrology under dis-cussion here has nothing to do with the occult, or even with daily horoscopes. My concern is not with any in-fluence, real or imagined, that the stars themselves might have on our lives, but rather with cycles of time and how these are recognizable in the position of the stars.

The measurement of time cycles was a matter of great importance to our forebears. They were also wise con-cerning other important matters (such as the vulnerability of the earth's ecosystem to global warming) which we ignore at our peril. Much of this knowledge has, unfortunately, been lost to sight over the ages. However, fortunately for us the ancients took the precaution of concealing what they knew in places and in ways that would ensure its preservation at least, if not its intelligi-bility to later generations. The keys that unlock this wisdom of the past are astronomy, archaeology and the perception that ancient art was not a form of self-indulgence but a means of conveying knowledge. Most if not all sacred buildings – pyramids, temples and the like – were constructed to conform to a secret canon known only to initiates. This body of law, which embraced such seemingly mundane matters as weights and measures, as well as the harmonics of proportion, numerology and astronomy, finds its expression throughout the world.

Though the canon as a whole has been lost, elements of it have come down to us in the works of Pythagoras, Euclid, Ptolemy of Alexandria and Vitruvius. These Latin and Greek writers, who were themselves initiates into the 'Mysteries', arcane systems of knowledge connected with religious belief and practice, were profoundly influenced, directly or indirectly, by the secret traditions of Egypt and Mesopotamia. These civilizations not only preceded that of ancient Israel but were, in some senses, its foster-parents: at the time of Joseph, so the Bible tells us, the Hebrews migrated from their more northerly lands to Egypt and settled there for some generations before being led out by Moses, during which time they adapted many Egyptian ways and customs. Egyptian and Mesopotamian civilization thus had an enormous influence on the development of Hebrew thought as it is expressed in the Bible. Indeed Moses, believed by Jews and Christians to have written the Pentateuch (the first five books of the Bible), is clearly stated as having been schooled in the wisdom of the Egyptians. This wisdom, or gnosis, would have included astronomy and astrology – the two subjects were not then divorced – as well as other aspects of the canon. Most importantly, Moses would have known that the maxim 'as above, so below' pertained to the laying out of Egyptian temples. He would have been well aware that sacred buildings, and indeed whole cities, were ideally designed in such a way that they should be microcosms of the macrocosm: models of the greater universe.

This gnostic inheritance passed secretly, from Egyptian and Mesopotamian sources as well as by way of early Judaism, into Christianity. Thus it is that the church (by which I mean the whole body of the Christian congregation and not any one denomination) knowingly or unknowingly inherited elements of the sacred canon. Though their descendants from the fourth century onwards were persecuted as heretics, the gnostics of Egypt and Mesopotamia were highly influential in the formation of the early church; indeed, many of their ideas have survived in a disguised form in the very texts that make up the New Testament. Consequently, by applying the keys of wisdom gained from the study of ancient Egyptian and Mesopotamian fragments we are able to unlock some of the most abstruse passages in the Bible. This is made much easier for us by the advent of modern computers and calculators, which can perform in moments calculations which even a generation ago would have taken days. Thus it is that we have available to us today the tools and the material to gain access to the innermost secrets of biblical prophecy.

Though a Christian I am not a fanatic, and certainly not a believer in the supremacy of any one church or denomination. In this book I attempt to present the often startling evidence which has come into my hands in as unbiased and logical a way as possible, so that any intelligent person may read the signs for him- or herself. I do not claim infallibility, nor that I am right in every single detail. However, I am sure that the factual evidence presented here is correct, even if at times I may have inadvertently made mistakes in its interpretation. It will be up to the reader to judge the case I make on its own merits.

CHAPTER 1

IN THE LAND OF THE PROPHETS

In 1972, following a long pilgrimage by bicycle to Israel, I spent some months working on a kibbutz – a collective farm, jointly owned by its members and run for the good of all. Though they have changed with the times, the kibbutzim were originally founded on socialist principles and in their early days had provided shelter and security for the thousands of mostly destitute Jews who had fled Europe in the aftermath of the Second World War. This security, however, had come at a price. Most of the kibbutzim were founded on uncultivated land – marshland or semi-arid desert which required tremendous effort to make it bloom. As if this did not make life for the first kibbutzniks hard enough, many of the kibbutzim were deliberately placed on Israel's borders with its hostile neighbours and so acted as front-line defences for the little country. Unlike, say, Tel Aviv or Haifa, these border kibbutzim were subject to regular commando raids and rocket attacks could be expected at any time. As a result the *sabras* who peopled these frontier settlements – young Israelis whose nickname likened them to wild cacti, prickly on the outside but soft and succulent within – had grown up knowing nothing else but a state of war, and were quite a wild bunch. Conscripted as teenagers, these young men carried sub-machine guns at all times. Rough and ready in their ways, they were the backbone of the Israeli army and still its most deadly weapon. When I arrived in Israel these gun-toting *sabras* were the most visible sign that the war with the

Arabs was by no means over; and there were other reminders, such as the occasional rocket attack on Kiryat Shemona, the nearest town to the kibbutz.

Kibbutz Kefar Szold was in Upper Galilee, on the edge of the Hula valley at the foot of the Golan Heights, close to Israel's north-eastern border with Syria. Prior to the Second World War the Hula valley, which enjoys a more temperate climate than most of Israel, had been a malarial swamp. Today it is a lush area of citrus groves and cotton fields. That the pioneer farmers had been able to transform this unpromising area into a productive paradise was a striking achievement and one of which the kibbutzniks were rightly proud. History is never long out of mind in this part of the world, for over the millennia invader after invader – Egyptian, Assyrian, Greek, Roman, crusader – has passed this way en route to or from Damascus and the cities of northern Mesopotamia. Upper Galilee is still strategically important today, for from this region emerge most of the springs and streams which supply the River Jordan with its life-giving water. One of these sources was by the ancient Canaanite city of Laish, which was captured by the ancient Israelites following the biblical Exodus and renamed Dan after the tribe who settled there. In the Bible it is famous as the most northerly city of David's Israel, Beersheba being the most southerly. Today Tel Dan is a nature reserve, the role of northern border town having passed to nearby Metula.

A few miles east of Dan and slightly to the south are the ruins of the ancient shrine of Paneas, built around a grotto from which flows another spring feeding the Jordan. Here the worshippers of Baal once revelled, to be replaced in Greco-Roman times by the cult followers of Pan. Shortly before the time of Jesus, Augustus, the first Roman emperor and nephew of Julius Caesar, entrusted the whole region of Upper Galilee to King Herod. He, in gratitude to his benefactor, erected a temple to the 'god' Augustus at Paneas. Philip the Tetrarch, who inherited

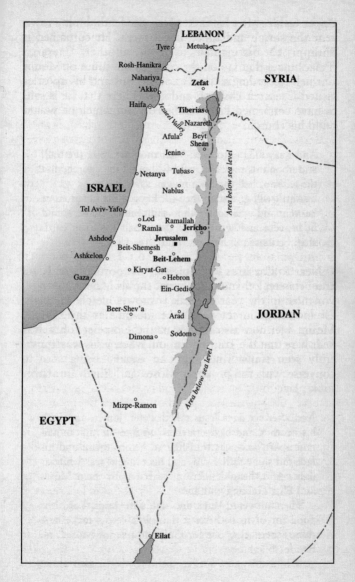

Upper Galilee after his father Herod's death, built a town near the shrine and called it Caesarea. He surnamed it Philippi to distinguish it from another Caesarea (Palaestinae) that lay on the coast to the south of Mount Carmel. According to the Gospels, Jesus and his apostles visited Caesarea Philippi, and it was here that he is said to have confirmed Peter as the rock on which he would build his church:

> And I say also unto thee, That thou art Peter [Petros], and upon this rock [petros] I will build my church; and the gates of hell shall not prevail against it.
>
> And I will give unto thee the keys of the kingdom of heaven: and whatsoever thou shalt bind shall be bound in heaven: and whatsoever thou shalt loose on earth shall be loosed in heaven. (Matt. 16: 18–19)

Near to Caesarea Philippi, over the border from Israel and between Lebanon and Syria, stands Mount Hermon. For most of the year its peak is snow-covered; the highest mountain in the Levant, it dominates the skyline. Mount Hermon also figures in the Gospels, for it was near here that the Transfiguration, when Jesus was apparently seen transformed into an angelic being able to converse with the prophets Moses and Elijah, probably took place:[1]

> And after six days Jesus taketh Peter, James, and John his brother, and bringeth them up into an high mountain apart, and was transfigured before them: and his face did shine as the sun, and his raiment was white as light. And, behold, there appeared unto them Moses and Elijah talking with him.
>
> Then answered Peter, and said unto Jesus, Lord it is good for us to be here: if thou wilt, let us make here three tabernacles; one for thee, and one for Moses and one for Elijah.
>
> While he yet spake, behold, a bright cloud

overshadowed them: and behold a voice out of the cloud, which said, This is my beloved Son, in whom I am well pleased; hear ye him.

And when the disciples heard it, they fell on their faces and were sore afraid.

And Jesus came and touched them, and said, Arise and be not afraid.

And when they had lifted up their eyes, they saw no man, save Jesus only.

And as they came down from the mountain, Jesus charged them, saying, Tell the vision to no man, until the Son of man be risen again from the dead.

And his disciples asked him, saying, Why then say the scribes that Elijah must first come?

And Jesus answered and said unto them, Elijah truly shall first come, and restore all things.

But I say unto you, that Elijah is come already, and they knew him not, but have done unto him whatsoever they listed. Likewise shall the Son of man suffer of them.

Then the disciples understood that he spake unto them of John the Baptist. (Matt. 17: 1–13)

Walking in the Golan nearly 2,000 years later, it seemed possible that Jesus and his apostles could appear at any moment, as though the Transfiguration had only just taken place. Their experiences and conversations seemed somehow to be still imprinted into the landscape of northern Galilee. This was my introduction to the Holy Land; but it would be another twenty-five years before I began to understand what the events described in the Gospels were really all about.

In 1972 Israel's remarkable victory in the Six Day War of 1967 was still fresh in minds and, as this campaign had led to the Jews taking possession of the old city of Jerusalem for the first time since they were expelled from it by the Romans in AD 70, there was a tangible feeling of prophecies being fulfilled. Even at that time there was in

31

Israel an atmosphere of what might be called millennial expectation, though the change of the centuries was still some three decades off. Indeed, for many the rebirth of the state of Israel and its success in capturing Jerusalem seemed to symbolize the birth of a new age.

Often, after my day's work picking grapefruit in the orchards of the kibbutz, I would take my Bible and walk along narrow paths to the heights. Here in the foothills of the Golan, with a view over much of the Hula valley, I would sometimes sit for an hour or more reading, pondering and watching the sun setting far to the west. In that direction lay Safad, which long before the formation of the present state of Israel was for centuries the capital of Galilee and an important centre for the study of the esoteric Jewish teachings known as the Kabbalah.

Beyond Safad, though not visible, stood Mount Megiddo. Possession of this prominent peak, which overlooks the fertile Jezreel valley, has been contested throughout history. Hieroglyphics on the walls of the Egyptian Temple of Karnac give details of a bloody war fought here in c.1468 BC by the pharaoh Tuthmosis III. The stronghold he built fell centuries later to King David of the Israelites. Under David's son Solomon, Megiddo became a prosperous city, one of the jewels in the crown. The Bible speaks of Solomon's 'cities of chariots and cities of horsemen' (1 Kings 9: 19); Megiddo must have been one of these, for traces remain of stables large enough to have held thousands of horses. Megiddo was again an important stronghold in Roman times, but afterwards fell into decay. It did not, however, lose its strategic importance and more recently, in the First World War, the British army fought a battle nearby. When General Allenby, who led these forces, was elevated to the peerage he took the title Lord Allenby of Megiddo.

According to the Bible, Allenby's will not be the last battle to be fought here. The Hebrew name Har-Megiddo ('Hill of Megiddo') is rendered into Greek as Armageddon. According to Revelation, the armies of the whole world will one day be drawn to Armageddon, where they will be destroyed by an earthquake such as has never before been seen:

> The sixth angel poured his bowl on the great river Euphrates, and its water dried up, to prepare the way for the kings from the east. And I saw issuing from the mouth of the dragon and the mouth of the beast and from the mouth of the false prophet, three foul spirits like frogs; and they are demonic spirits, performing signs, who go abroad to the kings of the whole world, to assemble them for battle on the great day of God the Almighty. ('Lo, I am coming like a thief! Blessed is he who is awake, keeping his garments that he may not go naked and be seen exposed!') And they assembled at the place which is called in Hebrew Armageddon.
>
> The seventh angel poured his bowl into the air, and a great voice came out of the temple, from the throne, saying, 'It is done!' And there were flashes of lightning, loud noises, peals of thunder, and a great earthquake such as had never been seen since men were on the earth, so great was that earthquake. (Rev. 16: 12–17)

Sitting in the hills of the Golan, where rabbit-sized rock hyraxes, called *schwanim* by the Israelis, played among the rocks, it was hard to imagine such an apocalyptic outcome to world history. But then, as if to emphasize the fragility of the current situation, an Israeli jet would go streaking past, shattering the peace and sending the *schwanim* scurrying for their burrows. Suddenly the biblical prophecies of a battle to end all battles at Armageddon did not seem so improbable.

Prophecy interested me even then; I was curious to know whether the events that were taking place in our own times, at the end of the twentieth century, really had been predicted millennia before, and, if so, what this might mean for our generation. Consequently, with little money and away from the distractions of television and newspapers, I spent much time studying my Bible. One prophecy in particular stood out – if only because it was Jesus himself who made it while talking to his apostles on the Mount of Olives a week or so before his crucifixion. It included a description of certain signs in the sky which would signify the end of our present age:

> For as the lightning cometh out of the east, and shineth unto the west; so shall also the coming of the Son of man be.
>
> For wheresoever the carcass is, there will the eagles be gathered together.
>
> Immediately after the tribulation of those days shall the sun be darkened, and the moon shall not give her light, and the stars shall fall from heaven, and powers of the heavens shall be shaken;
>
> And then shall appear the sign of the Son of man in heaven: and then shall all the tribes of the earth mourn, and they shall see the Son of man coming in the clouds of heaven with power and great glory.
>
> And he shall send his angels with a great sound of a trumpet, and they shall gather together the elect from the four winds, from one end of heaven to the other.
>
> Now learn a parable of the fig tree; when his branch is yet tender, and putteth forth leaves, ye know that summer is nigh:
>
> So likewise ye, when ye shall see all these things, know that it is near, even at the doors.
>
> Verily I say unto you, This generation shall not pass, till all these things be fulfilled.
>
> Heaven and earth shall pass away, but my words shall not pass away. (Matt. 24: 27–35)

Reading these prophetic words as the sun went down over the mountains beyond, I was filled with awe and foreboding. Could they indeed be referring to our own time? After all, the 'passing away' of heaven and earth could refer to the changing of the ages from Pisces to

Aquarius – an astronomical fact caused by the steady precession of the equinoxes. The precession is brought about by the attraction to the earth of the moon and planets which circle the sky just off the plane of the earth's movement around the sun. This causes the earth to wobble slightly on its axis, like a spinning top that is running down. Over time the sun's position at the spring equinox, the date when it crosses into the northern hemisphere, gradually shifts backwards through the zodiac. This movement of the sun's equinoctial point is barely perceptible, as an entire cycle of precession (360°) takes roughly 25,800 years. Over a period of approximately 2,160 years it will regress 30°. At the time of Jesus the spring equinox took place on the cusp of Aries and Pisces. Today it is still in Pisces but will soon move into Aquarius. This is why astrologers sometimes talk about the 'dawning of the Age of Aquarius'. All this is clear; but it still didn't explain what could be meant by the 'sign of the Son of man in heaven'. Was this meant to be a metaphysical sign, the appearance in the sky of a flaming cross or chi-rho symbol, for example?[2] Or could it also have an astronomical meaning? At the time I had no answer to this question.

Once the grapefruit-picking season was over, I left the kibbutz and went to Tel Aviv which, though no longer the capital of Israel, remains its most lively city. Here I spent several months working as a chef in the youth hostel on Bnei Dan Street. Like many people of my generation, I was fascinated by the East and regularly practised yoga. It was my intention to go on from Tel Aviv to Eilat, to take a ship to Kenya and to proceed from there to India, where I hoped to find a suitably qualified spiritual teacher. In the meantime, as the hostel was a busy place and a first port of call for many pilgrims – not all of them youthful – en route to the Holy Places, I met many interesting people.

For a couple of weeks there was a man staying at the hostel who stood out from the rest, not just because he was much older than most of the visitors but also because he seemed to radiate a different kind of energy. He would regularly sit on his own, in a corner, reading through and taking notes from a much-thumbed and annotated Bible. Dressed in jeans and a check shirt and always carrying the same canvas bag, he was clearly either American or Canadian. With his weather-beaten face, one could imagine him 'on the road', hitching lifts through the Bible Belt or jumping freight trains to Saskatoon. In short, on the surface he was the archetypal hobo, straight out of a Jack Kerouac novel. Few people would speak to him, perhaps fearing that he was a Jehovah's Witness or some other kind of religious crusader whose conversation would be out of sympathy with the 'free love' ideals of the Woodstock generation. Yet there was something else about this elderly traveller that drew my attention: he had the most extraordinary eyes. Bright blue and shining with an inner light, they gave out a spiritual lumin-escence. In later life I have met other people with this sort of eyes; invariably they are engaged in some kind of inner work or spiritual practice.

It was a week or so before I plucked up the courage to initiate a conversation with the old man by asking him in a semi-jocular fashion what he thought of modern Israel now that the Israelites had returned. He fixed me with a steady gaze and replied ominously, a sly smile creeping over his face: 'Some of the Jews may have returned, but Israel has yet to come. If you knew your Bible you would know this. Are you aware that there is a difference between Israel and Judah?' I had to confess that I didn't, and indeed that my knowledge of the Old Testament was sketchy to say the least. Clearly unsurprised by my reply – he probably expected no better from someone of my generation – he began turning over the pages of his own Bible and pointing out certain passages that he had marked, beginning in the Book of Genesis. He showed me the origins of twelve-tribed Israel: the patriarch Israel (originally called Jacob, brother to Esau), the son of Isaac and grandson of Abraham, had twelve sons; after the Exodus from Egypt, their descendants divided the land of Israel between them, each tribe receiving a portion.[3] He also showed me how the original Kingdom of Israel, as founded at the time of King Saul and consolidated under David, had been divided in two following the death of the latter's son Solomon. Of the original twelve tribes that made up David's Israel, ten, the northern ones led by the tribe of Ephraim, seceded to form a kingdom of their own. This new kingdom was still called Israel (in the Bible it is sometimes called Ephraim, after its leading tribe), but it now had its capital at Samaria, not Jerusalem. There were to be nineteen kings of this northern Kingdom of Israel from Jeroboam I (*c.*931–910 BC) to Hosea (*c.*732–723 BC).

Unfortunately, from the perspective of the Bible, the kings of Israel/Samaria led the people into idolatry. As God's punishment this Kingdom of Israel was destroyed by the Assyrians (*c.*722 BC) and its people taken captive. They were transported out of the Holy Land and re-settled, some of them in northern Mesopotamia (near Harran and on the Chabor river) but most in Medea, a province on the southern fringes of the Caspian Sea. At this point the 'ten lost tribes of Israel' disappear from the Bible narrative. 'The whereabouts of their descendants,' said my informant, 'remains a matter of great contention, although it is prophesied by Ezekiel that they will one day be rediscovered, come back to the Holy Land and be reunited with their brethren. In fact they have to return before the Second Coming of Jesus Christ if certain prophecies in the Bible are to be proven correct.'[4] Continuing his narrative, he informed me that the second, southern kingdom, which comprised only the tribes of Judah and Benjamin and retained the old capital of Jerusalem, was called not Israel but Judah. This kingdom continued in existence long after the destruction of Samaria, until it was finally brought to an end by the Babylonian king, Nebuchadnezzar II: the Nabucco of

Verdi's opera. Its inhabitants were also deported, this time to Babylon.

Realizing that I was in the presence of a biblical expert, I asked the old man about the prophecies made by Jesus in chapter 24 of Matthew's Gospel. He began his reply by explaining that in order to interpret the prophecies contained in the Bible it is first necessary to understand the language of symbolism. He reminded me that the fig tree, which features prominently in this prophecy, was a very important symbol which occurs in several different places in the Bible. 'Now, as everyone knows,' he said, 'the fig is mentioned in the Book of Genesis in the context of supplying Adam and Eve with their first clothes. It does, however, have other significances. Prophetically speaking, the fig tree represented the southern Kingdom of Judah, that is to say the Jews. This kingdom, as I have just told you, was in the main made up of only two tribes, Judah and Benjamin, though it did also include most of the Levites; they were priests and not land-holders like the other tribes.' He then pointed out that in Jeremiah chapter 24 there is a prophecy concerning two baskets of figs 'set before the temple of the Lord': 'One basket had very good figs, even like the figs that are first ripe: and the other basket had very naughty figs, which could not be eaten they were so bad.' The old man, by now visibly excited at having an audience, went on to explain what this was all about. In the context of this prophecy, the 'good figs' represented those Jews taken captive by the Babylonians who first looted Jerusalem c.597 BC, deposing the boy-king Jehoiachin (Jeconiah), who accompanied the captives to Babylon, and placing Zedekiah on the throne of Judah in his place. The 'naughty' figs were the seemingly lucky ones who remained behind with Zedekiah; however, because Zedekiah broke his treaty with Nebuchadnezzar, the king of Babylon, they were, in due course, treated much more harshly than the first. Jeremiah continues:

And as the evil figs, which cannot be eaten, they are so evil; surely thus saith the Lord, so will I give Zedekiah the king of Judah, and his princes, and the residue of Jerusalem, that remain in this land, and them that dwell in the land of Egypt:

And I will deliver them to be removed into all the kingdoms of the earth for their hurt, to be a reproach and a proverb, a taunt and a curse, in all the places whither I shall drive them.

And I will send the sword, the famine and the pestilence among them, till they be consumed from off the land that I gave unto them and to their fathers. (Jer. 24: 8–10)

'Jeremiah's prophecy did indeed come to pass,' the old man said, with relish, 'when ten years later the Babylonians again seized Jerusalem. This time they utterly destroyed the Temple of Solomon and slew King Zedekiah's sons in front of him. Blinding him, they then took the king and the remnant of the Jews, those who survived this campaign, into captivity. Thus was Jeremiah's prophecy about the figs fulfilled.'

The people of Judah remained in captivity until the Persian king Cyrus, a generation or two later, captured Babylon (539 BC) and allowed them to return home (c.520 BC) to Jerusalem to rebuild their temple. This reborn state of Judah continued as a vassal state of first Persia, then Greece and finally Syria (under the Seleucids), until 162 BC when, led by Judas Maccabeus, the Jews revolted. They were successful in gaining their independence and in extending the borders of Judah to encompass even more land than had been occupied by the tribes of Israel at the time of King David. However, this state also was not to last; Judah was soon beset by powerful enemies once more, this time from Rome.

The Hasmonean dynasty founded by the Maccabees was finally brought to an end in 37 BC by Herod the Great, a close ally of Rome (this was the King Herod who met the wise men from the East and ordered the killing of infants in Bethlehem). His kingdom, though larger than that of David, was in reality a Roman protectorate. After his death in 4 BC it was split into four parts. Judea, Samaria and Idumaea passed to his son Archelaus, who was given the title of 'ethnarch' (local/national ruler) by the emperor Augustus. When Archelaus was deposed in AD 7 this territory was merged with the Roman province of Syria and administered by a Roman procurator, who resided at Caesarea Palaestinae. Meanwhile, from 4 BC to AD 39 the provinces of Galilee and Peraea, the region on the east bank of the Jordan river, were ruled over by Herod Antipas, Archelaus' brother, who as ruler of a fourth part of the kingdom bore the title tetrarch. This was the King Herod who ordered the beheading of John the Baptist and later tried Jesus, presumably because, as a Galilean, the latter was one of his subjects. The fourth tetrarchy was that of Abilene, in south-western Syria. According to the Gospels, this was ruled over by a tetrarch called Lysanias. His true identity is disputed by historians, but he does not appear to have been a relative of the three surviving sons of Herod.

The biblical scholar, quoting from Luke's Gospel, went on to explain to me how Jesus, like Jeremiah before him, had used the symbol of the fig tree in one of his parables:

> He [Jesus] spake also this parable: a certain man had a fig tree planted in his vineyard; and he came and sought fruit thereon, and found none.
>
> Then he said unto the dresser of his vineyard, Behold these three years I come seeking fruit on this fig tree, and find none: cut it down; why cumbereth it the ground?
>
> And he answering him said unto him, Lord let it alone this year also, till I shall dig about it, and dung it:
>
> And if it bear fruit, well: and if not, then after that thou shalt cut it down. (Luke 13: 6–9)

The scholar explained at length that this parable referred to the mission of Jesus, who for three years preached in Judea – symbolically the 'vineyard' in which was contained the 'fig tree' of God, that is, the nation of the Jews. The 'Lord' was God, who had sent Jesus, and who was clearly annoyed at finding no 'fruit' (i.e. spiritually advanced people) on his fig tree of Judah. Jesus (the dresser of the vines) then asks that the tree be given another chance while his Gospel is preached.

The choice of the fig tree as a symbol is appropriate. Figs are self-fertilizing and produce fruits one year which will ripen in the next. Thus a good fig tree will always have fruits on it, though at different stages of ripeness. However, as anyone who has ever tried to grow figs will testify, a fig tree has to be properly cultivated right from the start. Its root-ball must be contained in a small area, and the tree must be planted in soil which is not too rich. If these two rules are not followed it will have a tendency to run to leaf and to produce no fruit. By analogy, the nation of Judah was planted by God in similarly tough conditions. Its roots were confined to a small area, the territory of Judea, which, with the exception of a few fertile valleys, was semi-arid or even desert and therefore low in fertility. Even so, by Jesus' day it had symbolically run to leaf and was not producing the required fruits.

In Matthew's Gospel the fig-tree analogy is taken further. Here patience with the fruitless fig tree has clearly once more run out, only this time, in a related story, it is Jesus himself who passes sentence on it:

And when he [Jesus] saw a fig tree in the way, he came to it, and found nothing thereon, but leaves only, and said unto it, Let no fruit grow on thee henceforward for ever. And presently the tree withered away.

And when the disciples saw it, they marvelled, saying, How soon is the fig tree withered away. (Matt. 21: 19–20)

41

'This same miracle of the cursing of the fig tree for bearing no fruit', the old man explained, 'is repeated in Mark chapter 11, so we are evidently supposed to take the story seriously. This curse, like that of Jeremiah centuries earlier, is to be taken quite literally, for in AD 70, little more than a generation after the crucifixion of Jesus, Jerusalem was again ransacked. This time it was the turn of the Romans. Like the Babylonians before them they utterly destroyed the temple, which had been rebuilt by Herod, and those Jews who did not die in the struggle were expelled from their homeland to become wanderers among the nations of the world.'

The scholar went on to explain that it was only after the Second World War, following the appalling European Holocaust, that the Jews were able to return to the Holy Land in substantial numbers, and in 1948 to re-found a state of their own. This eventual return of the Jews to their promised land was, he said, what was prophesied by Jesus in Matthew chapter 24, where he is reported as saying: 'Now learn a parable of the fig tree; when his branch is yet tender, and putteth forth leaves, ye know that summer is nigh.' 'The "putting forth of leaves" on the previously stricken fig tree of Judah', said the old man, 'represented the re-founding of the state of Israel and the Jews' subsequent repossession of their old capital city of Jerusalem in 1967.'

At that point I had to get back to work in the kitchen; and, as the learned American left the next day, I didn't have a chance for any more discussion with him. However, I was frankly amazed by what he had said in the short course of our single conversation. I had been brought up with a strict religious education and thought I knew my New Testament quite well, but no one had ever explained it to me in this way before. I re-read the last part of the prophecy in Matthew's Gospel: 'Verily I say unto you, This generation shall not pass, till all these things be fulfilled. Heaven and earth shall pass away, but my words shall not pass away.' I now reasoned that if the rebirth of the state of Israel really had been prophesied in this manner by Jesus himself, then it could mean that my own generation (those born around 1948) was the one that 'shall not pass away until all these things be accomplished'. With a notional life span of three-score years and ten, this generation born at the time of the re-founding of Israel – the first of the 'baby boomers', in other words – would not 'pass away' until 2018. Thus, if we accept that the fig tree symbolizes the nation of the Jews, and its 'putting forth of leaves' is symbolic of the re-founding of the state of Israel in 1948, then, according to the Bible, a final, prophetic period of seventy years would run out around 2018. This led me again to thinking about what might be meant by the 'sign of the Son of man in the heavens', which is supposed to herald the Second Coming of Jesus Christ at the end of this period. At the time I had no idea what this might be, and assumed that it must be some sort of supernatural phenomenon. A further twenty-five years would go by before I had the answer to this question. In the meantime my youthful adventures continued.

CHAPTER 2

A PYRAMID VISION

While living in Tel Aviv, to supplement my income from the hostel I had a second job sitting as a life model at a local art school. Though the work itself was both boring and poorly paid, at least my training in yoga made it quite easy to sit still for long periods. As a bonus I became quite friendly with several of the students attending the college, some of whom were my own age. One of them was a girl called Anna, who despite being a paraplegic and therefore confined to a wheelchair was one of the best artists in the class. As she spoke good English and was deeply interested in philosophy, I had several long conversations with her after class. Given my interest at that time in yoga, it was not long before the subject of India came up. She, it transpired, had grown up there, where her father had been a professor at one of the leading universities. Inevitably, I told her of my plans to visit the country and asked her for advice on places and people to see. I was very surprised and not a little put out by her reply.

'Adrian,' she said, 'don't do it. You're not ready mentally for such a journey. When my father was a professor in India we met many people such as yourself, Westerners full of enthusiasm and keen to learn about the mysteries of the East. The trouble is that, having grown up in the West, they didn't, and indeed couldn't be expected to, have an understanding of Eastern philosophy. This perhaps would not have mattered had they had a strong grounding in the culture of the West. Unfortunately, for the most part they had little understanding of Western philosophy either. With no definable or at any rate strong religious beliefs of their own, they attempted to fill the void with Hinduism, Buddhism or one of the other traditions of India. The result was almost invariably catastrophic for the individual involved. He or she would end up with two half-understandings of mutually incompatible belief-systems. They couldn't wholly abandon their Judeo-Christian inheritance without losing their own identity in the process, while at the same time they couldn't properly enter into the life of India because to those around them they were still foreigners, no matter how hard they tried to fit in. The result is that they would become totally confused and not a little unbalanced. Often they would end up as drifters, unable to settle down because they were so at sea within themselves. Also, most of them had at some time or other experimented with drugs as a quick way to enlightenment, and in India where cannabis and opium are readily and cheaply available it was all too easy for those of weak personality to slip into addiction and an early death. My father saw this happen many times with tragic consequences for the individuals involved. I would therefore recommend you strongly against going to India at this time. First study your own culture and what it has to offer – not just in a superficial way but in depth. Study Western ideas on self-development and undertake practices that will strengthen your will. Then, when you have attained a certain level of self-discipline and understanding both about yourself and the culture from which you come, you may be able to approach the East without falling into the same trap as the foolish young men my father used to meet.'

We only met on a few occasions but her words, spoken with candour and without any trace of bigotry, had a powerful effect. They set me on a course that was ultimately to lead to the most extraordinary discovery of my life: that the prophecies for the end of time really do refer to our own age.

I left Israel in May 1973, returning home to England for only a couple of months before setting off again, this time across the Atlantic. While travelling through Europe and then working in Israel I had made a number of friends – young people like myself, most of them Americans, who were out to explore as much as they could of the world and to have a bit of adventure in their lives before settling down. One of my new American friends was a girl called Christi, whom I met in Crete. Then in her early twenties, she had amazing blue eyes which, like those of the old scholar in Tel Aviv, shone with a special quality of spirit. On my way home I visited her in Germany, where she was studying at Stuttgart University, and she came back to England with me.

While in London Christi and I decided to pay a visit to the British Museum. This was to be a first time for us both, as although I lived in the capital and regularly visited art galleries such as the National and the Tate, I had never been to Britain's premier museum. The highlight of our visit, and one of the principal reasons for making it, was to see the mummy collection. So, having first marvelled at sculptures from Greece, Assyria and above all Egypt, we climbed the broad staircase leading from the entrance hall and wound our way through several rooms of Roman artefacts before suddenly finding ourselves confronted by rows of mummy cases. Some were empty; some still contained mummies, so carefully bound in their time-blackened bandages that it seemed a shame anyone should ever have thought of unwrapping such eternal parcels. Yet we could sense that all was not well. Although the mummies were behind glass, they still seemed to give off a curious smell of death and corruption. My heart began to race and a strange panic came over me. I felt pressure in my solar plexus which made it difficult to breathe; in sheer terror I rushed out of the room, and out of the building. Christi, who had had much the same experience, was by my side, and we both kept running until we were safely outside the black and gold railings which surround the museum compound. There we collapsed in a heap, puffing and panting, the strange feeling of psychic attack having passed.

Just what happened to us among the mummies I have to this day been unable to fathom. The room was crowded at the time, yet everyone else in there seemed to be oblivious to what we were experiencing. Whether we had encountered some sort of guardian entity or a manifestation of a 'Tutankhamun's curse' is a matter for conjecture. But I am in absolutely no doubt that the terror was real, and it did seem to be closely connected with the mummies. Since then I have, over the years, visited the British Museum on hundreds of occasions, and even been back many times into the room containing the mummies. On none of these visits has there been any recurrence of the strange terror I felt then, though to my nose mummies do still give off a strange smell of musty corruption. All I can suggest is that at that time in my life, when I was still regularly practising yoga, I was more psychically sensitive than I am now, and perhaps receptive to the anguish felt by one or more of the spirits associated with the mummies, either because of an untimely death or because their mortal remains had been removed from what should have been their eternal grave. Whatever it was, this experience was the beginning of what was to develop into a fascination with ancient Egypt that in later years has dominated my life.

During our short time together in London, Christi told me about her family and her roots in Oregon in the Pacific north-west of the United States. The land she described sounded not unlike Norway, which I had visited two years before, and I was not surprised to hear that it had been largely settled by Scandinavians. Her family was large and was of Irish-American stock though, surprisingly, they were not Roman Catholics. She talked about her parents with great affection, and it quickly became clear that she had inherited something special from them – the same something that shone out of her eyes in the spiritual look I had first noticed in her. Her father, she said, had spent years studying the paranormal in spiritual matters. In particular, he had developed a technique for past-life recall whereby he could put people into a mild trance state and enable them to remember events from previous lives. Apparently, though buried deeply in the subconscious, powerful events and especially traumas that had occurred in previous lives could continue to make their effects felt in the present. Such legacies of former experiences, she said, could explain otherwise irrational behaviour and phobias about certain people and places. This intrigued me. Having read several books about Edgar Cayce, the famous American 'sleeping prophet' who, in a similar trance state, had made amazing predictions concerning the changes to come at the end of the present age (in particular the imminent reappearance of Atlantis and the discovery of a secret chamber of records near the Great Sphinx of Giza), I was very keen to find out more. Thus it was that I found myself flying out to Oregon, both to see Christi and to meet her parents.

The state of Oregon turned out to be all that I had expected and more. As the plane approached Portland, the state capital, I could see the majestic cone of Mount Baker, an extinct volcano, poking above the clouds. Beyond, in the distance over the border with Washington State, were two other volcanic peaks: Mount Rainier and Mount St Helens. The three peaks were like enormous pyramids and, though asleep at the time, provided a pertinent reminder of our earth's violent past. In fact, this whole western area of the United States is geologically far from dormant. Among the predictions of Edgar Cayce which I had read were quite a number concerning earth changes in the United States. He had predicted that at the end of the twentieth century or soon after, much of both the eastern and western seaboards of America would sink beneath the waves and that a new channel would open up down its centre. This would enable the waters of the Great Lakes to flow down into the Mississippi Basin and hence to drain into the Gulf of Mexico rather than the St Lawrence seaway, as they do at present. While we may be thankful that these extraordinary prophecies have yet to come true, the explosive eruption of Mount St Helens on 18 May 1980 is a timely reminder that earth changes can be both sudden and violent. At the time I saw it from the window of the aeroplane it was a majestic peak, with an icy cone somewhat similar to Mount Fuji in Japan; today this has gone, and north of the mountain, in the direction that the explosion took, the area around the foot of the volcano is still a scene of devastation for many miles. It is only a matter of time before the other volcanic peaks in the Cascade Range erupt, perhaps with more serious consequences for such major cities as Portland and Seattle.

Christi's family owned a small farm overlooking a lake near Junction City. Her parents, both then in their mid-fifties, were remarkable people. Her mother, Alice, was the very archetype of the frontier housewife: knowing, resourceful and with an extraordinary presence that made her stand out from the crowd. Her father, Clarence, was a humble man, who had served his country in the Battle of Midway and still held to the old-style values. Honest, decent and hard-working are adjectives that came to mind, but there was something more than this: a depth of character that was above the ordinary. As well as running the farm (which was really only a small-holding), he was a senior manager at a local power station, but this was only his outside work, the face he showed to the world. His inner life was far more adventurous, as I was to discover.

Christi and her family were generous hosts, showing me round much of Oregon from the Pacific coast to Klamath Falls. However, what was of greater interest to me was Clarence's technique for past-life recall by means of hypnotic regression. As this can be dangerous in the wrong hands, I shall not describe how it was done, nor where he learned how to do it. Suffice it to say that it was very effective, though for me it had a most unexpected result. As I rested on their sofa, with Alice taking notes, Clarence put me into a deep trance and almost immediately my eyes began to move very fast in their sockets. At the same time images flashed up on to the inner screen of my mind. Along with these visual images came a sort of inner commentary, explaining what each symbolized. The images I saw, which I will not describe here, were quite intricate and formed 'movie sequences' that I could replay in my mind over and over again, like video samples. Some of them were universal in nature and could have come straight out of the Book of Revelation. Others were personal and, as I have since discovered, were prophetic of events that were to occur later in my own life. One of the most extraordinary, however, concerned the Great Pyramid of Giza, which at that time I had not yet seen and in which I had little interest. I did not realize then that I was looking at a symbol which would turn out to be of huge significance not only for me personally but also, as we shall see, for the whole world.

Looking back on these events after a gap of some twenty-five years, I have a better perspective on what these symbols meant. Given my interest in the Bible and in biblical prophecy, I can see now that it was not really surprising that in a deep state of trance my mind should tap into such themes in the collective unconscious. What I saw concerning the pyramid, however, was altogether different from what I was expecting in the way of past-life recall. In my dream-like vision I 'saw' the pyramid lacking a capstone and instead surmounted with the symbols of Christianity (the cross), Judaism (the six-pointed Star of David) and Islam (the crescent moon). Now of course, all three of these monotheistic religions stem from the patriarchal faith of Abraham and the prophets, most especially Moses who came out of Egypt.

It could therefore be argued that the pyramid, symbolizing Egypt, signified the wisdom of that country as taken to the Holy Land by Moses. In this sense the three related religions of Judaism, Christianity and Islam are underpinned by the teachings of Moses, symbolized by the pyramid. Yet there seemed to be more to it than this simple equation of pyramid with Moses. The commentary in my head that accompanied the image indicated that this was not really a symbol from the past but rather one of the future. According to this 'knowing' it would be through the pyramid, and what would be discovered there, that the great faiths of the West would eventually solve their differences and be reconciled. Thus this vision was essentially optimistic in tone and prophetic of something yet to happen. I was also 'told' that I would myself in some way be involved in this discovery. Of this there seemed to be no doubt, though at the time, knowing nothing about the pyramids, such an involvement seemed remote indeed.

During the three weeks that followed I had several more regressions, though none as vivid as this first. By the end of that period the summer was nearly over and, as there were other places I wanted to see before leaving America, I set off for California.

Leaving the forested mountains of Oregon I hitchhiked down to Los Angeles, staying with friends in the San Francisco Bay area en route. From LA I hitched along Route 66 to Chicago and from there went on to Wisconsin, where I had friends living in the little town of Racine. There I spent the winter, before heading back to England the following year. Racine had a very good library as well as a bookshop, and during the time I stayed there I read everything I could about the pyramids of Egypt, including a recently published book by Peter Tompkins, *The Secrets of the Great Pyramid*. I was amazed to discover from this that there was a long history of pyramid research and that much of this had focused on the possibility that the Great Pyramid in particular was closely linked with prophecies contained in the Bible. After my trance experience in Oregon, it became clear that this was an area of research I was going to have to investigate; but it would be a long time before I would actually visit Egypt myself. In the meantime I began reading all I could about the country and its religion, which had a profound effect on the development of early Christianity. This is not surprising given that, at the time of Jesus and for several centuries afterwards, Alexandria was the cultural and religious centre of the eastern Mediterranean. The importance of Egypt in the development of Jesus himself is hinted at in the Bible, not least because it was the country of exile for Mary and Joseph immediately after his birth. Could their choice of Egypt as a place of refuge have been a deliberate one? These were matters I now wanted to investigate.

In the Bible, Egypt is the only country outside the immediate region of Israel that Jesus is known to have visited. Taken there as a baby to avoid the wrath of Herod, he must have spent at least a few years of his infancy in that country before returning to Nazareth after Herod's death in 4 BC. (It is now generally accepted that Jesus was born in 6 or 7 BC, not at the end of 1 BC.) Mary and Joseph would most likely have waited a year or two after the king's demise before deciding it was safe enough to return, maybe in 2 BC. So we can surmise that Jesus was probably about five years old, maybe even older, when he saw Nazareth for the first time. In other words, he would no longer have been an infant but a young boy. Having lived in Egypt for virtually all of his life up to that point, he would very likely have been bilingual and able to speak Egyptian as well as his native Aramaic.

Jesus was by all accounts a very intelligent child. In Luke's Gospel we are told that every year he would go up with his parents to the Temple in Jerusalem at the time of the Passover. One year, when he was twelve, much to their dismay he stayed behind. Later they found him sitting with the learned elders, listening and asking

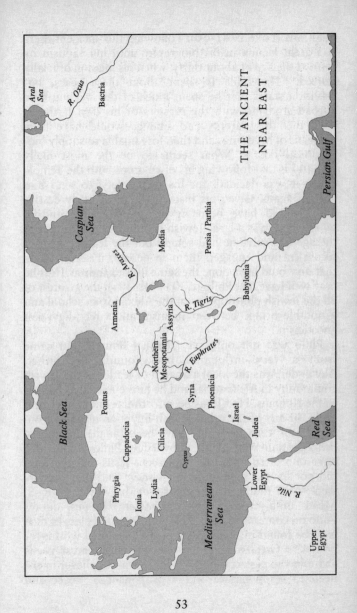

THE ANCIENT
NEAR EAST

Aral Sea

R. Oxus

Bactria

Persian Gulf

Caspian Sea

Media

Persia / Parthia

R. Araxes

R. Tigris

Babylonia

Armenia

Assyria

Northern Mesopotamia

R. Euphrates

Black Sea

Pontus

Syria

Phoenicia

Israel

Judea

Red Sea

Cappadocia

Cilicia

Cyprus

Phrygia

Ionia

Lydia

Lower Egypt

R. Nile

Mediterranean Sea

Upper Egypt

questions (Luke 2: 41–50). Following this incident there is a great lacuna in his biography until his baptism by John at the age of about thirty, when his mission officially started.[1] The Bible is silent about these years, but tradition states that he spent much of this missing time abroad studying with the masters of his day. If this is true, then his parents and siblings would have been ignorant of his doings and therefore unable to supply biographical details. What seems to be the most likely scenario is that following his discussions with the Temple elders it was decided, for his own safety, to send him abroad again. Given his history, the most likely destination would have been Egypt, probably Alexandria, where there was a large Jewish community. Given that at the age of twelve he had sought out the learned men of Jerusalem and engaged them in debate, it seems likely that he would have done the same in Alexandria. Thus he may well have met Philo (c. 30 BC–AD 40+), the greatest of all the Jewish philosophers of the Alexandrian school and a notable bridge between Judaism and Greco-Egyptian gnosticism.

Philo was not only very learned himself, but came from a very influential background. His father, Alexander, was the local alabarch or leader of the Jewish community in Alexandria, and he himself acted as banker to the Romans. Had Jesus been fortunate enough to meet Philo, or any of the other Jewish-Egyptian teachers from his school, then he would have been taught the gnosis, the Egyptian way of all knowledge. Philo would also have impressed upon the adolescent Jesus that the Jews did not have a monopoly on wisdom and that masters were to be found in many parts of the world. G. R. S. Mead, in his trilogy *Thrice Greatest Hermes*, quotes Philo on contemplatives: ' "Now this natural class of men is to be found in many parts of the inhabited world; for both the Grecian and non-Grecian world must needs share in the perfect Good." '[2] Philo was a believer in the need to study nature and a proponent of peace and 'turning the other cheek'. Mead quotes him at length on

> 'all those, whether among Greeks or non-Greeks, who are practisers of wisdom, living a blameless and irreproachable life, determined on doing injury to none, and on not retaliating if injury be done to them, in their enthusiasm for a life of peace free from contention.'
>
> Thus are they 'most excellent contemplators of nature and all things therein; they scrutinise earth and sea, and air and heaven, and the natures therein, their minds responding to the orderly motion of moon and sun, and the choir of all the other stars, both variable and fixed. They have their bodies, indeed, planted on earth below; but for their souls, they have made them wings, so that they speed through the aether, and gaze on every side upon the powers above, as though they were the true world-citizens, most excellent, who dwell in cosmos as their city; such citizens as Wisdom hath as her associates, inscribed upon the roll of Virtue, who hath in charge the supervising of the common weal . . .
>
> 'Such men, though [in comparison] but few in number, keep alive the covered spark of Wisdom secretly, throughout the cities [of the world], in order that Virtue may not be absolutely quenched and vanish from our human kind.'[3]

Among such worthy philosophers, Philo had in mind the Magi, the school of the wise men of Persia from whom came the three visitors to Bethlehem, as well as the yogis of India:

> 'While in non-Grecian lands, in which the most revered and ancient in such words and deeds [have flourished], are very crowded companies of men of worth and virtue; among the Persians, for example, the [caste] of Magi, who by their careful scrutiny of nature's works for purpose of the gnosis of the truth, in quiet silence, and by means of [mystic] images of piercing clarity are

made initiate into the mysteries of godlike virtues, and in their turn initiate [those who come after them]; in India the [caste] of the Gymnosophists,[4] who, in addition to their study of the lore of nature, toil in [the fields of] morals, and [so] make their whole life a practical example of [their] virtue.'[5]

Philo also admired the Essenes, whom we now know to have had a centre at Qumran on the Dead Sea and with whom Jesus and John the Baptist are thought to have been linked, for he writes: 'Nor are Palestine and Syria, in which no small portion of the populous nation of the Jews dwell, unfruitful in worth and virtue. Certain of them are called Essenes, in number upwards of 4,000 according to my estimate.'[6] In his own native land of Egypt mystics were especially plentiful, particularly among the Therapeuts, members of an esoteric school that had its headquarters near Alexandria and to which Philo makes special reference, suggesting that even if he were not one of their number himself, he was a close admirer. Mead has much to say on this subject, comparing Philo's account of Therapeutic teachings and practices with the written words of Jesus in the Gospels.[7]

The testimony of Philo, many of whose books written before Jesus' ministry in Palestine still survive, shows that there were teachers aplenty, in Judea, Egypt and elsewhere, for a young man of philosophical disposition to seek out. We can only conjecture on this, but it seems likely that, as in Jerusalem, the young Jesus would have met with and talked to elders of the Egyptian temples, seeking answers to his most burning questions and learning about their ancient mysteries. At Alexandria, then the intellectual capital of the world, he may have met Philo, who would have been middle-aged at the time. He would also have seen the temples and palaces built by Cleopatra and other rulers of the Ptolemaic dynasty. He would certainly have seen Cleopatra's Needles, the two tall obelisks which now stand one in London and the other in

New York. At that time these peripatetic monuments, which had originally been raised at Heliopolis more than 1,000 years earlier, stood before the Temple of the Caesarium in Alexandria, to which they had been moved by the Emperor Augustus in 14 BC. With his inquisitive mind, it seems certain that Jesus would have wanted to know all about these monuments: how they were made and why they had been erected. Likewise he would also have wanted to know about the pyramids, which even then were of such antiquity that the ordinary people had forgotten almost everything about them.

Jesus may also have ventured further south in Egypt to Asyut. This town, which in recent years has become a hotbed of Islamic rage, is still the home of a large and somewhat persecuted Coptic Christian community. It is here, according to Egyptian tradition, that Jesus, Mary and Joseph lived for most of their time of exile after the flight from Bethlehem. If so, Jesus would almost certainly still have had family friends and maybe even relatives living in the neighbourhood. From a base in Asyut it would have been relatively easy, had he wanted to, to sail up the Nile and visit Egypt's other famous cities and temples at Aswan, Philae, Denderah and Thebes. Here, like generations of other travellers before and since, he would have wondered at the great colossi of Memnon, the temples of Luxor and Karnac, the avenues of sphinxes and, in all he saw, the power and vanity of what was by then a civilization in its death throes.

All this is, of course, conjecture, for we have no firm evidence to back up traditional stories of Jesus' travels to Egypt, Persia, India and even Britain. All we have in the Gospels is evidence indicating that he was a well-educated man, tolerant of foreigners and critical of the establishment. As he also appears to have been in possession of strange, yogic powers over life and death, the ability to see into the future and a willingness to undertake a mission that he knew would lead to his own agonizing death, we may surmise that he was indeed initiated into the higher mysteries. Such people are the rarest of the rare, and it makes sense to think that Jesus was well prepared for his role. Accordingly, it seems to me more likely that he travelled widely, seeking instruction from whatever masters of wisdom he could find, than that he worked quietly in the back room of his father's carpenter's shop prior to launching his extraordinary mission. He would have needed to know about the roots of his own religion of Judaism in the teachings of Moses. He would have wanted to know all he could about the Egyptian religion too, realizing that beneath its veneer of superstition there lay a foundation of ancient wisdom. Philo, if he had met him, would have told him that the mysteries of Egypt owed their origins to Hermes Trismegistus, whom the Jews venerated as the patriarch Enoch. Armed with this understanding he would have wanted to know all about the origins of the pyramids and obelisks, understanding that they were raised for a special purpose perhaps not disconnected from his own mission of redemption.

Two thousand years later it has become clear, to me at least, that – strange as it may seem – at least some of the keys to the prophecies contained in the Christian Bible remain hidden in Egypt. In this respect I am convinced that the vision I had of the pyramid with its symbols at its top is highly relevant, and that the secrets it contains are directly related to our own times, as foreseen and prophesied by Jesus himself.

CHAPTER 3

HERMES AND THE PYRAMIDS

During the 1970s I became more and more interested in Egypt and more especially in that country's premier monuments, the pyramids. Like many others of my generation, I was sure that the pyramids contained a secret; that the reason they were built was not so obvious as it at first seems. What this secret might be I had no way of knowing, but it seemed to be linked with the idea of initiation into the Egyptian mysteries. However, the dream-vision I had had in America of a pyramid surmounted by the symbols of Christianity, Judaism and Islam implied that these extraordinary constructions were of great religious importance, not just for Egyptians but for us as well. I had a sense, heightened when I first saw them for real, that despite their great age the pyramids are more relevant to the present than to the past. For, like a working cathedral or church, they are in a sense still alive and functioning. It seemed likely, therefore, that their secret was not simply a matter of archaeology but of pressing concern for us today. I was later to discover that this sense of their still working in the present was correct, for they are the silent witnesses to the passage of the ages and prophets of the future.

The most famous of the pyramids, those at Giza, are the last remaining of the seven wonders of the ancient world. That they have survived to the present day is itself a marvel, owing as much to their colossal size and solid construction as anything else. The Great Pyramid alone, the largest of the three Giza giants, has been estimated to contain approximately 2.5 million tons of limestone and granite. How this material was cut, transported and used to build probably the most accurately aligned and symmetrical buildings in the world is still a matter of great debate. While the consensus view of most investigators is that it was built by a king called Khufu (or Cheops) some time during the middle of the third millennium BC, there is still wide disagreement as to both how and why he should have raised such a monument. The majority of professional Egyptologists are adamant that this pyramid, like all the others in Egypt, was simply a funerary monument. As far as they are concerned it is little more than a gigantic folly built by an autocratic and perhaps megalomaniac pharaoh, to act as the final resting place for his mummified corpse. Many amateur investigators, on the other hand, have remained unconvinced by this argument – not least because no trace of a mummy has ever been found in the pyramid – and have sought other purposes for its construction. Thus the pyramids in general and the Great Pyramid in particular have been claimed as everything from chambers of initiation to navigational aids for landing UFOs. Not surprisingly, though they will admit to the genius of their ancestors in constructing such perfect monuments, the Egyptian authorities charged with their preservation remain unimpressed by such interpretations.

One reason for this caution on the part of Egyptologists is that during late Victorian times the study of pyramids, or 'pyramidology', became the vehicle for some very strange speculation. Over time, pyramid research became less and less of a science and more and more of a philosophy or cult, so that before long the majority of mainstream scientists dismissed the whole subject as fraudulent. Pyramidologists were labelled 'pyramidiots', and it became a virtual kiss of death for the career of any aspiring Egyptologist to show the slightest interest in pyramids beyond the nuts and bolts level of how and when they were built. This position was clearly put in an interview for the BBC by the late Professor I. E. S. Edwards, a former Keeper of Egyptian Antiquities at the British Museum and one of the few modern Egyptologists to have taken an active interest in pyramid research.

> Pyramids in general are not very popular with Egyptologists because I think they are too plentiful. There are about a hundred of them. And also I think they have acquired something of a bad name because they have attracted so many cranks . . . I can't really offer any kind of opinion on the value of the work of the so-called pyramidologists – well, they are called pyramidiots, of course, so-called pyramidology. I can only say that most of what I can understand doesn't make much sense to me.[1]

In the same programme Dr Vivien Davies, the current Keeper of Egyptian Antiquities, indicated that the attitude of the younger generation of Egyptologists towards pyramid research was no less sceptical: 'I must confess I have never been somebody fascinated by the pyramids, though as a student one of course studied them. It is a curious thing, the Great Pyramid has this power over people. In my view it has the power of destroying common sense.'[2]

This scepticism amongst Egyptologists is not a new thing, as is clear from the writings of the Russian mathematician, journalist and mystic P. D. Ouspensky, who visited Egypt in 1914 on his way home to St Petersburg from India. He, like many others, while interested in astronomical theories was as dismissive of pyramidology as Professor Edwards some eighty years later. His observations are as applicable today as when he was writing:

> At the present time many interesting facts have been established concerning the Great Pyramid. But these

discoveries belong either to astronomers or mathematicians. And if it happens that any Egyptologists speak of them, there are only very few who do so, and their opinions are usually suppressed by others.

In a way the reason for this is understandable, for too much charlatanism has accumulated round the study of the astronomical and mathematical significance of the pyramids. Theories, for instance, exist and books are published proving that the measurements of the various parts and corridors inside the Great Pyramid represent the whole history of mankind from Adam to 'the end of general history'. According to the author of one such book prophecies contained in the pyramid refer chiefly to England and even give the length and duration of post-war cabinets.

The existence of such 'theories' of course makes it clear why science is afraid of new discoveries concerning the pyramids. But this in no way diminishes the value of existing attempts to establish the astronomical and mathematical meaning of the pyramids, in most cases so far only *the Great Pyramid*.[3]

Whatever its effect on common sense, over the centuries the Great Pyramid has attracted not only cranks but also some of the world's best minds. A colossal monument to the genius or folly of man, depending on your point of view, the pyramids have impressed as well as mystified travellers to Egypt throughout known history.

For most of its life the core of the Great Pyramid was shrouded in an outer mantle of white Tura limestone. This was stripped off by the Arabs following the forced opening of the pyramid by the caliph Al Mamoun in AD 820. (Legend has it that the limestone was recycled as building material for the mosques of Cairo.) With a mixture of luck and hard toil his men had succeeded in making their way into the system of chambers and connecting passageways familiar to today's visitors.

However, if they had hoped to find treasure, they were to be sorely disappointed. All that confronted them when they reached the inner sanctum of the King's Chamber was the solitary, empty sarcophagus that remains, even today, the sole piece of ancient furniture to be found inside the pyramid. Searches of the other two large pyramids of Giza, those of Khafre and Menkaure, proved equally fruitless; they too were stripped of most of their facing stones. Vandalized and ruined, the pyramids were once more abandoned to the desert sands, while for the next few centuries the Arabs and Mamelukes got on with the important business of building the glittering city of Cairo.

Though the Arabs seemed to lose all interest in the pyramids once it was discovered they were empty of treasure, they were still a subject of fascination for Europeans and continued, on occasion, to be visited and commented on by adventurers and travellers brave enough and bold enough to hazard a trip. Following the Italian Renaissance, and more specifically the rediscovery of the *Corpus Hermeticum*, which was brought to Florence after the fall of Constantinople in 1453, this interest became more focused. The *Corpus Hermeticum*, like the already known *Asclepius* and a few other frag-mentary works, was believed to have been written by Hermes Trismegistus. This name, which means 'Thrice Greatest Hermes', was what the Greeks called Thoth or Tehuti, the Egyptian god of science and writing. According to the *Hermetica*, Thoth/Hermes had written a number of books. This fact was well known in Europe long before the rediscovery of the *Hermetica* in the fifteenth century. For example, Lactantius, a Christian convert who flourished at the beginning of the fourth century and acted as tutor to Crispus, the eldest son of Constantine the Great, writes in his *Divinae Institutiones*:

Let us now pass to divine testimonies; but first of all, I will bring into court testimony which is like divine [witness], both on account of its exceeding great age, and because he whom I shall name was carried back again from men unto the gods . . .

The Egyptians called him Thoyth, and from him the first month of their year (that is September) has received its name. He also founded a city which even unto this day is called Hermopolis. The people of Pheneus, indeed, worship him as a god; but although he was [really] a man, still he was of such high antiquity, and so deeply versed in every kind of science, that his knowledge of [so] many things and of the arts gained him the title of 'Thrice-greatest'.

He wrote books, indeed many [of them], treating of the Gnosis of things divine, in which he asserts the greatness of the Highest and One and Only God, and calls Him by the same names as we [do] – God and Father.[4]

In the *Hermetica* Hermes is credited with having concealed important records in secret places. These, he prophesied, would later be discovered by the 'gods' Isis and Osiris. Some of his secrets would then be inscribed on obelisks and stelae (tablets) for the benefit of future generations. ''Tis they [Isis and Osiris] who will, says Hermes, learn to know the secrets of my records all, and will make separation of them; and some they will keep for themselves, while those that are best suited for the benefit of mortal men, they will engrave on tablet and obelisk.'[5] From this and other references, it was assumed by Renaissance scholars that the teachings contained in the *Hermetica*, if not transcriptions of what was written on the temple walls and obelisks of Egypt, were based upon these secret records of Thoth. The recovery of the Hermetic writings a thousand years after they had disappeared from Europe was regarded as providential, though it was to have serious religious repercussions.

Thoth/Hermes is a mysterious figure. He was considered important in the middle ages and even earlier because Christian and Muslim scholars alike identified him with the biblical patriarch Enoch – who, according to the Bible, had lived long before the time of Moses, being separated from Adam by only six generations. In the Bible Enoch remains an enigmatic figure, but he is clearly regarded as an important prophet as he is the only person in the Old Testament other than Elijah not to die but to be taken by God straight into heaven: 'And Enoch walked with God: and he was not; for God took him' (Gen. 5: 24). A much fuller account of his visions and prophecies is presented in the so-called Ethiopian Book of Enoch,[6] an apocryphal work clearly known at the time of Jesus as fragments of it have been found among the Dead Sea Scrolls, which all date back to at least AD 70 and most of which are probably decades older. He is also mentioned in the New Testament, in the Epistle of Jude, as a prophet of Judgement Day: 'And Enoch also, the seventh from Adam, prophesied of these [the fallen angels], saying, "Behold, the Lord cometh with ten thousands of his saints, To execute judgement upon all, and to convince all that are ungodly among them of all their ungodly deeds which the ungodly have committed, and of all their hard speeches which ungodly sinners have spoken against Him"' (Jude 14–15). As Enoch came before Moses, anything believed to have been written by him would be far more ancient than any of the texts contained in the Bible. Renaissance scholars did not have access to the Book of Enoch, though they knew it had once existed as it is mentioned by St Augustine. However, by equating Hermes Trismegistus with Enoch, they thought (wrongly, as it turns out) that they had rediscovered some at least of Enoch's writings. This implied that the texts of the *Corpus Hermeticum* were quite literally antediluvian, as according to the Bible Enoch had lived three generations before Noah.

Today we know that the texts of the *Corpus Hermeticum* date from no earlier than a century or two before the time of Christ and probably from a century or two after, so it is perhaps difficult for us to appreciate the excitement that these works generated in Renaissance Florence. As much of what they contain would at the time have been considered heretical, their impact must have been somewhat akin to that in our own time of the Dead Sea Scrolls, whose content has proved so controversial that they have yet to be properly published fifty years after their discovery. Little wonder, then, that Cosimo de' Medici ordered his chief translator of Greek texts, Marsilio Ficino, to put aside the works of Plato and to concentrate instead on the *Corpus Hermeticum*.

To the ancient Egyptians, Hermes (or, more properly speaking, Thoth), as well as being the god of writing who invented the hieroglyphs, was also the teacher who brought the sciences of geometry and architecture to humankind. Consequently, though the architect most closely associated with the building of pyramids, the most geometric of all buildings, was Imhotep,[7] their design was believed to have been inspired by Hermes. Thus it was that from the seventeenth century onwards many European scientists and mathematicians took a keen interest in the Great Pyramid of Giza. It was believed that in designing the pyramids Hermes/Enoch, being aware of the impending disaster of the Flood, had sought to preserve knowledge for future generations. It was his intention, so they reasoned, that as civilization was rebuilt and humankind again became capable of understanding the subtleties of what he had crafted, so scholars would be able to rediscover the lost knowledge he had hidden in the pyramids. European scholars hoped that by unravelling the mysteries of the pyramids, they would rediscover the ancient knowledge lost at the time of Noah's Flood, and in doing so would also find the answers to many questions that bedevilled science in their own day.

From the start European pyramid researchers have fallen into two categories. There have been those who, like the caliph Al Mamoun before them, have searched for concealed chambers inside the Great Pyramid –

sometimes even using explosives and causing irreparable damage in the process. Though the hunger for treasure persists, a more realistic desire has been that such secret chambers might conceal texts, either inscribed on their walls or hidden there by Khufu or some other follower of Thoth/Hermes. Other researchers, and these for obvious reasons have been in the majority, have been content to probe the pyramid using only their minds. Rather than searching for hidden chambers, they have sought to find hidden meanings in the size, geometry and measurements of the building itself (see colour illustration no. 4). Some of these researchers, such as Sir Isaac Newton, were eminent men of impeccable scientific credentials and it seems slightly odd that their work does not receive more attention from the modern scientific community – especially because it is directly relevant to one of the major concerns of science: the establishment of correct units of measurement.

Pioneering scholars of the early seventeenth century, concerned to set the new scientific methodology of experiment and observation on sound foundations, were extremely keen to establish a system of measures that would be not only universally accepted but also in harmony with nature. The final (though far from satisfactory) outcome of this quest is the metric system. This system is based upon the French metre, which is supposed to be exactly one ten-millionth part of a quadrant of a great circle running through the earth's poles and passing through Paris. It was well understood and easily provable by means of Euclidean geometry that a system of proportions could be devised from simple shapes such as squares, triangles and pentagons. But the 'Holy Grail' of mensuration (the study of measures) was the correct unit by which to measure length. Since it was accepted that God had created the world according to a fixed pattern of proportions, the search was focused on finding His unit of measure, the 'sacred cubit' that He had used in laying out the world. To people of a religious disposition who accepted the Bible as holy writ, it seemed natural that this divine unit of length would have been the same as that used by Noah when planning his Ark, by Moses for making the Ark of the Covenant, by Ezekiel for measuring the heavenly temple and by St John in describing the new Jerusalem in Revelation.[8] Unfortunately, Noah's Ark, the Ark of the Covenant and Solomon's Temple at Jerusalem no longer exist, while the city described in Revelation remains to be built; so it was not possible for seventeenth-century antiquarians to go out and measure any of these structures for themselves. However, the pyramids, most especially the Great Pyramid of Giza, were available for any intrepid explorer to play at being Ezekiel and to measure with a 'reed' or ruler. Since it was believed that the pyramids had been built using plans supplied by Hermes/Enoch, himself a recognized biblical patriarch, it seemed reasonable to suppose that they might have been laid out using the same unit of measurement as that employed by Moses and Noah. Measuring the pyramid should thus reveal the God-given 'sacred cubit'.

Perhaps because of the widespread belief, at least in certain elevated circles, that they were descended from the lost tribes of Israel, the British were very prominent in this type of pyramid research. The first of a number of British explorers to go to Egypt was John Greaves, then Professor of Mathematics at Gresham College in London. He set about surveying the Great Pyramid and its internal chambers using a ten-foot rule. His results were published in 1646 by Gresham College in a book entitled *Pyramidographia*. Sir Isaac Newton took Greaves's figures and, using these, tried to work out the cubit used by the Egyptians. From his measurements of the King's Chamber and the sarcophagus it contained, Newton deduced that the ancient Eyptians had made use of a cubit equal to 20.62 British inches. The length of this, the Egyptian 'royal cubit', would have been exactly 21 inches, their inch being slightly shorter than the

British.[9] Unfortunately, Newton's further investigations of the Great Pyramid were hampered by the inaccuracy of Greaves's external measures. He did, however, posit the use of another cubit which he estimated at roughly 25 inches. This 'sacred cubit' was to be resurrected centuries later by the proponents of pyramidology.

The pyramids of Egypt continued to be visited off and on by Europeans, but it was not until the time of the Napoleonic wars that more real progress was made in measuring these monuments. On 1 July 1798 Bonaparte landed in Egypt with his army, close to Alexandria. At first things went well for the French, who with their modern weaponry easily outgunned the Mameluke cavalry that opposed them in the Battle of the Pyramids. Napoleon was able to take Cairo and in three weeks had the whole country at his command. His victory, however, was to prove rather empty: for a month after his landing, on 1 August, the British under Horatio Nelson destroyed his fleet in the Battle of Aboukir. From then on Napoleon's further campaigning in Eygpt and Syria was doomed to failure. Ever the pragmatist, he abandoned his army to its fate and secretly returned to France, arriving at Fréjus in October 1799.

The purpose of Napoleon's foray into Egypt has never been properly explained. It is generally said that, realizing that an invasion of England was at that time an impossibility, he decided on the Egyptian adventure as a first step towards a conquest of the Near East. It is true that with access to the Red Sea he might have been able to interfere with British shipping and, more importantly, Britain's interests in India. However, as the newborn French republic had enough enemies already, extending the theatre of war to include Egypt would, at the very least, seem to have been very poor strategic thinking. One can only conclude that there were other, more subtle reasons behind this strange expedition, which on the face of it was really more in the nature of a publicity campaign than a serious invasion.

In fact, the Little General's interests in Egypt were much more esoteric than he was at the time prepared to admit. At the time of his Egyptian campaign, Napoleon was but a republican general and – nominally, at least – under the command of the civilian regime in Paris. Though a supremely able soldier, he nurtured greater ambitions. Two of his heroes were Alexander the Great and Julius Caesar. In 332 BC, already the victor of several important battles, Alexander, like Napoleon over two millennia later, came to Egypt. He was well received by the Egyptians, who viewed him as a liberator from the Persians. While in Egypt he visited the oracle of Zeus–Amon at the Siwa Oasis, where the priests were only too willing to confirm his special destiny as the son of a god. No doubt comforted by this divine endorsement, he went on to found Alexandria and to conquer almost the entire known world.

The story of Alexander's pilgrimage to Siwa was recorded by his biographers and would have been known to Napoleon. It is therefore not surprising that a story came to circulate that Napoleon's own destiny had been revealed to him in a similar way – not at Siwa, but while alone inside the Great Pyramid. He is said to have left the pyramid ashen-faced, as well he might if he had had a vision of his later history. That he would never tell anyone what was revealed to him while inside the pyramid only added to his mystique, and perhaps the sense that he was destined to be another Alexander.

In 48 BC Julius Caesar had followed in Alexander's footsteps. He was Rome's foremost soldier and politician, who seven years before had seized Gaul and dragged it into the Roman world. Probably Rome's greatest ever general, he had finally defeated his last serious rival, Pompey, at the Battle of Pharsallus. Pompey escaped to Alexandria, where he was murdered before Caesar could catch up with him. For Caesar there was nothing much left to do but to be entertained by a young Cleopatra, who came to him wrapped in a carpet. She became his mistress and he, recognizing her political talents, made her Queen of Egypt. This, and the unfortunate burning of the library of Alexandria soon after his arrival, was Ceasar's legacy to Egypt. Less widely appreciated is the clear effect that Egypt was to have on the future destiny of Rome. For, from the moment that Caesar set foot on Egyptian soil, something of the country's spirit entered into the Roman soul. Caesar visited the tomb of Alexander and wept over the latter's embalmed body – not so much from grief that his illustrious predecessor had died at the tender age of thirty-two, but rather that he himself was already in his fifties and had achieved less. Up to then, Caesar had been content to see himself as Rome's foremost general; but he now began to have real imperial ambitions. Like the pharaohs of Egypt, of whom Cleopatra was to be the last, he was now regarded (and perhaps regarded himself) as a god.

That on his return to Rome from Egypt Caesar was not content with being a mere dictator but had royal pretensions is borne out by the fact that he had a statue of himself set up among those of the seven kings of Rome. He also wore an embroidered robe and, like a pharaoh, adopted a throne of gold and a sceptre of ivory. During the feast of Lupercalia, Antony offered him a crown, which he feigned to reject. Subsequently an image of him was paraded along with those of the gods and his statue was placed in the Temple of Quirinus. This carried the legend 'To the Unconquerable God', a title which, though commonplace for a pharaoh of Egypt, was at that time considered by many as wholly inappropriate and even blasphemous applied to a Roman general.

Whatever divine powers Caesar might have possessed, these did not prevent his assassination at the hands of an outraged Roman Senate. But though his opponents were able to kill his body, they could not put the genie back in the bottle. Out of the turmoil that followed Caesar's assassination another 'god' arose: his nephew and successor Augustus. He too arrived victoriously in

Egypt after defeating Antony at the Battle of Actium. Cleopatra committed suicide rather than submit to whatever punishment he might have in mind; and with her died the Egyptian monarchy. The once proud land of Egypt was reduced to the status of a Roman province under the jurisdiction of a governor. Yet in many ways this was the end not of Egypt but rather of Rome. What had been a republic, albeit with many faults, was now turned into an empire. Where once the Senate and its elected officers had ruled supreme, balancing the power of generals, politicians and tribunes of the people, now there was only one real force in the land: the Emperor. A god in the eyes of his subjects, and maybe even in his own eyes too, Augustus was in effect the first acknowledged pharaoh of Rome. With him began a new dynasty, not just of Egypt but of the entire Mediterranean world. The Hawk of Egypt had, one might say, been reincarnated as the Eagle of Rome.

Napoleon greatly admired Caesar as well as Alexander, and was probably dreaming of following in their footsteps as early as 1797. Seen in this light, the conquest of Egypt could be considered an absolutely vital and necessary step in the creation of a new empire modelled on that of ancient Rome. Napoleon saw it as his destiny to restore the world to its former glory and remake it in the imperial traditions not just of Rome but of Egypt too. At the time of the Battle of the Pyramids he is said to have given his men a pep-talk telling them that forty centuries of history were looking down on them. It is evident from this and from other remarks he made around the same time that he saw himself as a latter-day Alexander or Caesar, and that he actively sought the support of Egypt in the fulfilment of his future destiny. Napoleon undoubtedly believed that his mission in life was to be a restorer of civilization and that part of this task of restoration would be the rediscovery of the ancient wisdom, which he, like many others both before and since, believed to be hidden in the sands of Egypt.

Napoleon was a freemason, as were many other leaders of the French Revolution. At the time, in the late eighteenth and early nineteenth centuries, freemasonry was a revolutionary philosophy with an agenda to change the world. Other master masons, such as George Washington and Benjamin Franklin, had masterminded the creation of the American Republic which was intended to be the ideal masonic state. Egypt was regarded as the original source of the philosophy underpinning modern freemasonry.[10] Even so, it was recognized by scholars of the time that, though freemasonry had preserved in secret certain traditional teachings, over the centuries much of the ancient wisdom had been lost. Napoleon undoubtedly wanted to recover this lost knowledge for its own sake, but he was also a shrewd enough politician to realize that by doing so he would greatly strengthen his own position at the head of the revolution. This seems to have been his real motivation in going to Egypt; and seen in this light, his conquest was in many ways successful.

At that time, some three decades before Champollion published his decipherment, the hieroglyphic language of the Egyptians was still a complete mystery. Various scholars, such as the Jesuit priest Athanasius Kircher, had tried to interpret them symbolically, but nobody knew what they really meant. Nevertheless, it was still generally believed that even if the hieroglyphs themselves could not be read, the mathematical knowledge of Thoth/Hermes was preserved in the dimensions of the pyramids. To bring to light this ancient wisdom, Napoleon brought along with his army a squad of scientists, or *savants* as they were called, whose task it was to research everything they could about ancient Egypt. Among them were the very cream of French academia, including mathematicians, astronomers, architects and artists. The *savants* travelled all over the country sketching temples, obelisks and other monuments, and recording for posterity the pictures inscribed on walls and ceilings. Like the British, the French were keen to establish the basis of the ancient Egyptian system of measures and in particular the true value of the cubit. To this end they made very careful measurements of the Great Pyramid. This task was made more difficult by the build-up of sand around the pyramid's base, and their figures, though better than those brought back to England by John Greaves, were still not entirely accurate.

As a result of their explorations around the Giza area, the *savants* found that the faces of the Great Pyramid were very accurately aligned north, south, east and west. Not only that, but the 45° diagonals that could be extended from its north-east and north-west corners enclosed the Nile Delta, while the south–north meridian running through the pyramid, if carried on northwards, neatly bisected the delta. This chimed with what is said about Egypt in the *Hermetica*. Here, in the course of a dialogue called *Kore Kosmu* (Virgin of the World), Isis explains to her son Horus how the Earth is laid out like a giant reclining woman. According to this doctrine, Egypt lay over the earth's heart, to the great benefit of its people.

> 'The Earth,' said Isis, 'lies in the middle of the universe, stretched on her back, as a human being might lie, facing toward heaven. She is parted out into as many different members as a man; and her head lies towards the south of the universe, her right shoulder towards the east and her left shoulder towards the west; her feet lie beneath the Great Bear, and her thighs are situated in the region which follows next to the south of the Great Bear . . .
>
> Now all these parts of the Earth are active in some respects, but sluggish in all else, and the men whom they produce are somewhat sluggish in intelligence. But the right holy land of our ancestors lies in the middle of the Earth; and the middle of the human body is the sanctuary of the heart, and the heart is the headquarters

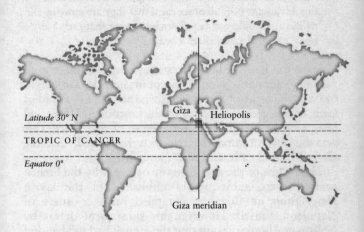

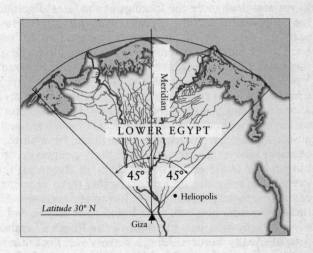

of the soul; and that my son is the reason why the men of this land [Egypt] while they have in equal measure all other things that all the rest possess, have this advantage over all other men, that they are more intelligent. It could not be otherwise, seeing that they are born and bred upon Earth's heart.'[11]

From this it seemed that the survey of the *savants* was in tune with ancient wisdom. If Egypt in general was thought to be at the heart of the world, then the Great Pyramid of Giza, at the apex of the delta on the junction of Upper and Lower Egypt, stood at the very centre of that heart. This was further confirmation, if any were needed, that the Great Pyramid embodied secret knowledge.

The results of the grand survey of Egypt by the French *savants* were subsequently published in the lavish *Description de l'Egypte*, compiled on the orders of Napoleon himself. However, his subsequent defeat by Nelson at Aboukir meant that the French had to abandon Egypt and once more the footings of the Great Pyramid were allowed to become entirely covered in sand. Thus, with the departure of the *savants*, pyramid study was back in the hands of adventurers. The most successful of these was a British guards officer called Colonel Howard-Vyse. He dug up part of the floor of the Queen's Chamber – to no effect – and then investigated the area above the ceiling of the King's Chamber. Here, a century earlier, another Englishman, Nathaniel Davison, had found a secret chamber. Suspecting there might be a further chamber above it, Howard-Vyse used gunpowder to blow a hole in the ceiling of this chamber. Repeating the exercise, he subsequently found a further three 'relieving' chambers, making a total of five including Davison's. All these chambers, however, were found to be empty, and a similar excavation into the floor of the King's Chamber proved equally fruitless. All this activity was not entirely in vain, though, for Howard-Vyse did find in one of the relieving chambers some cartouches containing the name

'Khufu' painted in red hieroglyphs on some of the blocks. As it was certain that these chambers had not been opened since the pyramid had been sealed in antiquity, this was good evidence that Khufu was indeed the name of the pharaoh who had had it built.

Howard-Vyse had greater luck outside the pyramid, where he had a team of workmen clear away some of the sand and debris from the centre of the north face of the pyramid. Though the French *savants* had found the original corner slots of the building, they had not bothered clearing the mound of material piled up between them. To his delight, Howard-Vyse now found some of the original casing stones, still in place and with the angle of slope intact. From these he was able to measure that the correct angle was 51° 51'. He knew from the French survey that the length of the base was about 763.62 feet. So, by simple trigonometry, he was able to ascertain that the true height of the pyramid when built should have been about 485 feet. His work finished, Howard-Vyse returned to England and published the results of his findings in two volumes under the title *Operations Carried on at the Pyramids of Giza in 1837*.

The 51° 51' angle was to turn out to have profound implications. In London John Taylor, a skilled mathematician as well as editor of the *London Magazine*, gathered together as much information as he could concerning measurements relating to the Great Pyramid. Dividing the length of the perimeter of the base by twice the height, he arrived at the number 3.144 – which seemed too close to the value of π (approximately 3.142) to be a coincidence. Once more it seemed that the ancient Egyptians were demonstrating their remarkable knowledge of mathematics. Furthermore, this finding had other implications. It meant that the pyramid had been built so that a circle drawn on the ground using its height as the radius would have had the same perimeter as the square base. In other words, the pyramid solved in a practical way the problem of how to 'square the circle', one of the supposedly insoluble mysteries of architectural mathematics.

Like the French *savants*, Taylor looked for a connection between the pyramid and the earth. He concluded that it was meant to be a model of the northern hemisphere, the perimeter of its base being in scale to the great circle round the equator, with the apex representing the North Pole. Taylor could see that, in practical terms, anyone constructing such a building would probably have used standard measures that would produce whole-number lengths for both the height and the perimeter. The strange thing was that neither the height nor the perimeter of the base was a whole number in either the standard or the royal cubit, let alone the British foot. Every schoolchild is taught that the value of π is approximately equal to 22 ÷ 7, but with his more advanced knowledge of mathematics Taylor knew that a more accurate value could be found from the relation 366 ÷ 116.5. By converting the perimeter of the pyramid into inches, Taylor found it came to 36,653.76 inches: almost exactly 100 × 366. This suggested that in the construction of the pyramids the Egyptians had used a 'pyramid inch' which was slightly longer than the English one of today to get a round figure of 36,600. Taylor reasoned that if they had been in possession of measuring rods 100 pyramid inches (PI) in length, then the pyramid's perimeter would be equal in length to 366 of these rods. As the solar year is roughly 366 days long, so the perimeter of the pyramid could be said to be its equivalent, with each day symbolized by one rod. According to this line of reasoning, the pyramid could be thought of as a gigantic calendar. Furthermore, a quarter of one of these rods would give a 25 pyramid inch 'sacred cubit': the very same measure proposed by Newton himself some two hundred years earlier.

Taylor's conclusion that the Egyptians who built the pyramid had made use of a cubit 25 pyramid inches in length was reinforced by the work of a British

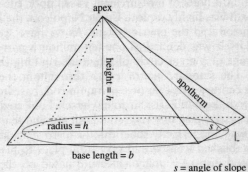

apex

height = h

apothem

radius = h

s

base length = b

s = angle of slope

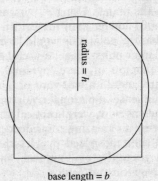

radius = h

base length = b

To construct a pi pyramid the perimeter of the base equals
$4 \times b$ and this is equal in length to the perimeter of a
circle drawn using the height (h) of the pyramid. Thus

$$4 \times b = 2 \times \pi \times h$$

This will only happen if the angle of slope (s) = 51°51'.
This is the angle of slope of the Great Pyramid of Giza.

astronomer, Sir John Herschel, the son of the Sir William Herschel who discovered Uranus. At that time the subject of standard units of measurement based upon the size of the earth was highly topical. Under Napoleon, the French had introduced the metric system. As we have seen, the metre itself was defined as one ten-millionth part of the quadrant of a great circle of longitude running through Paris. The standard metre length throughout the nineteenth century was that of a platinum rod, based on this definition, kept in Paris. Sir John Herschel objected to the metric system as a universal standard, arguing that as the earth was not perfectly spherical, the metre calculated on the established basis would vary from place to place. He proposed instead a unit of measure based on the polar axis of the earth, which would be invariable wherever you stood on the planet. Using a 'pyramid inch', whose length was 0.001 longer than the British inch, Herschel pointed out that the polar axis would be exactly 500 million of these larger units. To get a useful decimal system, he proposed that 50 of these 'pyramid inches' should make up a yard and 25 a half-yard or 'cubit'. No doubt there was some sense of national rivalry in all of this, for the British, then as now, were sceptical and suspicious of the metre. Yet by an amazing coincidence, if such it was, the inch and cubit proposed by Herschel were almost identical in length to the 'pyramid inch' and 'sacred cubit' proposed by Newton and Taylor.

Taylor's ideas were discussed at the highest level, but the sacred cubit and the pyramid inch were not accepted by the scientists of his day, whereas, despite Napoleon's defeat at Waterloo, the rival metric system has gone from strength to strength. However, even Taylor could not have guessed that his discovery (or some might say invention) of the pyramid inch was to have far-reaching consequences of a quite different sort. For its discovery was to spawn a whole new kind of pyramid research – the 'so-called pyramidology' derided so scathingly by Professor Edwards and other Egyptologists of today.

CHAPTER 4

THE PYRAMID AS GRAND
CHRONOMETER OF THE BIBLE

The 'pyramidiocy' of which Professor Edwards so disapproved began with Taylor's discoveries concerning the relationship between the circumference of the Great Pyramid and the perimeter of the earth. In Taylor's own eyes the rediscovery of the pyramid inch was a major breakthrough not just in pyramid research but in the reworking of a universal system of measurement: a system which had been inherited by the British. Yet his work was poorly received by his contemporaries and his paper on the subject was turned down by the Royal Society. However, in 1859 he did publish a book called *The Great Pyramid: Why Was It Built and Who Built it?* It was probably the latter part of this title that caused the most difficulty for scientists, for as a devout man who studied his Bible deeply, Taylor could only conclude that the pyramid must have been built by some divinely inspired prophet of God's chosen people. This time, however, it was not Enoch building pyramids to preserve knowledge, but rather some descendant of Noah. Not surprisingly, Taylor's ideas were well received by the British Israelites, whose movement, given the power of the British Empire at the time and its evident blessing by God, was becoming fashionable both in Britain itself and in the colonies. The fact that the pyramid inch differed by only one thousandth from the modern British inch was regarded as no coincidence but rather as evidence that the

British system of weights and measures had its origins in Egypt and had, along with much else besides, been inherited from the Israelites who left Egypt at the time of Moses.

One man who took these ideas very seriously indeed was the Astronomer Royal for Scotland, Charles Piazzi Smyth. A leading light both in astronomy and in the British Israel movement, he was very impressed with Taylor's work, especially his discovery of the pyramid inch and the sacred cubit of 25 such inches. Piazzi Smyth and Taylor had a very lively correspondence during the last few months before the latter's death in July 1864. The executors of Taylor's estate passed on to Smyth a number of his papers relating to pyramid measures, along with a treasured copy of Greaves's *Pyramidographia*. Thus in a very real sense Smyth inherited the mantle of esoteric pyramid research from the previous master of the genre. However, like Taylor before him, he was to find that this was not an easy burden to carry.

Smyth quickly realized that if this work were to be taken seriously, someone would have to go back to Egypt and re-measure the Great Pyramid, to make sure that the facts fitted the theory. Accordingly, in November 1864 he and his wife, equipped with the most modern surveying instruments yet to be taken to Egypt, embarked on an adventure that was to last for several months. Smyth measured just about everything he could: the dimensions of the chambers and Grand Gallery; the lengths of the passageways and their angles. He found, among other things, that the angle of the north-facing, descending passageway was 26° 18'. He realized that this pointed close to the pole, which as viewed from Giza is actually at an angle of 29° 51' to the northern horizon. Taking into account the precession of the equinoxes, he calculated that the descending passageway could have been orientated towards the star Alpha Draconis, which at c.2170 BC would, in its lower meridianal transits, have aligned with the shaft. This he took as evidence that the pyramid had been built at around that date.[1]

Keen to check up on the angle of slope of the pyramid itself, Piazzi Smyth searched among the debris at its foot for fragments of casing stones that had not been damaged. As best he could, given its damaged condition, he also studied the silhouette of the pyramid, and found that this gave an angle of 51° 50'. Comparing this result with the angle of 51° 52' 15.5" computed by Sir John Herschel from the dimensions of the casing stones in Howard-Vyse's report, he arrived at a mean figure of 51° 51' 14". This compared favourably with the measured angle of slope of one of the casing stones brought back to England by his friend Mr Waynman Dixon. This stone had been carefully measured and its angle of slope found to be between 51° 53' 15" and 51° 49' 55" – an average of 51° 51' 35". Other stones taken from the pyramid also showed the same angle of roughly 51° 51'. In similar fashion, Smyth took an average for the length of the northern base as measured by the French (763.62 feet) and by Howard-Vyse (764 feet), arriving at a figure of 763.81 feet. Using these averaged measures in his calculations gave a very accurate figure for π of 3.14159.

However, Smyth wanted to go one better than Taylor and to show that the perimeter of the pyramid (equivalent, as we have seen, to the circle drawn using its height as a radius) was equal to 365.24 and not 366 100-inch rods. This would show that it really was intended to represent the year, which properly has a length of approximately 365.24 days, not 366. To see if this were true required a more accurate measurement of the base than had hitherto been done. Unfortunately Smyth himself had to return to Britain, and so relied on some friendly Scottish engineers who happened to be in the area to carry out the work for him. They accordingly sent him the results of their survey giving a length of 9,110 inches (759.1667 feet). This was several feet shorter than either of the two previous measurements taken by the *savants* and Howard-Vyse. It was also rather too short for his 365.24 day theory; but, undaunted, he once more took an average between this reading and the 9,168 inches (764 feet) of Howard-Vyse, and in this way arrived at 9,140 inches – very close to the figure required to substantiate his hypothesis.[2] As far as he was concerned, the idea that the pyramid was intended to display special numerical relationships that embodied a knowledge of the dimensions of the earth and of π, and which symbolically linked it with the year, was proven. As this knowledge seemed out of keeping with what was then known of Egyptian civilization, he could only conclude that the architect who designed the pyramid was divinely inspired.

Smyth published his findings in a famous book entitled *Our Inheritance in the Great Pyramid* (1864) and the less well-known three volumes entitled *Life and Work at the Great Pyramid of Jeeze* (1865). Like Taylor's book before them, Smyth's publications were attacked by reviewers who regarded the notion that the builders of the pyramid were somehow divinely inspired as unscientific nonsense. In 1874 the Royal Society, disregarding Smyth's status as the highly esteemed Astronomer Royal for Scotland, meted out the same treatment they had given John Taylor and rejected his paper on the design of the Khufu pyramid. Refusing to be discouraged, Smyth went on to write and publish a book on that subject: *The Great Pyramid and the Royal Society* (1874). In 1884 he wrote a further book, *New Measures of the Great Pyramid*, presenting certain refinements to his deductions about the true height and other measurements of the pyramid.

Smyth's books were well illustrated with diagrams of the pyramid's interior, giving the lengths of the passageways and chambers in 'pyramid inches'. As we have seen, the reality of this unit of measure – as also the 25-inch 'sacred cubit' and 4-cubit or 100-inch rod – is still denied by academic Egyptology to this day; but that did not hinder its ready acceptance by others. The sacred cubit became the standard measure of the pyramidologists and they used it, or rather its inch divisions, to measure out history. The first to do this was another Scot: one Robert Menzies, who, after pondering Smyth's cross-sectional diagrams of the pyramid, came up with the idea that just as the perimeter of the pyramid could be thought of as representing the year, with divisions of one day to 100 pyramid inches, so also the lengths of the passageways and chambers were equally meaningful. Applying a formula of one pyramid inch to the year, he deduced that the lengths of the passageways represented prophetic time. As Smyth's calculations had indicated that the descending passageway had been aligned towards the star Thuban or Alpha Draconis in 2170 BC, this date was used as a marker. Less convincingly, it was deduced by Smyth that this date corresponded to two vertical wall-joints he had discovered in the walls of the descending passageway.

From these slender beginnings the whole school of biblical pyramidology was to grow. According to the pyramidologists, the foot of the pyramid symbolized the beginning of the world at the time of Adam and Eve which Archbishop Ussher and others in the seventeenth century computed at 4004 BC. From here there was a laborious climb up the outside of the pyramid to its entrance on the ninth course. The entrance here was taken as symbolic of the Flood of Noah's time and the destruction of the antediluvian world. The downward passage, leading to the subterranean chamber, represented fallen humankind on its way to hell. The sudden change in direction, where the ascending passageway leads upwards from the descending, was taken to represent the biblical Exodus under Moses. The ascending corridor itself was seen as symbolizing the Jewish Age, or the law of the Old Covenant of Moses. Its opening into the Grand Gallery represented the birth of Jesus and the beginning of the Gospel Age. This would end, so the pyramidologists believed, with the Second Advent of Christ, which would somehow correspond to the entrance into the King's Chamber.

Needless to say, none of this biblical speculation, which went far beyond the initial idea that Hermes Trismegistus had built the pyramids to preserve ante-diluvian records for the benefit of future generations, was acceptable to a scientific community now coming to terms with Darwin's theories of evolution. It also tainted Smyth's earlier finding concerning the likelihood that the pyramid's dimensions were, as Taylor had suggested, representative of the π proportion. The battle lines were drawn up, and the opponents of pyramidology were now to find their own champion in the man who was to become the father of modern Egyptology: William Flinders Petrie.

Like most of the early pyramid enthusiasts, Flinders Petrie was obsessed with measurements. Taking with him equipment perfected by his father, a mechanical engineer who was himself attracted by the ideas of Taylor and Smyth, Flinders Petrie set off for Egypt in November 1880. His was to be the most methodical survey to date, surpassing even that of Smyth. Using a theodolite and carrying out repeated measurements from a number of points around the plateau, he produced an accurate tri-angulation for all three pyramids. He was equally methodical in his measurements of both the inside and outside of the Great Pyramid, producing figures accurate to within a hundredth or even a thousandth of an inch.

Anxious to settle once and for all whether the claims of the pyramidologists that a sacred cubit of 25 pyramid inches had been employed by the Egyptians could be sub-stantiated, he had the rubble removed from the corners of the pyramid again, and also uncovered some more of the casing stones. Measuring not to the corners of the incised sockets, as Smyth had done, but rather to the edge of the pavement some 20 inches higher, he arrived at a figure for the base length of 9,069 British inches (755.75 feet), rather than the 9,140 inches (761.667 feet) published by Smyth. Taking a standard, royal cubit of 20.62 inches, such as was clearly used in the laying out of the King's

Chamber, and multiplying this length by 440, he arrived at a value of 9,072.8 British inches: close enough to his own measurement of the base length of 9,069 inches to be convincing. As for the height, 280 of these royal cubits were equivalent to 481.13 feet: almost exactly what had been found by the French nearly a century earlier. These results, apparently showing that the pyramid was built with a base length of 440 royal cubits and a height of 280, had the pleasing effect of confirming Taylor's theory concerning the use of the π proportion, while at the same time discrediting the sacred cubit and with it biblical pyramidology.

Petrie was now certain that pyramidology was not to be taken seriously, founded as it was upon false, or at least unproven, premises. The first of these was the existence of the pyramid inch as a unit of measure. The second was that the corridors and chambers of the Great Pyramid had been deliberately measured in such a way that their lengths in pyramid inches related to the unfurling of history. The third was that the descending corridor was aligned with the star Thuban as it would have been seen in 2170 BC; and the fourth was that this date was marked by vertical joints between blocks, not at the start but some way down the corridor. There was also the question why the pyramid builders should have wanted to record prophetically events relevant not to the Egyptians but rather the Israelites, who for most of the time were their sworn enemies. Given all of these factors, it is little wonder that pyramidology became known as pyramidiocy in an increasingly sceptical academic world. The Royal Society, which had earlier rejected papers by Taylor and Smyth, now found £100 available as a grant to enable Petrie to publish his results in 1883 in a book entitled *The Pyramids and Temples of Gizeh*. His reputation as the father of modern Egyptology was established, and his survey of the Giza monuments is still regarded as definitive.

Academic scepticism towards the ideas of the

pyramidologists could only increase as modern archaeology found its feet and more and more of the history of Egypt was brought to light. As discoveries have been made about the pyramids and their builders, so pyramidology has become increasingly irrelevant to any serious discussion of the pyramids. Indeed, one might have been forgiven for thinking that by the 1960s, given the rapid advances of post-war science, pyramidologists would be an extinct species. However, that would be to underestimate both their tenacity and their ability to reinterpret their base data. Even today, it seems, there are still scholars willing and able to jeopardize career and reputation in defence of the indefensible. And yet, for all their persistence, pyramidologists have never been able to explain satisfactorily the function of the other pyramids at Giza. If the Great Pyramid, which is not even central to the group, is a model of the world and chronometer of the ages, why did the Egyptians bother to build any more? Little did I know it back in the early 1970s, but in due course I was to find a plausible answer to this question, and many more besides.

An unfortunate side-effect of the discrediting of pyramidology itself has been the dismissal of the work of early pioneers, such as Piazzi Smyth, who remain tainted by association. The simple idea espoused by so eminent a scholar as Sir Isaac Newton, that the Great Pyramid contains a secret and that this is coded in numbers, has been all but lost under the voluminous weight of pyramidological speculation. Yet to say this is to state no more than what has always been believed about the pyramids since ancient times: that they were designed by Hermes to conceal knowledge for later days. Hermes, however, was also credited with writing books, some of which still exist in published form. These now became the object of my studies, for, as I was soon to discover, these writings, known today as the *Hermetica*, contain a hidden philosophy that descends from the secret gnostic tradition of the pyramid builders.

Throughout the 1980s I had little time or energy to think about pyramids as I pursued my career as a computer analyst and programmer. Though I did not entirely abandon esoteric studies, I was more concerned with the arcane numerology of how to pay the mortgage than with the measurements of the Great Pyramid. However, my long-term ambition was to be a writer and in 1991 I resigned my job and set about self-publishing *The Cosmic Wisdom beyond Astrology*, a book I had written a few years earlier. By now I was once more deeply immersed in Egyptian studies, and the following year I published a new edition of Walter Scott's English translation of the *Hermetica*. This was the collection of writings that had, according to Dame Frances Yates,[3] had a profound influence on the development of Renaissance Italy. I too had found these writings deeply inspiring, but even so I could not have anticipated the way that bringing them back into print now would change the direction of my life.

The *Hermetica* were written around the time of Philo; as noted in chapter 2, Jesus may even have read some of them. Though late in composition they are nevertheless important for Egyptian studies, as they throw light on the final phase of the ancient religion of the pharaohs. At the heart of this very complex system of beliefs and practices was the legend of Isis and Osiris. The Egyptian funerary liturgy was based on the death and resurrection of Osiris, a story of great poignancy with obvious Christian overtones. According to these legends, Osiris was an anthropomorphic god, sent to earth along with his sisters, Isis and Nephthys, and his brother, Set, by the father of the gods, Atum-Re, to bring the benefits of civilization to humankind. A wise and benevolent ruler, Osiris, in the tradition of Thoth/Hermes (who seems to have preceded him), instructed the Egyptians in the arts and sciences and instituted the rule of law or *Maat*. Osiris' role as bringer of civilization is described in the

Kore Kosmu, which, as we have already seen, takes the form of a Platonic dialogue between Isis and her son Horus:

> Thereupon Horus said: 'Tell me then, mother, how did earth attain to the happy lot of receiving the efflux [seed] of God?' – And Isis answered: 'Mighty Horus, do not ask me to describe to you the origin of the stock whence you are sprung; for it is not permitted to inquire into the birth of gods. This only may I tell you, that God who rules alone, the Fabricator of the universe, bestowed on the earth for a little time your great father Osiris and the great goddess Isis, that they might give the world the help it so much needed.
>
> 'It was they that filled human life with that which is divine, and thereby put a stop to the savagery of mutual slaughter.
>
> 'It was they that established upon earth rites of worship which correspond exactly to the Holy Powers in heaven.
>
> 'It was they that consecrated temples and instituted sacrifices to the gods that were their ancestors, and gave to mortal men the boons of food and shelter.
>
> 'It was they that introduced into men's life that mighty god, the Oath-god, to be the founder of pledges and good faith; whereby they filled the world with law-abidingness and justice . . .
>
> 'It was they that, having learnt from Hermes that the atmosphere had been filled with daemons,[4] inscribed [forms of words invoking the daemons] on hidden slabs of stone.
>
> 'It was they that, having learnt God's secret law-givings, became law-givers for mankind.
>
> 'It was they that devised the [initiation and training] of the prophet-priests, to the end that these might nurture men's souls with philosophy, and save their bodies by healing art when they are sick.[5]

The golden age of Osiris, however, was doomed not to last. His brother Set became jealous and slew the good Osiris, dividing his body into fourteen pieces and scattering these around Egypt.[6] Set, though like his brother a god from the sky, did not have the wisdom and compassion of Osiris, so that when he became ruler over Egypt lawlessness returned. All was not lost, however, for Isis secretly gathered the pieces of her dead husband's corpse and, binding these together with strips of linen, made the first mummy. Tricking the sun god into revealing his secret name, Isis invoked his power to resurrect Osiris for long enough that they could copulate. In this way she became pregnant with the divine Horus. After this final act, his task on earth having been accomplished, Osiris returned to the heavens. Isis, now a fugitive as well as a widow, hid among the bulrushes of the Nile delta, where nine months later she gave birth to Horus. He, when he had reached manhood, challenged his uncle Set to battle and eventually defeated him. Set was deposed and Horus became king of Egypt, once more establishing the rule of law.

The true lineage of Osiris having been re-established, all pharaohs thereafter were considered to be incarnations of Horus. When they died they expected to be transformed into Osiris by means of a complex series of rituals that involved mummification of the corpse, the uttering of spells by priests and the chanting of special invocations. Many of these ritual prayers are contained in the famous Book of the Dead,[7] which according to G. R. S. Mead should properly be called The Book of the Master of the Secret House – the 'Secret House' in question being the Great Pyramid, its master presumably Hermes Trismegistus.

The dictum that dominates all Hermetic thought and writing throughout the ages is the simple but profound statement 'as above, so below'. During the Renaissance, when alchemy came back strongly into vogue,[8] the so-called 'Emerald Table of Hermes' was closely studied.

The first verse of the 'Emerald Table' – a curious document of unknown origin that outlines the philosophical principles of alchemy – enumerates the theory of correspondences very clearly:

> True without deceit, certain and most true,
> What is below is like what is above and
> what is above is like what is below, for
> the performing of the marvels of the one thing.

As is clear from the passage of the *Kore Kosmu* quoted above, where the earth is described as a reclining woman with her heart in the place where Egypt is, the ancient Egyptians took the Hermetic dictum 'as above, so below' quite literally. They saw their country as representing on the ground what existed above in the heavens. This is actually stated in another text in the *Hermetica*, the *Asclepius*, where Hermes berates his pupil for not understanding the importance of Egypt as the Holy Land: 'Do you not know, Asclepius, that Egypt is an image of heaven, or, to speak more exactly, in Egypt all the operations of the powers which rule and work in Heaven have been transferred to earth below? Nay, it should rather be said that the whole Kosmos dwells in this our land as in its sanctuary.'[9]

Though the *Hermetica* gives us more than a glimpse of what was contained in the ancient Egyptian mysteries, yet there was much that remained concealed – as is clear from 'Libellus XVI' of the *Corpus Hermeticum*, which contains a letter from Asclepius to King Ammon.

> Of weighty import is this discourse which I send to you, my King; it is, so to speak, a summing up of all the other discourses, and a reminder of their teaching. It is not composed in accordance with the opinion of the many; it contains much that contradicts their beliefs. For my teacher Hermes often used to say in talk with me when we were alone, and sometimes when Tat was with us,

that those who read my writings will think them to be quite simply and clearly written, but those who hold opposite principles to start with will say that the style is obscure, and conceals the meaning. And it will be thought still more obscure in time to come, when the Greeks think fit to translate these writings from our mother tongue (Egyptian) into theirs. Translation will greatly distort the sense of the writings, and cause much obscurity. Expressed in our native language, the teaching conveys its meaning clearly; for the very quality of the sounds; and when the Egyptian words are spoken, the force of the things signified works in them. Therefore, my King, as far as it is in your power, (and you are all-powerful,) keep the teaching untranslated, in order that things so holy may not be revealed to Greeks, and that the Greek mode of speech, with its arrogance, and feebleness, and showy tricks of style, may not reduce to impotence the impressive strength of the language and cogent force of the words. For the speech of the Greeks, my King, is devoid of power to convince; and the Greek philosophy is nothing but a noise of talk. But our speech is not mere talk; it is an utterance replete with workings.[10]

This extract is a clear statement, if any be needed, that the Greek *Hermetica* does not contain the full import of the Egyptian mysteries, some of which, we must assume, are concealed by the play on Egyptian words of similar sounds but different meanings that is characteristic of the Pyramid Texts.[11] What is clear, and has always been so regardless of language, is that the Egyptians were masters of the Hermetic sciences of measurement: geometry and astronomy. This is confirmed by Clement of Alexandria, one of the church fathers who flourished in the late second and early third centuries. He also writes about the books of Hermes, and tells us that some of these concerned astronomy:

First comes the 'Singer' bearing some one of the symbols of music. This [priest], they tell us, has to make himself master of two of the 'Books of Hermes', one of which contains Hymns [in honour] of the Gods, and the other Reflections on the Kingly Life.

After the 'Singer' comes the 'Time-watcher' bearing the symbols of star-science, a dial after a hand and phoenix. He must have the division of the 'Books of Hermes' which treats of the stars ever at the tip of his tongue – there being four of such books. The first of these deals with the Ordering of the apparently Fixed Stars, the next two with the conjunctions and variations of Light of Sun and Moon, and the last with the Risings [of the Stars].

Next comes the 'Scribe of the Mysteries', with wings on his head, having in either hand a book and a ruler in which is the ink and reed pen with which they write. He has to know what they call the sacred characters, and the books about Cosmography, and Geography, the Constitution of the Sun and Moon, and of the Five Planets [Mercury, Venus, Mars, Jupiter and Saturn], the Survey of Egypt, the Chart of the Nile, the List of the Appurtenances of the Temples and of the Lands consecrated to them, the Measures, and things used in the Sacred rites.

After the above-mentioned comes the 'Overseer of the Ceremonies', bearing the cubit of justice and the libation cup [as his symbols]. He must know all the books relating to the training [of the conductors of the public cult], and those that they call victim-sealing books. There are ten of these books which deal with the worship which they pay to the gods, and in which the Egyptian cult is contained; namely [those which treat] of Sacrifice, First-fruits, Hymns, Prayers, Processions, Feasts, and the like.

After all these comes the 'Prophet' clasping to his breast the water-vase so that all can see it; and after him follow those who carry the bread that is to be distributed. The 'Prophet', as chief of the temple, learns by heart the ten books which are called 'hieratic'; these contain the volumes treating of the Laws, and the Gods, and the whole Discipline of the Priests. For you must know that the 'Prophet' among the Egyptians is also the supervisor of the distribution of the [temple] revenues.

Now the books which are absolutely indispensable for Hermes are forty-two in number. Six-and-thirty of them, which contain the whole wisdom-discipline of the Egyptians, are learned by heart by the [grades of priests] already mentioned. The remaining six are learned by the 'Shrine-bearers'; these are medical treatises dealing with the Constitution of the Body, with Diseases, Instruments, Drugs, Eyes, and finally with the Maladies of Women.'[12]

How close a link there is between these books of Hermes and the later *Hermetica* is debatable. Certainly there were large numbers of written texts contained in the library of Alexandria at the time of Clement which have since then been destroyed. We can only guess and hope that there may yet be other copies, written on stone or papyrus, concealed in hidden tombs, caves or chambers still to be uncovered. In the meantime there remains the Great Pyramid, believed by many to be an essay written on stone in the language of geometry and astronomy, to be examined and commented upon. Work in this fascinating area, as I was about to discover, had recently taken a surprising turn.

CHAPTER 5

THE ORION MYSTERY

In 1992, shortly after my edition of *Hermetica* was published, I had an unexpected phone call from a man called Robert Bauval. Although we were strangers we talked for over an hour, on subjects ranging from the pyramids to Frances Yates's book *Giordarno Bruno and the Hermetic Tradition*. During the course of our conversation, Robert informed me that he too had written a book and asked me if I would be interested in seeing it with a view to publication. When it arrived a few days later, I quickly realized that it contained some novel, not to say extraordinary ideas concerning the pyramids and the rebirth cult of the pharaohs.

What was particularly exciting about Bauval's work was his discovery that the concept of Egypt as an image of heaven was not just a philosophical conceit of the late Hermeticists. He had found evidence that during the Old Kingdom (*c.*3100–2200 BC) the pyramid builders had created a landscape that mirrored a portion of the heavens above: they had quite literally built a heaven on earth.

Central to this thesis was the idea the ancient Egyptians had conceived of there being a river in the sky which was the counterpart of their River Nile on earth. It was clear to Bauval that this celestial river, which the Greeks later called Okeanos and associated with the constellation of Eridanus, was originally seen in Old Kingdom times as the Milky Way. This was the heavenly river, or 'winding waterway', over which, according to the Pyramid Texts, the soul of the king was destined to be ferried.

> The Nurse-canal is opened, The Winding Waterway is flooded, the fields of Rushes are filled with water, and I [the dead king] am ferried over thereon to yonder eastern side of the sky, to the place where the gods fashioned me, where I was born new and young. (PT 343–4)[1]

> Hail to you Re [the sun-god], you who traverse the sky and cross Nut [the sky goddess and mother of Osiris], having traversed the Winding Waterway. I have grasped your tail for myself, for I am a god and the son of a god, I am a flower which has issued from the Nile, a golden flower which has issued from Iseion. (PT 543–4)

The importance of Egypt as the symbolic heart of the world has already been remarked on. It seems that the Egyptians also thought of their land as being like the pupil of an eye through which the light-stream of the universe passes. In other words, Egypt was a place of vision. This doctrine was concealed (though apparently not from the Greeks) in the alternative translation of *Kore Kosmu*, which, as well as meaning 'Virgin of the World', can also be translated as 'Eye-pupil of the Universe'. This alternative meaning is discussed by G. R. S. Mead in his *Thrice Greatest Hermes*.

> Egypt, the 'sacred land' *par excellence*, was called Chemia or Chem, Black-land, because of the nature of its dark loamy soil; it was, moreover, in symbolic phraseology the black of the eye, that is the pupil of the earth-eye, the stars and planets being regarded as the eyes of the gods. Egypt, then was the eye and heart of the Earth; the Heavenly Nile poured its light-flood of wisdom through this dark of the eye, or made

the land throb like a heart with the celestial life-currents.[2]

Mead, writing in 1906 and therefore not in possession of the latest translation of the Pyramid Texts, assumed that the Heavenly Nile was either the constellation of Eridanus or simply the ocean that was believed to stand above the celestial sphere. However, he did have something else to say on the subject which ties in with the idea of an analogy between the Milky Way and the River Nile: 'The Holy Land of those who had gone out from the body, watered by the Celestial Nile, the River of Heaven, of which the earthly river was a symbol and parallel, was divided into three regions, or states: (1) Rusta, the Territory of Initiation; (2) Aahlu, the Territory of Illumination; and (3) Amenti, the place of Union with the Unseen Father.'[3] I shall have more to say about this later.

It was Bauval's contention that the part of the Milky Way which interested the Egyptians most was the region that runs from the star Sirius alongside the constellation of Orion on up towards Taurus. This region of the sky seemed to correspond, in the Egyptian mind at least, to the area of the Memphite necropolis, that is to say the span of Old Kingdom burial grounds stretching along the west bank of the Nile from Dashur to Giza and down to Abu Ruwash. At the centre of this area was Giza; this, he determined, was the earthly equivalent of Rostau (Mead's Rusta), the gateway to the Duat or underworld.[4] Since Dr Edwards, for half a century the acknowledged expert on the pyramids, had written that 'by Pyramid times, Osiris had become identified with Sokar, the god of the Memphite Necropolis',[5] there was a clear connection between the pyramids and Osiris. Bauval knew that the Egyptians venerated the god Osiris as judge of the dead, and from the work of the acclaimed archaeo-astronomer Otto Neugebauer he discovered that they equated his star-form, or *sahu*, with the constellation of Orion.[6] Moreover, certain of the Pyramid Texts revealed that the

Egyptians believed that after death the pharaoh, provided he had passed certain tests, would ascend to the stars to become 'an Osiris'. Other texts stated that the pharaoh's soul will become a star in Orion.

> O king, you are this Great Star, the Companion of Orion, who traverses the sky with Orion, who navigates the Duat [nether world] with Osiris; you ascend from the east of the sky, being renewed in your due season, and rejuvenated in your due time. The sky has borne you with Orion . . . (PT 882–3)

> The King has come to you, O mother of the King, he has come to Nut, that you may bring the sky to the King and hang up the stars for him, for his savour is the savour of your son who issued from you, the King's savour is that of Osiris your son who issued from you. (PT 1516)

> In your name of Dweller in Orion, with a season in the sky and a season on the earth. O Osiris, turn your face and look on this King, for your seed which issued from you is effective . . . (PT 187)

Having grown up in Egypt, Bauval had long been interested in the Giza pyramids. As a trained building engineer he had wondered why they were arranged with the two larger ones more or less exactly on a diagonal but the smallest, that of Menkaure (Mycerinos), offset from this line. He could see that, from a constructional point of view, this architectural plan was unnecessarily complicated. It would have been easier and made more sense for the Egyptians to have built all three pyramids on the same north–south meridian or, failing this, at least on the same diagonal. There was also no obvious reason why the Menkaure pyramid should have been smaller than the other two. After all, as far as one can tell from this distance in time, Menkaure was just as powerful a pharaoh as his forebears. Why, then, would he want to build a pyramid that would be dwarfed for all time by the massive structures of Khufu and Khafre? All this puzzled Bauval for many years. Then one day, while camping in the Saudi Arabian desert, he saw overhead the constellation of Orion. In a flash of inspiration he suddenly realized that the three large pyramids of Giza had been built the way they were so that they would represent the three stars of Orion's Belt. For, just as there were two large pyramids on a diagonal line and a third smaller and offset to the west, so in the Belt there were two brighter stars with a third less bright and offset from the line linking the others.

This realization tied in with the idea that the Egyptians saw their land as being laid out after the manner of heaven. With the River Nile identified with the Milky Way, it made sense to think that the Egyptians had originally built pyramids to represent important stars on its 'bank'. Further research indicated that there was a similar stellar correlation with all the large pyramids of the Fourth Dynasty. While this pattern did not seem to apply to all the lesser pyramids of the Fifth, Sixth and later dynasties (there are, as Professor Edwards reminded us, nearly 100 Egyptian pyramids in all), it was clearly the case for the five recognized pyramids of the Fourth Dynasty (the three at Giza plus two at Dashur) and quite possibly for the two pyramids of Abu Ruwash and Zawyat al Aryan, which may also have been Fourth Dynasty.

Further confirmation that Bauval was on the right track came from the fact that it had been known since 1966 that the southern 'air shaft' from the King's Chamber was directed towards the point in the sky where Orion's Belt would clearly have crossed the southern meridian at the time the pyramid was built.[7] As the Pyramid Texts made clear that one of the beliefs of the cult of the pharaoh was that after death his soul would rise to the sky and become a star in Orion, this shaft seemed to provide a symbolic mechanism by means of which this could be accomplished.

Investigating the air shafts from the Queen's Chamber, which were originally blocked off by the Egyptians at both ends and re-opened at the bottom only in 1872 by a British engineer named Waynman Dixon, Bauval made another startling discovery. Whereas the southern shaft from the King's Chamber pointed towards the culmination of Orion's Belt, the equivalent shaft from the Queen's Chamber was aligned towards the culmination of Sirius. As this star, the brightest in the sky, was associated with Isis, the consort of Osiris, this alignment seemed to be no accident.

Further investigation on the north shaft, undertaken after Bauval and I had begun writing the book that was published in 1994 as *The Orion Mystery*, revealed that just as the northern shaft from the King's Chamber was aligned towards the then north star (Thuban or Alpha Draconis), so the northern shaft from the Queen's Chamber pointed towards the spot where daily the star Kochab (Beta Ursa Minoris) would make its upper alignment on the north–south meridian, a few degrees higher in the sky than the North Pole (see colour illustration no. 15). The constellation of Ursa Minor was represented by the Egyptians with a little ceremonial adze called a *meshtw*. This tool played a very important part in the funeral ceremony: it was used to cut open the bandages of the mummy and to 'open the mouth' of the deceased so that he could breathe anew and thereby be reborn. It was fashioned out of iron, a metal that was very rare at the time of the Old Kingdom. As far as we know the Egyptians at that time did not have the technology to smelt iron from its ore, so that the only source they had for this relatively hard metal was a certain type of meteorite. Since meteorites came from the sky, they regarded iron as a metal that belonged to the gods. The *meshtw* was therefore a sacred implement, imbued with the heavenly qualities of meteoritic iron. This connection was further strengthened by virtue of its being shaped like the Little Bear constellation (Ursa Minor), which seems to have been mystically linked to the jackal-headed god Wepwawet (or Upuaut), the 'opener of the ways'. There are several references to the use of the *meshtw* in the Pyramid Texts, of which the following is an example:

> O King, I open your mouth for you with the adze of Wepwawet, I split open your mouth for you with the adze of iron which split open the mouth of the gods. O Horus, open the mouth of this King! Horus has opened the mouth of this King, Horus has split open the mouth of this King with that wherewith he split open the mouth of his father, with that wherewith he split open the mouth of Osiris, with the iron which issued from Set, with the adze of iron which split open the mouth of the gods. (PT 13–14)

What was even more extraordinary was that, by means of computer simulation, Bauval was able to discover that at the time the Great Pyramid was built (we believe *c.*2450 BC), at the moment the star Kochab became aligned with the northern shaft of the Queen's Chamber, the Belt of Orion would be seen coming over the eastern horizon. In fact, to be more precise, Alnitak, or Delta Orionis, the southernmost star of the Belt and the one which according to the scheme of correlation would correspond to the Great Pyramid, would be rising. This seemed too striking a coincidence not to have been intentional. It also makes sense of others of the Pyramid Texts, for example: 'The libation is poured and Wepwawet [Ursa Minor?] is on high ... Raise yourself, Osiris the King [Orion?], you first-born son of Geb, at whom the Great Ennead [the nine gods of Heliopolis] tremble' (PT 1011–12). The implication seemed to be that the Queen's Chamber, far from being 'abandoned', as Egyptologists claimed, was somehow symbolic of the rebirth ceremonies to which the Pyramid Texts referred.

Indeed, we could imagine the mummy of the dead king being brought into the Queen's Chamber and the actual ceremony of the 'Opening of the Mouth' being performed on it using a *meshtw*. This, we felt sure, would have been done precisely as Kochab aligned with the northern shaft and Alnitak came over the horizon.

A further mystery connected with the Queen's Chamber emerged when Robert and I went to Egypt together to take photographs for our forthcoming book. Before going over we had heard from Professor Edwards that a German team were carrying out investigations of the air shafts. As the angles of these shafts were critical to the exposition of *The Orion Mystery*, we were anxious to meet them and to find out if they had re-measured these with greater accuracy than the Petrie survey conducted more than a century earlier. Accordingly we made contact with the engineer in charge of the work, a young man in his thirties called Rudolf Gantenbrink. He, it transpired, had been commissioned by the German Institute in Cairo, on behalf of the Egyptians, to look into the problem of better ventilating the Great Pyramid.

While the air inside the Great Pyramid has always been rather stale, the great increase in tourism in recent years has put an intolerable strain on the ancient structure. The moisture exuded in the sweat and breath of thousands of people every day has greatly increased the internal humidity. As a result the limestone core, which soaks up moisture like a sponge, has become waterlogged. This in turn has caused leaching of salts and, it is feared, a weakening of the overall structure. Gantenbrink, asked to come up with a solution to the problem, installed an extractor fan at the bottom of the southern shaft of the King's Chamber. This, it was hoped, would cause an airflow through the pyramid and gradually, over a period of time, dry it out.[8]

One important consequence of Gantenbrink's brief was that he was able to re-survey the shafts unhindered. To do this he built two devices, both of which he called

Upuaut – 'Opener of the Ways' – in recognition of the jackal-headed god, who as well as opening mouths was now to be called upon to open the air shafts or windpipes of the pyramid. The first machine was a fairly simple, sled-drawn video camera which, as the air shafts of the King's Chamber penetrate to the skin of the pyramid, he was able to pull up manually from the outside. The second, 'Upuaut 2', was a robot. This was a much more sophisticated mechanism, having its own traction and remote laser guidance system. This was needed in order to send the robot up the shafts from the Queen's Chamber, which are still open only at the bottom and have no exits to the outside of the pyramid. After several earlier attempts, on 22 March 1993 Gantenbrink sent this robot climbing to the very end of the southern shaft of the Queen's Chamber. To his and everyone else's surprise, the shaft not only turned out to be much longer than previously imagined (about 65 metres instead of 8) but it ended with what looked to be a little door, complete with copper handles.

Gantenbrink's discovery stunned the world when it leaked out a few weeks later. To the surprise of nobody except a few of the more sceptical Egyptologists, the press and indeed the public were as enthusiastic as ever about the possibility of new chambers being found inside the Great Pyramid. However, the announcement pleased neither the German Institute in Cairo nor the Egyptian authorities, both of whom felt that the normal protocols in this matter had been breached. Accordingly, though Rudolf Gantenbrink was now an international figure and a hero back home in Germany, he was banned from doing any further work at Giza and most especially from making any attempt at opening the tantalizing door – if such it was.

Robert and I became caught up in the slipstream of all this renewed interest in the pyramids, for, if truth be told, we had had not a little to do with alerting the press to Gantenbrink's historic discovery. He had sent Robert a video tape of the robot climbing the shaft and we had shown this first of all to the most eminent Egyptologists in Britain (including Drs Edwards and Davies of the British Museum and Dr Jaromir Malek of the Griffiths Institute in Oxford) and then to several reporters. With difficulty we kept the media away from our own work, for we didn't want the Orion correlation theory to become general knowledge before the publication of our book lest, taken out of context and without the detailed arguments in its favour, it should be dismissed as wishful thinking. We were determined to make sure that when it did come out the evidence, in its entirety, should be presented to the public in an authoritative manner. However, from our point of view it was fortunate that, because of the Gantenbrink affair and our involvement in it, we were contacted by Chris Mann from the religious broadcasting division of the BBC.

Chris, an affable and charming man and one of the most gifted producers in the corporation, immediately grasped the religious implications of *The Orion Mystery* and asked us if we would be prepared to make a programme for *Everyman,* the BBC's flagship series on religious matters. We agreed and in due course a programme was made in conjunction with the American Arts and Entertainment network (A&E); entitled *The Great Pyramid: Gateway to the Stars*, it was eventually shown in Britain in early February 1994. Based almost entirely on *The Orion Mystery*, it presented the thesis to an even wider audience than we could possibly reach with our book; it also included footage of Rudolf Gantenbrink's mysterious 'door', which, although it had attracted world-wide headlines soon after its discovery in March 1993, had hitherto remained unseen by the general public.

For the most part *The Orion Mystery* received positive coverage in the press – unusually for books in this genre, which all too often are ignored entirely. Neil Spencer, writing for *The Observer* of 6 February 1994, commented: 'For the status quo, this is the stuff of heresy, the latest example of the "pyramidiocy" of commentators like Piazzi Smyth and John Michell. Yet the case of Bauval and his co-author Gilbert, argued with modesty, is persuasive and scholarly.' Joanna Duckworth of the *Sunday Times* (27 February 1994) was also enthusiastic about what she called 'an absorbing and fascinating work of archaeological detection', and David Keys, archaeological correspondent for *The Independent*, devoted a whole page on 1 February, with graphics, to explaining the Orion correlation theory.

Not all the reviews were favourable, though; in an article published in the *Daily Telegraph* of 5 February 1994, Adrian Berry wrote: 'It [*The Orion Mystery*] is an honest work, but naive. I cannot believe its central hypothesis: that the three pyramids of Giza were positioned precisely to coincide with those of the three stars of Orion's Belt.' However, what had really annoyed him was not the central thesis of the book but something else: references we had made to how, because of precession, the way the skies looked to the pyramid builders was not exactly the same as the sky map they had laid out on the ground. This seemed to reflect the sky of *c*.10,400 BC rather than *c*.2500 BC when it is believed the pyramids were built. Berry went on: 'According to the authors, the period of 10,400 BC was what the Egyptians called the First Time, when they believed that gods became men. But this date, more than 7,000 years before the first pyramid was built, was many millennia before civilization and the invention of writing. Despite the authors' scholarship, I cannot believe this information could have been passed down so accurately through the ages.'

Mr Berry was perhaps not aware that geologists were already waging a war concerning the age of the Sphinx. Though we did not know it at the time we were writing *The Orion Mystery*, Robert and I had allies who would support us in the contention that the layout plan of the pyramids related to an earlier age than that of their actual construction. Even as *The Orion Mystery* was published, there were teams of explorers searching the vicinity of the Great Sphinx for one or more secret chambers in which might be concealed the records of a lost civilization.

The part of *The Orion Mystery* that seemed to cause more controversy than all of the rest of the book put together was the chapter entitled 'The Great Star-clock of the Epochs'. This was somewhat ironic, as we only included it as an afterthought; it was ancillary to the central argument concerning the Orion correlation and the use of the Great Pyramid in the Opening of the Mouth ceremony. The interest provoked by this chapter was out of proportion to its significance and at times threatened to overshadow the rest of the book. However, while Adrian Berry was sceptical, not all reviewers were unmoved by our arguments. Colin Wilson, writing in the *Evening Standard* of 10 February 1994, was positively enthusiastic about this aspect of the book, realizing that it buttressed the ideas of another independent researcher, John Anthony West, who was then suggesting that the Great Sphinx was much older than is generally imagined:

> Within the past few years, another maverick Egyptologist, John Anthony West, has persuaded a geologist from Boston University, Robert Schoch, to study the Sphinx. Schoch has finally become convinced that West and Schwaller[9] were right: the Sphinx is thousands of years older than is generally believed. A TV programme presenting these facts received top ratings in America last autumn.
>
> What has this to do with Bauval's theory? Over vast periods of time, the stars appear to change position, due to the earth's wobble (known as precession). The time the stars of Orion matched the pattern of the pyramids exactly was 10,400 BC. Bauval suggests that the pyramids were a star clock, whose hands first pointed to the date 10,000 BC, and that they pointed to this date because it was the time of the catastrophic events in Atlantis.

He throws off this theory very quickly and casually – quoting Plato and the modern clairvoyant Edgar Cayce – as if it is a mere footnote to his theory, and not even mentioning West's new evidence. But its importance cannot be overestimated. If Bauval is right, he has buttressed West's belief that ancient Egypt was founded by Atlantis survivors and that civilization is thousands of years older than we think. If his theory can be proved, it could be one of the greatest intellectual revolutions since the time of Charles Darwin.

With hindsight Wilson's enthusiasm for this aspect of *The Orion Mystery* was understandable as it turned out that he was then working on his own book concerning the Sphinx and its possible Atlantean connections. As in this book he argues the case for an older Sphinx, he naturally welcomed an astronomical theory that supported the idea of the pyramids of Giza recording a star-pattern going back to *c*.10,400 BC.

In our own book we had had nothing to say about the Great Sphinx, it not being directly relevant to the Orion correlation theory. We did not know John Anthony West, nor that the video based on his work, which challenges the current consensus that the Sphinx was carved at the time the pyramids were built (*c*.2500 BC) and that its head was sculpted in the likeness of the pharaoh Khafre, builder of the second pyramid, was to have a major impact on thinking about ancient Egypt. According to West's theory, the original Sphinx was carved many thousands of years before the building of the pyramids – possibly around 10,500 BC. The reason the head looks like that of an Egyptian pharaoh is that it was re-sculpted later – presumably at the time the pyramids were built. The evidence he presents for an earlier date for the original sculpture is the pattern of erosion not only of the Sphinx itself but also of the enclosure in which it sits. This, says geologist Robert Schoch, who was brought in by West to carry out this investigation, is characteristic of water erosion, and not air or sand erosion as had previously been thought. As there has been very little rainfall in Egypt since the period of the Old Kingdom (and indeed, for much of the past 5,000 years the Sphinx was buried up to its neck in sand and was therefore safe from erosion), they claim this as evidence for the Sphinx's greater antiquity.

At the time we were writing *The Orion Mystery*, we were unaware of this work on the age of the Sphinx. We had come to the idea that the 'First Time' or *Tep Zepi* of the Egyptians was more ancient than the pyramids from the writings of the Greek philosopher Plato, who died in 347 BC, and the extant fragments of the writings of Manetho, an Egyptian priest who lived slightly later, in the third century BC. Manetho's king lists, flawed as they are, remain the basis of Egyptian chronology to this day. However, his writings are known only from epitomes of his work contained in the writings of Eusebius and others. The king lists do not begin with the First Dynasty pharaoh Menes, who is thought to have lived around 3100 BC; there is a whole period of some 25,000 years prior to this when Egypt is said to have been ruled successively by gods, demi-gods and the 'spirits of the dead'. The exact periods Manetho gives for these different rulerships seem to be somewhat arbitrary, but it is clear that Egypt had a long history prior to the beginnings of the First Dynasty *c.*3100 BC.

Manetho is supported in his chronological framework by Plato, whose works are the earliest known to mention the lost city of Atlantis. In his dialogues the *Timaeus* and the *Critias*, which were written towards the end of his life, Plato gave what he believed to be a truthful account concerning the demise of this great city-state. Plato claimed that the story of Atlantis came from Solon, the law-giver of Athens, who had visited Egypt during his period of exile (*c.*590 BC). According to Plato, or rather Critias, who narrates the dialogue, Solon met with certain priests at the Egyptian city of Sais. There, in the course of a discussion about the relative antiquities of their countries, he was told the story of an Atlantean invasion of both Egypt and Greece that had taken place some 9,000 years earlier. The island home of the Atlanteans was said to have been beyond the Pillars of Hercules, somewhere out in the Atlantic Ocean. It was destroyed in a single day as a result of a catastrophic event, one so terrifying in its effects that not only did Atlantis itself sink beneath the ocean but the inundations caused by its destruction wiped out civilization in most of the world. According to the priests of Sais, it was only in Egypt that records of these terrible events were preserved.

Naturally, Plato's account is considered mythical by most scholars; but this has not prevented his story of Atlantis from achieving worldwide appeal. Ever since it was written, and especially over the past couple of hundred years, people have been speculating on the geographical location of Atlantis. Equally, many people have wondered about the lost records of Atlantis, said by Plato to have been preserved in Egypt and referred to by the priests of Sais. Research on the subject was given new impetus in the 1930s, when the psychic clairvoyant Edgar Cayce – mentioned above in chapter 2 – began giving 'life readings' for people which apparently referred to Atlantis. Cayce would go into a sleeping trance; then, while he was in this state of apparent unconsciousness, his assistants would ask him questions concerning the health or welfare of his clients. He, still to all intents and purposes asleep, would give replies to these questions, his subconscious mind apparently accessing some sort of historical 'memory bank' that according to him existed in the ether. The readings he gave were scrupulously recorded by his assistants and preserved in volumes which are now kept at the ARE (Association for Research and Enlightenment) centre in Virginia Beach that was founded to perpetuate his work. Many of his replies gave prescriptions for medications, often quite exotic and entirely unknown to him when conscious, to treat the physical infirmities of his clients. However, sometimes he would refer to the 'previous lives' of individuals and to how this or that experience from the past was affecting their lives in the present. Many of these past-life readings were said to have taken place in either Egypt or the lost continent of Atlantis or both. By analysing and comparing these readings, which number about 20,000, his followers were able to build up a detailed picture of Atlantis and of how, even before it sank beneath the waves, much of its knowledge was transferred to Egypt. Of course, this could all be dismissed as so much imagination – were it not that, though his responses emerged over a period of some thirty years, the picture of the past that they painted bore a marked continuity of style and content. Given this evidence, it has to be admitted that at the very least his imagination was consistent.

According to the Cayce readings, a party of Atlanteans, knowing that their own country was to be destroyed, came to Egypt. There, in partnership with other immigrants from Asia and with the indigenous peoples of Africa, they established a new civilization. In Egypt they built and buried a 'Hall of Records' close to the Sphinx, which according to Cayce was sculpted around 10,500 BC. This, as Adrian Berry was quick to point out in his critique of *The Orion Mystery,* is some 7,000 years before civilization proper is supposed to have begun in the Nile valley. Yet Cayce's story of the sinking of Atlantis, the beginnings of civilization in Egypt and the burial of secret records, improbable as it at first seems, does echo some of what is said both in the *Hermetica* and in other classics of world civilization. It is not hard to see that the story of the Atlantis flood parallels that of Noah in the Bible, of Utnapishtim in the *Epic of Gilgamesh,*[10] and of Deucalion, the Greek 'Noah' who was regarded as the father of the Hellenic race. Similarly, the idea of buried records from Atlantis matches the notion of a secret cache of 'books of Hermes', buried for safety by Thoth/Hermes at the time he is said to have brought civilization to Egypt.

The quest for the remains of a mysterious, antique civilization (Atlantis by any other name) was also the subject of research by Graham Hancock, a friend of John Anthony West. Graham met Robert and myself while we were busy writing *The Orion Mystery* and became very interested in the theory connecting the pyramids with Orion. He was quick to appreciate the importance of the Orion correlation theory, and in particular the idea that the pyramids supported a date of *c.*10,500 BC for the start of civilization. Accordingly, he and Robert teamed up to write a follow-up book to *The Orion Mystery* called *Keeper of Genesis*. My own work, meanwhile, was taking my attention east of Egypt towards Mesopotamia as I re-engaged in a quest for the mysterious Magi, the 'wise men' who visited Bethlehem at the start of Matthew's Gospel. I had more than an inkling that they were connected with the same mystery tradition as the philosophers who wrote the *Hermetica*, and indeed Robert and I had often discussed this. However, what I was now to discover in Mesopotamia went far beyond even my expectations in the light it was to throw on esoteric Christianity.

CHAPTER 6

THE KINGS OF THE EAST

Robert Bauval's theory that the pyramids of the Fourth Dynasty were constructed to make a map on the ground of the region of the heavens incorporating the Orion constellation and the nearby Hyades star group reminded me of something I had read about twenty years earlier, shortly before I went on pilgrimage to Israel. This was a story recorded in G. I. Gurdjieff's book, *Meetings with Remarkable Men*. An Armenian Greek who had grown up at the end of the nineteenth century on the border between Russia and Turkey, Gurdjieff was an unusual amalgam of parts: a searcher after mysteries and at times also a tsarist spy, at the turn of the century he travelled all over the Near East and even as far as China and Tibet on a quest for secret knowledge. According to his own testimony he met up with a number of otherwise unknown masters and became an initiate of a secret society called the Sarmoung (or Sarman) Brotherhood. Later, during the 1920s, he became famous as a guru operating from a priory just outside Paris.

Though Gurdjieff died in 1948, his ideas lived on in a book by the same P. D. Ouspensky who had earlier visited the pyramids, called *In Search of the Miraculous: Fragments of an Unknown Teaching*. Based on lectures given by Gurdjieff at St Petersburg and Moscow during the First World War, it became a cult best-seller in the 1970s. I first read this book in 1971 and was immediately struck by the coherence of the ideas it expressed, which were so different from the empty vapours of much 'New Age' literature. Like Ouspensky, I was anxious to find the 'miraculous' and felt strongly that Gurdjieff's ideas were, as by his own admission, not all of his own creation. I was sure that he had indeed found some hidden source (or, as he would call it, a 'school') where the ancient wisdom was still taught. The question was, what was this school and where was it based?

Most commentators on his work (and there have been many, including a large number of his former students) write that Gurdjieff probably learned most of what he taught from one or more of the Sufi orders, such as the Naqshbandi, that were active in the Near East at the time he was making his search. I was not so sure. While it was clear from his books that he had visited many Sufi monasteries or *tekkes*, I was not convinced that Sufism, at least as generally known, was the source of the core ideas, particularly those concerning cosmology, that made up his system. For one thing, Gurdjieff himself was a Christian and stated that his 'system' was 'esoteric Christianity'. Although he claimed to have visited Mecca and to have travelled widely in Islamic countries, there is no evidence that he converted to Islam. Indeed, his requiem service was held in the Russian Orthodox cathedral in Paris and he was buried in a Christian cemetery. Had he been a Muslim convert it seems unlikely that this would have been his wish; and yet without his being a professed Muslim it is equally unlikely that any Sufi group would have unveiled to him its inner traditions and secrets.

To resolve the mystery of where Gurdjieff obtained his system it seemed to me that we needed to ignore the claims of his later followers and to look for clues in his own writings and those of Ouspensky, his star pupil and first biographer. These sources indicate two things: first, Gurdjieff's great interest in Egypt; and second, his belief that the Christian religion, at least in its outer manifestations, owed as much (if not more) to Egypt as to Judea.

This latter conviction is clear from one of the conversations he had with Ouspensky, recorded in *In Search of the Miraculous*:

'Generally speaking we know very little about Christianity and the form of Christian worship; we know nothing at all of the history and origin of things. For instance, the church, the temple in which gather the faithful and in which services are carried out according to special rites; where was this taken from? Many people do not think about this at all. Many people think that the outward form of worship, the rites, the singing of canticles and so on, were invented by the fathers of the church. Others think that this outward form has been taken partly from pagan religions and partly from the Hebrews. But all of it is untrue. The question of the origin of the Christian church, that is, of the Christian temple, is much more interesting than we think . . .

'The Christian church, the Christian form of worship, was not invented by the fathers of the church. It was all taken in ready-made form from Egypt, only not from the Egypt we know but from one which we do not know. This Egypt was in the same place as the other but it existed much earlier. Only small bits of it survived in historical times, and these bits have been preserved in secret and so well that we do not even know where they have been preserved.'[1]

Gurdjieff's interest in Egypt was more than academic. In the semi-autobiographical *Meetings with Remarkable Men* he tells the story of how he found one of the keys to the secrets of Egypt in the course of a search for the location of an ancient monastery in northern Mesopotamia. During this adventure he stayed at the home of an Armenian priest while his travelling companion, another Armenian called Pogossian, recovered from a spider's bite. The priest showed his visitors an old map, drawn on vellum or animal skin, of 'pre-sand

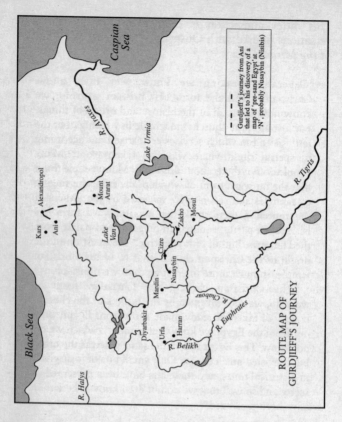

Gurdjieff's journey from Ani that led to his discovery of a map of 'pre-sand Egypt' at 'N', probably Nusaybin (Nisibis)

ROUTE MAP OF GURDJIEFF'S JOURNEY

Egypt'. This map, the priest said, had been in his family's hands for generations, having been passed on to him by inheritance from his great-grandfather. In *Meetings* Gurdjieff tells us that he was so excited when he saw this map that he waited until the priest had gone out and then surreptitiously made a copy of it on oiled paper which he sewed into the lining of his jacket. Thus prepared, he abandoned for the time being his earlier search for the secret brotherhood and immediately headed off for Egypt. Once there he began an intensive study of the pyramids and Sphinx, which he now believed dated from a time before Egypt became engulfed in sand.

Gurdjieff's story of the map and of how its discovery had influenced his quest for knowledge had impressed me greatly when I first read it. Though he makes no further mention of it in his writings, it was clearly of great importance. It was clear from his actions that Gurdijeff's interest in Egypt was mainly centred on the pyramids, which have for many centuries been engulfed in sand. I could only conclude that 'pre-sand Egypt' referred to a time when they were free from sand. Given that we could now see that pyramid fields were themselves a map of the region of the sky in the vicinity of Orion, it was more than tempting to think that his map was also of the pyramid region and that what had so excited him was the realization that it indicated the same thing. Now, after working on *The Orion Mystery*, I began to suspect that what he might have seen and found so fascinating in the house of the Armenian priest was an ancient map of the pyramids, showing their connection with the Orion constellation. That such a map should have turned up in Mesopotamia was not really surprising. After all, the *Corpus Hermeticum* had been preserved until about the eleventh century at Harran, the Mesopotamian city where, according to the Bible, Abraham tarried on his way to Canaan and where he subsequently buried his father Terah. The people who had looked after these Hermetic texts, regarding them as sacred scriptures, were called Sabians. Star-worshippers (their name is said by some to derive from the Egyptian word *s'ba*, meaning 'star'), they were in possession of other Greek texts besides these – on subjects including medicine, alchemy and mathematics – which they subsequently translated into Arabic. In this way many classical works lost to the West were preserved. The Sabians are also said to have made regular pilgrimages to Egypt to worship at the pyramids. Putting two and two together, I began to suspect that the map Gurdjieff had stumbled upon,

117

although it may have itself been a copy of some other even more ancient document, had probably been drawn by a Sabian.

Looking more closely at Gurdjieff's itinerary, I concluded that the place where the Armenian priest must have lived (which Gurdjieff enigmatically calls 'N') was a town in south-east Turkey now known as Nusaybin.[2] In Roman times Nusaybin was called Nisibis and it was of great strategic importance. From the middle of the second century BC it was the residence of the kings of Armenia, before it was subsumed into the Roman Empire by Trajan in AD 115. It was to change hands several more times, between Rome and Parthia, before eventually being surrendered for good by the Roman emperor Jovian in AD 363. At that time, as part of the Parthians' price for allowing a Roman retreat, the entire population of Nisibis, most of whom were Christians, was forced to leave and find new homes to the west. However, in AD 489 there was a movement of people in the opposite direction, when the diophysite-leaning 'School of the Persians' at Edessa was closed and its followers moved back to Nisibis, where they either founded a new academy or reinvigorated one already there.[3] It seemed to me quite possible that the Sarmoung Brotherhood, to which Gurdjieff alluded and which seemed to be connected with Nisibis, was not a Sufi society at all but was descended from this essentially Christian academy. Furthermore, an even older name for Nisibis was Soba. Could this, I wondered, and not the Egyptian word *s'ba*, be the origin of the name Sabian? Could the so-called Sabians of Harran have been descended from earlier migrant 'Sobians' from Nisibis?

With these possibilities in mind I was beginning to see a link – a tenuous one, it is true – between the Sabians of Harran, the Christian School of the Persians at Nisibis and Gurdjieff's Sarmoung Brotherhood. All or any of these groups could have been interested in the stars and have preserved knowledge of the connection between

Orion and the pyramids of Egypt in the form of a map of 'pre-sand Egypt'. However, so far this was all just conjecture. I realized that the only way to judge whether or not Gurdjieff's story of this map was remotely feasible was to make the long journey to Nisibis/Nusaybin myself. For various reasons the trip could not be made immediately; but eventually, in October 1995, my wife Dee and I set off in pursuit of further enlightenment.

Not surprisingly, given its position on the Syrian border very close to Iraq, Nusaybin turned out to be strongly Arabic in character. A dusty place of low buildings (none seemed to be over two storeys in height), it was surrounded on all sides by the northern Mesopotamian plains with a dramatic backdrop of mountains some miles to the north. The streets were crowded with people, many of them traditionally dressed; more Tijuana than San Diego, it had the air of a border town in the old Wild West. On the surface at least, there was little evidence that this had once been a major centre of learning in the Christian, Muslim or any other tradition. The overwhelming sense was of people trapped in a time-warp; I felt that the place could not have been very different a century ago when Gurdjieff himself journeyed through these parts.

The Christians in this area of Turkey and Syria, which along with parts of Iraq and Iran is claimed as their homeland by the Kurdish people, are called Suriani and are members of the Jacobite church, named after James (Jacobus) Baradeus, the sixth-century bishop of Edessa. Their numbers are diminishing fast as people migrate to Istanbul and the other big cities of Turkey in search of work and to get away from the Kurdish 'troubles'. The few thousand who remain are under the religious jurisdiction of a patriarch resident in Syria. To serve their religious needs there is still one church in the town, the rest having been either turned into mosques or demolished altogether. Today there are no Armenians in this area of Turkey, the massacres of 1916 and the subsequent exodus of any who somehow managed to survive that holocaust having seen to that. However, the Armenian and Jacobite churches have much in common, and in 728 at a council of the Armenian church at Manzikert, a union was established between them. Thus any Armenians remaining in the town would have attended the sole surviving church. This church, I suspected, was probably the place where Gurdjieff and Pogossian saw the strange map of Egypt.

When we eventually found it, hidden down a side street and not far from a border checkpoint, the church at Nusaybin was a strangely haunting place. It was a very old building and, no doubt to protect it from vandalism, was hidden behind a high enclosing wall. On entering the compound we were greeted by a middle-aged woman with a small child in tow. She turned out to be the caretaker and, for a modest tip, showed us round. The building was more like a small fortress than a church. One could imagine the frightened citizens hiding here during the long wars between Rome and Parthia that dominated the fourth century. Certainly it looked old enough to have been in existence in those far-off times. The windows had all been bricked up for security and it was very dark inside; however, once our eyes had become accustomed to the gloom, we could see that the building had some interesting features. The walls looked as though they had once been painted – but so long ago that any colours had long since worn off or become hidden under a thick covering of candle soot. There were several doors with rounded archways decorated with carefully carved leaves in ornate Byzantine style. In front of a simple altar was a small lectern, and on this was a Bible with a large, metallic cross placed on it to hold open the pages. An embroidered cloth depicting the Virgin Mary hung in front of another lectern, adding a little colour to the sombre surroundings but also a touch of melancholy. One had the sense that the life had all but gone out of this

Christian community, leaving only memories behind. Before long, perhaps within a generation, the congregation would die out completely, and then the church would be taken over by others to be either demolished or put to some other use. It seemed a sad ending to nearly 2,000 years of Christian faith in these parts.

What was particularly strange about this church to us as Westerners was that it had no spire or tower, not even an apex roof. Instead it was crowned with a small apartment, the residence of the priest when he was at home. (The parish now being so small, it does not have a resident priest of its own but shares one with neighbouring towns.) It was not very large, but it had in front of it a roof-terrace which provided a comfortable sitting area at times when the sun was not shining too strongly. This feature strengthened my growing conviction that this was the apartment where Gurdjieff had stayed and where he was shown the map, for in *Meetings with Remarkable Men* he describes how the convalescent Pogossian was able to sit outside on the priest's terrace during the day. We did not see (nor did we expect to see) any trace of the old priest's map. After more than a century of comings and goings at the church, it would have been more than remarkable if we had. However, I had seen enough to feel sure that this church was where Gurdjieff had seen it.

Leaving Nusaybin, we headed northwards to the town of Mardin in the foothills of the Taurus mountains. Here we visited another very ancient foundation, known after the colour of its brickwork as Deyrul Zafaran, 'the Saffron Monastery'. It was first built in AD 495 – six years after the expulsion of the School of the Persians from Edessa to Nisibis. Of great interest to us was a pre-Christian temple still visible in the basement. This features a window which, according to our guide, was illuminated by the rising sun. Whether this occurred at the spring equinox or the solstice he didn't say; but it was proof, if any were needed, that in these parts remnants of ancient religious beliefs and practices lie just below the surface. Leaving Mardin, we followed Gurdjieff's route westwards, to the city now known as Sanliurfa ('Illustrious Urfa' – Urfa for short), formerly called Edessa by the Greeks.

As mentioned above, in AD 363, following the disastrous defeat of the Emperor Jovian, Nisibis (and presumably Mardin as well) was surrendered to the Persians. The local population, who had been loyal to Rome, were permitted, indeed compelled under the terms of the treaty, to leave the town in a mass evacuation. In scenes reminiscent of modern-day Bosnia, the refugees made their way west; many of them settled in Edessa, where they established the 'School of the Persians'. It seems to have been called this because, as far as the resident population of Edessa was concerned, the immigrants from Nisibis were Persians, their home town now being firmly in the Parthian Empire. In reality, they were mostly either Armenians or Christianized Assyrians – 'Aisors', as Gurdjieff calls them. As the school was Nestorian in outlook,[4] it also seems to have received pupils from abroad, particularly the Parthian Empire, where Christianity was a minority religion and the dominant sect was Nestorian. As a consequence it was famous throughout the world as a centre of learning and a place where the knowledge of the East, particularly of Persia, was made available to the West. As far as the mainstream church was concerned, however, the Nestorians were heretics; and, as we have seen, in 489 the School of the Persians was closed on the orders of the Emperor Zeno and its adherents driven back over the border to Nisibis. I suspected, however, that there might still be some traces of its existence at Urfa.

Returning to Urfa, which we had visited briefly the previous year (on which occasion I had been so unwell that we had had to abandon any thoughts of investigating the city), was the highlight of our trip to northern Mesopotamia. As Gurdjieff says that after he left 'N' (Nusaybin) he headed straight for Smyrna (Izmir) en route to Egypt, he must have passed through Urfa, which lies on the main road west. He would not, alas, have been able to stay as we did at the Hotel Harran, which was not built until the 1960s; but he would, like us, have enjoyed drinking *cai* and eating the honeyed sweetmeats that are a speciality of the area. As he was interested in archaeology and the town has many unique and fascinating features, it seems more than likely that he would have spent at least a few days here before journeying onwards.

Originally called Orhay before the Greeks renamed it Edessa, Urfa is an extremely ancient city, its origins lost in the mists of time. It was already very old when Alexander the Great invaded the Persian Empire in 334 BC and annexed this whole region. After he died his empire was divided between his generals and Mesopotamia passed to the lot of Seleucus. In *c.*302 BC he founded a number of cities in Syria and Mesopotamia with the name Antioch, the most famous being the western capital of the Seleucid Empire, which in Roman times was to rival Athens and Alexandria in importance. Edessa was one of the other cities founded, or rather re-founded, under the same name at this time. On later coins of the dynasty it is called 'Antioch by the Callirhoe' (Antioch by the beautiful flowing [water]) – a reference to the spring-fed stream and fish-ponds at the centre of the city. However, its original name was Orhay or Ursu, translated by some as the biblical 'Ur of the Chaldees' and it is from this name that the modern name Urfa is derived.

When the Seleucid Empire abandoned Mesopotamia in 129 BC and withdrew to Syria, the province of Edessa, or Osrhoene as it was then called, though theoretically under Parthian suzerainty, became a small kingdom in its own right. It was ruled by a line of 'toparchs', many of whom were called Abgar, and continued to be so governed, at least nominally, right up until its incorporation into the Roman Empire as a *colonia* by Caracalla in AD 214. From then on until its final conquest by the Turks in 1146,

Edessa was the most important stronghold in northern Mesopotamia. In part this was due to its location and the near-impregnability of its citadel, but also important to its survival was the year-round availability of clean water from natural springs. For these reasons it was known as the 'Eye of Mesopotamia', the jewel which any power wishing to become dominant in the area had to have under its control.

The toparchs of Edessa were early converted to Christianity. According to an ancient legend Abgar V, who was lame and suffered from an incurable disease – possibly leprosy – wrote a letter to Jesus inviting him to come to Edessa and settle there. He is said to have sent this letter via his secretary, called Hannan, who according to one of the versions of this story was also the court artist. Hannan is said to have brought back to Abgar a likeness of Jesus on a headscarf, or 'Mandylion', along with the Master's reply saying that while he himself could not come to Edessa, once his mission was fulfilled an apostle would be sent to cure the king. In due course, after the events of Calvary, an apostle named Addai or Thaddeus arrived at the Edessan court and Abgar was miraculously healed. In later accounts of this miracle it was said to have been achieved with the help of the head-scarf, which was no longer described as a simple portrait drawn by an artist but a likeness of Jesus imprinted on the cloth after his baptism in the Jordan. The Mandylion was an important relic at Edessa, certainly from the sixth century onwards and probably from long before that. It was believed that as long as it remained in the city, Edessa would not fall to its enemies. Subsequent events proved this hope false: the city changed hands many times even before the removal of the Mandylion by the Byzantines in 943.

Aided by the presence of the Mandylion, Edessa rose to become one of the most important theological centres of the Christian world. Its cathedrals and churches were said to rival those of Constantinople itself, and its libraries were on a par with those of Antioch and Athens. Yet, unlike those cities, it was in daily contact with people from the east. Trade routes from India and the lands of the Parthian Empire ran through northern Mesopotamia, and Edessa was one of the most important stopping-off points for merchants. Its bazaar, which is still the largest in eastern Turkey, would then have been a lively place of discussion. It is therefore not surprising that Edessa was a major centre for philosophical debate, both between different Christian sects and between Christians and the pagans who were their neighbours to the east and south. Certainly if a brotherhood of initiates were active in the area of northern Mesopotamia, Edessa would have been their city of choice from which to operate.

A major conduit for the transmission of knowledge from east to west and west to east was, as we have seen, the School of the Persians, whose professors and students were famed throughout the world for their knowledge. The original site of this school was at the foot of the citadel next to the famous fish-ponds known as the 'Pools of Abraham'. Today these holy ponds, with their tranquil tea-gardens, make a pleasant oasis away from the dust and heat of the city; at the height of Edessa's fortunes, however, they would have been inside the grounds of the palace. Not surprisingly, these ponds have an interesting story associated with them. According to this legend the patriarch Abraham (or Ibrahim, as he is known locally) was born in a cave beneath the citadel, where the spring that feeds the pools rises, and Orhay or Urhay, meaning 'Ur of the Chaldees', was the original name of the city. In a footnote to his extremely valuable book *Edessa, the Blessed City*, Professor J. B. Segal writes: 'Basil, cited by Michael the Syrian, declares: "After the flood, in the time of Noah, King Nimrod . . . built Orhay. He called it 'Ur', that is 'town', and as the Chaldeans lived there he added 'hay', that is 'that town [of the Chaldeans]', just as Urshalem (Jerusalem) signifies 'town of Shalem'."'

According to the legend, when Abraham reached manhood he was arrested by Nimrod and imprisoned on the citadel, which is known today as the 'Throne of Nimrod'.[5] On top of the citadel, overlooking the city and at the edge of a sheer natural cliff face, are two massive Corinthian pillars. These, though dating from the reign of Abgar the Great at the end of the second and beginning of the third century AD, are nevertheless associated with the legend of Abraham who lived nearly two millennia earlier. Nimrod, it is said, had him tied between the two pillars and then, when the young man still refused to do his bidding, cast him off from the top of the citadel to what ought to have been his certain death. Fortunately for Abraham, the earth opened to give birth to the fish-pond that carries his name, and he splashed down harmlessly in the water.

Now, while the story of Abraham's imprisonment and subsequent fall into the ponds is obviously mythical, it is not without interest. For although there is no reference in the Bible to Abraham's ever having been tied between columns, this does happen to another mighty man of Israel: Samson. Weakened through being shorn of his hair by the treacherous Delilah, he was captured and blinded by the Philistines. Not noticing that his hair had regrown while he had been imprisoned, his captors tied him between two pillars of the Temple of Dagon. Realizing that this would be his last chance to carry out a mighty deed, Samson prayed to God that his strength might return to him for one last time. Then, flexing his muscles, he pulled down the pillars of the temple so that he and many thousands of the Philistines perished together.

Whether or not there ever was a strong man called Samson who warred against the Philistines, traditional enemies of the Israelites, is immaterial; the story is obviously to be understood symbolically. What is important about this biblical myth is that its central figure is the Hebrew version of an archetype which is also identifiable in the Greek myths as Orion, the giant son of

Poseidon. For Orion, like Samson, was also considered to be invincible until he fell under the spell of a woman – in his case Merope, the daughter of the king of Chios. He too was blinded; but, unlike Samson, his sight was restored by the sun god Helios. Later, out hunting, Orion was accidentally slain by Artemis, the moon goddess; he was then turned into a constellation, forever hunting the wild bull, Taurus, and followed by his faithful dogs, the constellations of Canis Major and Canis Minor.

In *Hamlet's Mill*, their brilliant essay on the precession of the equinoxes and its relevance to mythology, Giorgio de Santillana and Hertha von Dechend recognized that both the story of Orion and the adventures of Samson were really to be understood as stellar myths.[6] They pointed out that the lion which Samson is said to have killed probably represented the constellation of Leo, which rises close to Orion. The 'jaw-bone of the ass' with which he killed a thousand Philistines was in reality, they argued, the Hyades star-group. This is shaped like a jaw-bone and is part of the Taurus constellation which lies on the ecliptic and is even closer to Orion than Leo. They also identified King Nimrod, who is described in the Bible as 'a mighty hunter before the Lord', as another manifestation of the same Orion archetype, indicating that this constellation was an important cultural element in Mesopotamian mythology, as it was in the Egyptian and Greek.

With these considerations in mind, it became clear to me that the story of Abraham tied between the pillars of Edessa probably harked back to some earlier story involving Nimrod himself, that is to say the Samson/Orion figure, tied between the pillars. In this case it would originally have been Nimrod and not Abraham who survived a fall into the fish-ponds below the citadel. The meaning of this legend became clearer when Dee and I made a thorough investigation of the columns for ourselves. Using a compass, we discovered that they were orientated so that the north–south meridian ran exactly at right angles to an imaginary line linking the two columns. This meant that standing on top of the citadel between the columns and looking over the city we were facing directly north. Conversely, when we were at ground level (in fact by the fish-ponds, where once the School of the Persians had stood) looking upwards at the columns, we were facing south. Remembering how at the Great Pyramid there were shafts pointing towards the transit positions of important stars, I suddenly realized that the gap between the columns could have been used by the ancients for just this purpose. With the aid of an appropriate watch tower it would have been possible to observe the constellation of Orion as it passed between the columns.[7]

This seemed to me to be the real mystery concealed in the legend of Abraham's bondage between the pillars. The story referred to the constellation of Orion which could be seen every night, at different times depending on the season, passing between the pillars. Using the SKY-GLOBE computer program to look at the skies as they would have appeared in Edessa at the time the pillars were erected (c.AD 200), I was able to see that around 12 September, Orion would be between the pillars at dawn. By 23 November, as the sun was between Scorpio and Sagittarius, he would make his transit at midnight. Then, as the sun entered the sign of Pisces, at around 21 February, he would be between the pillars at sunset. Through much of the late spring and summer he would be invisible, as the sun would be in this quadrant of the sky, obscuring Orion from view. I could see from all this that the pillars of Edessa could have been used as a chronometer, making use of the appearances of Orion to herald each season in turn.

These movements of Orion seem to have had more than passing significance for the local ruling dynasty. Immediately behind the pillars, on top of the citadel, there are the remains of what looks to have been a small, stepped platform. On this could have been placed a throne, so that the ruler of the city could have sat here with Orion passing over his head. The connection between Orion and the religious practices of Edessa is not an idle guess. It is known that at Edessa worship of a god called Marilaha took place. The authority of the local king, or *budar* as he was known, depended on the blessings of Marilaha. Firm establishment of the king's lineage was symbolized by his stool, which acted as a throne, and by a pillar which was set up next to it. The placing of pillars and stones to support the claims of local potentates was a universal practice in northern Mesopotamia, not confined to Edessa alone. At an archaeological site called Sumatar Arebesi, which is close to Urfa and seems at one time to have been a major religious centre, important inscriptions have been preserved. One reads: 'In the month of Shebat in the year 476 [i.e. February AD 165], I, Tirdat bar Adona, ruler of the 'Arab, built this altar and set a pillar to Marilaha for the life of my lord the king and his sons and for the life of Adona my father.' Another reads: 'In the month of Shebat in the year 476 ... we set this pillar on this blessed mount and erected the stool for him whom my ruler feeds. He shall be *budar* after Tirdat the ruler and he shall give the stool to him whom he feeds. His recompense shall be from Marilaha. And if he withholds the stool, then the pillar will be ruined. He, the god, lives.'[8] The king mentioned in the first text would have been that of Edessa who would have been overlord to Tirdat, local ruler of the Arabs of the area in question. It is evident that the stool and pillar are to be seen as important cult objects signifying divine sanction from Marilaha as long as the pillar should stand.

According to Professor Segal, the name Marilaha simply means the 'Lord God'; another title for this same deity, known throughout Mesopotamia, was Be'elshamin, 'Lord of the heavens'. A stool and pillar connected with Marilaha appear in miniature on a coin dating from the reign of Elagabalus (AD 218–22). Thus worship of God under this name must still have been flourishing in Edessa at the time when the pillars were placed on top of the citadel. This is long after the city had first been converted to Christianity, which according to local legends occurred soon after the Crucifixion. This would suggest that even in Christian times Marilaha was accepted as a proper title for God.

The setting up of royal pillars in honour of God is strongly reminiscent of the story in the Bible in which Jacob set up a similar pillar of his own at Bethel, where earlier (Gen. 12: 8) Abraham had pitched his tent. 'And Jacob set up a pillar in the place where he [God] had spoken with him, a pillar of stone; and he poured out a drink offering on it, and poured oil on it' (Gen. 35: 14). Jacob raises a stone ostensibly as a witness to the promises made to him by God, but also presumably to stake his claim to rule over this land given by God to Abraham. Jacob, it should be remembered, had just returned home after spending fourteen years of his life in the household of his uncle Laban. He lived at Harran, some 40 kilometres south of Edessa, with which city it would have at that time shared the same stellar religion, so he would have been steeped in the local customs. Harran is most famous for its temple of the moon, but according to the sixth-century poet Jacob of Serug, another deity was worshipped here: 'Mari [lord] of his dogs'. It seems likely that this 'lord' was the constellation of Orion the Hunter, and that he is to be identified with the Marilaha of Edessa. Thus, as in Egypt with the worship of Osiris, Orion would appear to have been seen as in some way representing God in stellar form. This would explain how, as we shall see in later chapters, Jacob himself comes to be identified with Orion.

As we wandered around the streets of Urfa, it was becoming apparent to us that there was a clear historical line of transmission linking this area, which included Harran and Nisibis as well as Urfa itself, to a religion associated with Orion. Throughout this region Marilaha, also known as Be'elshamin or 'Lord of the heavens', was worshipped as the supreme God with a status above the planets. His symbol in the sky, or perhaps the place where his heaven was thought to be located, seems to have been the Orion constellation. Thus, just as the Egyptians venerated Orion as the star-form of Osiris, their god of the dead, so these northern Mesopotamians had a similar veneration for that same constellation as being connected with their own high god, Marilaha. Since Abraham was believed to have come from these parts, it is scarcely surprising that aspects of the ancient Orion religion remain attached to his legends, albeit in disguised form. With the advent of Christianity, most especially of the Orthodox church in which there was little place for old, pre-Christian star cults, the belief that the God of Abraham was somehow uniquely connected with Orion was driven underground. However, knowledge concerning Orion continued to be part of the secret teachings of the star-worshipping Sabians of Harran. They stayed obstinately pagan right up until the final destruction of their city by the Mongols in the thirteenth century, and certainly in the sixth century continued to revere the 'Lord of his dogs'. As they also preserved the *Hermetica*, the writings of Hermes Trismegistus or Thoth, whom they considered to be the same personage as the biblical Enoch, it is clear that they would have known quite a lot about the Egyptian mysteries. This explains why they made regular pilgrimages to Egypt for the purpose of studying the pyramids and suggests that they probably knew all about the Orion connection. Nor were they the only ones. The Nestorian-leaning School of the Persians, forced out of Edessa and re-established in Nisibis, is almost certainly to be identified with Gurdjieff's Sarmoung Brotherhood – which explains how it was that a map of 'pre-sand Egypt' should turn up in the possession of an Armenian priest in this town.

The connection between Abraham and Urfa is also important for another reason. Following their exodus from Egypt, his descendants, the Israelites, were guided by a line of prophets. Foremost among these was Elijah who, like Samson, was something of a 'wild man of God'. He famously sacrificed a bull (Taurus) and is described in the Bible as wearing a rough garment with a belt. Later I was to discover that these clothes are covert allusions to his connection with another secret 'school of Orion' that probably had its antecedents in Urfa at the time of Abraham and has continued into the present under the guise of the Jewish Kabbalah. This, however, belongs to another chapter of this quest; first my attention was to be occupied in unravelling the secrets of another small kingdom of northern Mesopotamia, which at the time of Jesus and shortly before I believe to have been the centre of the School of the Magi. This kingdom was called Commagene.

CHAPTER 7

THE SANCTUARY OF A MAGUS

Leaving Urfa behind us, Dee and I made our way over the great River Euphrates. We had only a sketchy idea of what lay ahead, but were keen to visit some even more spectacular ruins in a place called Commagene, to the north of Edessa on the west bank of the river. Like Osrhoene, the province of which Urfa/Edessa was the main town, this had for a time, following the decline of the Seleucid Empire and prior to the arrival in force of the Romans, been an independent principality. Though today Commagene is mostly a barren wasteland of eroded hills and valleys, at one time it was densely forested and rich in agriculture. In those halcyon days, which seem to have lasted for centuries after Alexander's conquest and into the time of its independence, it gave birth to a syncretic religion all of its own. The inventor of this was a king of the first century BC called Antiochus I Epiphanes. Quite a lot is known about him, not just because he is mentioned by the Jewish historian Josephus but because of the many imposing monuments he left behind.

After a long drive over bumpy, pot-holed roads we eventually found ourselves at one of the most important archaeological sites in the region: Arsameia-ad-Nymphaeum, the winter capital of the kingdom of Commagene. From where our taxi parked we scrambled up a steep hill to arrive at what appeared to be a very modest collection of ruins, called today 'Base Site III'.

133

The most striking feature of this site was a remarkably well-preserved relief of a Commagene king (probably Antiochus' father, Mithridates I) shaking hands with the god Hercules (readily identifiable from his lion-skin pelt and the large club that he carried in his left hand). At right angles to this relief there was a wall bearing an extremely long text written in Greek. This inscription was very impressive to look at, and clearly its contents must have been important; otherwise Antiochus would have been satisfied with having this information recorded in books. He obviously wanted to make sure that his message would be readable in centuries to come, long after the demise of his kingdom. I was not able to read the Greek, but from the translation given in an English-language guidebook I learned that Base Site III was in fact a shrine. The inscription explained, among other things, that this shrine had been set up by Antiochus in honour of his father, Mithridates, and gave details of the duties of his priests. The inscription also said that Antiochus was inaugurating a new 'royal birthday' for the kings of Commagene, to be celebrated at the same time each year.

Below this inscription there was another most curious feature: the mouth of a deep shaft. Running into the mountain at an angle of 35°, the passage was big enough for a person to enter. Little seemed to be known about it, but from another guidebook I was able to ascertain that it is 158 metres long and that a thorough excavation carried out in the 1950s had revealed nothing at its bottom. It seemed that for decades archaeologists had been mystified by this shaft, speculating that it was unfinished and had been dug to afford an escape route in time of invasion from the sanctuary to the valley below. In fact there is absolutely no evidence for this theory, which flies in the face of reason. Anyone wishing to make a hasty escape from the mountain under attack from above would have needed not a tunnel but rather fleetness of foot. If the enemy's forces were concentrated below in the valley, then it would surely have been folly to descend into their midst. Indeed, had such a tunnel been completed then it could have been used by invaders as a means for gaining entrance to the sanctuary.

A second, more plausible theory was that it had been intended as a burial shaft for the remains of King Mithridates, in whose honour the sanctuary had been constructed. Unfortunately, this theory too is unsupported, for when the shaft was dug out, no bones or other remains were found at its bottom. A third suggestion was that it might have been intended as a well; but there is no water at the bottom of the shaft, and if this was its purpose it seems strange that it was constructed at an angle and with steps inside – unless, of course, people were expecting to walk up and down inside the 'well' bringing buckets of water to the surface. If this were the case, then they might just as well have walked down the outside of the mountain to the stream-fed river at its foot, whence they could have used pack animals to carry amphorae full of water back up the hill – something impossible in the narrow confines of the shaft.

Dee and I had visited Base Site III the previous year and had been much troubled by this shaft. It seemed to us that none of the reasons put forward for its construction made much sense. Remembering that the shafts in the Great Pyramid were angled to align with the stars, we had thought this shaft too might have had a stellar purpose. Unfortunately, on that first visit we had not thought to bring a compass with us and had not taken note of the direction in which the opening faced. However, after we had returned home to England, I discovered that were it to have been angled towards the south, then at the time the shaft was dug – probably between 60 and 35 BC – it would have marked the transits of Sirius. This seemed almost too good to be true; and so, indeed, it turned out to be, for on our second visit in 1995, this time with a compass in my hand, I discovered that the shaft faced west and not south. Accordingly the Sirius theory, attractive as it was, had to be abandoned.

However, this was not to be the end of the matter. While at Base Site III on this second occasion, which was during the late afternoon, we noticed that the sun was low in the western sky. Thinking about this, we realized that on certain days at certain times, it should have been possible for the sun briefly to illuminate the bottom of the shaft. We had seen something similar to this the previous year at Monte Alban in Mexico, where a 'shadow tube' directed vertically into the sky was used to mark the moment when the sun reached its highest elevation. We also knew that when he made his celebrated calculation of the earth's circumference, Eratosthenes made use of the fact that on the summer solstice no shadow was cast by the sun down a well at Syene, because Syene was close to the Tropic of Cancer and so at noon that day the sun would be directly over-head. It therefore seemed to us that Antiochus, or more probably one of his priests, had arranged for the digging of the shaft at Arsameia for a similar reason: to mark the day when the sun would cast a ray of light right down to the shaft's bottom. Because the shaft was so long (approximately 158 metres) it would have been pinpoint accurate as such a sun shadow-meter. In other words, far from being an escape route or burial tube, the shaft was some sort of solar telescope which would enable an observer at its bottom to identify a specific day of the year. The question now was: which day?

Back home, I consulted SKYGLOBE again – and this time I was more fortunate. I discovered that there were two days in the year when the sun would perform this feat, crossing the western sky with an elevation of exactly 35°: one when it was on its way north towards the summer solstice, and the other, about two months later, when it was returning back south. To my surprise, the first date turned out to be 27 May, when the sun was standing directly over the outstretched 'arm' or 'club' of

Orion. This seemed to echo the relief of the king shaking hands with Hercules, and also fitted the Greek myths which tell us that Hercules was, after his death, given a constellation in the sky – not, I now suspected, the dim northern constellation that we today call by the name of Hercules but more likely the brilliant Orion. I believed now that Hercules, like those other heroes, Samson and Osiris, was represented in the sky by the Orion constellation. Accordingly I dubbed the area on the ecliptic over Orion's outstretched right arm the 'shake-hands' position.[1] Given that the monument at Base Site III was a sanctuary built in honour of Mithridates, the deceased father of King Antiochus, it seemed rather obvious that the shake-hands position represented the former's ascension to the stars. Thus, just as the Great Pyramid had a shaft running from the King's Chamber to take the pharaoh's soul to the Belt of Orion, so the shaft at Arsameia had a similar function in taking the soul of the dead King Mithridates to the position on the ecliptic where the sun passed over the outstretched hand of Orion. This was, of course, further evidence of the importance of the constellation of Orion in the religious thinking and traditions of Mesopotamia; but, more than this, it indicated that, like the Egyptians, they believed that their dead monarchs were taken up into the stars.

As if this were not enough, I soon discovered that the shaft at Base Site III had another secret in store. The second date in the year when the sun would shine down the shaft was even more intriguing and indicated further Egyptian influences. It turned out to be 28 July: the day when the sun would have been in conjunction with Regulus, the giant, red star at the heart of the constellation of Leo. This again was clearly no accident; for on the 'shake-hands' relief the king was shown dressed in all his finery with several references to Leo. At his waist was a dagger belt with five lion's heads surrounding it, which seemed to be an allusion to the fact that Leo is the fifth sign of the zodiac, and he wore a crown with five rays radiating from it and a little lion sculpted on its side. Clearly, then, the constellation of Leo was important to these kings, and I formed the opinion that the 'royal birthday' of the kings of Commagene, which the inscription over the shaft said was to be celebrated each year, was to be held on this very day, when the sun joined its strength to the king's star Regulus (see colour illustration no. 10).

Further investigation into the likely reasons for choosing the Regulus conjunction for the birthday of the kings suggested that this rite was probably of Egyptian origin. It is well known that the Egyptians celebrated the crowning of a new king as the 'Birth of Horus'. In Egypt, Horus' birthday was celebrated when the star Sirius made its first appearance at dawn, heralding the annual flooding of the Nile.[2] Yet what had not been remarked upon, as far as I knew, was that in Old Kingdom times the sun–Regulus conjunction occurred precisely at this juncture. I realized that the reappearance of Sirius at dawn, after its period of invisibility, represented Isis coming out of confinement after the birth of her son Horus. However, Horus was not directly connected with Sirius but rather with Regulus, the principal star of Leo. This had obvious connections with the symbol of the lion-sphinx as guardian of the pyramids and watcher of the horizon.

The lion symbolism at Commagene was not confined to the shrine at Arsameia, but was strongly apparent at the most important monument built by Antiochus: his Hierothesion or 'Holy Seat'. A visit to this monument had been our prime reason for going to Commagene, for I was convinced that it too contained a secret. The Hierothesion of Antiochus I Epiphanes stands on Mount Nimrod, the highest peak in the old kingdom of Commagene. It features a large tumulus, or conical pyramid, built from heaped-up fragments of white limestone. At the foot of the tumulus, seated in rows on the east and the west sides of the monument, are colossal statues of the gods. Somewhere inside the tumulus, though his remains have yet to be unearthed, it is believed that Antiochus lies buried. Glittering in the morning sun, this funeral mound was visible for miles and must have served as a sort of beacon to his countrymen, reminding them always of their king. Dee and I had visited this 'pyramid of Turkey' the previous year – though not without difficulty: the Turkish army's heavy-handed response to Kurdish demands for autonomy and the recent kidnapping of several tourists by the Kurds had made the whole region a no-go area as far as most travel companies were concerned. Indeed, tour operators we spoke to in western Turkey were adamant that we should stay clear of what was now a very dangerous place. However, we were not to be put off and made our own arrangements. As our reward, we had the Hierothesion entirely to ourselves.

It is difficult to describe the extraordinary feeling generated by this strange monument, especially on a first visit. To reach it we had had to hire a local minibus to drive us up a long, pot-holed track paved unevenly with cobble-stones. Eventually, after several bone-shaking miles, we reached the car park at the top of Mount Nimrod. But this was not the end of the ordeal: we now had to hike for some twenty minutes in the thin, mountain air to reach the summit. Breathless and drenched in sweat from the steep climb, alone on the mountain except for our guide, in silence broken only by the howl of the wind and the crunch of our own footsteps on the many scattered fragments of shattered limestone, we turned the last corner to be greeted by a most amazing sight: the Eastern Terrace. To our left as we walked on to the terrace, seated with their heads at their feet like decapitated kings, were statues of the gods which carried both Greek and Persian names: Zeus/Ohrmazd, Aries/Artagnes, Apollo/Mithras and others. It was still very cold up there, even though it was May, and there were drifts of snow lodged behind the statues and wherever else the sunshine could not reach. All around us, as far as the eye could see, were stretched the mountains of the Anti-Taurus range, peaks which to us, in our elevated position by the side of the gods, looked like so many footstools.

As at Base Site III, Antiochus had been more than thorough in recording his motives for posterity. Both the backs of the statues and their thrones were heavily inscribed with texts in Greek, explaining to all and sundry his purposes in erecting this strange monument. These had been translated by two Turkish scholars in 1883, soon after the rediscovery of the Hierothesion during a topographical survey, and parts of the translation were included in a local guidebook. One extract reads as follows:

> I [Antiochus] have always believed that piety is, of all the virtues, not only the one of which possession is most sure, but also the one where the pleasure is most gentle for mortals; it is piety which constitutes the happiness of power and which makes its use enviable and, during all of my life, I have been seen to have respect for the gods, like the most faithful guard of my royalty, and an incomparable delight for my heart . . .
>
> Thus I justify in erecting, close to the celestial thrones [i.e. the heavens] and on foundations inaccessible to the ravages of time, this tomb where my body, after having aged in the midst of these blessings, will sleep in eternal rest separated from the pious soul flying off to the celestial regions of Jupiter–Oromasde [Ohrmazd].
>
> I resolve to consecrate this place to the erection of seats for all the gods alike, in order not only to raise there in the memory of my ancestors monuments which you see, but also so that devout people dedicated to superior spirits, will constantly have before their eyes, as a witness of my piety, this same place, where they will have the same feelings. It is thus why I have erected these statues in divine forms which you see, to

Jupiter–Oromasde, to Apollo–Mithras–Helios–Hermes, to Artagnes–Hercules–Ares, and to my homeland, the fertile Commagene . . .

The reason why Antiochus gave his gods multiple names, in both Greek and Persian, was that he was anxious to unite the population of his kingdom. Some of his subjects were descended from the Greeks who came to Anatolia following the conquests of Alexander; others were Asians who had previously lived under the Persian Empire. Each group had its own religious beliefs. Antiochus sought to please both by developing a syncretic religion that brought together both Greek and Persian elements. This, he hoped, would gradually win support from the people and greatly aid the process of fusion between the two disparate groups. His attempt was probably unsuccessful; not until some centuries later did the unity of religion for which he strove come about when the Roman Empire converted to Christianity.

On the Hierothesion the seated thrones of the gods were flanked on either side by pairs of eagles and lions, one of each on each side of the group. These heraldic beasts probably represented the divine guardians of the Greek and Persian royal families, from both of which Antiochus claimed descent. According to his proclaimed genealogy, Antiochus was descended on his father's side from Darius III, the last of the Persian kings, who was deposed by Alexander the Great in 331 BC, while his mother's family tree had links back to Philip II of Macedon, the father of Alexander. Forming a parade leading up to the thrones were bas-relief processions of Antiochus' ancestors, shown dressed in Persian or Greek costume as appropriate. The gods themselves were not just metaphysical abstractions but were related to the planets, the 'celestial thrones' to which Antiochus wished his soul to ascend; the most important was Jupiter (Zeus), which he equates with the Zoroastrian god of light, Ohrmazd.

141

Antiochus' great interest in astrology is clear from a remarkable bas-relief accompanying the second set of enthroned gods to the west of the tumulus. This relief, known as the 'Lion of Commagene', shows the figure of a standing lion with various stars placed on or near its body. On its neck is a crescent moon, above its back are three planets, shown as larger (presumably indicating brighter) stars. These are named as Mars, Mercury and Jupiter. The Lion of Commagene was analysed in the 1950s by two German archaeo-astronomers, Otto Neugebauer and H. Hoesen, who published the results of their research in a paper entitled 'Greek Horoscopes'. Not surprisingly, they recognized the lion as representing the constellation of Leo: 'That the lion represents the constellation of "Leo" cannot be doubted since the 19 stars which are depicted on or near the body of the lion agree very nearly with the positions of the 19 stars assigned to this constellation in the so-called Catasterisms of Eratosthenes.' More importantly, they were able to show that the positions of the planets and moon on the relief indicated that what was being represented was not just an arbitrary depiction of Leo but rather a definite sky pattern relating to a certain date. This date they calculated as -61 July 7th; or, according to the Gregorian rather than the astronomical calendar, 7 July 62 BC. They were, however, making their calculations before the days of modern computers. Using SKYGLOBE to check this date, I found that although the moon would have been in Leo on 7 July, the 6th gave a better fit as it would then have been below the head, as depicted on the relief.

The date represented by the lion was not linked to either of those indicated by the shaft at Arsameia; according to Neugebauer and Hoesen, it was related to the king's coronation. This seems rather strange, as it is known from historical records that Antiochus I was already king of Commagene long before 62 BC: he had been an ally of the famous Mithridates VI, king of

Pontus, who had fought a bitter war against the Romans, attempting to end their influence in Anatolia. Defeated by Lucullus in 69 BC, Mithridates escaped to Armenia, but was finally defeated by Pompey around 66 BC and committed suicide in 64 BC. Pompey's famous 'reorganization of the east' took place shortly afterwards and Antiochus, realizing that if you can't beat them you had better join them, declared himself to be a Romanophile. For this piece of political realism Pompey allowed him to retain his throne and kingdom, no doubt regarding a friendly Commagene as a useful buffer state between Parthia and the Roman possessions to the west. It was this peace treaty between Antiochus and Pompey, argued Neugebauer and Hoesen, which was celebrated as a 'coronation' by Antiochus and recorded in the Lion Horoscope.

I found this conclusion hard to accept, for why would Antiochus want to celebrate what was in effect a defeat? Though no doubt pleased that Pompey did not depose him but rather allowed him to retain his throne, it nevertheless seems unlikely that he would have wanted to advertise the fact of his weakness for posterity – especially in the privacy of his own sanctuary on Mount Nimrod, which would never be visited by the Romans and could therefore earn him no favours. Antiochus, like all the other minor kings of the region of northern Mesopotamia and Anatolia, had an agenda of his own. This was to maintain as far as possible his independence from outside interference, which meant that he had to play off Rome against Parthia. Though he describes himself as a 'Romanophile' in the inscription at Arsameia, it is a historical fact that in 40 BC he allied himself with the Parthians when they invaded Judea and sought to rescue the princess Mariamne, the last in the line of the Hasmoneans, from the clutches of King Herod. As Herod was Rome's chosen client to rule over Judea, this put Antiochus once more at odds with Roman policy. Thus, although he had previously allied himself with Pompey in the latter's civil war with Caesar, he could scarcely be called a committed Romanophile. When the Parthian invasion failed and Herod was securely on his throne and married to Mariamne, Antiochus reaped the whirlwind. In 38 BC Mark Antony invaded Commagene, assisted by an eager Herod; Samosata, the capital city, was sacked and Antiochus deposed. What happened to him afterwards is rather unclear. Certainly an Antiochus of Commagene was executed in Rome in 29 BC on the orders of Augustus, the nephew of Julius Caesar. This may have been his son, Antiochus II; but if it was Antiochus I, as seems more likely, then his body was probably never buried in his prepared final resting place.

Whether or not Antiochus was buried inside the tumulus on Mount Nimrod, the evidence of this and other monuments shows that he was deeply involved in astrology. As we have seen, Egyptian influences are apparent in the angling of the shaft at Base Site III so that it indicated the position of the sun on the birthday of Horus, while Greek influences appear in the choice and costume of the statuary, with Mars shown as Ares, Orion as Hercules, the sun as Apollo and Mercury as himself – a philosopher after the tradition of Hermes. Furthermore, the connection between the shaft and Orion was extremely important in the light of what we had already discovered at Urfa and other sites in northern Mesopotamia. It was clear that Antiochus was fully aware that this constellation represented a desirable place in the sky to which the soul of his father should be directed. That he was able to represent both the birth and the ascension of the king by means of a single shaft was a stroke of genius made possible only by the location of Arsameia and only at that precise time. Little wonder, then, that he felt his kingdom was especially blessed by the gods; for only at its latitude could such an alignment be accomplished. That he got himself into hot water politically on many occasions suggests that he was not a particularly worldly-wise ruler. Unlike Herod, who

1 Mount Hermon where the 'fallen angels' came to earth.

3 The author by the waterfall near the source of the Jordan.

2 The shrine at Paneas, the biblical Caesarea Philippi.

The Origins of Pyramidology

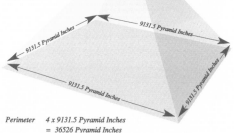

Perimeter	4 x 9131.5 Pyramid Inches
	= 36526 Pyramid Inches
	1 Rod = 100 Pyramid Inches
Therefore	36526 Pyramid Inches = 365.26 Rods
Therefore	1 Rod represents 1 Year
Sacred Cubit	$\dfrac{Rod}{4}$ = 25 Pyramid Inches

According to Pyramidology, measurements of passages and chambers in 'Pyramid Inches' correlate with history as 1PI = 1 year

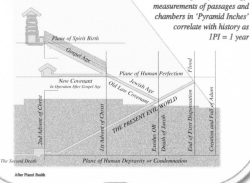

After Piazzi Smith

5 The pyramids of Giza and Khufu's royal barge of the sun. The angle of the oars represents rays of sunlight and echoes the pyramid's slopes.

6 The *Great Sphinx*, the head possibly remodelled after the Middle Kingdom Pharaoh *Sesostris III*.

7 The western terrace of the Heirothesion of Antiochus I Epiphanes.

8 The lion of Commagene showing planets and moon in the constellation of Leo, 6 July, 62 BC.

9 Base Site III at Arsameia: the 'shake-hands' position of Hercules and the Commagene king.

The Shrine at Arsameia

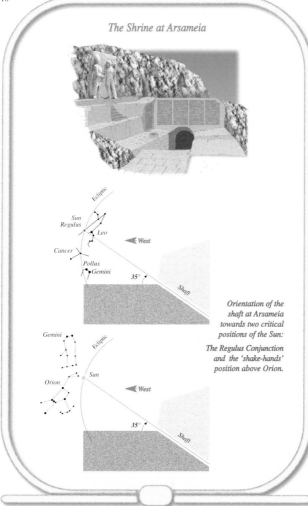

Orientation of the shaft at Arsameia towards two critical positions of the Sun:

The Regulus Conjunction and the 'shake-hands' position above Orion.

11 The Temple of Luxor with an avenue of sphinxes leading to
the pylon of Ramses II.

12 Hypostyle hall of Karnac
Temple with obelisk of Hatshepsut
in the background.

13 The obelisk of Senusert I at
Heliopolis on the site of the Temple
of the Phoenix.

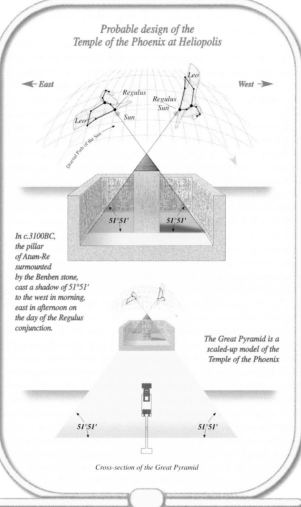

Probable design of the Temple of the Phoenix at Heliopolis

← East

West →

Leo

Regulus

Regulus
Sun

Leo

Sun

Diurnal Path of the Sun

51°51'   51°51'

In c.3100BC, the pillar of Atum-Re surmounted by the Benben stone, cast a shadow of 51°51' to the west in morning, east in afternoon on the day of the Regulus conjunction.

The Great Pyramid is a scaled-up model of the Temple of the Phoenix

51°51'   51°51'

Cross-section of the Great Pyramid

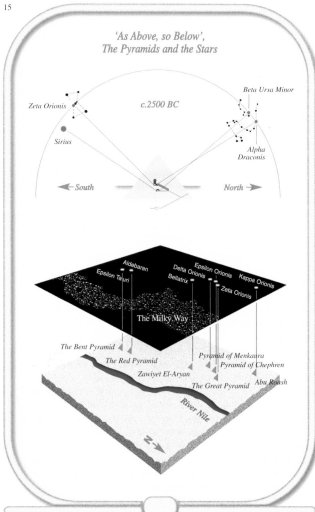

'As Above, so Below',
The Pyramids and the Stars

always seems to have landed on his feet and been adept at judging shifts in the balance of power, Antiochus constantly found himself on the wrong side. Yet it was clear to me as I visited his Hierothesion who, from the point of view of the people, would have been the better king. Herod might have been politically adroit but he was a tyrant who would tolerate not the least suggestion of opposition.

I was now beginning to see that Commagene was of supreme importance as regarded my own quest for the Magi, the wise men who visited the infant Jesus at Bethlehem. Although the attempt by the Parthians to capture the Hasmonean princess Mariamne had failed and she had subsequently been forced to marry King Herod, this did not mean that Persian influence had disappeared from the Holy Land. It remained particularly strong in Galilee, which at the time of Jesus' birth had a fairly mixed population including many rather obscure sects of Persian origin. Mariamne was murdered by King Herod in 29 BC on suspicions of adultery with his brother-in-law. He had already killed her brother, the high priest Aristobulus, in 35 BC and the Hasmonean line was effectively extinguished when he had his own sons by Mariamne, Alexander and Aristobulus, executed in 6 BC. The Parthians – the Persians – were not disinterested observers of these events. Given the opportunity, they were keen to promote the cause of any would-be king of Judah who would stand in opposition to the Romanophilic Herodians. This could explain why the Magi went in search of the baby Jesus.

Throughout all this intrigue-filled period in the first century BC, the little kingdom of Commagene was in the front line of the simmering conflict between Rome and Parthia. It seemed to me more than likely that, for all his Romanophile protestations, secretly Antiochus was always a member of a 'Persiaphile' federation. This federation, which may have been quite a loose affair, had previously looked to Mithridates of Pontus as its political leader. He was married to the daughter of Tigranes, king of Armenia, and almost certainly was related to Antiochus through the latter's father, Mithridates I of Commagene. The defeat and death of Mithridates of Pontus left a vacancy as champion of the Persian/Anatolian tradition. I believe that Antiochus realized this and promoted himself to fill that role. His 'coronation', if such we may call it, in 62 BC would not have been as king of Commagene but as manifest (Epiphanes) head of this secret Persian/Anatolian brotherhood.

Through my own researches concerning Commagene I became convinced that the organization with which Antiochus was involved, and possibly even headed, was not merely political. I suspected that this organization was, like the later School of the Persians, connected with Gurdjieff's Sarmoung Brotherhood and that it was dedicated to preserving the wisdom of the East in the aftermath of Alexander's invasion and the subsequent Hellenization of Asia.[3] I also suspected that the Magi or 'Three Wise Men' of the Christian Nativity story were later ambassadors from this essentially religious organization. The political reality at the time of the Nativity was that the three kingdoms of Commagene, Armenia and Osrhoene were fighting for their very survival in the face of the growing power of Rome. I could envisage a scenario in which a group of Magi, the wise men of the East, were keen to secure a more favourable succession to the Judean throne at a time when everybody knew Herod would soon die. Being astrologers and seeing portents in the sky, they knew that a great soul, a putative 'King of Judah', was about to be born. To this end, like emissaries sent out in search of a baby Dalai Lama, they made their way to Bethlehem. There they met up with Mary and Joseph, providing them with the necessary money and contacts in Egypt to ensure that their baby would be safe from Herod's persecution and to lay the foundations for his future education. Later, the young Jesus would be free to visit the wise men of his time, perhaps even the same men who had come to Bethlehem. Then, or so they promised, they would teach him the secret traditions of the East. As subsequent research was to show, this must have included secret teachings concerning the constellation of Orion.

Yet this scenario, pleasing as it is, is clearly not the full story. For, as I was now to discover, there are some astonishing astrological ideas hidden in the simple account given in Matthew's Gospel, which turns out to have been based on Jesus' own birth horoscope.[4]

That the Magi were astrologers is made clear in Matthew's Gospel, where they are said to have followed a bright star on their journey from the East to the stable of Bethlehem. Matthew's insistence that Jesus was born at Bethlehem seems at first contrived and unnecessary, but he had good reasons for saying this. According to Matthew's account Jesus was, through his father Joseph, a lineal descendant of King David and therefore by implication the true-born king of Israel. To emphasize this point Matthew lists the generations from Abraham to Jesus, and then makes the following curious statement: 'So all the generations from Abraham to David were fourteen generations, and from David to the deportation to Babylon fourteen generations, and from the deportation to Babylon to the Christ fourteen generations' (Matt. 1: 17). The implications of this are clear. Abraham was patriarch of the Hebrews, but during the first fourteen generations there was no line of David ruling over the House of Israel. Though kingship was first given to Saul, he and his line were quickly rooted out and David placed in his stead. From him proceeded all the later kings of Judah, with a promise given by God in chapter 7 of the Second Book of Samuel: 'And your [David's] house and your kingdom shall be made sure for ever before me; your throne shall be established forever.' This promise is repeated, though on condition of good behaviour, in chapter 2 of the First Book of Kings: 'If your sons take heed to their way, to walk before me in faithfulness with all their heart and with all their soul, there shall not fail you a man on the throne of Israel.' Yet in spite of these promises the line of David was seemingly brought to an end at the time of the Babylonian captivity when Zedekiah, the last king of Judah to be descended from him, was blinded and taken in chains to Babylon, his sons having been slain before him. Where now was a 'man on the throne of Israel'?

Matthew's answer to this conundrum is Jesus, who was descended from David through the line of Joseph the carpenter. The fourteen generations separating Jesus from the disastrous Babylonian captivity when the Jews ceased to have a king are set in parallel with the period of fourteen generations between David and Abraham. Jesus is the new King David, and for this reason he has to be born at Bethlehem in Judah, the city where David, son of Jesse the Bethlehemite, was also born.

Over the centuries there has been much speculation as to the identity of the Star of Bethlehem followed by the Magi, but the most convincing explanation remains that first given by the astronomer Johannes Kepler. He took the view that it was almost certainly a rare conjunction of the planets Jupiter and Saturn in the sign of Pisces, which occurred throughout the summer months of 7 BC and again in December. Thus the birth of Jesus would have taken place in that summer, three years before the death of King Herod in 4 BC and not at year 1 BC on the Christian calendar. Looking into this matter further and using the SKYGLOBE program, I was able to see that the conjunction of Jupiter and Saturn referred to by Kepler was in fact the only significant stellar event around that time. Given the interest of the Egyptians, the Mesopotamians and probably others throughout the Near East in the day the sun rose conjunct with Regulus as the birthday of kings, it seemed reasonable to suppose it was this day specifically that would have interested the

Bethlehem Magi. In 7 BC the Regulus day fell on 29 July. What was even more interesting, though, was that at dawn on this day there were only three planets visible above the horizon. Two of these were Jupiter and Saturn, still very close together and forming the conjunction known as the Star of the Magi, while the third was Mercury.

From all this it became obvious that the Matthew story of the Magi contained a hidden astronomical message. I could see that the three gifts that they were said to have brought to the stable of Bethlehem could represent the astrological influences of these three planets: frankincense for Mercury, gold for Jupiter and myrrh for Saturn. But the message went much further than this: in fact, a large area of the dawn sky seemed to be representative of the events at Bethlehem. There was a symbolic correspondence between what was happening in the sky and on earth. It was the old Hermetic message 'as above, so below' – but this time, rather than concerning the gods of Egypt, the message was Christian. Thus the star Sirius, which in Egypt had represented Isis, now clearly symbolized Mary, the mother of Jesus. Orion, who as Osiris had been the stellar consort of Isis, was now symbolic of Joseph. Procyon, the brightest star of Canis Minor (which I equated with Nephthys, the sister of Isis) was now Mary's midwife. The three kings were the three planets, and the three 'shepherds' who attended the stable in Bethlehem were also present in the sky as the stars Capella (in Auriga) and Castor and Pollux (in Gemini). These stars are higher up in the sky to the north of the ecliptic (in the hills) and, like shepherds walking before their flocks, rise before the stars of Leo.

Even the animals were not left out. The stable itself represented the zodiac, with the ox as Taurus, the sheep as Aries and, as I subsequently discovered from reading in William Drummond's *Oedipus Judaicus*, the donkey as Cancer. Nor did the astrological significance stop here;

for in the Nativity story the baby Jesus is laid in a manger, the place or 'house' where the animals would get their food. Now, Bethlehem means 'House of Bread' in Hebrew, and it was a town of Judah, historically the lion tribe of Israel. Thus the manger in Bethlehem could be equated with the star Regulus in Leo. The laying of the baby Jesus in his manger therefore symbolized the conjunction of the sun with Regulus in Leo.

Thus it became clear to me that the symbolism of the familiar Christmas card scene, the Adoration of the Magi, had a symbolic significance far beyond what is generally realized. Not only that, it implied that the birth of Jesus had the same significance as that of a Horus king. I was truly staggered by these findings, which flowed out of the simple application of the Hermetic philosophy 'as above, so below' to the Magi story. It now seemed obvious that whether or not any actual Magi visited the stable in Bethlehem (and it is entirely possible that they did), the reason Matthew included the story in his Gospel was because of this hidden symbolism which implied that Jesus was a king. I was more than intrigued by this, and began to wonder if other stories and prophecies in the Bible could have had a stellar meaning too. I was to discover not only that this was indeed so, but also that esoteric astrology, of the sort discussed in the last two chapters, revealed a whole systematic chronology for the 'end of days'. Astrology, and not the 'pyramid inch', was the true master-key sought in vain by the nineteenth-century pyramidologists. With its help I was able to understand how the pyramids recorded time and also to start decoding not only the Gospels but even that most obscure of all prophetic works, the Book of Revelation.

All this, however, was a long way off. First I had to return to Egypt to make a fresh study of the pyramids and obelisks in the light of the understandings I had gained in Commagene. I was now to discover real evidence that the pyramids had deep significance for the solar as well as the astral religion of the Egyptians.

CHAPTER 8

NEEDLES OF STONE

Dee and I visited Luxor in 1993. At that time our principal interest was in the Old Kingdom pyramids, and indeed our main reason for going to Egypt was to take photographs of them for *The Orion Mystery*. However, we couldn't come to Egypt without seeing at least some of the important remains of the New Kingdom (currently believed to span the period from 1600 to 1100 BC). As well as the famous Valley of the Kings, we were particularly interested in the Temple of Karnac, which stands on the outskirts of Luxor. This collection of buildings consists of three temple complexes dedicated to the Theban trinity of gods – Amun-Re, his wife Mut and their son Khonsu – and is, after the pyramids, probably the most massive of all ancient Egyptian monuments. It was in continuous use for at least 2,000 years, during which time Amun-Re rose in prestige to become the most important god in Egypt. Alexander the Great consulted his oracle at Siwa, the Greeks equating him with Zeus, their own father of the gods. Naturally enough, the priesthood which served Amun-Re benefited greatly from his elevation in rank to become the most powerful institution in the state.

Amun, however, had usurped the title of Re, 'sun god'. Originally, according to an Old Kingdom creation myth, Re was a separate god entirely who sprang from a cosmic egg laid by a celestial goose on the primeval mound at Wnw or Hermopolis Magna.[1] Amun – also given the alternative spellings of Amon or Amen – was originally one of an older group of gods: the ogdoad (group of eight) of Hermopolis. He was a god of the air, and, according to the earlier Hermopolitan creation myth, a son of the self-created Thoth/Hermes. His cult centre was Thebes – or Waset, as it was known to the Egyptians prior to its renaming by the Greeks after 331 BC. At the time of the Old Kingdom this was quite a minor city. As it grew in power and prosperity during its golden period of the Eighteenth Dynasty, so did Amun's cult, which now merged with that of the sun god *par excellence*, Re (or Ra) to give the hybrid god Amun-Re. By promoting their local god in this way, the Theban priesthood was able to assert its prestige throughout the country. As a result the city's temples became extremely wealthy institutions, able to afford to build on the sort of lavish scale unseen since the construction of the pyramids 1,000 years earlier. Across the river the Valley of the Kings, which lies below a hill shaped like a natural pyramid, became the preferred burial place of the pharaohs. It was here in 1922 that Howard Carter discovered the tomb of Tutankhamun and all its fantastic treasures.

Karnac was not the only temple at Waset. At the centre of the modern-day city stands the impressive Temple of Luxor, built by Amenhotep III but added to by later pharaohs, most notably Ramses II. This temple is built on an axis, that runs roughly north-east from its adytum or 'holy of holies', through various courtyards and gateways, to emerge in a large plaza.[2] Beyond this the axis carries on along an avenue of human-headed sphinxes. This avenue, which is not all visible today as it runs for several miles underneath the present-day town, linked the temple with its neighbour: the even larger and more impressive Temple of Karnac.

It was primarily to see these two temples that Dee and I had come to Luxor. Arriving in the evening and with not much time available, we made our way straight to the

Temple of Luxor. It was quite late by the time we arrived but thankfully, although the *son et lumière* had finished, it was still open. As it was relatively free of tourists and hustlers, we were able to walk along the avenue of sphinxes and savour the full impression of what it must have been like in New Kingdom times to approach this grand building undistracted. Greeting us at the entrance to the temple were two enormous seated statues of Ramses II. Hugely impressive, they loomed above us in the gathering darkness. Behind them was a colossal gateway or pylon built by Ramses, celebrating his victory in the Battle of Kadesh. The tapering sides of this structure would once have been joined at the top by a cross-beam carrying a representation of a winged disc, emblematic of the rising sun. In a relief carved on the front of the pylon the king could be made out in his full glory as he rode in his chariot and, according to his boasts, single-handedly defeated the enemies of Egypt. Ramses was not one to sell himself short where his posthumous reputation was concerned, and to emphasize his glory he had raised a towering obelisk in front of each seated statue. Unfortunately for Luxor, the right-hand obelisk was removed to Paris in 1833, leaving the Temple of Luxor in an amputated condition. However, as the two obelisks were of different heights, even when they were both present the entrance to the temple would have had a curiously asymmetrical feel.[3]

The purpose of Egyptian obelisks is still one of the great mysteries of the ancient world. Even the mechanics of how they were cut, transported and raised is the subject of debate among Egyptologists. The reason why Ramses placed heteromorphic obelisks in front of his extension to the Temple of Luxor has never been explained. As usual, it is generally assumed that this was a matter of whim. That they served some sort of commemorative function is not to be doubted as they carry inscriptions telling us of the pharaoh's pious intentions. Those on the obelisk now resident on the busy roundabout of the Place de la Concorde in Paris, on the spot where once the guillotine stood, have been translated by Wallis Budge and published in his book *Cleopatra's Needles and other Egyptian Obelisks*. According to him, the hieroglyphs on the central line of the east face translate as follows:

Ra-Her-aakhuti [Re-Heracte], Mighty Bull of Ra, crusher of the Asiatics, lord of the Vulture and Uraeus Crowns [Upper and Lower Egypt respectively], who wageth war against millions, the bold-hearted Lion, the Golden Horus, great one of victories over every land, the King of the South and the North, User-Maat-Ra, the Bull on his boundary, who maketh every land rise up and come before him by the command of his august father Amen. The son of Ra, Ra-mes-su meri-Amen, made [this obelisk] for him that he might have life for ever.'4

With variants, the other lines of text from this and the other faces of the obelisk were much the same – all of them beginning with the same address to 'Ra-Her-aakhuti, the Mighty Bull'. At the time we viewed its companion at Luxor we had little idea why Re-Heracte should have been called 'Mighty Bull' but later it was to become clear that this title was an important clue to the purpose of the Egyptian obelisks.

The next day we went to the Temple of Karnac to see two other, slightly older obelisks. From the entrance, to the west of the main building, we walked through several forecourts, each fronted by massive pylons, before reaching the Hypostyle Hall, one of the great buildings of the New Kingdom. Like most Egyptian temples of the period it was open to the sky, but inside there was a positive forest of columns, each of gigantic proportion and stylistically modelled on lotus shoots. The shafts of the columns were covered in hieroglyphs, no doubt of enormous importance to the initiated priesthood who could read them; but their most obvious feature, besides their size, was that they invited one to play games of hide-and-seek. Whether such frivolity had been permitted in ancient times must be a matter of debate. However, as in all such cases – a hypostyle hall was a feature of most large temples of the period – it represented the papyrus swamp in which the young god Horus was hidden prior to his attaining manhood and overthrowing his usurping uncle Set. It therefore seems natural that whatever ceremonies were conducted here should have had an element of concealment, perhaps culminating in the final appearance of a priest dressed up as Horus from behind one of the pillars.

Leaving the columns behind us we walked on eastwards, and soon found ourselves by the two obelisks. The larger of these was an enormous pink granite needle which had been placed there on the orders of Queen Hatshepsut. Like the remaining obelisk of Ramses II at the Temple of Luxor, it had originally been one of a pair.[5] However, unlike the Ramses obelisk, this one featured vignettes (illustrative drawings) as well as hieroglyphic texts. Also like that other one – and, it would seem, all other obelisks with readable texts – that of Hatshepsut was dedicated to the sun god, Amun-Re, who was instantly recognizable by virtue of his tall, plumed crown. The vignettes drawn on the pyramidion or tip of the obelisk showed Hatshepsut kneeling before him, he with his hand protectively upon her shoulder. Other vignettes on the main body of the obelisk depicted the queen, her father (Tuthmosis I) and her nephew (Tuthmosis III) making offerings to the sun god. The hieroglyphic texts written down each side of the obelisk have again been translated by Budge. Those on the front or west face read as follows:

The Horus, Usritkau, Lord of the Vulture and Serpent Crowns [i.e. chosen by the goddesses Nekhebit and Uatchit], Flourishing in years, the Horus of gold, Divine one of crowns, King of the South and the North, Lord of the Two Lands, Maat-ka-Ra. She made [them] as her monument for her father Amen, Lord of Thebes, setting up for him two great obelisks before the august pylon [called] 'Amen, mighty one of terror.' It is worked [i.e. covered over] with a very great quantity of shining, refined copper, which lights up Egypt like Athen [i.e. the solar disc]. Never was the like made since the world began. May it make for him, the son of Ra, Hatshepsut, the counterpart of Amen, the giving of life, like Ra, for ever.[6]

The reference to Queen Hatshepsut as 'him' and a 'son' rather than a 'daughter' of Re (or Ra) is most telling. Though following the death of her father, Tuthmosis I, and husband, Tuthmosis II, she was for many years the undisputed ruler over Egypt, for ceremonial purposes she had to maintain the pretence that she was a man. Thus on her obelisks and in most of her other official portraits she is shown wearing a false beard, as though she were a king and not a queen.

Walking around the Hatshepsut obelisk in the morning light was for me a profoundly moving experience. It must have been even more startling when it was first raised, for then, as the inscription informs us, it would have been capped with copper so that its gleam would have been seen from a very great distance. From the amount of workmanship that went into it, it seemed unlikely that it had been raised by Hatshepsut as a mere display of one-upmanship. From the tone of the inscriptions, as well as the references to the reflective copper cap lighting up Egypt 'like the Athen', i.e. the disc of the sun, it was obvious that the queen's obelisks fulfilled a definite function that was primarily connected with a solar cult and had little or nothing to do with stars. This cult does not seem to have originated at Thebes but, like so much else, was imported from Lower Egypt.

It was Tuthmosis I, Hatshepsut's father, who had

raised the first obelisks at Thebes. One of his obelisks stood nearby that of Hatshepsut in the Temple of Karnac, and we looked at this next.[7] According to Budge, this had also originally been one of a pair. The inscriptions upon the front (westernmost) side are not dissimilar from those found on the Hatshepsut obelisk and read as follows:

> Horus, Mighty Bull, beloved of Maat; King of the South and the North, Akherperkara, emanation of Amen. He made [them, i.e. the obelisks] as his monument to his father, Amen-Ra, Governor of the Two Lands [i.e. Egypt]. He set up to him two great obelisks at the two-fold doorway of the house of the god [i.e. temple]. The pyramidion caps were made of *tcham* metal [Electrum] . . .[8]

The inscriptions on the right and back sides of the obelisks are very similar, again addressing 'Horus, the Mighty Bull', but the left or northern side is rather different and hints at the origins of the obelisk cult.

> Horus, beloved of Ra, crowned with the White Crown; lord of the vulture crown and the serpent crown, the adorer of Temu, diademned with crowns; King of the South and the North, Lord of the Two Lands, Akheperkara, made of Ra; the Horus of gold, great of strength, mighty of valour, flourishing for years in the Great House of Maat; son of Ra, Tuthmosis diademned like Ra, divine governor of Anu [On], beloved of Amen-Ra, lord of the thrones of the Two Lands, endowed with life like Ra for ever.[9]

Here, besides the frequent allusions to Ra/Re, the sun god, there is mention of Anu – Heliopolis – the ancient city in the suburbs of Cairo which, as we would discover a few days later, boasts an even older obelisk: that of

157

Senusert I. It would seem therefore that the idea of raising obelisks originated in Heliopolis; Tuthmosis I merely brought this idea back to Thebes. This seems to indicate that he encouraged, even if he did not originate, the syncretism between Amun and Re. All this is confirmed by Budge, who writes:

> Tuthmosis I was the first king who set up obelisks in Thebes, and in view of the later religious history of the XVIIIth Dynasty his action seems to show that he was favourably disposed to the doctrines of the priesthood of Heliopolis, and that he wished to link the cult of Ra with that of the Theban god Amen. As Usertsen I [Senusert I] had set up a pair of obelisks before the house of Ra at Heliopolis, so Tuthmosis I set up a pair before a pylon of the temple of Amen.[10]

This is important, as it indicates that even though the obelisk as an art form reached its height in Thebes it originated in Heliopolis, several hundred miles further down the River Nile and much further than Thebes from the granite quarries of Aswan. However, as the granite-lined King's Chamber and the Temple of the Sphinx attest, moving granite long distances was not a problem for the ancient Egyptians. It is therefore not as strange as it initially seems that the first known obelisk is that of Senusert I (or Usertsen, as Budge calls him) at Heliopolis. On our return from Luxor we went to see this obelisk for ourselves, as well as its companion temple dedicated to that most mystical of birds, the phoenix.

The city of Heliopolis was at the time of the Old Kingdom the most important religious centre in the whole of Egypt. According to a famous legend, reported by the Greek historian Herodotus, the ancient Egyptians believed that every 500 years a strange bird, called the 'Bennu' (translated as 'phoenix' by the Greeks), would fly to Egypt from Arabia bringing with it the wrapped, embalmed body of its parent. It would take this strange

THE EGYPTIAN PHOENIX, OR BENNU BIRD

package or 'egg' to Heliopolis, where it would be burned and its ashes buried in the Temple of the Phoenix. Then, out of the ashes, another phoenix would be born. There are variations on this legend,[11] and it is clear that Herodotus did not fully understand the symbolism implicit in what the priests of Heliopolis told him. Nevertheless, it is undoubtedly true that his report is based on ideas prevalent in Egypt at the time.

The legend of the phoenix laying an egg was connected with a very ancient cult surrounding a mysterious stone called the Benben. This was kept at Heliopolis before it disappeared around the time the pyramids were built. In *The Orion Mystery* Robert Bauval and I argued that the phoenix legend probably originated with the appearance over Egypt of some celestial body – perhaps a comet – and the discovery by the Egyptians of an oriented meteorite. This meteorite was probably made of iron and roughly conical in shape as a result of its burning its way through the atmosphere. This, we believed, was the true origin of the Benben cult.

There was also at Heliopolis a sacred pillar, symbolizing the erect phallus of Atum, the father of the gods. The meteorite or Benben seems to have been seated on top of this pillar, apparently symbolizing Atum's seed or semen. According to the ancient myths of Heliopolis, Atum, the first and invisible god, is supposed to have created the universe through masturbation. His semen or ejaculate was the primal stuff from which everything else, including the other gods, was made. The root word 'ben' means son or seed in many Middle Eastern languages. The Benben stone, which as a meteorite had an extra-terrestrial origin, seems to have been looked upon by the Egyptians as being of the primal stuff of the universe, a frozen portion of Atum's seed left over from this first creation. It was therefore placed on top of the phallic pillar as a reminder of that first creation when Atum ejaculated and created the universe. The pillar of Atum with the Benben sitting on top of it is what seems to be represented in the determinative hieroglyph for On or Heliopolis, which depicts a pillar with a protuberance on the top of it.

Ånnu

Heliopolis

Although the original Benben stone disappeared at about the time the pyramids were built, it bequeathed its name to the pyramidions that sat on the top of the pyramids, and also the pyramidal tips of obelisks.[12] There was therefore a close etymological linkage between the Benben stone of the early Dynastic Age, the pyramids of the Old Kingdom and the obelisks of the Middle and New Kingdoms. It was tempting to think that in all cases the pyramidions represented the same thing: the 'seed' or semen of Atum, the cosmic creator, made manifest as his offspring Osiris and sent to earth to carry out his mission of civilizing humankind. This being the case the Benben, like the pyramids, was emblematic of Osiris and therefore somehow linked to the stellar religion of Orion.

It was this essentially Osirian theory for the origins and meaning of the Benben that we presented in *The Orion Mystery*. Yet this interpretation, plausible as it is, is clearly not the whole story. In ancient Egypt, hand in hand with the Osirian cult of the dead, there was a solar cult of the living. The west bank of the Nile, and in particular the pyramid fields, represented the land of the dead, the kingdom of Osiris. However, the east bank, where Heliopolis stood, symbolized the world of the living under the ever-watchful eye of Re, the sun god. Thus while the pyramids symbolized Orion, the star form of Osiris and his place of ascension in the sky, Heliopolis was connected with the worship of the sun god under his varied names of Atum, Re-Heracte and Khepera. When we wrote *The Orion Mystery* we had neither time nor space to go into all of this in a book that was essentially about the stellar cult of the Old Kingdom. Yet it was clear to me even then that it would eventually be necessary to address the question of the solar aspects of the Egyptian religion too if we were ever to obtain a holistic view. For while Osiris/Orion is clearly of great esoteric interest, the solar focus of most of the temples used by the living, and indeed of the obelisks, is clear for all to see.

I had also another interest in Heliopolis. On our return from Luxor, Dee and I paid a visit to the little church of the Materiya. Though of relatively recent construction, it commemorates a legend of great antiquity and of particular interest to Christians. According to this legend, during the Flight to Egypt, when Mary, Joseph and the infant Jesus fled from Bethlehem to escape the wrath of King Herod, they rested at Heliopolis. The Virgin Mary, in despair that her child might die from thirst, scratched at the ground at the foot of the tree under which she sat. Immediately a fountain of water appeared where she had dug and she was able to give water to the child. A variant on this strange story is told by Budge:

From time immemorial Heliopolis formed the terminus of the caravan roads from the north, west and south, and was in consequence a flourishing trade centre. It is probable that it was the capital of the 'kings of the North', i.e. Lower Egypt, in pre dynastic times. It was the home of many cults, first and foremost among which was the cult of the Sun-god, whose various forms were, in early times, called Khepera, Atem, etc.

The Hebrews called the city 'On' or 'Aven' (Gen. xli. 45, 50; Ezech. xxx. 17), and 'Beth Shemesh' (Jer. xliii. 13), or 'House of the Sun', and it will be remembered that Joseph married a daughter of Potipherah (in Egyptian *Pa-ta-pa-Ra*, 'The gift of Ra'), a priest of On (Gen. xli. 45, 50; xlvi. 20). There is a famous well or fountain at Heliopolis in which, according to tradition, the Sun-god Ra bathed his face when he rose for the first time on the world. This well is still to be seen at Matariyah, which the Arabs call ''Ain ash-Shems', i.e. 'Fountain of the Sun'. It is stated in the Apocryphal Books that the Virgin Mary rested by this well, and drew from it the water with which she washed the clothes of her Child, and that wherever the water fell balsam-bearing plants sprang up; drops of the oil made from them were always mixed with the water used in baptising Christians. Tradition also says that when the Virgin and Child approached Heliopolis during the flight from Palestine all the idols in the city fell down on their faces and did homage to them.[13]

The obelisk of Senusert I was not one of the 'idols' which fell at this time, for it was still standing when Dee and I visited Heliopolis in 1993. Today it, along with what remains of the nearby Temple of the Phoenix, stands in a little park, an island of ancient tranquillity amid the housing blocks of modern Heliopolis. Obelisks look more powerful at home in the Egyptian sunshine than they do under the drizzly, grey skies of London, Paris or New York. As I gazed up at its glinting tip in the noonday sun, it was obvious that it was intended to serve as a solar instrument. Yet at the time it was not at all clear to me how this functioned. It was only after visiting Arsameia and seeing the shaft built by Antiochus that I suddenly realized what the obelisks were for and how they were used: they were intended to be time-keepers, just as was the shaft of Antiochus in faraway Commagene on the River Euphrates.

As we have seen, Antiochus' strange shaft at Arsameia points west, not south, and at the time it was dug it aligned with a point in the sky which the sun would cross when it was conjunct with the star Regulus in Leo. On this day and at the precise moment that the sun crossed the east–west axis, it would have shone straight down the shaft. Because the shaft was so long (approximately 158 metres), it would have been a highly accurate sun shadow-meter. The imagery and the inscriptions at Arsameia indicated that this conjunction of the sun with Regulus was considered to be of the utmost importance as it represented the king's 'official birthday'.

In my book *Magi* I presented the case for believing that the idea that the birth of the king should ideally take place when the sun was conjunct with Regulus was a common conception throughout the Middle East. On this basis I argued that in the Gospel story of the Nativity, the optimal date for the birth of Jesus and the visit of the Magi or 'three wise men' was 29 July 7 BC.[14] It was also clear that the day the sun rose in conjunction with Regulus was connected with the first appearance of Sirius at dawn, which had always been the start of the Egyptian calendar. This was not at all surprising, as at the time of Antiochus strenuous efforts were being made in the east to change over from the lunar Macedonian calendar to the solar Egyptian calendar. In Egypt the Regulus conjunction symbolized more than just the king's birthday; it was the New Year. In Commagene they measured this by means of a shaft in the hillside, but equally the year could have been tracked by measuring the length of a shadow cast by a pillar or even an obelisk. This, I could now see, was how time was tracked in Egypt.

Now, it is fairly obvious that any tall post or standing stone will cast a shadow and it is hardly an original idea to suppose that obelisks could have been used as giant sundials in order to tell the time. However, the varying length of the shadow cast by the sun at noon each day could have been used as a calendar as well. For as the sun makes its annual journey through the zodiac, from the winter to the summer solstice, so at noon it reaches a point higher and higher in the sky. Consequently, noon-time shadows become shorter and shorter the closer one gets to the summer solstice. In a sunny country like Egypt, an obelisk could have been used as a calendrical device merely by marking on the ground the length of the noon shadow on different days in the year. To know the day of the year, you would only have to observe where the shadow fell on that day. As the length of the noon shadow is related geometrically to the angle of the sun in the sky, i.e. its 'altitude', it is indirectly indicative of this too.

The sun crosses the celestial equator at the equinoxes. On the first day of spring it passes into the northern hemisphere, while on the first day of autumn it moves back into the southern. Equinox is Latin for 'equal night'. On these two days of the year the night is the same length as the day, because the sun is directly over the equator. If you were standing at some point on the equator, then on these days you would observe the sun passing directly overhead at noon. Were you to raise an obelisk there, you could measure this moment precisely, for the sun would cast no noon shadow. Go further north and, because the sun will be lower in the sky, there will be a shadow. The further north you go, the lower the sun will appear and consequently the longer the noon shadow it will cast. The Egyptians seem to have made use of this simple fact when they raised their obelisks.

Confirmation that the equinox was important in the

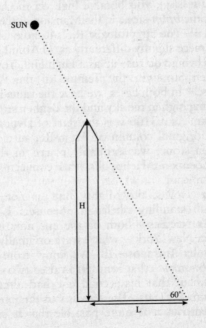

NOON EQUINOCTIAL
SHADOW AS CAST BY OBELISK
AT HELIOPOLIS

solar religion of the Egyptians and most especially in the cult of the obelisk is clear from the inscriptions at the top of nearly all of the ones I had seen in Luxor. Almost invariably these began with the appellation: 'Horus, Mighty Bull . . .' Looking at the computer program SKY-GLOBE, set to Cairo in Egypt, it was obvious why this should be. From around 4150 to 1850 BC the spring equinox took place while the sun was in the constellation of Taurus the Bull. At the start of the Dynastic period in Egypt, at around 3100 BC, the sun at the equinox would have been just above the Hyades, i.e. between the horns of Taurus.

Utterance 600 of the Pyramid Texts seems to make allusion to these connections between obelisks and the rising sun – and the Benben stone – as it begins: 'O Atum-Khoprer [the morning sun depicted as a scarab beetle climbing the sky], you became high on the height, you rose up as the *bnbn*-stone in the Mansion of the "Phoenix in" On . . .'[15] The Egyptologist R. T. Rundle Clark translated this piece slightly differently as 'O Atum! When you came into being you rose up as a High Hill, You shone as the Benben Stone in the Temple of the Phoenix in Heliopolis.'[16] In both cases, we have the same idea of the sun climbing high in the sky and the Benben stone shining like the sun. As *c.*3100 was the start of Dynastic Egypt, when the original column of Atum-Re, surmounted by the Benben stone, was probably placed in the Temple of the Phoenix at Heliopolis, this connection seemed highly significant.

Though 'Horus, the Mighty Bull' is not addressed on the still standing obelisk of Senusert I, he is on Cleopatra's Needles – both on the one now in London and that in New York – which were originally raised at Heliopolis by Tuthmosis III. We know from surviving ancient monuments that Senusert I raised two obelisks at Heliopolis, but that his second one had already fallen down before AD 1201. The remains of this obelisk have disappeared, but it is quite possible that it carried the

'Horus, Mighty Bull' type of address and that where we meet this declaration on New Kingdom obelisks it was a carry-over from Old and Middle Kingdom times when the spring equinox occurred while the sun was in the sign of Taurus.[17]

The connection between the goddess figure in Egypt, whether we think of Isis or Hathor, and the sun in Taurus is made clear by the head-dress that she wears. Frequently this shows the solar disc between the horns of a cow or bull, and seems to be a representation of the spring equinox in Taurus. Further evidence that this is what the Egyptians had in mind is provided by the legend in which Isis tricks the sun god Re into revealing his secret name of power. Bitten by a snake or stung by a scorpion, in order to be healed from his pain Re had to tell Isis his name of power; with this she was able to resurrect her dead husband Osiris long enough for them to have sex, as a result of which she became pregnant with Horus. Now, the scorpion goddess was called Selkhet, an aspect of Isis herself. She was personified as the constellation of Scorpio, which is opposite to Taurus in the zodiac and at the time of the Old Kingdom would have contained the autumnal equinox position of the sun. The wounding of Re by either a snake or a scorpion signifies the start of autumn and the diminishing of solar power as the days shorten. The sun's strength carries on diminishing until the winter solstice, when the days start to lengthen once more. However, daylight only overtakes darkness again when the sun comes back to the spring equinox, which in Old Kingdom times occurred when it was between the horns of the bull as 'Horus, Mighty Bull'.

One of the important things about the location of Heliopolis is that it lies close to the 30° N circle of latitude (30° 06' to be precise). This position, as I was to discover when I began doing more work with the SKY-GLOBE program on returning from a later trip to Egypt, has certain interesting implications. For one thing, it means that when the sun is directly over the equator, it climbs to a noon angle in the sky of almost exactly 60° as viewed from Heliopolis.[18] What this means is that at the equinox the length of the noon shadow and the height of the obelisk casting it form a precise geometrical relationship of 1 : √3. This geometrical relationship is extremely important mathematically as it derives from a figure known as the *vesica piscis* or 'dish of fish' and gives rise to a whole system of architectural geometry known as *ad triangulum*. The geometry of the *vesica piscis* is directly related to the six-pointed Star of David. In numerology the number 6 is often associated with the sun, and it is therefore interesting to see that this six-fold geometry is produced by the sun on the equinox at Heliopolis, 'the City of the Sun'.[19]

The sun god Re had an even deeper secret than this, which would have been revealed to the Egyptians if they had studied the shadows cast by an obelisk or similar device at Heliopolis for long enough: precession. At the time of the Old Kingdom the spring equinox took place in the sign of Taurus the Bull, but when Moses was alive

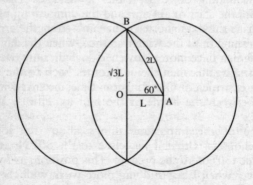

THE *VESICA PISCIS*

(*c*.1364 BC?) the spring equinox had already moved into the sign of Aries, the Ram. Today, and for the past 2,000 years or so, the spring equinox occurs in Pisces. Thus throughout the Christian era the *vesica piscis* has been generated by the spring shadow at Heliopolis when the sun is in Pisces, a 'dish of fish'. This is one reason why the early Christians adopted the symbol of the fish as one of their secret signs. Soon, however, the sun at the spring equinox will be moving into Aquarius, and when this happens the symbol of the fish, which we associate with the Christian era, will be as outdated as that of the bull or ram as an emblem for the equinox.

In sacred geometry, the *vesica piscis* is often associated with the Virgin Mary. Esoterically the 'dish of fish' can also be likened to a 'fish-pond', and indeed this may be the origin of the legend concerning Mary discovering the well at Heliopolis and either giving water to Jesus or washing his clothes. The sacred nature of the well at Heliopolis belongs to a myth much older than Christianity for, as we have seen, the city was closely associated with the sun god, Re-Heracte. That he washed his face at the well of 'Ain ash-Shems when he rose for the first time seems to be an earlier version of the legend in which the baby Jesus is watered and his dirty linen washed.

What seems significant about the myth of the scorpion of Isis stinging Re is that during the Old Kingdom the sun would also have cast a 60° shadow when it was at the autumn equinox in Scorpio. Thus the secret name of Re which Isis needed to know is clearly connected with this angle. His secret name is really a number and that number is $\sqrt{3}$. By using it she is able to generate the *vesica piscis* and thereby regenerate Osiris.

There seems also to be a connection here with another myth concerning Osiris, whose dismembered phallus was said to have been eaten by an oxyrhynchus fish. Because of its loss, in order to consummate their union and thereby become pregnant with Horus, Isis had to fashion a prosthetic phallus for her husband. Esoterically this can be linked with the original pillar of Atum, the archetype of all later obelisks and itself symbolic of a phallus. Furthermore, for Horus to be born on the day when the sun was conjunct with Regulus in Leo, Isis would have needed to have been impregnated nine months earlier. This would have occurred, symbolically or actually, when the sun was in Scorpio and close to the equinox.

The sexual symbolism would seem to go further once we recognize that the prosthetic phallus fashioned by Isis was really the pillar of Atum-Re, symbolizing that god's member. The *vesica piscis* represents a fish, but also clearly symbolizes the vulva of Isis. In a symbolic act of intercourse, this encloses the pillar. When the sun reaches the correct angle of 60°, as it does on the autumn equinox, it illuminates the top of the pillar which shines brightly as Atum-Re symbolically ejaculates his seed or *benben*. By the theory of correspondences, 'as above, so below', the god-woman Isis becomes impregnated also by virtue of knowing the secret names, or rather numbers, of Atum-Re. In this way she is able, nine months later, to give birth to Horus, son of Osiris but also the 'seed of the seed' (*benben*) of Atum.

We therefore have within this legend of Isis some sort of secret tradition concerning the wounding of the sun god at the autumn equinox, the reappearance of Orion (Osiris) as a winter constellation and the birth of Horus, the son of Osiris, all linked with the waxing and waning of the annual solar cycle. The pillar or obelisk at Heliopolis seems to have been the method by which this cycle was marked and thereby in some sense controlled. As I was soon to discover, this was only one level of the secret, esoteric teaching of Heliopolis; there was more to come. With these discoveries in mind I turned my attention back to another conundrum that we had touched upon in *The Orion Mystery*: the numbers of the sanctuary of Thoth, also at Heliopolis. For it was something hidden in this sanctuary that had apparently inspired the design of Khufu's pyramid. I was now beginning to think that these numbers of Thoth might be given by the surviving obelisk. Little did I know it then, but this was the key I had been looking for to open the doors to the next level in understanding the function of the pyramids themselves.

CHAPTER 9

THE BARK OF RE

It was a bright morning in 1997 when with some friends I found myself once more trekking towards the pyramids of Giza. This time it was not the Great Pyramid we had come to see, but rather one of the most extraordinary archaeological discoveries of the twentieth century: an intact Old Kingdom boat. This boat, which was found on the south side of the pyramid, dismantled and buried in a specially prepared pit, has its own little museum. Reassembled, it was an awe-inspiring sight, not so much for what it is (though this is interesting enough) as for its age – approximately 4,500 years old.

Close examination of the boat reveals that it was not some specially made ceremonial craft but a working vessel of a sort that might have been used by the pharaoh himself when cruising the Nile. It was made entirely of wood and without the use of nails: its timbers were secured with knotted ropes, giving the impression that it had been sewn together like a bag. This method of construction is not as impractical as it seems at first sight, for once the timbers became wet they would have expanded to close off any gaps between them and the ropes would have held them securely together. It has also been noted that it would have been possible to dismantle such a boat and to carry it across the desert separating the Nile from the Red Sea. With its high prow and stern, the vessel seems to have been intended to contend with sea waves rather than for river travel alone. Such a boat could have been used to sail down the coast of Africa or out into the Mediterranean. The question remains, though: why did Khufu, or perhaps a successor, have it dismantled and buried close to the Great Pyramid?

The answer could involve some religious purpose, for after all the pharaoh's body had to be brought across the Nile for burial. Thus we read in the Pyramid Texts:

> O sounding-poles of Horus, O wings of Thoth, ferry me across, do not leave me boatless . . . (PT 515)

> O Kherty of Nezat, ferryman of the 'Ikht-bark which Khnum made, bring me this, for I am Sokar of Rostau,[1] I am bound for the place where dwells Sokar who presides over Pdw-s. (PT 300)

It is possible that the boat by the pyramid was such a ferry boat, even the actual one used to bring the body of Khufu up or down the Nile in preparation for his burial at Giza. It may be that the boat, having been used for this purpose, was then dismantled and buried so that it would never be used again for more mundane tasks. Nevertheless, its burial by the pyramid implies that it had some further symbolic significance.

Egyptologists believe the craft to have been intended as a representation of the symbolic boat used by the sun god Re when sailing through the skies. This seems a distinct possibility, given that in some of the Pyramid Texts it is stated that the pharaoh would, after his death and rebirth as a god, travel in the bark of Re, and that he might even take over the place of the sun god to pilot it through thickets of reeds.

> I am pure, I take my oar to myself, I occupy my seat, I sit in the bow of the ship of Two Enneads, I row Re to the West, and he establishes my seat above the owners of doubles, he records me as above the living. (PT 469)

I fly up as a bird and alight as a beetle; I fly up as a bird and alight as a beetle on the empty throne which is in your bark, O Re. Stand up and remove yourself, O you who do not know the Thicket of Reeds, that I may sit in your place and row over the sky in your bark, O Re. When you ascend from the horizon, my sceptre will be in my hand as one who rows your bark, O Re. (PT 267)

It is clear from this and other texts that the idea of the sun travelling in a boat across the sky – the 'waters above', as it is described in the Bible – was fundamental to Egyptian thinking. Re was visualized as rising at dawn in his day-boat and sailing through the sky. At sunset he would disembark and change over to his night-boat. He would then sail through the underworld defeating and killing the demons of the night. This idea of the sun travelling by boat is hardly surprising given that the River Nile was the principal highway of Egypt and everyone, from king to slave, would have frequently gone backwards and forwards across it by boat.

The image of the bark of the sun god sailing through the sky stayed with the Egyptians throughout the long period of their civilization. The boat of Khufu reveals what they probably had in mind: a wooden vessel with a mast and sail to carry the boat upstream, in the direction of the prevailing wind, and oars to paddle across the 'winding waterway' – the Milky Way, the celestial equivalent of the River Nile. The oars of Khufu's bark are sharply pointed and can be seen hanging over the side of the boat. One can vividly imagine teams of slaves paddling with all their might as they took this craft on its last ceremonial journey across the Nile to his pyramid.

The constituent parts of the bark of Re had their own symbolic meanings. For example, the mast was likened to the phallus of an extremely fierce baboon god called Babi. In the Coffin Texts he is described as the eldest son of Osiris and in the earlier Pyramid Texts his phallus symbolizes the bolt on the door of heaven.

Because I know the name of her [the *nsmt*-bark's] mast;
it is the phallus of Babi. (CT 473)

To become Babi in the realm of the dead. N. has cleared
the night, the midnight stars tremble at him, he having
appeared mighty and equipped as Babi, the soul of the
'Iknt of Him who is in darkness, the 'Iknt of N. in his
hand, it belongs to the Lord of the night sky. The Lords
are afraid of him, men tremble at him, because N. is
Babi, Bull of the baboons, and he who shall see him
shall not live. (CT 668)

The phallus of Babi [door bolt] is drawn back, the doors
of the sky are opened, the King has opened the doors of
the sky because of the furnace-heat which is beneath
what the gods pour out. (PT 313)

The fact that Babi was regarded as being a baboon
suggests that originally he was connected with Thoth,
who as well as being represented as ibis-headed was
also depicted as a baboon. Babi's erect phallus-mast
is also clearly linked, symbolically speaking, with the
phallus of Atum-Re and hence with the original pillar of
Heliopolis or On.

Today at Heliopolis there is little for the tourist to see
other than the Middle Kingdom obelisk of Senusert I and
the remains of a small temple. This temple, which Dee
and I looked at on our first visit to Heliopolis, perplexed
us greatly at the time. For while it is said to be the
remains of the famous Temple of the Phoenix, it is quite
small and below ground level. In fact it looks rather like
an empty ornamental pond, and one might be tempted to
think this was its original function were it not that its
walls are heavily inscribed with hieroglyphs. These make
it clear that this was indeed once the Temple of the
Phoenix and that it was probably on this spot that
the original pillar of Atum once stood. Looking at this
little temple, it was clear that it was not because the

surrounding area has, over the centuries, been buried under mounds of rubble and dirt that it was below ground level. Strange as it seemed, the Temple of the Phoenix, or at least this part of it, had always been subterranean. The question was: why?

In several of the Hermetic writings there are references to Thoth – or Hermes Trismegistus, to give him his Greek/Latin name – burying secret records. Thoth was not one of the Heliopolitan gods as such, but had his principal sanctuary at Wnw or Hermopolis Magna. In Egyptian papyri he is shown as the scribe of Osiris, but the implication in the Hermetic writings is that though in heaven he became the vizier of Osiris, on earth he belonged to an earlier epoch. As the biblical Enoch lived many centuries or perhaps even thousands of years before Moses, so Thoth predated the Heliopolitan gods Isis and Osiris. Indeed, he is said to have left behind on earth certain records that would later be found by them: ' "They [Isis and Osiris]," said Hermes, "will get knowledge of all my hidden writings, and discern their meaning; and some of these writings they will keep to themselves, but such of them as tend to the benefit of mortal men, they will inscribe on slabs and obelisks." '[2]

In our book *The Orion Mystery*, Robert Bauval and I drew attention to an ancient document called the 'Westcar Papyrus', which relates a similar story of a search for secret 'records' pertaining to Thoth that took place during the Pyramid Age. As an appendix to our book we reprinted an article by Alan Gardiner,[3] one of the most eminent Egyptologists of his day, addressed to his former teacher, Professor Adolf Erman. Professor Erman was famous, among other things, for his translation of the Westcar Papyrus, which is stored in a Berlin museum. This papyrus is very important, for while it dates only from New Kingdom times, it is generally believed that it was copied from an original which was written during, or soon after, the reign of the Old Kingdom pharaoh Khufu, who built the Great Pyramid.

The part of this long document that interested both us and Gardiner concerns the story of how Khufu called upon the services of a magician named Djedi. According to the Westcar, Khufu wanted to know from him the ''*ipwt* of the *wnt* of Thoth' so that he could 'have the same for his pyramid'. Djedi replies that though he did not know this information himself, he knew where it could be found – inside a flint box in a room called 'Revision' in Heliopolis:

> Then said King Cheops (namely to Djedi): What of the report, thou knowest the number of the *'ipwt* of the *wnt* of Thoth? And Djedi said: So please thee, I know not the number thereof, O sovereign my lord, but I know the place where ... And His Majesty said: Where is that? And Djedi said: There is a box of flint in a room called 'Revision' in Heliopolis; (well,) in that box![4]

This passage had been translated from the Egyptian by Professor Erman, but there was still some doubt in Gardiner's mind concerning its true meaning. According to him the *wnt* was some sort of special building or sanctuary at Heliopolis considered sacred to Thoth. He deduced this partly from the similarity of the word *wnt* to Wnw, the Egyptian name for Hermopolis Magna, and partly from a determinative attached to the word which indicated a chamber. More problematic was the meaning of *'ipwt*. Previously a Dr Crum had found a Coptic word, *epo*, in association with other words with meanings such as 'doors', 'bolts' or 'keys'. Since that time *'ipwt* had been translated as 'locks', and it had been assumed by Professor Erman and others that the contents of the flint box that so interested Khufu were the keys to these locks. Gardiner, using mostly philological arguments, set out to correct this assumption. He deduced that what Khufu had really wanted to know was the *number* of the secret chambers of Thoth, so that what had presumably been contained in the flint box was a papyrus holding this information. What use Khufu made of this information is not stated, but one has to presume that he did somehow make use of it in the construction of his pyramid. As Gardiner writes: 'What ambition could have fired Cheops (Khufu) more than to possess in his own pyramid a replica of the mysterious chambers in the hoary sanctuary of the god of Wisdom?' What indeed?

This, I had thought, was the end of the matter – until, unexpectedly, I came across another translation for the word *'ipwt*. For yet another meaning of this term, or at least of its root word *'ipw*, related not to locks, bolts or even numbers but rather to the oars of Re's barge. This I discovered in a totally serendipitous way when reading through the Coffin Texts. Spell 360, like many others, is full of maritime references: 'BEING INTERRED IN ON. These are the oars of Re with which he rows the old ones, and he will not be flooded, he will not be scorched. I am these oars of Re with which he rows the old ones' (CT 360). In an interesting footnote R. O. Faulkner, from whose translation of the Coffin Texts this spell is taken, states that the word he translates as 'oars' is *'ipw* and that this was a very archaic usage at the time the text was written (Middle Kingdom). The words *'ipw* and *'ipwt* are very similar; an extra 't' usually implies nothing more than the feminine as opposed to the masculine gender. It therefore seems more than likely that the literal translation of *''ipwt* of the *wnt* of Thoth' was 'oars of the sanctuary of Thoth'. This makes little sense until we think of the sun-boat being rowed on its way through the sky. The *'ipwt* might then be thought of as rays of the sun acting as its symbolic oars.

Egyptologists are fond of the idea that the shape of the pyramids represented rays of the sun coming down through the clouds, and that the pharaohs might have believed that by building pyramids in imitation of this phenomenon they were constructing a stairway that would enable them to climb up and join the sun in his boat. As Professor Edwards put it in his *Pyramids of Egypt*:

These great triangles forming the sides of the Pyramids seem to fall from the sky like the beams of the sun when its disk, though veiled by storm, pierces the clouds and lets down to earth a ladder of rays.

When standing on the road to Saqqara and gazing westwards at the Pyramid plateau, it is possible to see the sun's rays striking downwards through a gap in the clouds at about the same angle as the slope of the Great Pyramid. The impression made on the mind by the scene is that the immaterial prototype and the material replica are here ranged side by side.[5]

At the time we were writing *The Orion Mystery* we had been very sceptical about this analogy, which seemed to imply that the pyramids were solar symbols. Yet I now came to see that there could be something in it after all, especially after talking to an Egyptian who claimed to have seen this very phenomenon at the pyramids. This idea has profound mathematical implications that I could now see might have had a bearing on the construction of the pyramids. If you imagine the rays of the sun coming through the clouds, then clearly the angles they make with one another – or, to use Professor Edwards's terminology, the slope of the 'immaterial prototype' – will be dependent on the altitude of the sun. As the sun rose higher and higher in the sky, so the angle of slope would become more and more acute, giving a steeper and steeper pyramid.

This thought brought back to my mind the image of oars being used to propel the sun-boat through the sky. Could it be, I thought, that the ancient Egyptians viewed the sun's rays as the 'immaterial' oars of Re's hypothetical boat, changing their angle relative to the earth as it rose higher and higher into the sky? Certainly the rows of oars in Khufu's very real boat would have been held out more widely when lifted from the water and plunged back in steeply. There would indeed have been a rhythm to their movement involving a variation of their angle of dip analogous to the increase and decrease of the angle of the sun's rays. If this line of reasoning were correct and the word *'ipw* was, as Faulkner maintained, archaic Egyptian with the literal meaning of 'oars', then by analogy the *"ipwt* of the *wnt* of Thoth' at Heliopolis probably also referred to the sun's rays, or more especially to their angle in relation to something in the secret chamber. In this case Gardiner's alternative translation of 'numbers' would refer to these angles, which could be measured using the relative lengths of shadows cast by a pillar or obelisk. I had already found one of these angles: 60°, which was the angle of the 'oars' at noon on the equinox and which was derived from the $1:\sqrt{3}$ relationship; but I suspected there would be other numbers of Thoth of equal or even greater significance. What could these be?

Gardiner was not merely speculating when he suggested that the Westcar Papyrus referred to a tradition that there was a document actually written by Thoth hidden in a box at Heliopolis. That Thoth was believed to possess such a box containing some sort of secret documents is indicated in the Coffin Texts. In spell 992 (unfortunately with some lacunae in the text), the deceased seeks to become Thoth's secretary:

'TO BECOME THE SECRETARY OF THOTH AND TO OPEN WHAT HIS BOX CONTAINS. My nt-crown is my reward, my reward. I am [. . .] Re-Atum, I have come so that I may reckon up the signs [. . .] I will open what it contains. The seal is broken, [The cord (?)] is cut [. . .] words. I am he who is over exhaling, Lord of the breath of the Great One [. . . I] sit [. . .] I open the chest of the Great One, I break the seal [the Lord of Right]. I open what the boxes of the god contain. I lift out the documents, for I am a lord who exhales.[6]

Though this text dates from the Middle Kingdom rather than the Old, it is not unreasonable to believe that Djedi, if he is more than a fictional character, might have known of a similar box, perhaps hidden in a temple at Heliopolis and containing secret documents connected with Thoth. There can be little doubt as to what this temple would have been. The god Thoth was usually symbolized by an ibis and, as we have seen, he was believed to have laid the egg of creation from which the sun was hatched. The place where this 'egg-laying' took place was a primeval hill or island rising out of the flood-waters of Nun. On what was believed to be the site of this cosmic creation, his sanctuary of Hermopolis Magna (Wnw) – modern-day El Ashmunein – was built. In another version of what is clearly at root the same myth, the egg of creation is laid by a goose, the Great Cackler. This story of the egg of creation has been analysed by the late Dr Rundle Clark of Birmingham University in his book *Myth and Symbol in Ancient Egypt*:

> The egg was invisible, for it took shape before the appearance of light. In fact the bird of light burst forth from the egg.
> 'I am the Soul, the creation of the Primeval Waters . . . my nest was unseen, my egg was unbroken,' for the generation of the egg took place in the time of non-being.
> There was another version of the myth in which the egg was laid by a goose, the Great Primeval Spirit. This bird was 'the Great Cackler' whose voice broke the silence – 'while the world was flooded in silence'.[7]

The third bird to lay an egg is of course the Bennu or phoenix of Heliopolis. Like the ibis, it makes its nest on top of an island, this time the primeval hill of Atum at Heliopolis. The word *bennu* is made of two words, *ben-nu*, and seems to mean 'son of (or seed of) Nu'. In ancient Egyptian cosmology Nu was a primeval god of the deep. Wallis Budge describes his attributes as follows:

Nu represents the primeval watery mass from which all

the gods were evolved, and upon which floats the bark of 'millions of years' containing the sun. This god's chief titles are 'Father of the gods' and 'begetter of the great company of the gods'. He is depicted in the form of a seated deity having upon his head disk and plumes.[8]

In each case the egg-laying bird is aquatic; the egg is laid in a nest on a hill rising out of the primeval waters, and it hatches to give birth to either the sun or a bird of light. Given all these correspondences, it is fairly obvious that in all three cases we are dealing with the same fundamental myth, with slight adaptations depending on location. Thus the phoenix myth of Heliopolis is closely connected with the perhaps even older story of the Thoth-ibis laying its egg at Wnw or Hermopolis Magna. In his article Gardiner made no reference to exactly what the secret chamber of Thoth might have been, saying only that it was at Heliopolis. Given that the phoenix myth seems to have been modelled on the earlier story of Thoth's egg at Hermopolis, I became convinced that the word *wnt* was indeed derived from Wnw and that it had the literal meaning of 'nest'. Thus the *wnt* or sanctuary of Thoth at Heliopolis, where Djedi told Khufu he would find the *'ipwt*, whatever that might be, is probably to be identified with the 'nest' in which the phoenix or *bennu* bird had laid its 'egg'. This 'nest' would, of course, be the Temple of the Phoenix, whose remnants I had seen in 1993. This would seem to be the most likely place where a flint box containing secret numbers would have been stored. The next question now was: what were these numbers?

As we have seen, Antiochus' strange shaft at Arsameia points west, not south, and at the time it was dug (*c*.62 BC) it would have aligned with a point in the sky which the sun would cross when it was conjunct with the star Regulus in Leo. On this day (then 28 July, now 24 August), at the precise moment that the sun crossed the east–west axis, a ray of sunlight would have shone right down to the bottom of the shaft. The imagery and the inscriptions at Arsameia indicated that the conjunction of the sun with Regulus represented the king's 'birthday' – real or imagined – which during the first century BC would therefore have been celebrated on 28 July. The idea that the birth of a king should ideally take place when the sun was conjunct with Regulus seems to have been a common conception throughout the Middle East. As we have seen the optimal date for the birth of Jesus and the visit of the Magi or 'three wise men' was on 29 July 7 BC.

It was also clear that the day the sun rose in conjunction with Regulus was connected with the first appearance of Sirius at dawn, which had always been the start of the Egyptian calendar. This was not at all surprising as at the time of Antiochus strenuous efforts were being made in the east to change over from the Macedonian Lunar calendar to the Solar Egyptian. The conjunction with Leo therefore symbolized more than just the king's birthday; it was the New Year. In Commagene they measured this by means of a shaft in the hillside but equally the year could have been tracked by measuring the length of a shadow cast by an obelisk. This, I could now see, was how time was tracked in Egypt.

Realizing that, just as at Commagene, the angle made by the sun when conjunct with Regulus might have been significant to the priests of Heliopolis, I decided to investigate this possibility. To do this I reset SKYGLOBE with the sky as it would have appeared on 'Regulus day' in the Cairo area (which includes Heliopolis) during the Old Kingdom. A promising start was that the computer showed that the culmination of the sun at noon in the southern sky was about 82.9°. This would give a tangent of 8, so that at midday an obelisk of 8 cubits in height would have cast a shadow of 1 cubit in length. This suggested that the 8:1 relationship could be one of the 'ipwt or secret numbers of Thoth.

This in itself was surprising; but there was more to come. To my amazement I then discovered that in the morning and afternoon of Regulus day, at the two moments when the sun crossed the east–west axis, the angle formed between the sun's 'height' and the horizon was between 51.8° and 51.9°. Unfortunately the SKY-GLOBE program is only accurate to a tenth of a degree, but even so this was an astounding discovery. For 51.85° equals 51° 48', which is almost exactly 51° 51' in degrees and minutes: the so-called p angle used in the construction of the Great Pyramid. Thus on Regulus day at around 3100 BC, representing the birth of Horus and at the start of Dynastic Egypt when the original Pillar of Atum was raised at Heliopolis, the sun would have been exactly east in the morning and again exactly west in the afternoon when it was at the perfect pyramid angle of 51° 51' (see colour illustration no. 14). It would have culminated at noon at an angle near enough to 82° 52', so that a column of 80 cubits in height would cast a shadow exactly 10 cubits in length. This all seemed too precise to be a coincidence, particularly as in the cult of Heliopolis the sun god Re was worshipped in three forms: Khepera, the scarab or morning sun, Heracte or the Horus-hawk at noon and Atum-Re in the afternoon. It became obvious that Khepera must have been worshipped between dawn and when the sun crossed the eastern axis, Heracte when it was at its height in the south and Atum after it crossed the western axis.

This conclusion had other important implications to do with calendrics, for one of the functions of the priests of Heliopolis was to maintain an accurate calendar. Realizing this, I became convinced that the priests of Old Kingdom Egypt must have used the shadows cast by the Pillar of Atum-Re to tell them when was the correct day on which to celebrate the birthday of Horus. Traditionally, as noted above, the start of the Egyptian year was marked by the first appearance at dawn of the star Sirius after its seventy-day period of invisibility.

However, if one simply counts the days from one rising of Sirius to another the calendar quickly diverges from the heavens, for the simple reason that whereas Sirius (or any other star for that matter) will return to its start point every twenty-four hours and will therefore complete a notional 'year' in exactly 365 days, the sun takes slightly longer to complete its annual cycle – roughly 365.24 days. In our modern Gregorian calendar we get around this discrepancy by adding an extra day every four years, with other rules to govern the addition of a day at the end of a century. It would appear, however, that the later Egyptians did not do this. Their calendar was divided into three seasons of four months each, with each month equal to thirty days. This gave a civil year of 360 days, to which they added five extra, intercalary days to give a total of 365. Because they did not take into account the extra quarter-day, the Sirius or Sothic year (from Sothis, the Greek name for Sirius) moved ahead of the solar year by 1° every four years. With the solar clock running slow, their 'New Year' would not come back into line again for 1,471 years, a period which is referred to as a Sothic cycle.

Much has been made of this discrepancy by Egyptologists as a means of developing a supposedly accurate chronology for ancient Egypt.[9] On the basis of very slim evidence indeed it has been deduced that the ancient Egyptians were incapable of creating a sensible calendar that would properly fit their months and seasons to what was really happening in the skies above and with nature on the earth. It is assumed that they allowed their calendar to slip round, decade by decade and century by century, so that over time they were celebrating their festivals at completely wrong times of the year. This would be the equivalent of our celebrating 1 January on 1 July, and Easter at Michaelmas. On the face of it this would seem to be a nonsense for people whose calendar was solar and not lunar. In any case, the evidence, such as it is, that the Egyptians allowed the

New Year to slip in this fashion, dates to no earlier than the Middle Kingdom: to 1872 BC at the very earliest. There is no evidence at all that the pharaohs of the Old Kingdom celebrated the New Year at any other time than when the Nile flooded following the heliacal rising of Sirius. At that time this would have coincided with the day when the sun rose in conjunction with Regulus in Leo; in other words, on the birthday of Horus. The shadows cast by the Pillar of Atum at Heliopolis would have marked this date with pinpoint accuracy. It is therefore reasonable to assume that one of the tasks of the priests of Heliopolis was to tell both king and people the right day to celebrate New Year, not on the basis of any mere counting of days or even the observation of the heliacal rising of Sirius *per se*, but rather from their own clock: the Pillar of Atum-Re in the Temple of the Phoenix.

Unfortunately, by 1872 BC, although the obelisk at Heliopolis would still have cast shadows of the right length when the sun was conjunct with Regulus, this event would have taken place some eight days later than the first appearance of Sirius. It may also have no longer corresponded with the flooding of the Nile, the most important event, practically speaking, in the Egyptian year. There is also the fact that many temples, including those at Heliopolis, had been destroyed following the collapse of the Old Kingdom (*c.*2181 BC?) and prior to the renaissance that occurred with the start of the Middle Kingdom (*c.*1990 BC). The surviving obelisk at Heliopolis, raised by the pharaoh Senusert I, dates from the Middle Kingdom and was probably put up as part of his programme of restoration. However, it is entirely possible that during the intervening First Intermediate Period, the cultural hiatus between the Old and Middle Kingdoms, the knowledge of how the original Pillar of Atum and its Benben had been used to pinpoint the equinox and the sun–Regulus conjunction, the true birthday of Horus, had been lost.

Though obelisks still had a symbolic and ceremonial importance as divine phalluses, the later Egyptians of the New Kingdom and after seem no longer to have understood how to use them properly. Evidence for this is that they now went ahead and raised obelisks in the new capital of Thebes even though at this location, which is nearly 5° south of Cairo, obelisks would not have cast meaningful shadows either at the equinoxes or on Regulus day. That the Middle and New Kingdom pharaohs were merely copying traditions that properly belonged to an earlier age at Heliopolis is further indicated by the inscriptions on these later obelisks which, as we have seen, praise Horus as a 'Mighty Bull'. During the Old Kingdom, when the spring equinox occurred in the sign of Taurus, this was no doubt an appropriate title; but by 1872 BC the equinox was already moving into Aries. Certainly by the time of Queen Hatshepsut, Tuthmosis III and Ramses II this title was anachronistic: Horus should have been called a 'Great Ram'. Presumably tradition demanded that the old title be retained even though it no longer bore any relationship to what was happening in the skies above Thebes.

With these preliminary observations in mind, I now turned my attention back to the original Temple of the Phoenix at Heliopolis. The fact that on Regulus day the sun would be at an altitude of 51° 51' as it crossed the east–west axis has many important ramifications, not least of which is the effect this would have had on the design of the temple housing the Pillar of Atum with its Benben stone crown. For *The Orion Mystery* our illustrator Robin Cook, an expert on Old Kingdom geometry, sketched a rough drawing of how he thought this temple might have looked. However, this picture gave no indication of the actual dimensions of the temple. This was something I now began to investigate.

CHAPTER 10

THE KEYS OF THE SANCTUARY

Rudolf Gantenbrink, the German scientist who discovered the little 'door' hidden at the top of the southern shaft from the Queen's Chamber, had, at the time he made his discovery, total access to the Great Pyramid. In 1992–3, as described in Chapter 5 above, he carried out a thorough survey of the monument. Having analysed the results of this survey, he came to the rather surprising conclusion that the pyramid's architect had used plans that were scaled down to one-fortieth of the final size of the pyramid. Subsequently, in an article published in the magazine *Quest for Knowledge*, he wrote:

> The heights of all construction points [of the Great Pyramid] are essentially one 40th of the basic width of the pyramid or one 40th of their height or, in two cases, even one 40th of both (these designate the construction points of the upper air shafts). This is all the more surprising when we consider that the base of 440 ells [cubits] when divided by 40 produces 11, and the height of 280 ells when divided by 40 produces 7. Two exceptions apart, as we have already seen, all distances of the same length are divisible by 7 or 11 or both. This clear sub-division into 40ths leads us to suspect that the architect of the Cheops Pyramid worked in a scale of 1:40 when placing his plan on papyrus.[1]

Gantenbrink's discovery that all major measurements

of the Great Pyramid (e.g. the height from the base of the Queen's and King's Chambers, the junction of the descending and ascending corridors, etc.) were divisible by 40 to give a whole number of cubits implies that the pyramid itself is a scaled-up version of a smaller model. The question is, what was this smaller model?

It is generally admitted, even by orthodox Egyptology, that Khufu's pyramid was built with an angle of slope of 51° 51'. As we have seen, in *c.*3100 BC this was the angle to which the sun rose as it crossed the east–west axis on Regulus day, and it could have been measured using a pillar. It is also the angle that gives the p relationship, such that the circumference of a circle drawn using the height of the pyramid is the same as the perimeter of the square base. The actual height of the pyramid was 280 cubits, while its base length was 440 cubits.[2] This gives a ratio of height to base of 7:11 and these, being the critical numbers for generating such a pyramid, would appear to be the 'secret numbers of Thoth' which Khufu and Djedi were seeking in the flint box at Heliopolis. Yet, while it is entirely possible that there was such a box and that it contained a document recording this information – perhaps even, as envisaged by Gantenbrink, a huge papyrus, with dimensions given in a scale one-fortieth of those used in the pyramid – there is another way that these numbers could have been concealed: in the dimensions of the temple itself.

According to all accounts, the original Pillar of Atum was quite short and stubby. If it had been 6 cubits high and had been surmounted by a pyramidion or *benben* of 1 cubit in height, then on Regulus day, when the sun was in the east or west, this would have cast a shadow of 5.5 cubits in length. A square temple based on these measurements, with the pillar in its centre, would have had sides 11 cubits long, giving a perimeter of 44 cubits. The base dimensions of such a temple would therefore have been exactly one-fortieth of the size of the Great Pyramid. This, it seems to me, is the scale model as proposed by Gantenbrink.

189

A further connection with sacred numerology is given by the dimensions of the boat of the sun as described in Pyramid Text 519:

> O Morning Star, Horus of the Nether world, divine Falcon, *w3d3d*-bird whom the sky bore . . . you having a soul and appearing in the front of your boat of 770 cubits which the gods of Pe bound together for you, which the eastern gods built for you.

The length of this boat, 770 cubits, is exactly $7 \times 11 \times 10$ and therefore contains within it the sacred numbers of Thoth: 7 and 11. As we have seen, the mast of the boat was likened to the phallus of Babi; the tip of the mast, which casts its shadow on the prow of the boat, would therefore equate with the Benben stone at the top of the Pillar of Atum. The Benben stone is sometimes likened to the heart of Re, i.e. the sun, and also to the soul of Osiris. It also represented the egg of the phoenix, which was incubated at Heliopolis by the rays of the sun as they shone off its surface. According to the phoenix legend, the egg was really the embalmed body, or Osiris-form, of the phoenix's own parent.

Furthermore, since the relationship of length of shadow to height of an obelisk, or other vertical post, when the sun is at the critical (pi) elevation of 51° 51', is bound by the ratio of 14 : 11, the length of shadow cast by a mast of height 490 cubits high would be $490 \times 11/14 = 385$. Since 385 is exactly half the length of the boat (770 cubits), this would appear to be intentional. Thus the dimensions of the sun-boat, like those of the Temple of the Phoenix, were highly symbolic. This being so, it seems likely that its metaphorical oars or *'ipw* were indeed thought of as representing descending rays of sunlight.

From all of this we can see that it was the relative dimensions of the sanctuary of the phoenix itself that Khufu was incorporating in his pyramid. His pyramid was a scaled-up version of the *wnt* of Thoth, with the 'oars' or *'ipwt* of sunlight made solid as the sides of a pyramid, in place of a *benben* perched on top of a pillar, surrounded by the walls of a temple, which together yielded the dimensions of pi. If the rays of the sun had delineated the 'immaterial prototype' in the seclusion of the sanctuary of the phoenix, Khufu's pyramid did indeed turn this into a 'material replica', as Professor Edwards had suggested (see colour illustration no. 5).

Whether or not Khufu actually opened a flint box and took from it a papyrus scroll on which were drawn the plans of the temple as envisaged by Thoth must remain a matter of conjecture. It is just possible that this is so, and that the plans, the box or both were later concealed inside the Great Pyramid. They may even still be there, in a secret chamber – perhaps even one behind the 'door' discovered by Gantenbrink. On the other hand, it could be that the so-called 'flint box' was really something else entirely. The use of flint to make a box seems highly unusual, given its flaky character and fragility. Generally speaking, flint was employed in the manufacture of tools such as axe- and arrowheads. However, flint does have another characteristic: its ability, when struck, to create sparks and hence to light fires. It is therefore, properly speaking, a 'fire-stone', and it could be that this is a better translation of the Egyptian word rendered as 'flint'.

Now, we know that in building the pyramids the Egyptians used several different types of stone: ordinary limestone for the core; white, Tura limestone for the casing stones; and granite for the lining of the King's Chamber. These different stones seem to have had symbolic meanings. There was a definite hierarchy of stones that paralleled the order of elements, so that the lighter, less dense limestone represented the physical world and the more dense granite the spiritual realms. This idea is also reflected in the belief that iron was a heavenly metal and the substance from which the bones of the gods were made.

There was also a secret alchemy of shape that seems to have persisted right up until the Renaissance. According to the alchemists, the world was formed from four elements: earth, water, air and fire. Each of these elements was associated with a shape, earth, for example, being associated with the square or cube. By the same line of reasoning, the element of fire was symbolized by the triangle, which in three dimensions becomes a pyramid. Alchemy, at least in its Western version, was the invention of the Egyptians, its name being derived from Al-Chemia – Chem or Khem meaning Egypt. It therefore seems likely that the theory of elements and their shapes, though discussed by Plato in his *Timaeus*, derives ultimately from Egypt. If this is so then the pyramid shape, and more particularly the pyramidion or *benben* which sat on top of the pyramid, symbolized the element of fire.

We know from surviving examples that the pyramidion put on top of each pyramid was generally made of black granite, perhaps as a substitute for meteoritic iron. 'Fire-stone' is a description which could equally apply to the *benben* stone itself as it glinted like the egg of a phoenix in the fiery light of the sun. Thus the *benben* and 'flint box' could well be the same thing. In this case it would be the dimensions of the shadows cast by the 'box' which would have been important – it would not need to have been hollow nor to have contained anything. The room called 'Revision' by Djedi, which translated literally would mean 'repeated vision', must have been inside the Temple of the Phoenix, where each year those present would have seen repeated the same shadow-dance of the sun. This, therefore, had to be the sanctuary, or *wnt*, implying that the phoenix or Bennu, the 'son of the deep', was really Thoth wearing different feathers from his usual ibis form.

All this gives a new twist to the Khufu/Djedi story. The scenario that now presents itself is this. Khufu has decided he wants to build his pyramid using the numbers of Thoth, and asks Djedi what these are. Djedi replies that off-hand he doesn't know, but that they are to be found from the dimensions of a sanctuary at Heliopolis, the *wnt* of Thoth, called 'Revision'. The *'ipwt* are associated with, rather than concealed inside, a 'fire-stone' (the Benben) which is kept hidden from public gaze inside this sanctuary. It seems likely that the stone, which was probably a meteorite, was kept separately from the pillar of Atum and was only placed on top of it at certain times – maybe once a year, maybe less often – that represented the appearance of the fiery phoenix in the temple. Thus the dimensions of Thoth were kept a secret from even the priesthood, as without the added height of the Benben the sacred 7:11 relationship would remain concealed.

Djedi knew this, and he also knew that it would be a waste of time bringing the 'flint box', the Benben, to Khufu for the latter's inspection. Just as in *Raiders of the Lost Ark* Indiana Jones had to place a special crystal on top of a measuring rod and use this to focus the rays of the sun on to a certain spot, so the measurements of the shadows cast by the Benben stone had to be made inside the *wnt* on the appropriate day as it stood on the pillar of Atum if the correct numbers were to be ascertained. The attempt must have been successful; for, scaled up forty times, these measurements give the right dimensions for Khufu's pyramid, which was indeed built in accordance with the rays of the sun and the numbers of Thoth as given on Regulus day.

Corroborating evidence that the Benben stone contained in its measures the secret of the pyramids is to be gleaned from a further account contained in the Westcar Papyrus. Here Djedi predicted that it would be not he, but rather the eldest of the children in the womb of a priestess called Reddjedet, who would bring the flint box to Khufu. This leads on to the story of the birth of Reddjedet's triplets: Userkaf, Sahure and Neferirkare, who later became the first pharaohs of the Fifth Dynasty. These pharaohs built their pyramids not at Giza but rather at Abusir, a few miles further south and nearer to the older necropolis of Saqqara. In *The Orion Mystery* we suggested that the choice of this site was influenced by their desire to build pyramids representing the 'head' of Orion, which consists of a similar grouping of fairly dim stars. However, there is another aspect to this, which is that these pharaohs of the Fifth Dynasty, though they built much smaller pyramids than those of their illustrious forebears of the Fourth, instituted a revived solar cult, erecting sun temples at Abusir, characterized by stumpy obelisks of a type that must have been based on the original Pillar of Atum at Heliopolis. It has been suggested by Egyptologists that the advent of the Fifth Dynasty saw the eclipse, at least for a time, of the stellar cult of Osiris and the emergence of the solar cult of Re. Whether or not this is true, the pharaohs of the Fifth Dynasty continued to build pyramids with angles of slope near to if not exactly the perfect pi angle. This would suggest that any changes in emphasis were more subtle than has been suggested.

The pyramids of the Fourth Dynasty themselves had a solar as well as a stellar function. During the night they were stars of Orion/Osiris; but during the day they were replicas of the Benben stone and emphatically solar in aspect. In view of the angles produced by the sun on certain days at Heliopolis (and of course Giza, which is on nearly the same latitude), it would appear that the Great Pyramid, which has a slope giving the pi relationship, could also have acted like a giant obelisk. When the sun crossed the eastern or western axis on the morning and afternoon of Regulus day, the angle of its shadow would have exactly matched the slope of its opposite face. To anyone standing at the bottom of the west face of the pyramid and looking up, at the precise time the sun crossed the eastern axis, it would for a short time have seemed to sit on top of the pyramid. Then, for an instant, the west face, which had previously been enveloped in shadow, would suddenly be bathed in light. Conversely, an afternoon observer standing next to the eastern face would see the sun again sit on top of the pyramid but then, at the moment it crossed the western axis, the eastern face would suddenly go dark.

What this means in practical terms is that at the precise moment when the sun crossed over the east–west axis of the pyramid the west face would be illuminated; bear in mind that at the time of its construction the Great Pyramid was faced with white Tura limestone and one can begin to imagine how startling this change would be. Not only that, the change from dark to light would have been visible from a great distance. In the afternoon the situation would have been reversed: at the precise moment that the sun crossed back over the east–west axis, the eastern face would suddenly pass into shadow. This would also have been visible from a great distance, only this time when viewed from the Nile valley to the east. In this way the pharaohs of the Fourth Dynasty honoured the father of the gods, Atum-Re, as well as his great-grandson Osiris. Their main function, though, was to assist the ascent of the pharaoh's soul so that he could take his place among the stars.

The realization that in building his pyramid with an angle of slope of 51° 51' Khufu was aligning it with the sun as it would appear on Regulus day was exciting to say the least. For one thing it meant that the pyramid was as much to do with life as death, with the birth of the divine Horus as well as the rebirth of his father Osiris. The pyramid was concerned very much with the ascension of the soul, in Egyptian a *khu* or *akh*, a word associated with radiance and light. This is explained very succinctly by Egyptologist Mark Lehner in his recent book *The Complete Pyramids*:

> The Pyramid Texts speak of the king ascending to Nut, the sky goddess, leaving 'a Horus', a new living king, behind him. Joining the stars the king becomes an *akh*. *Akh* is often translated as 'spirit' or 'spirit state'. It derives from the term for 'radiant light', written with

the crested ibis, as though the crest transforms the
ordinary ibis bird of the *ba*. The *akh* is the fully
resurrected, glorified form of the deceased in the
Afterlife. *Akh* is also a word for 'effective', 'profitable',
'useful'. The reunion of the *ba* with the *ka* [other subtle
bodies] is effected by the burial ritual, creating the final
transformation of the deceased as an *akh*. As a member
of the starry sky, called *akh-akh* in the Pyramid Texts
and the New Kingdom Book of the Dead, the king is
free to move on over the earth . . .

The names of pyramids show that they were per-
ceived as places of ascension and transformation.
Khufu's was *Akhet*, the 'Horizon' of Khufu. Built on the
word *akh*, the name signified not just the horizon but
the 'radiant place' of glorification.[3]

This is certainly true; but the name Akhet or 'Horizon' of
Khufu has further levels of meaning. It should not be
supposed that the pyramid was called Akhet simply
because the soul of Khufu was looking out from it
towards the horizon. Rather, as we have seen, the
pyramid itself was a 'horizon' over which the sun would
pass in such a spectacular manner on Regulus day.

The name Akhet is also clearly linked with another
important symbol in the religion of the ancient
Egyptians: the double lion or *aker*. This symbol shows
two lions, one facing east and the other west. Between
them is a horizon with the sun seated on top of it.
According to R. T. Rundle Clark, the double lion symbol
was a manifestation of Shu and Tefnut, the first children
of Atum-Re. This is borne out by the Pyramid Texts,
which contain the following statement in Utterance 301:
'The accustomed offering cake is still yours, O Atum and
Double Lion! You two that have created your own divine
selves and powers!'[4] Rundle Clark points out that in a
later gloss it is added that Shu and Tefnut were 'the pair
who engendered the gods and put them in their proper
places'. In a very real sense the Great Pyramid can be seen

RUTI OR DOUBLE LIONS OF EAST AND WEST

to represent this horizon, with the two all-important positions of Leo, one to the east, perhaps representing Tefnut, and the other to the west, flanking it and maybe symbolizing Shu.

Though Shu was usually shown in human form, Tefnut retained her leonine characteristics throughout the period of ancient Egyptian civilization, always being shown with the head of a lioness. These two, who taken together formed the *aker* or double lion symbol, were Atum's first-born, progeny of his first ejaculation. As Lehner points out in the passage quoted above, Khufu's pyramid was a place of radiance. It therefore seems more than significant that it was when the sun was conjunct with Regulus in Leo and crossing the east–west axis that it would have been at the critical angle of 51° 51' in the sky and there-fore illuminating Khufu's pyramid with no shadow. This seems to have originally symbolized the ejaculation of the lion god or Atum at the time of the first creation, and consequently the coming into being of Shu and Tefnut.

The word Akhet, which is translated as 'horizon', had a further meaning of 'inundation'. This is what the first month of the year was called, and since this was heralded by the heliacal rising of Sirius at the time of the Regulus conjunction, one must assume that it was so called because of the important solar alignments at this time. Within the context of the Osiris religion, which seems to have been a later development from the original lion cult of Atum, the conjunction of the sun with Regulus became associated with the birth of Horus, son of Isis. At this time of year the inundation of the Nile would happen, and as this also occurred at the time of the first appearance of Sirius, it was connected, metaphorically speaking, with Isis breaking her waters.

The connection with Thoth in all this becomes obvious when we consider the root word *akh*, which roughly translates as 'soul' or 'spirit'. The Egyptians believed in the existence of several different 'higher bodies' or modes of being that came into their own after the death of the physical. The *ka* represented the 'double' of the person, perhaps what occultists today would call the 'etheric body'. Higher than this was the *ba*, which was symbolized by a human-headed hawk, often depicted as hovering over the mummy. Closely linked to the *ka*, the *ba* would survive death but still partook of funerary offerings. We should perhaps call it the 'astral body' in modern parlance. Higher than both of these 'bodies' was the *akh* (also transliterated as *khu*) with the general meaning of soul or body of light. This, as Mark Lehner explains, was shown as a crested ibis and was considered to be the eternal part of man. It was the desire of pharaohs and probably of other Egyptians that after death their highest body should take up its existence among the stars, as one of the *akh-akhs*. The hieroglyph for such a group of souls shows a gathering of three crested ibises together. This represented the 'company of the gods', most especially the gods of Heliopolis. Under the right circumstances the *akh* of the deceased could expect to join this illustrious company.

When we visited Heliopolis for the first time and explored its small subterranean temple, we saw a number of instances of this hieroglyph inscribed on its walls. It is tempting to think that the word *akh*, and even more *akh-akh*, is onomatopoeic and derives ultimately from the sound made by wading birds when gathered together in a muddy lagoon. Such a place seems to be one of the images the Egyptians had in mind when thinking of their heaven. They thought of 'Isles of the Blessed' washed by the waters of the celestial Nile, the Milky Way. This was the abode of souls which, like the ibises and herons of the Nile valley, periodically migrated. From this abode of souls in the sky came Thoth as well as the Bennu (the two were probably one and the same) who as an ibis laid the egg of creation. All this had happened far in antiquity, long before the emergence of Dynastic Egypt.

Thoth, whom the Greeks identified with Hermes and the Hebrews with the patriarch Enoch, was said to have taught mankind the ways of salvation; he was also, as we have seen, believed to have hidden certain records either at Heliopolis or in some other place nearby. According to the *Hermetica* the anthropomorphic gods of Heliopolis, Osiris, Isis, Nephthys and Set, came to earth much later than Thoth. All except Set, who turned out to be a prince of darkness, upheld the rule of law. Isis and Osiris found some of the records of Thoth and used these in their teachings, engraving their knowledge on stelae and obelisks. On their deaths they returned to their place of origin, once more to become *akh-akhs* or stars in the sky.

The later pharaohs of the Fourth Dynasty, most especially Khufu, rediscovered some of the knowledge left behind by the 'gods' and built the pyramids of Giza. These pyramids were intended to represent the stars of Orion's Belt, which it was believed was the place to which Osiris had departed. However, the Great Pyramid had a further symbolic function. Its dimensions were based upon certain measurements preserved at the more ancient Temple of the Phoenix in Heliopolis. Here the secret numbers of Thoth/Hermes could be discerned from studying the shadows cast by the Benben stone on the day the sun was in conjunction with Regulus. This was the secret revealed to Khufu by the magician Djedi, and using it they were able to rediscover the sacred numbers of Thoth, 7 and 11, the ratio of which gives the perfect pi angle: 51° 51'.

Khufu's pyramid, which employs this perfect angle, was a place of illumination and a centre for transformation, perhaps not only for himself but for others as well. Representing both the lowest of the Belt stars, Alnitak, as well as an updated version of the Temple of the Phoenix at Heliopolis, it was a hybrid, symbolizing both the metamorphosis of the dead pharaoh into an *akh* and his projection towards the Belt of Orion, as well as the handing on of power to his successor, the next Horus. How the stellar transformation was achieved, using rituals such as the 'Opening of the Mouth' ceremony, is explained in *The Orion Mystery*. The way in which the Regulus conjunction governed Egyptian thinking is the other side of the coin. It indicates that the Egyptian religion was not just a matter of caring for the dead but had deep meaning also for the living. What I did not expect, but was now to find, was that the other pyramids were also involved in this process and that together they had a message for our own time.

The day after visiting Khufu's boat I found myself back in the centre of Cairo at the Egyptian Museum. Here, filling the galleries and overflowing into the gardens outside, are stored the country's greatest antiquities, including most of the contents of the tomb of Tutankhamun. In the midst of so much splendour it is difficult for anything not made of gold to stand out; but one piece that does is the near life-size statue of Khafre, builder of the second pyramid of Giza. This effigy occupies pride of position in the Old Kingdom rooms and is without doubt one of the greatest works of art in the world. Made of green diorite, an extremely hard stone, it is carved with a smoothness that would have been difficult to achieve had it been modelled out of clay. The muscular strength of the pharaoh's physique, coupled with the benevolent expression of his face, combine to give the impression of a monarch who was not only fit and confident in himself as god's deputy on earth but also one who was loved by his people.[5]

The only effigy which has been found to date of Khafre's predecessor Khufu is a tiny statue, just 3 inches in height, discovered at Abydos by Flinders Petrie. Menkaure, who built the third pyramid at Giza, was better served, with a series of reliefs each showing him with a pair of goddesses. It seems that he had originally commissioned one of these for each of the forty-two *nomes* or counties of Egypt, but if this was so the set was never completed. Two examples are to be seen in the Egyptian Museum; but, fine as they are, they cannot compare with Khafre's statue. In a similar fashion, though it is smaller than the Great Pyramid of Khufu, because it stands on higher ground Khafre's pyramid – from a distance, at least – dominates the Giza group. Paradoxically, although it was built later, the Khafre pyramid occupies the key position on the plateau, and it is certainly tempting to think that it occupies the site of some former structure, one which may have been thousands of years older than the pyramids we see today.

Unlike the Great Pyramid, that of Khafre has retained some of its casing stones, those near to its apex. From these it has been possible to measure with great accuracy its angle of slope, which turns out to be 53° 10'. This is over 1.25° steeper than Khufu's pyramid, once more inviting the question: why? The standard explanation of Egyptologists is that by building a steeper-sided pyramid Khafre was able to obtain a greater height over a smaller base. The steeper angle enabled the Egyptians to economize both on materials and manpower. However, closer examination reveals that there was far more to it than this. By building his pyramid with an angle of 53° 10' Khafre was making a sacrifice: for his pyramid would now not have the sacred pi angle incorporated in its building. When I thought about this it seemed inconceivable that he would have risked compromising his ideals for the sake of a minor economy – certainly when he was already investing heavily in terms of materials and manpower. There had to be another reason.

Suspecting that there might be astronomical factors at work again, I once more ran SKYGLOBE with settings for Cairo at the epoch of *c.*3100, with the sky orientated towards the east and the cursor set at an angle of 53.2°. Paging the sun round one day at a time, it didn't take me long to discover that it would have reached this angle exactly on the summer solstice. In the epoch in question this would have occurred about eleven days after the Regulus conjunction. However, just like the equinox and for the same reasons of precession, the position of the sun relative to the stars at the time of the solstice moves over time. At *c.*2450, when the evidence of the air shafts suggests the Great Pyramid was built, the solstice would have taken place three days after the Regulus conjunction. By 2280 BC the solstice meridian would have run straight through Regulus. However, even before this, say around 2370 BC, the position of the sun at the solstice would have been very close to Regulus. In any event, it is clear that the Khafre pyramid was built with a slope that would be correct for the summer solstice, whether or not it was seen at the time as conjuncting Regulus.

This result, though not entirely unexpected, was nothing short of sensational. For while it could be argued that the match between the slope of the Great Pyramid and the angle reached by the sun in the east and west when conjunct with Regulus at the perfect pi angle was nothing more than a coincidence, it seems inconceivable that when the Egyptians, for 'reasons of economy', gave the Khafre

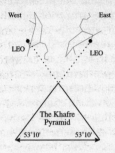

The slope angle of the pyramid (53°10') is such that it
casts no shadow on the day of the summer solstice between
the time the sun crosses the east axis in the morning and the time
it crosses the west axis in the afternoon.

pyramid a different slope, this would also have accidentally corresponded to the correct angle for an alignment
with the sun on the summer solstice. There could be only
one sensible explanation: that within the solar as opposed
to the stellar aspect of the pyramid cult, if the Great
Pyramid represented the birth of Horus, then the Khafre
pyramid was intended to be celebratory of the solstice.

Using the same program I now turned my attention to
the third pyramid of Giza, that of Menkaure, which had a
slope angle of 51° 20' 25" – slightly shallower than that of
the Great Pyramid. SKYGLOBE indicated that this
pyramid would have been illuminated some seven days
before the Regulus conjunction, when the sun was entering
Leo and over the outstretched paw of the lion. Taking these
results together, it was clear that the three pyramids
together would have marked out the sacred month of the
lion, which at that time pivoted around the summer
solstice.

These alignments with the sun in Leo indicated that all

three pyramids had a solar as well as a stellar aspect. What we were seeing was a supreme example of the symbolist's art, in which the architect (or architects) had combined in the same group of megalithic pyramids the central mysteries of the cults of Re and Osiris. That the pyramids still also represented the stars of Orion's Belt I had no doubt. After all, it is typical of Egyptian mysticism to combine symbols, so that the same object could have multiple interpretations. Like the Pyramid Texts, which speak in their confused way about a solar as well as stellar religion, so it would seem that the pyramids fulfilled dual functions as shadow markers and as models of the stars. This, however, was not the end of the story. As I was now to discover, they also had a prophetic purpose relating to our own times. The key to this was the enigma of the Sphinx.

CHAPTER 11

THE GAZE OF THE SPHINX

A few days after visiting Khufu's boat I found myself standing below the looming presence of the Great Sphinx of Giza. The modern age has not been kind to this old statue; its flanks continue to be eaten away by pollution, and despite restoration work costing millions of pounds (at the time of this visit it was surrounded by scaffolding) it seems that little can be done to preserve it in perpetuity. There is a danger that its neck, which is much weakened, could give way and consequently it could soon lose its head. It is already without a nose, rumoured to have been blown away by a cannon shot fired by Napoleon's troops during target practice. Its beard, too, has been lost – though part of it, which ought surely to be returned, is now in the British Museum. It was therefore with some sadness that I looked on this vast statue, realizing that ours might be the last generation to see it exposed to the elements and not enclosed in a building of some sort.

It had been two years since the Sphinx and I were last together, when Robert Bauval and I had been filming some night shots for the BBC programme *The Great Pyramid: Gateway to the Stars*. At that time it had appeared somewhat aloof and uninterested in our work; now it seemed more friendly and less intimidating than I remembered. Whether this was a trick of the light or a consequence of the fact that I was with a lively group of people, it was difficult to say. What was clear was that my relationship with this amazing statue had somehow changed from straightforward awe to puzzled incredulity. Like a million others before me I wondered at the wistful smile and the steady gaze towards the east. The Sphinx seemed to be looking beyond this world to the workings of time itself, and while it was by no means easy to read the mind of his creator, it was clear that the Sphinx was in deep meditation.

At this point my reverie was disturbed by a tug on the sleeve; as I turned round my gaze was met by the beaming face of a young boy selling souvenirs. Pointing gleefully at the Sphinx before us, he held out his hand. In it was a plastic replica intended to be both a paperweight and a pencil sharpener. The object was ugly beyond belief and a poor advertisement for Egypt's premier statue. It was not just a model but an Egyptian version of the familiar 'snowstorm' toys I remember from my own childhood. It consisted of a brightly painted sphinx enclosed in a clear plastic dome which was filled with some heavy, oily liquid. At the bottom of the vessel was a layer of golden sand which, when the object was shaken, swirled about like a sandstorm. Then, after a minute or so of frantic activity, the sand would settle back down around the feet of the unfortunate sphinx. As a final indignity a pencil sharpener occupied the little sphinx's posterior. The paperweight/pencil sharpener, though a mockery of its original, was, in a way, truthful to its subject. For the real Sphinx too has seen many sandstorms, and indeed has spent most of its life with just its head poking above the desert landscape. And while it has no obvious function, it is known to conceal an empty grotto in its hindquarters (like the pencil sharpener?) It is also rumoured to be standing guard over a secret chamber below.

'Where are you from?' The inevitable question came from the young boy at my side. Usually I would brush aside this all too familiar question with a cursory 'Japan!' This would serve to confuse over-pushy vendors long enough for me to make a hasty escape, for there are not many Japanese who are Caucasians over 6 feet tall and speaking English as their first language. This time, however, perhaps because the boy seemed so young, I replied: 'England'. 'England very good,' came the expected reply; 'Paul Gascoigne, Gary Lineker!' I cast my mind back to when I had first visited Israel in the early 1970s. Then, too, one would be accosted by young vendors in the markets of Jerusalem or Bethlehem with the initial question 'Where are you from?' Then, after you had answered 'England', you would get the inevitable reply: 'England very good: Bobby Charlton!' Some things, it seems, never change, and one of them is the association in young Middle Eastern minds of England with football.

Fortunately I was saved from having to buy the hideous sphinx by another member of our party who found it amusingly kitsch and who, after some haggling, managed to purchase it for a couple of dollars. But by then we had been surrounded by a large party of schoolgirls, who for some reason must have thought we were film stars. Not at all shy, as one might expect given Arabic protocol, they greeted myself and Roy Bird, who as proprietor of the magazine *Quest* had organized the current trip with myself and John Anthony West as guest speakers, with handshakes all round. Before long we were being pressed to sign postcards, exercise books and whatever else might come to hand. Eventually we were rescued by their teacher and allowed to join John West and the rest of our party at the top of the Sphinx enclosure.

John, now in his sixties, continues to be a thorn in the side of established Egyptology. A pioneer very much in the traditions of Howard Carter, who also spent much time prior to his discovery of Tutankhamun's tomb guiding tourists around the heritage sites of Egypt, his tours are unique experiences. With his trademark pith helmet and walking cane, he is himself a familiar sight throughout Egypt and is greeted everywhere as 'Doctor', not because of any medical expertise or a PhD but in recognition of his great knowledge and familiarity with his subject matter. His tours are not orthodox by any means, and people attending them are instructed in alternative theories. Many of these originate from the work of Schwaller de Lubicz, who spent a lifetime studying the temples and other works of art of ancient Egypt and whose books, most of which are still available only in French, remain controversial decades after his death.[1]

Schwaller's pioneering work on the symbolism implicit in Egyptian monuments such as the Temple of Luxor, which he renamed the 'Temple of Man', inspired West to carry out certain researches of his own. His starting point was a comment made by Schwaller in one of his books to the effect that the Sphinx was very much older than is generally thought, this being borne out by the severe water erosion evident both on the sides of the statue itself and on the enclosure surrounding it. Looking closely, West could see for himself clear evidence for this erosion, which seemed to have been caused by surface water falling as rain on to the top of the Sphinx and forming rivulets running down its sides. To him at least it was obvious that for these streams to have created the sort of erosion visible today, the Sphinx would have to have witnessed frequent and heavy showers. Yet it is also clear that throughout its known history Egypt has been a very arid country, relying on the Nile to provide it with its water supply. The only explanation that made sense was that the rainfall necessary to have eroded the Sphinx in this way must have fallen millennia earlier – perhaps as early as 10,000 BC – at a time when geologists believe the climate of Egypt was much wetter than it is today. Realizing that he might be on the threshold of an extremely important discovery, West published his findings in a book, *Serpent in the Sky*. He also enlisted the help of Dr Robert Schoch, an American professor of geology, who confirmed that the erosion patterns to be seen on both the Sphinx itself and its enclosure were consistent with water rather than wind erosion. This seemed to indicate a date for the carving of the Sphinx of at least 6000–7000 BC, with a possibility that it could go back to as early as 10,500 BC.

West's re-dating of the Sphinx has placed Egyptology in a quandary. How could it be so old, it has been argued, when there is in Egypt no recognizable evidence – in the form of pottery, habitations, tools, etc. – for a civilized culture at the time specified? A further criticism of the 'early Sphinx' theory is that its head was very obviously modelled on that of a pharaoh. The consensus is that it was based on that of Khafre, the pharaoh who is believed to have built the central pyramid of the Giza group. If this is so, it is argued, then the Sphinx must have been carved at the same time as his pyramid was built, which would be some time between 2700 and 2400 BC.

West opposed this simple deduction on two counts. First, a close analysis of the features of the Sphinx's face and a comparison of these with Khafre's famous statue by a chief forensic officer from the New York Police Department showed that the models for the two works of art were different individuals. The police officer found that the Sphinx had a pronouncedly prognathous jaw, typical of many black Africans, and that this as well as the general proportions of the head differed noticeably from the statue of Khafre in the Cairo Museum. The second point was that the head of the Sphinx, which is nowhere near so severely eroded as the rest of the statue, is proportionately much too small for the leonine body. In response to this anomaly, West suggested that the Sphinx could have originally been furnished with a simple lion's head, one in proportion with its body; much later, perhaps during the time of Khafre, this could have been re-sculpted in the image of an Egyptian pharaoh. If this were so, then there was little except for prejudice on the part of Egyptologists to tie the Sphinx's original construction to the pyramid age. Even though its head was recognizably meant to be that of an Egyptian pharaoh, its lion's body could indeed date back to much earlier –

perhaps even to 10,500 BC, as suggested by the psychic clairvoyant Edgar Cayce.

To establish his case in the face of heated opposition from the Egyptological establishment, West needed all the support he could get. The timely publication in 1994 of *The Orion Mystery*, with its few paragraphs suggesting that the pyramids were built in such a way that they mirrored the position of Orion at a date of 10,500 BC, provided him with further ammunition. Prior to the publication of *The Orion Mystery*, Robert and I had met up with another writer, Graham Hancock, who like West was keen to find supporting evidence for an antique civilization dating back to the epoch *c.*10,500 BC. In May 1994 all four of us got together at West's house near New York, where we discussed his Sphinx erosion theories and the current state of play with regard to the opening of Gantenbrink's mysterious 'door' inside the Great Pyramid.

Robert and I had had no idea what hot water we were getting into when we suggested in *The Orion Mystery* that there was evidence for an early date of *c.*10,500 BC for the start of Egyptian civilization. The theory we set out in that book was at root a simple one that explained the layout of the Fourth Dynasty Giza pyramids as representative of the Belt of Orion. The further elaboration that they may have mirrored the sky of 10,500 BC rather than that of 2,500 BC proved to be highly contentious and, unfortunately, gave certain critics a welcome target on which to focus their attacks. Yet it was not without substance; and I was now to find further evidence that not only the pyramids but also the Sphinx marked time.

In *Keeper of Genesis*, the book they went on to write jointly while I was working on *Magi*, Robert and Graham drew attention to the fact that during the New Kingdom the Egyptian name for the Sphinx was Hor-em-Akhet, which was shortened to Horakhti (Heracte) and later rendered into Greek as Harmarchis. During New

Kingdom times the Sphinx as Heracte was worshipped as a god, and offerings were made in his sanctuary. The ancient Egyptians, certainly those from these later times but maybe their forebears as well, believed that the statues of gods were somehow inhabited by their spirits. In the *Asclepius* dialogue, one of the writings contained in the *Hermetica,* it is stated that by making 'living' statues, men are copying the work of God.

> *Trismegistus* ... Mankind is ever mindful of its own parentage and the source whence it has sprung, and steadfastly persists in following God's example; and consequently, just as the Father and Master made the gods of heaven eternal, that they might resemble him who made them, even so do men fashion their gods in the likeness of their own aspect.
>
> *Asclepius.* Do you mean statues, Trismegistus?
>
> *Trismegistus.* Yes, Asclepius. See how even you give way to doubt! I mean statues, but statues living and conscious, filled with the breath of life, and doing many mighty works; statues which have fore-knowledge, and predict future events by the drawing of lots, and by prophetic inspiration, and by dreams, and in many other ways; statues which inflict diseases and heal them, dispensing sorrow and joy according to men's deserts.[2]

The statues of pharaohs were of this sort, intended to provide an alternative anchor for the spirit besides the mummified corpse. (Indeed, it is for this reason that their statues were often mutilated by those who came later, to prevent the spirit from entering them.) And it would appear that the Sphinx, too, was regarded as just such a living statue, the embodiment of the god Heracte or 'Horus on the Horizon'; as such it was felt to be capable of conferring his gifts, most especially those of rulership.

Following the collapse of the Old Kingdom the Sphinx fell into disrepair and, as its body sits below ground level inside its own excavated enclosure, it quickly became buried in sand with only its head protruding. This seems to have been the situation when Tuthmosis IV, a New Kingdom prince, had a dream in which he met with the spirit of the Sphinx. He was told that if he cleared away the sand and restored the statue, it would ensure that he became the next pharaoh. Tuthmosis did as he was asked and in due course the Sphinx was seen to have kept its side of the bargain. In gratitude Tuthmosis, now pharaoh, had a stela carved, recycling a lintel from the doorway of Khafre's old mortuary temple for the purpose, to record his dream and how he had restored the Sphinx. He had this stela set up close to the chest of the statue so that all later visitors would be reminded of his good works. This stela has proved to be very controversial, but we do know from it the full name of the Sphinx in antiquity. On line 9 of the inscription the statue is called Hor-em-Akhet-Kepri-Re-Atum – shortened in line 13 to Atum-Hor-em-Akhet.[3]

The name Hor-em-Akhet-Kepri-Re-Atum is possibly the origin of the famous 'riddle of the Sphinx' with which Oedipus was challenged, in the much later Greek legend: 'What creature walks on four legs in the morning, on two at noon, and on three at evening, and is weakest when it walks on most?' Oedipus' answer was 'man', for as an infant he is weakest and crawls on all fours. At his strongest he walks on two legs, and as an old man he has three legs as he leans on a stick. The riddle of the Sphinx would, however, seem to be of much greater antiquity than this Greek myth, for in Egypt the answer could just as easily have been 'the sun' as 'man'. The ancient Egyptian sun god was worshipped at dawn in the form of Kepri, a crawling dung-beetle, at noon as the two-legged hawk, Re-Heracte, and in the evening as Atum, who was usually depicted as an old man leaning on a stick. Thus it would seem that the riddle of the Sphinx, at least the original Sphinx of Giza, is really connected with the daily cycle of the sun and not with man at all.

As we have already seen, according to Egyptologist

Mark Lehner the Egyptian word *akhet,* which is generally translated as 'horizon', derives from the root *akh,* a word which means among other things 'radiant light'. Hor-em-Akhet, which is usually translated as Horus on the Horizon, can thus also mean Horus of the Radiant Light. It is also well established that the father of the gods, Atum, who in later times is depicted as an old man with a stick, was originally represented in the form of a lion.[4]

On the dream stela of Tuthmosis IV the king is shown twice, wearing different crowns and making offerings to two separate sphinxes. That he should make double offerings is strange, as there is only one Great Sphinx at Giza. However, sphinxes were normally placed in pairs to guard the entrance gates of temples and it has been argued that the Great Sphinx was itself once one of such a pair.[5] According to this hypothesis the second sphinx, being destroyed by a lightning bolt or some other such act of God, was never replaced. Unfortunately, attractive as this idea is, it does not seem tenable, for there seems to be little evidence on the ground for there ever having been a second sphinx. It seems more likely that the paired sphinxes to which Tuthmosis makes his offerings represent the repeated constellation of Leo, with the sun at the solstice in the east in the morning and again in the west in the afternoon. This makes sense, for the two children of Atum, Shu and Tefnut, were also often depicted with the heads of lion and lioness respectively.[6] These twin lions, the children of Atum, are referred to as the Rwty (or Ruti), the 'double lion god' in the Pyramid Texts:

> You have your offering-bread, O Atum and Ruti,
> Who yourselves created your godheads and your persons.
> O Shu and Tefenet [*sic*] who made the gods,
> Who begot the gods and established the gods:
> Tell your father [Atum]
> That the King has propitiated you with your dues.
> You shall not hinder the King when he crosses to him
>   at the horizon,

For the King knows him and knows his name;
'Eternal' is his name; 'The Eternal, Lord of the Year'
   is his name.
(PT 301)

From this it is clear that Shu and Tefnut stand one in
the east and the other in the west, where they guard the
rising and setting of the sun. The king must have considered it necessary to make separate offerings to the Ruti
or double-lion guardians of the horizon at the different
times of day when the sun crossed the east–west axis.

There is, however, a further twist to all of this. While
it is true that the Sphinx watches the rising of the sun
every day, it is only at the equinoxes that its gaze is truly
aligned with this event, for only then does the sun rise
exactly in the east. As we have seen, at the time of the
Old Kingdom when the pyramids were built
(*c.*2700–2200 BC), the spring equinox took place with the
sun in Taurus and the autumn equinox with it in Scorpio.
Given this fact it seems strange that the Egyptians of the
Old Kingdom should have carved a lion-bodied statue
to face the equinoctial sunrise. A man-headed bull, or
minotaur, might have seemed more appropriate. This is
one of the arguments in favour of believing that the Great
Sphinx predated the pyramids by many millennia. For it
was during the period of approximately 11,000–8100 BC,
long before the start of Dynastic Egypt and the building
of the pyramids, that the constellation of Leo would have
risen with the sun at the spring equinox.

Around 8700 BC the sun would have risen in the east
conjunct with the star Regulus. As this conjunction was
connected, astrally speaking, with the birthday of the god
Horus, son of Osiris, I had, like Robert and Graham,
been tempted to think that this was the date for the carving of the Sphinx. However, the discovery that the shaft
at Arsameia, though aligned to catch rays from the sun
on the day of the Regulus conjunction, was pointed
towards the western sky with an inclination of 35° and

not horizontally, caused me to think again. What if the Egyptians of the Old Kingdom had also been less concerned with the position of the sun on the horizon at sunrise than with its conjunction with Regulus? What if the Great Sphinx were not so much looking at the horizon and watching the dawn but observing the sun crossing the east–west axis? If this were the case then the date of 8700 BC for when the sun rose in the exact east conjunct with Regulus would be irrelevant; what would be of more significance would be the altitude of the sun as it crossed the east–west axis. As we have seen, in *c.*3100 BC the sun made an angle of 51° 51' on Regulus day, but by the time the Khafre Pyramid was built, or soon after, this had shifted to 53.2°, with the Regulus conjunction occurring on the summer solstice. Could this be what the Sphinx was watching?

There was yet another aspect to this conundrum. As already noted, according to West, Schoch and others who support the idea of a super-antique Sphinx, its head was probably leonine before being re-carved in the image of a pharaoh. Egyptologists such as Mark Lehner, who holds the opposing view that the Sphinx was carved as a whole and is no older than the pyramids, believe the head was always that of the pharaoh Khafre. Yet what nobody seems to have considered is a third alternative: that it might have been re-carved even later than the pyramid age.

That the Sphinx does not look anything like Khafre, particularly when viewed in profile, is evident to anyone who cares to compare it with his statue. Yet it is clearly intended to represent a pharaoh, as it wears the *nemes* scarf and once sported a beard and Uraeus, or rearing cobra, on its brow. All of these devices are part and parcel of the uniform of a pharaoh. This, however, does not mean that the Sphinx's head was modelled on Khafre, or even that it was intended to represent a pharaoh from the Fourth Dynasty. The *nemes* scarf and Uraeus were standard accoutrements for the Middle and New

Kingdom pharaohs too, as these kings consciously modelled themselves on the by then legendary Fourth Dynasty rulers. There is, for example, a statue from Deir al Bahri, the Valley of the Queens, of the Twelfth Dynasty (Middle Kingdom) pharaoh Amenemhet III wearing the *nemes* and Uraeus. The Colossi of Memnon, the magnificent seated statues of the Eighteenth Dynasty pharaoh Amenophis III, which stand in splendid isolation across the Nile from Luxor, also wear the *nemes*. The even more famous gold mask of his grandson Tutankhamun shows the young pharaoh wearing all of the above with the addition of a vulture's head, symbol of Upper Egypt, alongside the rearing cobra. At the Nineteenth Dynasty temple at Abydos of Seti I, father of Ramses II, the king is depicted in his reliefs wearing the *nemes*, the Uraeus and the false beard. We therefore have a situation where the Sphinx's head may have been re-carved not at the time of Khafre, or indeed of any other Old Kingdom pharaoh, but at almost any time in Egypt's long history. The question then is: why was the lion given the head of a man?

There is one very obvious answer to this which again relies on astronomical observations. As we have seen, during Old Kingdom times (*c*.2700–2200 BC) the constellation of Leo marked the summer solstice. One argument for the Sphinx's being very much older than is generally supposed is that you have to go back to a period before *c*.8000 BC before Leo is seen to rise directly in line with the gaze of the Sphinx (the star Regulus would have risen due east *c*.8800 BC). At the time the pyramids were built Leo rose well to the north of the east–west meridian and was not facing the Sphinx at sunrise. However, by about 1800 BC, roughly the time of Senusert III, there was another stellar phenomenon to be seen in the eastern skies. At this time the head of Orion would have been seen to rise in the east directly in the line of sight of the Sphinx. As the earliest known human-headed sphinxes – apart from the Great Sphinx of Giza –

date from around this time, it is tempting to think it was then that the head was re-carved. We know from the surviving remains at Heliopolis and elsewhere that the Twelfth Dynasty pharaohs were very active in restoring Old Kingdom temples. It seems likely that they would have paid some attention to the Great Sphinx and its accompanying temple.

From SKYGLOBE we can see that throughout the period of the Middle Kingdom the Regulus conjunction once more gave the pi angle of 51° 51' as the sun crossed the east–west axis. (This is because Regulus, which had moved up to its most northerly position at around 2280 BC when its conjunction with the sun corresponded with the summer solstice, was now moving back south.) This is probably why the Middle Kingdom pharaoh Senusert I raised the first obelisk at Heliopolis, where it would cast a shadow giving that angle. The surviving statue of Senusert III from Deir al Bahri shows him to have had quite a prominent prognathous jaw, so it seems likely that the Sphinx was re-carved in the likeness of either him or one of the other kings of the same Middle Kingdom Twelfth Dynasty who shared this facial feature. A close comparison of surviving statues of these pharaohs with the Sphinx would probably show which one it is intended to represent.

By combining the recumbent lion figure with the head of a man, the Egyptians would have been making a powerful statement about the importance of Orion as the archetypal pharaoh: Osiris. Thus, like the pyramids, the Great Sphinx of Giza would seem to have symbolized the mysteries both of Leo and of Orion, of the exoteric and the esoteric, the kingdom of this world and of the next. However, the Egyptians were not the only ones to venerate the lion as embodying the power of the king; so too did the Israelites when they established the throne of David. Abraham, the patriarch of Jews and Arabs alike, visited Egypt and his great-grandsons settled there. Most commentators agree that Moses led the Israelites out of

Egypt at some time during the reign of the New Kingdom pharaoh Ramses II. When he did so, it would seem that he brought with him many of the secret teachings of the Egyptians, including those concerning the lion.

CHAPTER 12

THE WANDERING LION OF ISRAEL

According to the Bible, at the time when Jacob, the younger son of Isaac and grandson of Abraham, was himself an old man, his favourite son Joseph became vizier of all Egypt. Joseph was a wise and forbearing personality gifted with prophetic insight. As a result he prepared the Egyptians for a serious famine that was about to strike the entire region, so that, unlike the Israelites back in Canaan, they had large grain stores to tide them over the hard times. Joseph's brothers, who had earlier sold him into slavery, came to Egypt seeking to purchase food for themselves and their livestock. They approached Joseph, whom they didn't recognize, and explained their plight to him. In a gesture of magnanimity he invited them to bring back his entire family and to settle in Egypt. Some generations later, by which time the Israelites had become slaves of the Egyptians, Moses was born. He was brought up as an Egyptian prince but became a national leader of his own people, the Israelites, and set about winning back their freedom. By means of a series of plagues called down on the heads of the Egyptians, Moses persuaded the pharaoh of his day, who in the Bible is unnamed, to allow the Israelites to leave Egypt and return to Canaan.

These momentous events are recorded in the books of Genesis and Exodus, but unfortunately the Egyptian records, unless they have been misunderstood and mistranslated, appear to make no mention of these matters.

Thus it is far from clear how this biblical story fits into the accepted history of Egypt as rediscovered by modern-day Egyptologists. It is generally acknowledged, however, that the arrival of the Israelites in some way corresponds with the so-called Second Intermediate Period of Egyptian history which followed the collapse of the Middle Kingdom. During this time, which is thought to stretch from c.1750 BC to c.1560 BC, Egypt was ruled over by an Asiatic people called the Hyksos or 'Shepherd Kings'. These foreigners are thought to have come from eastern Anatolia – probably Armenia – bringing with them advanced techniques of chariot warfare. It seems likely that the Israelites arrived in Egypt during, or perhaps at the beginning of, the period of Hyksos rule. They may even be identified as Hyksos themselves.

The dating of the Exodus of the Israelites from Egypt is also uncertain. We know that the rule of the Hyksos was brought to an end by the princes of Thebes, who rallied the native Egyptians to overthrow the foreigners. Thus began the rule of the illustrious Eighteenth Dynasty and the emergence of the New Kingdom. Though some of the Hyksos were no doubt driven out of Egypt at this time, others were probably enslaved. This could be the origin of the story of Israel's enslavement prior to the Exodus. The Bible does provide some clues; using the genealogy of Jesus as provided at the start of Matthew's Gospel, and knowing as we do that the fall of Jerusalem to the Babylonians occurred in 586 BC, it is possible by working backwards from this event to arrive at a date of c.1364 BC for the Exodus.[1] This is in the right area for the Eighteenth Dynasty, so we may assume that the pharaoh with whom Moses had to deal was one of those belonging to this dynasty, possibly Tuthmosis III.

Using a date of c.1364 it is possible to analyse what was happening in the sky at the time of the Exodus. Over the period of roughly 450 years from 1800 BC to 1364 BC, the constellation of Leo had, because of precession, continued to drift gradually south. Thus by the time of the

Exodus the solar shadow giving the true 51° 51' angle was happening at Heliopolis about four days before the conjunction of the sun with Leo. The New Kingdom rulers of Egypt could no doubt live with this, but the movement of Leo had other implications that could be exploited by those, such as Moses, who understood astronomy. In the Book of Exodus we are told how Aaron, Moses' brother, possessed a staff which could turn into a serpent. The priests of the Egyptians had similar rods which also could become serpents; however, Aaron's was evidently more powerful than theirs and consumed them:

> And the Lord spoke unto Moses and unto Aaron saying,
>
> When Pharaoh shall speak to you, saying, Shew a miracle for you: then thou shalt say unto Aaron, Take thy rod and cast it before Pharaoh, for it shall become a serpent.
>
> And Moses and Aaron went in unto Pharaoh, and they did so as the Lord had commanded: and Aaron cast down his rod before Pharaoh, and before his servants, and it became a serpent.
>
> Then Pharaoh called the wise men and the sorcerers: now the magicians of Egypt, they also did in like manner with their enchantments.
>
> For they cast down every man his rod, and they became serpents: but Aaron's rod swallowed up their rods. (Exod. 7: 8–12)

For those of us of a rational mind, the story of miraculous rods which turn into serpents is unbelievable. We can only imagine, and this has been suggested, that what the pharaoh and his magicians witnessed was a hallucination projected on their minds by the more powerful sorcery of Moses and Aaron. However, there is a more rational explanation than this, once it is realized that the Hebrew word *mopheth*, here translated as 'miracle', really means 'sign'.

The Egyptian religion was, as we have seen, highly inventive in its use of colourful symbolism to describe abstract ideas. Like most ancient cultures it understood the contest between light and dark as symbolic of the struggle between good and evil. The Good was personified by light, symbolized by the sun god Re himself or his regent on earth, the hawk-headed god Horus, who was believed to be physically incarnated in the living pharaoh. The personification of Evil or Chaos was represented, as in the Bible, by the primeval serpent, which was called Apep or Apopis by the Egyptians. The Apep serpent manifested as darkness, and in *The Book of the Dead* and other places it was regarded as an obstacle which had each day to be cleared from the path of Re's bark as it sailed through the underworld. Various gods were invoked to carry out this necessary task, and in the course of the rituals described in *The Book of the Dead* Apep is symbolically defeated and hacked to pieces, as he evidently had been at the beginning of creation. This, however, was clearly not the end of the matter as far as the Egyptians were concerned. While alive, the pharaoh was regarded as the incarnation of Horus, and it was therefore his duty to uphold the rule of light. How, then, in practice was he, not being a luminous body like the sun, to show his power over the serpents of darkness?

One possible way seems to have been through the manipulation of shadows, and most specifically the shadows cast by pyramids and obelisks. The association between the darkness of a shadow and the chaos of Apep, the archetype of all serpents, was probably strengthened in the Egyptian mind by the fact that snakes will often hide in dark corners and crevices. As we have seen, the pharaohs raised obelisks extolling Re-Heracte, 'the Mighty Bull'. These obelisks of the pharaoh would cast, on certain days, shadows of specific lengths. In this way the darkness of the shadow, itself a mini-serpent, was brought into the service of the gods of light and order, thereby emphasizing their dominion over chaos.

The removal of poisonous snakes from houses was another important and symbolic function of the priesthood, and even today is a task whose practitioners are highly revered in Egypt. To capture a snake, use is made of a long stick with a fork on one end. This is used to pin down its head so that the snake-charmer can get close enough to grip the creature tightly by the neck and to put it into a sack or basket. Usually the snake is later set free in the desert, the realm traditionally ruled over by Set, the tempestuous brother of Osiris. This method of catching snakes seems to be a very ancient craft, and has probably not changed much since pharaonic times. Statues and paintings of the pharaohs and their wise men often show them carrying a special staff called a *waz*-sceptre. Like a snake-charmer's staff, this sceptre had a curved fork at the bottom end. The *waz*-sceptre seems to have had a mainly ceremonial function, but it could have been used for pinning down snakes in just the way practised by snake-charmers today. However, it could also have been used as a *gnomen* by means of which it would have been possible to tell the time. Held vertically in the sunlight, the staff would cast a shadow and this would extend from it in just the way that the body of a snake would stretch out from its pinned-down head. Thus it seems likely that when the Bible says that Aaron cast down his staff and it became a serpent, what it is really referring to is the shadow, or 'serpent', that the rod cast when put before the light of the sun. It would seem that the pharaoh's magicians were able to do likewise, but Aaron's rod cast a longer shadow and therefore consumed these lesser 'serpents'. This can only have been true if Aaron's staff was longer than theirs. If so, this would have been for a reason; and that reason seems to have been linked with Moses' greater knowledge of astronomy.

As we have seen, at the time of the Old Kingdom, when the pyramids were built, the Regulus conjunction occurred when the sun was at an angle of 51° 51' as it crossed the east–west axis. As a result a rod of 7 cubits in length, held vertically, would have cast a shadow of 5.5 cubits in length. Using this length as a radius, a circle with a circumference of 44 cubits could have been drawn on the ground. By 1364 BC the height of the sun as it crossed the east–west axis in its Regulus conjunction was no longer 51° 51' but had fallen to about 51° 6'. As a result, to obtain a shadow of the same length (5.5 cubits) it would be necessary to shorten the staff to approximately 6.82 cubits instead of 7.

Not fully understanding the importance of the geometry implicit in the 14:11 relationship (which contains the numbers of Thoth, 7 and 11), the Egyptian sorcerers must have shortened their staves to accommodate the new reality and make sure that the shadows were of the traditionally correct length. Thus they would have been using staves of the new length, 6.82 cubits, to obtain shadows of 5.5 cubits in length on Regulus day. Aaron must have had a staff of the true length: 7 cubits, perhaps worked out from the dimensions of the Temple of the Phoenix at Heliopolis. This would have given the correct length of shadow of 5.5 cubits when the sun was at 51° 51', as it would have been some two or three days earlier. On Regulus day it would have cast a shadow of approximately 5.65 cubits – long enough to consume the shorter shadows, or 'serpents', cast down by the staves of the sorcerers. From this we can see that the first skirmish or conflict between Moses and the Egyptian hierarchy concerned standards. Not only was Moses instructed in all the wisdom of the Egyptians, as St Stephen, the first of the Christian martyrs, says in the Acts of the Apostles (Acts 7: 22) but he was clearly a true initiate after the order of Thoth/Hermes/Enoch. The challenge he posed to the Egyptians was not one of superior magic, but rather one of understanding the true Hermetic principles behind the numbers of Thoth.

According to the Book of Exodus, Moses led the

Israelites out of Egypt into the wilderness, where they wandered for forty years. The most memorable event that occurred during this time was the receiving at Mount Sinai of the Ten Commandments. This peak, today called by the Arabs Gebel Musa or the 'Mountain of Moses', is the highest peak in the Sinai peninsula. Here Moses is supposed to have met with God. What may or may not have transpired between Moses and his Creator, including the detailed instructions given to him concerning the designs for the Ark of the Covenant, need not concern us here. What is important for our present purpose is the location of Mount Sinai itself, at latitude 28° 32' north and longitude 33° 59' east. The SKYGLOBE program reveals that at this location in *c.*1350 BC the sun would have crossed the east–west axis with the 51° 51' pi angle on the day it was conjunct with Rho-Leonis, the 'back paw' of Leo. Thus if Aaron or Moses had erected a staff 7 cubits in length on this day it would have generated the magic circle of 44 cubits in perimeter or a square of sides 11 cubits: the sacred numbers of Thoth/Hermes.

The importance of the Leo constellation in the birth of the Israelite nation and to the tribe of Judah in particular is made clear much earlier in the Bible, in the Book of Genesis. In the prophecies of Jacob (Israel) to his children and the nations which will rise from them he says: 'The sceptre shall not depart from Judah, nor the ruler's staff from between his feet' (Gen. 49: 10). Judah was the 'lion tribe' of Israel, and it therefore seems significant that a staff raised on Mount Sinai at the time of the liberation of the Israelites from their bondage in Egypt should cast the perfect shadow at the time the sun was conjunct with the paw of Leo.

This, however, is not the end of the story. The first capital of the Israelites after they left Egypt and once more occupied the land of Canaan was Shechem, a city in the hill country of Samaria and now called Nablus. Here there was a piece of land which Jacob had long before bought from the sons of Hamor. The story is told in Genesis:

> And Jacob came safely to the city of Shechem, which is in the land of Canaan, on his way from Paddan-Aram; and he camped before the city. And from the sons of Hamor, Shechem's father, he bought for a hundred pieces of money the piece of land on which he had pitched his tent. There he erected an altar and called it El-Elohe-Israel [God, the God of Israel]. (Gen. 33: 18–20)

At Shechem Joshua, who was Moses' successor as leader of the Israelites, called on the people to swear an oath to the God who had brought them out of Egypt. In recognition of this he raised a stone to bear witness to their oath. The bones of the patriarch Joseph were also buried here, in what had previously been Jacob's sanctuary.

> And the people said to Joshua, 'The Lord our God we will serve, and his voice we will obey.' So Joshua made a covenant with the people that day and made statutes and ordinances for them at Shechem. And Joshua wrote these words in the book of the law of God; and he took a great stone, and set it up there under the oak in the sanctuary of the Lord. And Joshua said to all the people, 'Behold, this stone shall be a witness against us; for it has heard all the words of the Lord which he spoke to us; therefore it shall be a witness against you, lest you deal falsely with your God' . . .
> The bones of Joseph which the people of Israel brought up from Egypt were buried at Shechem, in the portion of ground which Jacob bought from the sons of Hamor the father of Shechem for a hundred pieces of money; it became the inheritance of the descendants of Joseph. (Josh. 24: 24–32)

The significance of Shechem can again be seen from the stars. At the time of Jacob, which we can notionally date at around 1600 BC, it can be seen astrologically that at Shechem the sun would have sat in the 'shake-hands' position, that is, over the outstretched right hand of Orion, at exactly 30° above the horizon in the east or the west. This would seem to be the Jacob connection, for as we have seen he is closely associated with Orion; indeed, an alternative name for Orion's Belt is 'Jacob's Staff'. During this epoch the sun would have culminated in the south with an angle of 60° at the time it was in Taurus. This may be why Shechem was associated with the 'bull tribe' of Joseph.

By the time of Joshua things had changed, but what was significant in this era (c.1300 BC) is that the sun, as seen from Shechem, was now making an angle of 45° when between the stars Rho-Leonis and Regulus. Once more the lion connection with Israel was being emphasized. The great lion-king of Israel was of course David, who lived c.1000 BC. He captured Jerusalem and established his capital city on the flanks of Mount Zion. To emphasize the importance of Jerusalem in relation to its neighbour cities such as Shechem he had the Ark of the Covenant brought there from Shiloh. His son Solomon carried on the work of turning Jerusalem into the national capital and at around 900 BC built the first temple, in which was housed the Ark containing the tablets of Moses bearing the Ten Commandments. Again, this has astrological importance; for by then, in the Jerusalem area, the sun made an angle of 45° when it was in conjunction with Regulus.

Solomon raised two great pillars, called Jachin and Boaz, at the front of his temple. These seem reminiscent of the paired obelisks which, as we have seen, were normally placed in front of Egyptian temples and which at Heliopolis would have cast significant shadows. Jachin and Boaz were each 18 cubits in height and carried capstones of either 4 or 5 cubits (the Bible text is a little unclear on this point; see Exodus). Because the sun would have been at a height of 45°, the shadows cast to the east and west by these pillars would have been the same as their height on the days when the sun was conjunct with Regulus. This seems to have been deliberate, emphasizing the sacred nature of Jerusalem as a city of the lion. Thus it was that David and Solomon between them established Jerusalem as the capital of Israel. The importance in all of this of the lion symbol, that is to say the constellation of Leo, is borne out in the prophetic name Ariel, meaning 'lion of God', which Isaiah gives to the city of Jerusalem.

The right of the House of David to govern Israel was not undisputed. As can be seen from the books of Samuel and 1 Kings, David and Solomon dealt ruthlessly with their enemies, and as long as they were alive Israel remained united. However, following the death of Solomon the Israelites gathered at the old capital of Shechem, and instead of accepting his son Rehoboam as king, ten of the twelve tribes opted instead for Jeroboam, a strong-man from the tribe of Mannaseh. From this time onwards the kingdoms of Israel and Judah were split. The ten-tribe nation making up the northern kingdom of Israel, now called Samaria, was subsequently ruled over by the dynasty of Jeroboam until its deportation by the Assyrians in c.732 BC. The lion tribe of Judah, along with its neighbour, the tribe of Benjamin, remained loyal to the descendants of David and Solomon. The Jews, as they were now to be called, never forgot the glory days of David and Solomon; nor, it would seem, the importance of the constellation of Leo on the standard of their nation.

I found unexpected confirmation of the importance of the lion symbol in Israel in the course of a trip to the Holy Land which I made in 1998 (about which more will be said in a later chapter). During the course of this trip I visited the town of Safad, which is the highest in the land and one of the sacred cities of Israel. It is so dignified not because of its altitude but rather for its history as a centre of Jewish culture during the long period of the diaspora. Prior to the fifteenth century Spain had been a major centre of Jewish learning, in particular of that secret branch of study known as the Kabbalah. However, from 1478 onwards the Jews came under increasing pressure from the Spanish Inquisition either to convert to Christianity or to leave the country. As a result many of these Sephardic or Spanish Jews (including the family of the great philosopher Spinoza) settled in the Netherlands. Others went to Palestine and in particular to Safad, where there was already a thriving Jewish community. As a consequence, Safad became the major centre of Kabbalistic learning in the world – a tradition that still survives to this day.

One of the principal teachers to establish a school at Safad was Adoni Rabbi Yitzhak Luria, often referred to by the acronym of 'Ari' (meaning 'lion'). He was born in Jerusalem in 1534 but moved to Cairo, where he studied the Kabbalah along with more conventional Jewish teachings. In 1569 he moved to Safad in order to attend the school of another Kabbalist called Rabbi Moshe Cordeviero. Following the latter's death, Rabbi Ari took over the school and taught the secrets of the Kabbalah to a select circle of students. After he died a synagogue was built on the site, then an open field, where he and his followers had gathered together on the Sabbath. It was this synagogue, called the Ha'Ari Ashkenazi, which I came to Safad to see.

The synagogue itself turned out to be an inconspicuous building on the lower slopes of the town, which from the outside could easily be mistaken for a house. The inside was not unlike a church, densely packed with benches with an altar at one end. On this altar there was a tabernacle or 'ark' containing, as is usual, the sacred scrolls of the Torah. I could not see these scrolls as they are protected from public view by a blue velvet curtain. However, the designs on the curtain itself were most intriguing and seemed to indicate that someone, perhaps

229

an initiate from the school of Ari, knew about the connection between Jerusalem and the constellation of Leo. At the centre of the design was a pair of slabs covered with Hebrew writing which I took to represent the Ten Commandments of the Mosaic Law. At the time of the Temple of Solomon these were kept inside the Ark of the Covenant, housed in the Holy of Holies. They were the most valuable possession of the Israelites, the memorial of the Mosaic Covenant. Indeed, the Temple itself was really no more than a container for the Ark and these precious tablets of the Law. As we have seen, in front of the Temple of Solomon stood two pillars, Jachin and Boaz, which would have cast significant shadows when the sun stood at exactly 45° in the east and west on Regulus day. The designs on the curtains graphically confirmed the Leo connection with the Temple of Jerusalem, for on each pillar there stood a rearing lion (see colour illustration no. 20).

On returning to England at the end of this trip I consulted a Jewish friend of mine and asked him if this design was common to all synagogues. He replied that while the overall design of synagogues is standard, in that there is an altar, an ark containing the rolls of the Torah and a symbolic curtain shielding these from view when not in use, how this curtain is embroidered is a matter of personal taste. While it is certainly possible that it is merely an accident of design that this particular curtain shows lions standing on the columns, it is also tempting to think that knowledge of the Regulus conjunctions and their importance in the design of the Temple at Jerusalem was part of the secret knowledge passed down from ancient times by the Kabbalists and known to Ari, the 'lion' of Safad.

This becomes even more likely when we come to realize that the Kabbalists seem to have known a great deal about signs in the sky, not least the importance of Orion. Jesus, who came from Nazareth which is not far from Safad, was also addressed as 'Rabbi', and so it should come as no surprise that much of this knowledge passed, in secret form, into Christianity. Matthew spoke of certain signs that we should look out for to tell us of the end of the age, but his instructions are in code and not easy to understand. Breaking these codes was to be the next task in my quest; when I did so they revealed, contained in the Christian Gospels, a profound knowledge of the same secret astrology.

CHAPTER 13

THE HOLY LAND REVISITED

In late November 1998 I returned to the land of Israel for the first time since 1973. Much had changed with the passage of time; some things, however, had not. As the country was still officially at war with at least some of its neighbours, there were still gun-toting *sabras* to be seen everywhere. But the balance of the population had changed. Whereas on my earlier visit Jews of European and American descent had seemed to predominate among the Israeli population, and these were for the most part secular in outlook, recent mass immigrations from Russia, Africa and other places had altered the ethnic mix. The Haredim or ultra-orthodox Jews, immediately recognizable by their black suits, side-locks and prayer shawls, were also far more in evidence, especially on the streets of Jerusalem. Little loved by the majority of Israelis they, like the Pharisees of Jesus' time, clearly believed that they alone occupied the moral high ground. Because they held the balance of power in Israel's political system, they exercised influence out of all proportion with their numbers. The passage of a quarter-century had also changed the Arabic population of the occupied territories. Though they were still, on the outside at least, friendly towards foreigners, one could sense their inner frustration and anger with what seemed to them an indifferent and hostile world. In the Arab markets of Jerusalem this rage was channelled into aggressive salesmanship that made even the souks of Cairo seem pleasantly civilized.

There were more subtle changes, too. Twenty-five years earlier there had been a sense that this was the land of Christ; notwithstanding the presence of the country's other major faiths of Islam and Judaism, there was then still an overwhelming atmosphere of Christian piety in the streets of Jerusalem and Bethlehem, and above all in the region around the Sea of Galilee. One sensed that the churches, many of them grown from seeds sown at the time of Constantine the Great and his saintly mother Helen, had such deep roots that, like the ancient cedars of Lebanon which once supplied materials for Solomon's Temple, they would never disappear. Yet today, though the church buildings are still there (indeed, many have been recently rebuilt and are more beautiful than ever), changing attitudes have introduced an air of uncertainty. For example, how many people today really believe that the Basilica at Bethlehem marks the spot of Jesus' birth? Or that the Church of the Holy Sepulchre in Jerusalem covers the spot where he was crucified and buried? Yet it was to recover these churches, which must be among the ugliest in Christendom, that in 1099 Jerusalem was seized by the armies of the First Crusade and its Jewish and Muslim population massacred. To today's Christian pilgrims such misplaced zeal may seem repugnant, but it is still the driving force in the politics of the region. The Jewish fundamentalists who are attempting to settle the West Bank and are building new villages around Jerusalem have taken over the mantles of the First Crusade's leaders Godfroi, Bohemond, Baldwin and Tancred. They, not today's Christians, are the modern counterparts of the medieval crusading fanatics; and, as a result of their influence, the Holy Land is once more, to all intents and purposes, a crusader state without the cross.

For all this, Israel was noticeably richer than it had been twenty-five years earlier. The infrastructure was much improved; the people were better dressed than I remembered, and the cars they drove were both newer and much more plentiful. There were many more hotels, shops and restaurants, and everywhere the towns seemed to have grown enormously. Yet for me these changes highlighted a feeling of artificiality I remembered experiencing before. In what was arguably the most sacred landscape in the world, the cities and towns were notable for their brutal architecture and almost total lack of any aesthetic pretensions.

This time I had travelled to Israel by plane, landing at Eilat. Located at the head of the 'finger' of the Red Sea called the Gulf of Aqaba by the Arabs and Gulf of Eilat by the Israelis, on the edge of the Sinai peninsula, this is Israel's southernmost city. A playground for those seeking winter sun and snorkelling, it is also a major port. My intention was to spend a day or two there before heading north. While I intended to revisit Bethlehem and Jerusalem, what I most wanted to do was to journey northwards along the roughly north–south line linking Eilat with Metula, Israel's most northerly city.

Eilat itself turned out to have changed beyond all recognition since I had seen it in 1973, when it was scarcely more than a building site. At that time it had been possible to sleep on the beach with the stars overhead for company. Young students and travellers such as myself would spend several months working on construction sites until they had saved enough money to continue their journey to India. It was then a relatively simple matter to work a passage on one of the many cargo ships sailing down the coast of Africa to Mombasa, and from there one could take ship to Bombay. This had been my intention, too, when I first arrived, but I had quickly decided that it was not as sensible a plan as it had seemed. There was a rough side to life in Eilat, which was unlike anywhere else in Israel: in many ways it resembled a gold-rush town in Arizona or one of the other states of the 'Old West'. Travellers were regularly being robbed of money and possessions by the many vagrants who were even poorer than themselves, and fights were common. Indeed, on my first day in the town I had had a supermarket bag containing nothing more than a little bread and a few tomatoes stolen from under my nose while I was busy sunbathing. A Dutch friend of mine from the kibbutz had purchased a share in a rough shanty on the dunes, where there was a more permanent encampment used by construction workers as well as itinerants. Though only made of wood the building seemed relatively secure as it had a stout padlock. My friend paid over quite a lot of 'key-money' for a billet in this small but relatively safe building and into it, much to the envy of her friends who had to keep their own possessions by them at all times, she entrusted her ruck-sack. However, on returning to camp that evening we had a sense that all was not well. This feeling of foreboding was quickly confirmed when we discovered that the shanty had been burnt to the ground. All that was left of what had been the stoutest building on the dunes was a charred ruin. Though nobody was hurt by what was clearly an arson attack, my friend had lost everything – including her passport. All that she had left were the clothes she was standing in and what money she had in her pocket.

Memories of these and other events crossed my mind as I surveyed the new Eilat. Today there is no trace of the places where they happened. Where once there were dunes, there is now a large shopping mall. The small hotels which were being built then are now dwarfed by newer and much larger buildings, the five-star hotels that fringe the best areas of the beach – where sleeping is now forbidden.

Leaving Eilat behind me I boarded an Egged Bus, still the most common form of travel thoughout all Israel. My destination was the Dead Sea, where I planned to stay for a few days before going on to Jerusalem. The land we passed through was mostly arid, though here and there, where there was water, there were kibbutzim growing dates, citrus fruit and other produce. For most of our journey the terrain was flat, a plain sandwiched between two ranges of mountains: one in Israel and the other in the Hashemite Kingdom of Jordan. Only as we approached the Dead Sea itself did this plain, known as the Arava, begin to rise appreciably. Shortly afterwards the road plunged steeply downwards, past the salt peaks of Sodom (one of which is called 'Lot's Wife') to the south-western fringes of the Dead Sea itself. We were now, though you wouldn't guess it from the topography, at the lowest point on earth: over 400 metres below sea level. We passed the remains of Herod's great fortress of Masada, where once, on his orders, the Hasmonean Princess Mariamne had been held prisoner and later the Zealots had committed suicide rather than be taken prisoner by the Romans. A few miles further on were the ruins of Qumran, where the Dead Sea Scrolls were discovered.

Throughout the long drive along the rim of the Dead Sea, a route which I remembered well and which had not changed much in twenty-five years, I was fascinated by the geology of the landscape. On either side of the sea there were steep cliffs, occasionally cut by intersecting wadis. Where there was a small, spring-fed stream, such as at Ein Bokek or Ein Gedi, the land was verdant; but for the most part the sea lived up to its name, surrounded as it was by barren desert. The cliffs themselves were an interesting sight, showing stratified layers of rock. These bands, some thick and some thin, often ran for many miles. They were shades of muddy brown in colour, and while some of them seemed to be limestone others were clearly of a weaker, more friable material. At Qumran, which I explored, the limestone cliffs had been hollowed out into caves, a job presumably made easier by the weakness of the intermediate layers. It was easy to see why the Essenes had chosen this remote spot for a community: it had a reliable, if limited, supply of fresh water which, with some ingenuity, they had been able to channel both for their own use and to irrigate their crops. Less obvious was why it had taken so many centuries for

236

their caves to be rediscovered and their writings brought to light.

Leaving the Dead Sea valley, the bus began its long ascent to the hills of Judea, in which nestles Jerusalem. There I checked into a cheap hotel near to the Jaffa Gate, which lies on the western side of the old city. A day or two later I found myself winding back down the precipitous road, now a dual carriageway, that leads from Jerusalem to the Jordan valley. It had been my intention to visit the site of Jesus' baptism, which is traditionally believed to have taken place at a point between the town of Jericho on the West Bank and a village called Bethany on the East. Unfortunately, because of the continuing political tension in the area this stretch of the river, which formed a border between the Israeli 'Occupied Territories' and the State of Jordan, was out of bounds. The nearest I could get to the River Jordan was the Allenby Bridge, a few miles upstream from the site of the baptism. As a compromise I hired a Palestinian taxi and set off for Jericho and the Greek Orthodox Monastery of the Temptation, which is supposedly built over the cave where Jesus, immediately after his baptism, spent his forty days in the wilderness. It was there that I was to gain further insights into the extraordinary ministry of Jesus.

It was now over twenty-five years since I had first visited Israel and had sat in the foothills of the Golan contemplating biblical prophecies. At that time and in that place it had seemed that anything was possible. There had been an all-pervading atmosphere of imminence, a sense that at any moment Jesus Christ might appear wearing sandals and a long flowing robe. Now, back in the Holy Land so many years later, pieces of the puzzle were falling into place. I was at last finding some plausible answers to the questions that had so obsessed me then – questions such as: What did Jesus mean when he said, 'Where the carcass is there the eagles gather'? And what might be

237

the 'sign of the Son of man in heaven' that he said would herald his second coming? At the time I was writing *Magi*, in 1995, although I had some insights concerning the Ascension of Jesus to the 'right hand of the Father', I still had only vague answers to these questions. I remembered, however, that in chapter 16 of Matthew's Gospel Jesus castigates the Pharisees and Sadducees for not understanding certain signs of the times. In this chapter he makes a cryptic comment about Jonah which seems to be connected with the later prophecies about signs in the sky:

> And the Pharisees and Sadducees came, and to test him they asked him to show them a sign from heaven. He answered them, 'When it is evening, you say, "It will be fair weather; for the sky is red," and in the morning, "It will be stormy today, for the sky is threatening." You know how to interpret the appearance of the sky, but you cannot interpret the signs of the times. An evil and adulterous generation seeks for a sign, but no sign shall be given to it except the sign of Jonah.' So he left them and departed. (Matt. 16: 1–4)

I had always been intrigued by this passage. What on earth could be meant by 'the sign of Jonah'? And was this sign intended for his own 'adulterous generation' or for one yet to come? If the latter, could it indeed connect with the later prophecies in Matthew chapter 24, where Jesus talks unambiguously about the end of the age and the eagles drawn to a carcass? It was all very mysterious. I decided further research on Jonah was called for.

Jonah probably lived during the seventh century BC when the Assyrian Empire was at the height of its power. According to the Bible he was ordered by God to go and prophesy at Nineveh, which at that time was the Assyrian capital. Preaching morals to tyrants is seldom a very safe thing to do, and naturally enough Jonah was scared, especially as the Assyrians had a very bad reputation for cruelty; so he refused to go, and instead tried to escape by ship to Tarshish (Cadiz). God, not disposed to allow such a transgression by one of his prophets, caused such a storm at sea that eventually the crew, recognizing Jonah as the reason for their discomfort, threw him overboard. This might have been his end, were it not that he was swallowed whole by a whale. He now had to spend three days and three nights inside its belly, praying for forgiveness, at the end of which time he was vomited out on to dry land. Once more Jonah was bidden to go to Nineveh, and this time he heeded the call. At the Assyrian capital he prophesied to the people that in forty days their city would be overthrown. Appalled, they donned sackcloth and ashes and repented of their sins – whereupon God, much to his prophet's annoyance, relented. Jonah's response to this great act of leniency was to go off and sulk. For this he was again reproached, this time for his lack of compassion. The story ends with God saying: 'Should I not pity Nineveh, that great city, in which there are more than a hundred and twenty thousand persons who do not know their right hand from their left, and also much cattle?' (Jonah 4: 11).

The story of Jonah, then, has many twists and turns; but it was still not clear to me what its basic message was, nor what could be the 'sign of Jonah' spoken of by Jesus. The explanation given in the Bible (Matt. 12: 40) is that Jesus was here prefiguring his own burial for three days and three nights prior to his Resurrection from the belly of the earth. However, there seemed to be more to it than this. For one thing, unlike Jonah, Jesus took his mission seriously from the start and made no attempt to escape his fate. Also, he was entombed for a maximum of thirty-six hours after his crucifixion – only half the period Jonah is said to have spent in the belly of the whale, an event which itself taxes all credulity. And while Jonah's preaching at Nineveh brought about a change of heart in its king and people, no such repentance was forthcoming when Jesus preached in Jerusalem. Far from donning sackcloth and ashes, the authorities of the time put him to death. The analogy between Jesus and Jonah seemed rather weak, and I was sure that the 'sign of Jonah' was something else.

Reading on in chapter 16 of Matthew's Gospel I found a further clue as to what this sign might be. Here, shortly before the story of the Transfiguration on Mount Hermon, Jesus has a conversation with his disciples concerning his true identity:

> Now when Jesus came into the district of Caesarea Philippi, he asked his disciples, 'Who do men say that the Son of man is?' And they said 'Some say John the Baptist, others say Elijah and others Jeremiah or one of the prophets.' He said to them, 'But who do you say I am?' Simon Peter replied, 'You are the Christ, the Son of the living God.' And Jesus answered him, 'Blessed are you, Simon Bar-Jona! For flesh and blood has not revealed this to you, but my Father who is in heaven. And I tell you, you are Peter, and on this rock I will build my church, and the gates of Hades shall not prevail against it. I will give you the keys of the kingdom of heaven, and whatsoever you shall bind on earth shall be bound in heaven, and whatsoever you shall loose on earth shall be loosed in heaven.' Then he strictly charged the disciples to tell no one that he was the Christ. (Matt. 16: 13–20)

This passage has interesting implications both for Simon Peter's relationship with John the Baptist and for the nature of the 'sign of Jonah'. John and Jonah are basically the same name; the sign of Jonah could therefore be connected with the mission of John the Baptist, whose call 'Repent, for the Kingdom of Heaven is at hand' echoes the earlier prophet Jonah's preaching to the Ninevites. Confirmation that this is probably what was being hinted at is provided by Robert Young's *Analytical Concordance to the Holy Bible* – an invaluable source for

anyone seriously interested in researching the Bible –
which tells us that the Hebrew name Jonah means 'dove'.
This would seem to be a clear allusion to the story of
Jesus' own baptism by John, when a dove landed on him
and a voice from heaven said: 'This is my beloved Son
with whom I am well pleased.' It is thus reasonable to
conclude that it was not Jesus himself who was to be
compared with Jonah of old but rather his cousin the
Baptist, who as at the time of Nineveh called people to
repentance. This much was clear; but it was not yet
obvious what the 'sign of Jonah' was.

A further clue is to be found in the mythology of
Mesopotamia. The Sumerians and later the Babylonians
had a legend, rather similar to the Osiris legend of Egypt,
that civilization had been brought to Mesopotamia by
teachers, called 'Annedoti', who came out of the Persian
Gulf or Erythrean Sea. The form of these Annedoti, who
according to some writers – notably Robert Temple in
The Sirius Mystery[1] – may have been extra-terrestrial in
origin, was half-fish and half-man. The leader of the
Annedoti was called Oannes, and each night he would
retire back into the Persian Gulf where he would sleep
under water. This demi-god is depicted on Assyrian
cylinder seals and reliefs. He has a man's body, but
wrapped around this is a second body, that of a fish.[2]
Curiously enough, the name Oannes is the root from
which is obtained the name John (Ioannes or Joannes in
Greek). Could Jonah, who came out the belly of a fish,
and John the Baptist, who (like a half-fish?) stands up to
his waist in the River Jordan baptizing, be in any way
linked with the myth of Oannes, the Annedotus? This
was a question that I could not immediately answer.

The references to John the Baptist are also telling
in another way. Prior to meeting Jesus, Simon Peter and
his brother Andrew had been among that prophet's
disciples. John had been the first to declare, at the time of
Jesus' baptism, that the latter was the Christ. This piece
of information had evidently been revealed to him

241

OANNES, MESOPOTAMIAN GOD OF CIVILIZATION

spiritually, and it would seem from the passage from Matthew's Gospel quoted above that Peter too was now being spiritually guided towards the same understanding. At the time this conversation takes place John is already dead, having been executed on the orders of Herod Antipas. Taking all these matters into account, could it be that in calling Peter 'Bar-Jona', Jesus is not referring to his physical father but is rather suggesting that Peter has inherited the mantle of John, his former teacher?

This somewhat convoluted analysis becomes clearer when we examine in more detail the story of Jesus' Nativity at Bethlehem. It has to be remembered that the Gospels were written at a time when the church was one small sect in a sea of cults jostling for support. As it was competing for converts among the Gentiles, Matthew (and the other evangelists) needed to show that their messiah fulfilled the expectations not only of the Jews but also of the surrounding nations. From the evidence in Commagene it is clear that one of these expectations was that the right time for a king to be born was at dawn when the sun was conjunct with Regulus. As we saw in the previous chapter, 29 July 7 BC seems to be the chosen date of the Nativity. On that day alone the stars would have been in the right position for the birth of a king (the Regulus conjunction) and there would have been three planets visible at dawn (Jupiter, Saturn and Mercury), two of them in conjunction forming the single, very bright 'Star of Bethlehem' followed by the Magi. The pattern of stars at dawn on 29 July, 7 BC so clearly fits with the ancient conception of the birth of a 'lion king' that I was absolutely certain that it was this date which Matthew had in mind when writing his Gospel. The learned among the pagan Greeks, Egyptians and others would very likely have understood the subtle, unspoken message written between the lines of his Gospel: that Jesus was born to be a pharaoh or king.

Yet if the Nativity took place in summer, why do we celebrate Christmas in the middle of winter and not in

July or August? The answer to this is quite simple, and again has to do with the church's need to win converts. Our date for Christmas, 25 December, was originally a pre-Christian, winter solstice festival held in honour of the birth of Sol Invictus, the 'unconquered sun'. It was also the birthday of Mithras, an Anatolian/Persian god whose cult was extremely popular throughout the Roman Empire during the first and second centuries AD. The adoption of 25 December as Christmas was a pragmatic move made by the church during the fourth century after Constantine the Great made Christianity the official religion of the Empire. In order to appease public opinion in Rome and elsewhere, where the people were used to having a party on this day, the previously pagan festival celebrating the winter solstice was made the birthday of Christ. Prior to this time the official festival of Christmas, still held to by the Orthodox church, was 6 January, the feast of the Epiphany. However, this feast too was originally celebrated not as the supposed birthday of Jesus but rather as his baptism by John. In Greek Επιφανια (Epiphania) means 'manifestation', usually of something supernatural. The feast of the Epiphany originally had nothing to do with the arrival of wise men at the stable in Bethlehem, but commemorated the manifestation of the Holy Spirit as a bright light at the time of Jesus' baptism in the River Jordan. This story is told in chapter 1 of John's Gospel:

> The next day he [John the Baptist] saw Jesus coming toward him, and said, 'Behold the Lamb of God, who takes away the sin of the world! This is he of whom I said, "After me comes a man who ranks before me, for he was before me." I myself did not know him; but for this I came baptizing with water, that he might be revealed to Israel.' And John bore witness, 'I saw the spirit descend as a dove from heaven, and it remained on him. I myself did not know him; but he who sent me to baptize with water said to me, "He on whom you see

the Spirit descend and remain, this is he who baptizes with the Holy Spirit." And I have seen and borne witness that this is the Son of God.' (John 1: 29–34)

The same story is contained in the Gospel of Matthew, but with some differences of detail. Again the baptism is accompanied by the manifestation of the Holy Spirit in the form of a dove descending on to Jesus:

> Then Jesus came from Galilee to the Jordan to John, to be baptized by him. John would have prevented him, saying, 'I need to be baptized by you, and do you come to me?' But Jesus answered him saying, 'Let it be so now; for thus it is fitting for us to fulfil all righteousness.' Then he consented. And when Jesus was baptized, he went up immediately from the water, and behold, the heavens were opened and he saw the Spirit of God descending on him; and lo, a voice from heaven, saying, 'This is my beloved Son, with whom I am well pleased.' (Matt. 3: 13–17)

Prior to about AD 350 the baptism of Jesus took precedence over his birth, which does not seem to have been celebrated at all until the second century. Once more there is some vagueness about the actual year in which Jesus was baptized, but there are good reasons for believing that it took place in AD 26.

According to the Gospel of John, Jesus' baptism happened shortly before the wedding feast of Cana, which was followed a few days later by the feast of the Passover. For this latter festival Jesus is said to have gone up to Jerusalem, where he got into an argument with the money-changers in the Temple. In a heated exchange with the Jewish elders, he claimed that if they destroyed the Temple, he could raise it up in three days. Their reply that this was impossible as 'it had already taken forty-six years to build', is one of the keys to a correct chronology, for we know that King Herod

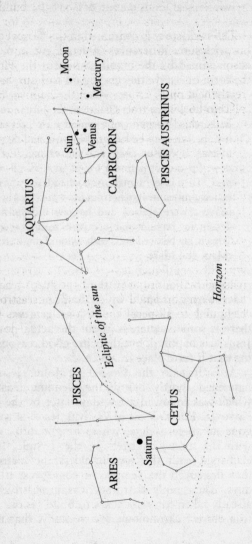

STELLAR SIGNATURE OF THE BAPTISM OF
JESUS, 6 JANUARY AD 26

Moon

Mercury

Sun

Venus

AQUARIUS

CAPRICORN

PISCIS AUSTRINUS

PISCES

Ecliptic of the sun

Horizon

CETUS

ARIES

Saturn

came on to the throne of Judea in 38 BC and that he began the temple project in the eighteenth year of his reign. This gives us a start date for the building of 20 BC and forty-six years on brings us to AD 26 for the Passover following Jesus' baptism. As the Passover took place around the time of the spring equinox, we know the baptism must have been earlier than this. Thus, assuming that the early church festival of the Epiphany was correctly held on 6 January, then the baptism by John took place on 6 January AD 26.

That this 'rebirth' of Jesus by the descending Holy Spirit is what we ought to be celebrating on 'Old Christmas' (i.e. the Epiphany) I had no doubt, but I had discovered something else: like the real Nativity on 29 July 7 BC, this date was 'star-correct'. Using the SKY-GLOBE computer program I had found that on 6 January, although the sun was in the constellation of Capricorn, it was also under the 'hand' of Aquarius, the water carrier, because these two constellations overlap. Also on this date the planet Venus was in conjunction with the sun; though it would not have been visible, being masked by the bright glare of the sun, its position could have been computed by a competent astrologer. I was beginning to suspect that St Matthew was such a man, for the bird associated with Venus is the dove – the very bird which John is said to have seen come down from heaven to land on Jesus. Since the Hebrew word for dove is *jonah* there was a double possibility, astrologically speaking, with both John (Aquarius) and the dove (Venus) representing the 'sign of Jonah'. However, there was yet more to come before this part of my investigation was complete.

Down in Jericho it was a hot day, even though it was now December. My taxi dropped me at the foot of a steep cliff, and from here it was a stiff climb up a staircase to the Greek monastery which perched like a bird's nest high on the cliff face. By the time I arrived at the top I was bathed in sweat and quite breathless, but exhilarated at the same time.

I was greeted at the door by a young monk – one of only two residents in a building which had accommodation for over a hundred brothers. Through lack of recruitment the monastery seemed to be dying. Nevertheless, I was given a gracious welcome by the monk, who offered to be my personal guide. We went first into the main church, which was a dark sanctuary lit only by candles. Bidding me to be silent for a few minutes, he lit a few more candles and then began to chant some prayers. Around the walls, over the altar – indeed, anywhere that there was a space, it seemed – there were icons of the saints. The gold paint on these holy images glowed in the candle-light, which together with the chanting made for a strangely antique atmosphere. I too said some prayers; then my guide took me to the inner sanctum of the building. In contrast to the main chapel, it was a light, airy room with windows to the outside. Its focal point was a little altar over a large, flattened stone. Above the altar, between two pillars, was a picture of Jesus. He was wearing a red tunic beneath a sky-blue mantle and appeared to be dancing with joy (see colour illustration no. 19). 'This place that you are in,' began the monk in halting English, 'is the cave in which Christ lived during the forty days he spent in the wilderness. Two of his temptations took place here and for the third he was transported bodily to the Temple in Jerusalem. The stone which you are looking at was his bench that he sat on while he was being tempted.' With these words he knelt down and solemnly kissed the stone. Feeling slightly self-conscious but not wanting to offend, I followed suit and kissed it too. These formalities over, he left the room so that I could have some time there to myself, perhaps to remember the many times I have succumbed to much easier temptations than those which Jesus confronted.

The story of the temptation of Christ occurs in chapter

4 of Matthew's Gospel, immediately after the story of the baptism:

> Then Jesus was led up by the Spirit into the wilderness to be tempted by the devil. And he fasted forty days and forty nights, and afterwards he was hungry. And the tempter came and said to him, 'If you are the Son of God, command these stones to become loaves of bread.' But he answered, 'It is written, "Man shall not live by bread alone, but by every word that proceeds from the mouth of God."'
>
> Then the devil took him to the holy city, and set him on the pinnacle of the temple, and said to him, 'If you are the Son of God, throw yourself down; for it is written, "He will give his angels charge of you, and on their hands they will bear you up, lest you strike your foot against a stone."'
>
> Jesus said to him, 'Again it is written, "You shall not tempt the Lord Your God."' Again, the devil took him to a very high mountain, and showed him all the kingdoms of the world and the glory of them; and he said to him, 'All these I will give you, if you will fall down and worship me.' Then Jesus said to him, 'Begone, Satan! For it is written, "You shall worship the Lord your God and him only shall you serve."'
>
> Then the devil left him, and behold angels came and ministered to him. (Matt. 4: 1–11)

It was hard to credit that the events here described had actually taken place inside the room in which I was now standing, which though a cave is now fronted by a wall. Yet few of the events described in the Bible can be placed with any certainty, and it was possible, even if not probable, that Jesus had spent time in this wilderness sanctuary overlooking the Jordan valley. If so, then it was even possible that the stone I had kissed had served as his stool and had been one of those he had been tempted to turn into bread.

At the time I was writing *Magi* I had thought long and hard about these temptations of Jesus. It was clear to me that the devil represented his own lower nature, that is to say his ego, looking for an easy way out from what was going to be a difficult and painful mission. The three temptations themselves seemed in some way linked with the gifts of the Three Kings, of frankincense, myrrh and gold, which by my analysis represented the influences of the three planets of his birth: Mercury, Saturn and Jupiter. Thus the transformation of stones into bread would be a misuse of magic, the power of Mercury; to challenge death by recklessly jumping from the pinnacle of the Temple was to fall for the temptation to misuse the power of Saturn, which among other things is said to confer longevity; and the planet of the emperor, that is to say the 'King of the World', was Jupiter. Thus I could see that by overcoming these temptations Jesus was symbolically moving beyond the realms of the planets, that is to say the 'lower heavens'. In doing so he was affirming his willingness, come what may, to meet a higher destiny: to become the vehicle for the work of the 'higher Logos', the 'Word' of his Father who stood above the planetary spheres.

This much I had worked out, at least to my own satisfaction, in 1995; but shortly before coming to Israel three years later I had begun to see the baptism and temptation of Christ in a different way that went beyond even this mystical interpretation. The key to this new interpretation was the knowledge that the baptism took place on 6 January AD 26 with, as we have noted, the sun in the sign of Capricorn but under the hand of Aquarius.

The zodiacal constellation of Capricorn is represented as a goat. This is important, as it was customary in biblical times to make use of goats in rituals of atonement for sin. Whereas sheep were invariably used as blood-offerings, goats were not always sacrificed but could take on a different role as 'scapegoats'. The sins of Israel would be symbolically placed upon the head of a goat, which would then be set free in the wilderness – probably to die of starvation. Under the kings of Judah this seems to have been considered a necessary part of the process of cleansing the nation of Israel. The origins of this practice go back to the time of Moses. In chapter 16 of Leviticus, Aaron, Moses' brother, is instructed by God in the correct practice of this ritual of atonement:

> He [Aaron] shall put on the holy linen coat, and he shall have the linen breeches on his body, be girded with the linen girdle, and wear the linen turban; these are the holy garments. He shall bathe his body in water, and then put them on. And he shall take from the congregation of the people of Israel two male goats for a sin offering, and one ram for a burnt offering.
>
> . . . Then he shall take the two goats, and set them before the Lord at the door of the tent of meeting; and Aaron shall cast lots upon the two goats, one lot for the Lord and the other for Azaziel. And Aaron shall present the goat on which the lot fell for the Lord, and offer it as a sin offering; but the goat on which the lot fell for Azaziel shall be presented alive before the Lord to make atonement over it, that it may be sent away into the wilderness to Azaziel.
>
> . . . And when he [Aaron] has made an end of atoning for the holy place and the tent of meeting and the altar, he shall present the live goat; and Aaron shall lay both his hands upon the head of the live goat, and confess over him all the iniquities of the people of Israel, and all their transgressions, and all their sins; and he shall put them upon the head of the goat, and send him away into the wilderness by the hand of a man who is in readiness. The goat shall bear all their iniquities upon him to a solitary land; and he shall let the goat go in the wilderness. (Lev. 16: 4–9)

Azaziel, to whom the scapegoat is sent, is mentioned in the Book of Enoch as one of the Nephilim ('Watchers' or

'Fallen Angels') who came to earth and begat children with the 'daughters of men'. Like the Annedoti of Mesopotamia, they are said to have taught men science. However, in the Book of Enoch their influence, particularly that of Azaziel who taught the skills of warfare and enticement, is considered malign.

> Moreover Azazyel [*sic*] taught men to make swords, knives, shields, breastplates, the fabrication of mirrors, and the workmanship of bracelets and ornaments, the use of paint, the beautifying of the eyebrows, the use of stones of every valuable and select kind, and of all sorts of dyes, so that the world became altered.
>
> Impiety increased; fornication multiplied; and they transgressed and corrupted all their ways.[3]

In words remarkably similar to those found in the Hermetic book the *Kore Kosmu*, where the earth appeals to God because men have polluted her with their spilt blood, the 'men, being destroyed, cried out; and their voice reached to heaven'. Their cries are heard by the good angels – Michael, Gabriel, Raphael and others – who take the message to God.

> Thou hast seen what Azazyel has done, how he has taught every species of iniquity upon earth, and has disclosed to the world all the secret things which are done in the heavens.
>
> Samyaza [leader of the Nephilim] also has taught sorcery, to whom thou hast given authority over those who are associated with him. They have gone together to the daughters of men; have lain with them; have become polluted; and have discovered crimes to them. The women likewise have brought forth giants. Thus has the whole earth been filled with blood and iniquity.
>
> And now behold the souls of those who are dead, cry out. And complain even to the gate of heaven.[4]

For these crimes God sentences Azaziel to be bound and cast out into the desert. This damnation of the devil is connected with the necessity of the Great Flood, for at the same time God tells Noah that while he is going to send a flood to destroy life on earth, his seed will be saved.

> Then the Most High, the Great and Holy One spoke, and sent Arsayalalyur to the son of Lamech [i.e. Noah], saying, Say to him in my name, Conceal thyself. Then explain to him the consummation which is about to take place; for all earth shall perish; the waters of a deluge shall come over the whole earth, and all things which are in it shall be destroyed. And now teach him how he may escape, and how his seed may remain in all the earth.
>
> Again the Lord said to Raphael, Bind Azazyel hand and foot; cast him into darkness; and opening the desert which is in Dudael,[5] cast him in there. Throw upon him hurled and pointed stones, covering him with darkness; There shall he remain for ever; cover his face, that he may not see the light. And in the great day of judgement let him be cast in the fire.
>
> Restore the earth, which the angels have corrupted; and announce life to it, that I may revive it. All the sons of men shall not perish in consequence of every secret, by which the Watchers have destroyed, and which they have taught, their offspring.
>
> All the earth has been corrupted by the effects of the teaching of Azazyel. To him therefore ascribe the whole crime.[6]

At the time of Jesus the Book of Enoch was widely read, and indeed fragments of it have been found among the Dead Sea Scrolls. These, or at least some of them, probably belonged to the community at Qumran, which is believed to have been Essene. As it seems almost certain that this 'school' trained John the Baptist (and possibly also Jesus himself), it is almost certain that both of them would have been familiar with the Book of Enoch. Curiously the caves (there are many of them, not just one) hollowed out in the cliff face by the Monastery of the Temptation are very similar to those at Qumran. We know that these were used by hermits in the early days of Christianity, and it seems likely that they date from before this time. It is therefore quite possible that the caves here were used by hermits from Qumran and that Jesus retired to one of them after his baptism.

In the story of Jesus' temptation we are told that he confronted the devil. From the passages cited above it is not hard to see that this desert-living devil is probably to be understood as Azaziel. We therefore have a connection between the archetypal 'scapegoat' sent into the wilderness to Azaziel, and Jesus, who is baptized when the sun is in the sign of Capricorn (the goat) and who meets with the devil (Azaziel) in the wilderness. By this reading of the stars, Aquarius symbolizes John, while Jesus, as usual, is symbolized by the sun. This time, however, the sun occupies the sign of Capricorn, which seems to indicate that Jesus is the scapegoat who takes on himself the sins of the world. Jesus has powers, and when he meets the devil he is confronted with both a challenge and a choice. He can succumb to temptation, in which case he is guaranteed an easy life – possibly even becoming emperor of Rome; or he can turn his back entirely on the things this world has to offer and walk the lonely path leading to Calvary. It would seem from all of this that in this story with its astrological parallels we are once more seeing the old Hermetic dictum 'as above, so below', this time being enacted quite literally in the life of Jesus. What at first sight appears to be a simple story of a man under-going a baptism, a ritualistic washing away of sins, actually masked a deeper truth concerning the heavens.

Leaving the Monastery of the Temptation and making my way back down to the waiting taxi, my thoughts returned once more to the story of Jonah and the whale, and the reference to a sign. Then it occurred to me that one possible clue to this riddle is that the constellation of Aquarius stands next to Cetus – the whale – over which stretches Pisces, the fish. This seems to imply a connection between Aquarius (as John or Jonah) and the profession of fisherman. Both Andrew and Peter were fishermen prior to becoming apostles and this, in a way, links them with the baptizing sign of Aquarius.

The link with fishes and fishermen was certainly important, for at the time of Jesus the spring equinox took place in the sign of Pisces, at which time the sun would pass over the top of Cetus the whale. Could this, I wondered, be what Jesus meant by the sign of Jonah: the beginning of the age of Pisces? While this was certainly a plausible theory, I was still not convinced that it was the full answer, which I felt would go even deeper. Cetus, the whale or sea-monster, is, as one might expect, a very large constellation: while it swims away from Aquarius and its main body lies under the constellation of Pisces, its head reaches up to Aries. I was to find out later that this connection between Cetus and the constellation of Aries has very deep significance. Accordingly, it is my belief now that the sign of Jonah has a very specific meaning with relevance for our generation as well as that living at the time of Jesus. What this meaning might be will be described in a later chapter; first we need to discuss another prophecy of Jesus: that a body or corpse would be found where eagles gather.

CHAPTER 14

AT THE CENTRE OF THE WORLD

Back in Jerusalem I checked into one of the oldest hotels
in the city: the Petra, which though run down is not
totally without charm. Like an ageing film star who in
her youth shared her bed with many of the greats, it has
played host to many famous travellers and writers,
including Ernest Hemingway; now though I had my own
small room, the dormitories were full of back-packers
from all over the world, which brought back pleasant
memories of my own youthful adventures.

The Petra may have fallen on hard times, but it still
enjoys an almost unrivalled prospect over Old Jerusalem,
and after unpacking I climbed up to the roof to see the
view of which I had heard so much. It turned out to be
even better than I expected. Spread out before me were
the rooftops, domes and minarets of all Jerusalem. To
the left, in a more or less northerly direction, lay the
Church of the Holy Sepulchre; east of this, not quite
directly in front of the hotel, was the Dome of the Rock.
It looked like a gigantic wedding cake, or a golden bauble
glittering in the afternoon sunshine. It outshone by far
all the other buildings one could see, with the possible
exception of a Russian Orthodox church in the distance
on the side of the Mount of Olives, whose onion domes
were also gilded. There could be no doubt that the Dome
of the Rock, at least from the outside, was still the most
important and beautiful building in Jerusalem; and its
location was such that it was visible from miles around.

I decided it was high time I paid it a visit.

Brushing aside hawkers, I plunged down David Street, a pedestrian walkway which for most of its length takes the form of a staircase with gift shops in either side. Presently the street came to a junction, and after a few false turns I eventually found myself in front of the most sacred place in Judaism: the Wailing Wall. Security was tighter than I remembered it in the 1970s, but this was hardly surprising given the sensitivity of the area and the ever-present danger of terrorist attack. I walked across to a checkpoint, where I passed my camera bag through a scanner and allowed myself to be frisked. These formalities completed, I was soon standing on the Temple Mount close to the Al Aqsa mosque, which had once been the headquarters of the Knights Templar.

The Haram ash-Sharif, as the Temple Mount is known to Muslims, was not quite as I had expected. For one thing it was swarming with children, for whom the main area beneath the level on which the dome stood functioned as a park. Here they were allowed to play football and other games, seemingly oblivious to the supposed sanctity of the site. I suspected that there was more than a little politics involved in this. At present the Israelis dare not challenge the possession of the Harem by the Muslims for fear of provoking what could easily turn into a world war. As a result, religious Jews cannot enter its precincts to pray in the space once sanctified by the ancient temple; instead, they have to content themselves with chanting by the Wailing Wall and pressing scribbled notes into its cracks. By allowing their children to play football in the holy precincts it looked as though the Palestinians were inadvertently rubbing salt into the wound, insulting the Jews praying below. Such, unfortunately, are the ways in which politics, religion and daily life are inextricably mingled in this most complex of cities.

Walking up the steps from Al Aqsa, I found myself in front of the Dome. I had brought a compass with me and

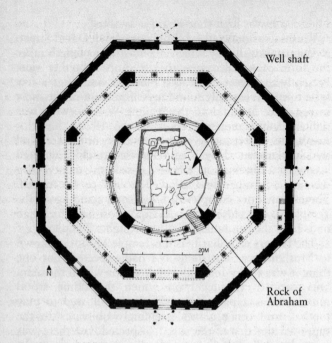

Well shaft

Rock of
Abraham

GROUND PLAN OF THE DOME OF THE ROCK

was therefore able to confirm that this was the southern
side (the building is eight-sided) and that it was, like the
Great Pyramid, truly orientated towards the cardinal
directions. I walked around the building several times,
taking pictures from various angles, before making my
way to the entrance, which is on the western side. Not as
large as it looks from the distance, inside the building was
very much as I remembered it. Beautifully proportioned
and carpeted throughout, it was clearly designed in such
a way as to invite peregrination. Today, of course,
Muslims all address their prayers to Mecca, where
pilgrims circumambulate the mysterious stone known as
the Ka'ba. This, however, has not always been the case;

at the time the Dome was built (between AD 681 and 691), by the Umayyad Caliph Abd al-Malik, Mecca was in the hands of his rival Ibn az-Zubayr. As pilgrims from territories controlled by the Umayyad caliphate were temporarily banned from Mecca, al-Malik had to make other provisions and built the Dome as an alternative centre of devotion. Here, over the rock of Abraham from which Mohammed was believed to have ascended to heaven in a dream, he built a mosque around and in which pilgrims could circumambulate, as had been their custom at Mecca. Later, after it became possible for Muslims to go to Mecca again, the Dome at Jerusalem became of lesser importance, though it still retains the prestige of being the third holiest place in Islam.

This much you will find in most history books on the subject; however, there is more to the Dome, as I had learned from a remarkable book entitled *Architecture, Mysticism and Myth,* written by William Lethaby, Surveyor of Westminster Abbey from 1906 to 1928. It is a collection of essays on certain recurrent architectural themes, one of the most important of these being the near-universal idea that the most sacred of buildings put up by a civilization or culture stands at what is considered by the people in question to be the centre of the world. Lethaby notes that the Iron Pillar of Delhi, the Altar or Temple of Heaven in Peking and the Temple of Apollo at Delphi were all at one time or another considered to be at the centre of the world. However, for the West at least, the city that best exemplifies this idea of the world's centre is Jerusalem; and within Jerusalem it is the Temple Mount that lies at the very navel of the world. He writes:

Jerusalem has been to Jews and Christians the centre of the world, 'beautiful for situation, joy of the whole earth'. What the Temple was as a centre of worship is shown by Solomon's dedicatory prayer and by Daniel's open window toward Zion. The following is the direction as to prayer in the Talmud: 'Those who are in foreign countries beyond the borders of Palestine ought in praying to turn their faces towards the sacred land as it is written, "They shall address their prayer to Thee by the way of the land which Thou hast given to their ancestors" (1 Kings viii. 48). Those who dwell in Palestine direct their countenance towards Jerusalem, for it is written, "They shall pray unto Thee towards the city which Thou hast chosen." Those who make their prayer in Jerusalem turn towards the mount of the Temple, as it is said in the same verse, "And the house which I have builded in Thy name." Those who are upon the mount of the temple turn towards the Holy of Holies. "They shall address their prayer to Thee in this place, and Thou wilt hear it in heaven Thy dwelling place, Thou wilt hear it and pardon." Hence it follows that those of the north should turn towards the south, those of the south towards the north, the men of the east towards the west, the men of the west towards the east, so that all Israel shall turn in the act of prayer.'[1]

Lethaby goes on to explain that the reason why the Temple Mount of Jerusalem was so important was that it was considered to be the location of the foundation stone of the world. Borrowing a metaphor from the *Kore Kosmu*, the old rabbis thought of Jerusalem, and most especially the Temple itself, as being the eye-pupil of the world. It was the *kibleh* (point of adoration) of Moses and was revered as such by both Christians and Jews. At the time of Mohammed it nearly became the Islamic *kibleh* as well, in place of the old Arabic centre of Mecca; the Prophet, however, thought better of this, fearing that it would increase the temptation of his followers to convert to either Christianity or Judaism. As all this is very well explained by Lethaby I shall quote him in full:

But not only was it [Jerusalem] a ceremonial centre; it was geographically in the midst of the earth; and the following from the Talmud (Hershon) shows that the

Rabbis of the Temple had an omphalion [navel] stone, and that it was built not only on *a* rock but *the* rock.

'The world is like the eyeball of man; the white is the ocean that surrounds the world, the black is the world itself, and the pupil is Jerusalem, and the image of the pupil is the Temple.'

'The world's "foundation stone" sank in the depths under the Temple of the Lord, and upon this the sons of Korah used to stand and pray.'

'The land of Israel is situated in the middle of the world, and Jerusalem in the centre of the land of Israel, and the Temple in the centre of Jerusalem, and the Holy of Holies in the centre of the Temple, and *the foundation stone on which the world was grounded is situated in front of the ark.*'

'When the ark was removed a stone was there from the days of the first prophets; it was called *Foundation*. It was three digits high above the earth.'

... In Jerusalem the 'Dome of the Rock,' *El Sakhrah*, occupying the traditional site of the temple sanctuary, surrounds a mass of the living rock, the bare summit of Mount Moriah, which for about sixty by forty feet crops out of the beautiful paving; under it is the 'Well of Souls'; and the Turkish Pacha told Sir Charles Warren 'it lay on the top leaves of a palm tree, from the roots of which spring all the rivers of the world.' Nusir-i-Khusran, who visited the sites in 1003 AD, says that God commanded Moses to make this stone the *kibleh*, and later Solomon built the temple about it as a centre. From it the four doors open, as an early pilgrim says, to the four quarters of the world. In Mohammedan tradition this rock is the world's foundation stone. It is known to them as the *kibleh* (point of adoration, centre) of Moses. Mahomet thought at first of adopting it in the place of the old Arab centre of Mecca, well understanding the religious need of such an omphalos to Eastern thought, as in it the idea of separation from others is most forcibly expressed. The Prophet says,

'Verily although though shouldest show unto those to whom the Scripture hath been given all kinds of signs, yet they will not follow thy kibleh, neither shalt thou follow their kibleh; nor will one part of them follow the kibleh of the other.' At the last day, however, even the black stone of Mecca will come as a bride to the rock of Jerusalem, and thus arises any confusion there may be as to the world centre of Islam.[2]

That the site over which stands the Dome of the Rock should be important to all three of the great faiths which owe their origins to the Abrahamic covenant is beyond dispute. However, what was especially interesting is that such a rock is called here a *kibleh* – a word so similar to 'Kabbalah' as to suggest a common root. Could it be, I wondered, that part of the secret Kabbalah concerned the role and destiny of Jerusalem? When I re-published Lethaby's book myself in 1993 I had no definite answer to this question, but I was already beginning to think it must have been so.

After a few days more in Jerusalem and a visit to Bethlehem, I once more boarded an Egged bus, this time heading north along the Jordan valley for Tiberias. As before the bus wound down the steep road from Jerusalem to join the main highway running between Eilat, the Dead Sea and Galilee. With Jericho to our left I peered out of the window to the right, in the general direction of where Jesus was baptized by John. This area, still hundreds of metres below sea level and known as the Plain of Jericho, is highly fertile. At the time of Herod the Great it was famous for its groves of palm trees from which balsam, a soothing base used in many ointments, was manufactured. Mark Antony, who took over the administration of the eastern parts of the Roman Empire after the murder of Julius Caesar, much to the annoyance of Herod, gave these groves to his lover Cleopatra. Today most of this land is still suffering from the after-effects of Israel's many wars with its neighbours. Entrance to and from Jericho is controlled by armed police, and the fact that the Jordan itself forms the border between Israel and the Hashemite Kingdom means that the immediate vicinity is highly militarized. Time and the peace process will no doubt change this, but in the meantime the Palestinians, who administer Jericho, have found a new way of making a living and drawing funds away from rich Israelis: they have opened a casino. One can only wonder what John the Baptist would have made of roulette, poker and baccarat.

Signs for the Allenby Bridge, one of only three crossing points from Israel into Jordan, brought to mind an earlier prophet than John: Elijah. He too had wanted to cross the Jordan – but in his day there was no bridge. Undaunted, he took off his mantle and with it struck the waters, which obligingly parted. Accordingly he and his disciple Elisha were able to walk over without so much as getting their feet wet. The fact that this miracle took place in the vicinity of where, centuries later, John baptized Jesus was clearly no accident. For in the course of researching *Magi* I had found evidence to suggest that John the Baptist was an initiate in the mould of (or even the reincarnation of) Elijah. Like John, Elijah had been rough-robed and very much a 'wild man of God'. In fact the descriptions of both prophets, John and Elijah, link them to a certain stereotype which also includes Samson, whose name means 'distinguished' or 'strong'. As noted in chapter 6 above, Harvard professor Giorgio de Santillana and his associate Hertha von Dechend have convincingly demonstrated that the story of Samson is really to be understood as an astronomical allegory. According to them Samson, like Elijah and John, represents the constellation of Orion. The Hebrew name for Orion is *kesil,* meaning 'strong', and the mythical Greek hero Orion the Hunter was, like the biblical Samson, a strong-man.

The story of Orion the Hunter, an archetype deeply rooted within the human subconscious, goes back to the very origins of civilization. One has only to think of the fictional Tarzan, whose home is the jungle and whose friends are the animals, or of Superman, the comic-book hero who comes from the stars and fights against wrong-doing, to see the Orion/Samson archetype at work even today. It certainly goes back to the dawn of history and is probably to be recognized in the legends of Sumeria. In the *Epic of Gilgamesh* the Orion archetype is recognizable in the form of Enkidu. He, like Samson, begins life as a wild man of superhuman strength. Like Tarzan, Enkidu is a friend of the beasts and he annoys Gilgamesh, king of Erech, by setting free ensnared animals. To capture this wild man Gilgamesh orders that a temple prostitute be taken to the watering hole where Enkidu regularly drinks and that she seduce him with her charms. This she does and Enkidu, driven wild with desire, experiences sex for the first time. Then, after seven days of constant orgy, he discovers that a change has come over him. The animals who were his friends now shun him, and he finds that he has become anxious to join the company of men. Accordingly the prostitute persuades him to cast aside his clothing of skins, to shave himself and be anointed with oils. Thus civilized he is led to Erech, to the court of Gilgamesh. There the two heroes, Gilgamesh and Enkidu, who are perhaps to be understood as different aspects of the same basic archetype, have a wrestling match. After this they become firm friends and set out together to hunt down a fearsome monster called Humbaba. The *Epic of Gilgamesh* is the oldest surviving poem of its type known to us. From the many versions of it preserved on clay tablets it is clear that it was widely known and recounted throughout the period of Mesopotamia's greatness. It seems likely, therefore, that the story of Samson as we have it ultimately derives from this earlier legend.

In early Christian times the 'wild man' archetype is to be recognized in the legend of St Christopher. He too was a giant, converted and civilized – in this case by a hermit rather than a prostitute. Born in Syria, Christopher (which means 'Christ-bearer'), realizing that he himself was not of the right temperament for the life of a hermit but nevertheless wanting to serve his fellow men, decided instead to devote himself to the charitable work of carrying travellers over a river. Years went by without event, until one day a small child asked to be carried across the swollen river. Christopher took the child on his shoulders, and initially there was no problem. However, as they got further out into the river the child became increasingly heavy, so much so that the giant feared he might collapse under the enormous weight pressing down on him. When they eventually reached the other bank, he scolded the child, saying: 'Had I carried the whole world on my back it would not have been heavier.' The child was, of course, Jesus Christ, and he replied: 'Don't wonder at it. You carried not only the world but also he who made it!' After this event Christopher became a saint, and is indeed still the patron saint of travellers.

The pope has recently abolished the feast of St Christopher, rightly believing him to be a mythological figure rather than a real, historical personage. His feast used to be celebrated in the Western church on 25 July. In the Eastern church, which it would seem often understands such matters better, the feast of St Christopher is held on 9 May. This earlier date clearly indicates his connection with Orion, for it seems likely that the Christopher legend is based on a very old myth that goes back to long before the Christian era to Old Kingdom Egypt. At around the time the pyramids were built (*c.*2700–2200 BC), each year on 9 May the sun would have been standing in the 'shake-hands' position, directly over the outstretched hand of Orion. As it is at this time midstream over the Milky Way, Orion does, symbolically speaking, carry the sun, i.e. the creator of the solar system, including the earth, over the river of heaven. As we have seen on other occasions, Jesus Christ is often symbolized, astrologically speaking, by the sun. Thus, within the framework of the Christopher myth, we can think of the infant Jesus, his radiant head symbolized by the sun, sitting on the shoulders of the real giant: Orion. Orion's upstretched right hand can be visualized as steadying the child sitting on his shoulders, while his left hand grasps his staff tightly as he struggles across the river (see colour illustration no. 18).

This is exactly how St Christopher is depicted in countless paintings. Indeed, it was normal before the Reformation to have such a picture or even a statue of the giant Christopher placed near to the entrance of a church or cathedral. Not many of these icons survive, but I was pleased recently to see such a picture inside the Catholic cathedral of Antwerp in Belgium. This is entirely appropriate, as that city has its own legend about a giant who once controlled the flow of river traffic in and out of the River Scheldt. According to this legend, the giant lived on the banks of the Scheldt and exacted a toll from any boat that wanted to sail into or out of its mouth. He exerted his control by means of a great chain spanning the river, which he raised or lowered depending on whether or not the toll had been paid. On one occasion a young hero refused to pay the toll. Instead, he fought with the giant, chopped off his right hand and threw it on to the opposite bank of the river. From then on the giant was unable to pull up his chain and boats could sail freely on the Scheldt. The city of Antwerp, its name meaning 'hand-thrown' in Flemish, is said to have been founded on the site where the giant's hand landed. (The hand of the giant remains a city symbol and is a popular subject for artists; a large sculpted version is to be seen in the city's main square.) Again, the connection between the giant and Orion becomes clear once it is realized that the latter's 'hand' lies half-way across the Milky Way and that it grips the ecliptic, or 'chain', along which the sun moves over the river of heaven. From all these stories we can see that the giant Orion standing on the bank of the river is a familiar theme that crops up in the mythology of many places, in Europe as well as in the Middle East.

As we have seen, the prophet Elijah is linked with the Orion archetype and it is therefore not surprising that his story is connected with a river. At the end of his mission, after they have crossed the Jordan, Elijah promises his mantle to Elisha provided he observes him leaving the earth. Then, in a great swirling of fire, a chariot appears and Elijah is taken up to heaven.

> When they had crossed [the Jordan River], Elijah said to Elisha, 'Ask what I shall do for you, before I am taken from you.' And Elisha said, 'I pray you, let me inherit a double share of your spirit.' And he said, 'You have asked a hard thing; yet if you see me as I am being taken from you, it shall be so for you; but if you do not see me, it shall not be so.' And as they still went on and talked, behold a chariot of fire and horses of fire separated the two of them. And Elijah went up by a whirlwind into heaven. And Elisha saw it and he cried, 'My father, my father! the chariots of Israel and its horsemen!' And he saw him no more.
>
> Then he took hold of his own clothes and rent them in two pieces. And he took up the mantle of Elijah that had fallen from him, and went back and stood on the bank of the Jordan. Then he took the mantle of Elijah that had fallen from him, and struck the water, the water was parted to the one side and the other; and Elisha went over. (2 Kings 2: 9–14)

This story of Elijah's ascension seems to be an allegory concerning the rising of the sun and the fading out of the stars at dawn. In antiquity the sun god was often depicted as being drawn along in a fiery chariot by celestial horses. It seems to me that Elijah's disappearance as the chariot arrived is a coded reference to the fading of the stars of Orion at sunrise.[3] Elisha inherited the mantle of Elijah and it is significant that the first miracle which he performed was once more to part the Jordan so that he could go back to Jericho. It is also noteworthy that John the

Baptist carried out his Jordan mission near Jericho, at approximately the same spot where Elijah and Elisha are said to have crossed over. Again, this implies that he too is to be thought of as an initiate of the same school as Elijah and Moses, that other great divider of waters.

Little is said in the Bible about Elijah's own origins other than to describe him as a Tishbite, i.e. as having come from Tisbeh (a city believed to have been in Gilead, a mountainous district east of the Jordan between the Sea of Galilee and the Dead Sea); yet great pains are taken to describe the clothes he wore. As we have seen, his mantle or cloak was inherited by his pupil Elisha, signifying the passing on of his prophetic powers to the next generation. Elijah's other clothes are clearly symbolic of his role as a prophet in the lineage of Samson and other 'wild men of God', for when a messenger of the king is sent to find Elijah he returns saying that he wore 'a garment of hair cloth, with a girdle of leather about his loins'. Similarly, John the Baptist 'wore a garment of camel's hair, and a leather girdle around his waist'. That this mimicking by John of the earlier prophet was quite intentional and meant to link his mission in people's minds with the promised return of Elijah is clear when one reads the first few verses of Matthew chapter 3:

> In those days came John the Baptist, preaching in the wilderness of Judea, 'Repent, for the kingdom of heaven is at hand.' For this is he who was spoken of by the prophet Isaiah when he said, 'The voice of one crying in the wilderness: Prepare the way of the Lord, make his paths straight.' (Matt. 3: 1–3)

Further light is shed on this passage later in Matthew's Gospel where it is stated categorically, by none other than Jesus himself, that John the Baptist was the reincarnation of Elijah.

Jesus began to speak to the crowd about John: 'What did you go out into the wilderness to behold? A reed shaken by the wind? Why then did you go out? To see a man clothed in soft raiment? Behold, those clothed in soft raiment are in kings' houses. Why then did you go out? To see a prophet? Yes, I tell you, and more than a prophet. This is he of whom it is written, "Behold, I send my messenger before thy face, who shall prepare thy way before thee."

'. . . For all the prophets and the law prophesied until John; and if you are willing to accept it, he is Elijah who is to come. He who has ears to hear let him hear.' (Matt. 11: 10–15)

However, over and above this, the description of both Elijah and John the Baptist as roughly clothed and belted is in keeping with the Orion/Samson archetype. The belt is one of the most important descriptive features of the constellation of Orion, and the reference to John's belt seems to link the Baptist with a secret school of prophets – a 'School of Orion' – that possibly stretches back to the time of Enoch. This school, if such we may call it, seems to have influenced many brotherhoods spread throughout the Near and even Far East, not just Elijah's 'school of the prophets'. In a book about the great Sufi poet and mystic Mevlana Celaleddin Rumi, I found evidence to suggest that these ideas concerning Orion are not dead even today.

Rumi is famous as the founder of the order of the Mevlevi dervishes, whose *tekkes* or monasteries once flourished throughout Turkey and Mesopotamia. It is well known that their whirling dance is intended to be symbolic of the motion of the planets around the sun, but what is not often talked about is the way that the dress of these Sufi mystics and of other dervishes is connected with an ancient Orion cult:

Many authors tend to interpret the dancing of the dervishes by the planetary system. For instance one makes the following remark: 'We might connect the dance of the dervishes who, eight in number, move round an orbit, though in contrary direction, perhaps in accordance with a Mohammedan precept. In these dervishes and their dance . . . we may see a survival of the mystic Cabiri, "the Seven Great Ones," or planetary gods, revolving around the green centre of the terrestrial globe.'

Another sharing this opinion comments: 'This, the dervishes hold, expresses the harmony of God's creation, in an ecstasy of spiritual love, of communion with the eternal.'

Another writer comments on the belt worn by some of the dervishes called the *Kamberiye* (the belt is worn in the memory of Kamber, Ali's [i.e. the grandson of Mohammed's] groom): '. . . the three stars of Orion's Belt, denoting the seasons of the year . . . appear again in the girdle of three strands of Munja grass which every Brahmin at his initiation ties around his waist with three knots, saying as he does that they represent the three stars of Orion's belt . . . This three-knotted girdle, called the *Kamberiah*, is worn by all sects of dervishes in South-Western Asia, who are the modern representatives of the ancient dancing priests.'[4]

The fact that Brahmins wear a *kamberiah* would rather seem to contradict the assertion that the *kamberiye* of the dervishes is so named after Ali's groom. The similarity of names would suggest that both belts must have the same origin and are themselves related to the prototype of the eastern *kamarband* or 'cummer-bund' as we would call it in English, which during the days of the Raj was worn, as part of their ceremonial dress, by British officers. This belt, consisting of many folds of muslin or brightly coloured cloth, is still worn in India to this day. Further proof that the *kamberiye* or knotted belt of the dervishes goes back to long before the advent of Islam is that Zoroastrians, the modern descendants of the ancient Magi, wear a kind of knotted belt or cord similar to the *kamberiye* as a symbol of membership of their religious community:

> It had been, it seems, an Indo-Iranian custom for men on initiation to put on a woven cord as a sign of their membership of the religious community ... All Zoroastrians, men and women alike, wear the cord as a girdle, passing three times round the waist and knotted at back and front. Initiation took place at the age of fifteen; and thereafter, every day for the rest of his life, the believer must untie and retie the cord repeatedly when praying. The symbolism of the girdle (called in Persian the 'kusti') was elaborated down the centuries; but it is likely that from the beginning the three coils were intended to symbolize the threefold ethic of Zoroastrianism, and so to concentrate the wearer's thoughts on the practice of his faith.[5]

The author quoted here, Mary Boyce, does not tell us what might have been the further elaboration 'down the centuries' of the symbolism implicit in the *kusti*, but it seems probable that, like the *kamberiah* of the Brahmins, it was connected, metaphorically speaking, with the belt of Orion. Brahminism predates Zoroastrianism, so it is evident that the wearing of such a belt or girdle is a very ancient custom. It seems likely that Zoroaster and his followers were familiar with the importance of the Orion constellation, perhaps from contact with an earlier esoteric school.

Further clues to the connection between Orion and the secret traditions of the Hebrews are contained in *Oedipus Judaicus* by Sir William Drummond (1770–1828).[6] As he points out:

> We know that Joseph was a diviner; and there are many circumstances from which we may conclude, that Jacob was an astrologer ...

271

It appears from Eusebius[7] that tradition, at least, represented Israel as an astrologer, who believed himself under the influence of Saturn. Even at this day, the three great stars in Orion are called *Jacob's staff*, and the milky way is familiarly termed *Jacob's ladder*.[8]

Drummond doesn't say which are the 'three great stars' in Orion, but it would seem most likely that he means the belt. The verse in question, which comes shortly before Jacob's dream of angels going up and down the ladder, is Genesis 32: 10: 'I [Jacob] am not worthy of the least of all the steadfast love and all the faithfulness which thou [God] have shown to thy servant, for with only my staff I crossed the Jordan; and now I have become two companies.' In this verse and what follows Jacob, who is returning home to Canaan after a long sojourn with his uncle Laban at Harran, draws attention to the fact that whereas when he left he had nothing but his staff, he returns with a large family. The connection between the Belt of Orion and this staff seems obscure until it is realized that this is a euphemism for Jacob's phallus. What he is really saying is that his 'staff', i.e. his phallus, has been fruitful in generating further branches on the family tree. This again hints at a connection with ancient Egyptian mythology, wherein the Belt of Orion seems at times to have been similarly considered to represent the phallus of Osiris.

The connection between Jacob (or Israel, as he is shortly to be called) and the constellation of Orion is apposite. As Drummond remarks, the holy planet of the Israelites was Saturn, which they called 'Sabaoth'. This name is derived from the term Sabbath (or Shabbath), which means 'cessation'. Its day of the week was Saturday or 'the Sabbath', the day of cessation when no work was to be done. This was partly a reminder that on the seventh day of creation God rested, but it is also linked to the belief that Saturn, as the seventh planetary sphere from earth, was the last before one reached the zone of the fixed stars, the throne of God himself.

Astrologically speaking, the influence of Saturn is considered to be one of the most difficult to deal with. In the past astrologers considered its influence to be wholly malevolent, but today there is a greater understanding that Saturn exercises more of a 'policing' role, in that its function is to bring wrongdoing to account. Thus in her book *Saturn: A New Look at an Old Devil*, the modern astrologer Liz Greene writes:

> In traditional astrology Saturn is known as a malefic planet. Even his virtues are rather dreary – self-control, tact, thrift, caution – and his vices are particularly unpleasant because they operate through the emotion we call fear. He has none of the glamour associated with the outer planets [Uranus, Neptune and Pluto] and none of the humanness of the personal planets [Mercury, Venus and Mars]. In popular conception he is devoid of any sense of humour. He is usually considered to be the bringer of limitation, frustration, hard work, and self-denial, and even his bright side is usually associated with wisdom and the self-discipline of the man who keeps his nose to the grindstone and does not commit the atrocity of laughing at life. By his sign and house position [i.e. position in the sky at birth] Saturn denotes those areas of life in which the individual is likely to feel thwarted in his self-expression, where he is most likely to be frustrated or meet difficulties. In many instances Saturn seems to correspond with painful circumstances which appear not to be connected with any weakness or flaw on the part of the person himself but which merely 'happen', thereby earning the planet the title, 'Lord of Karma'. This rather depressive evaluation remains attached to Saturn despite a most ancient and persistent teaching which tells us that he is the Dweller at the Threshold, the keeper of the keys to the gate, and that it is through him alone that we may achieve eventual freedom through self-understanding.[9]

The image referred to here of Saturn as the guardian of the threshold comes about because traditionally (before the discovery of Uranus in 1781) it was believed to be the ruler of the outermost planetary sphere. It therefore represented the possibility of either jumping out of the solar system to the wider sphere of the fixed stars or, more likely, reincarnating back on earth. In Greek cosmology Saturn was called Chronos and, as 'Lord of Karma', took on the function of the Grim Reaper, or he who decides when our allotted time is used up. To the Romans, who borrowed much of their mythology from the Greeks, Saturn was personified as 'Father Time' and was usually depicted as an old man carrying a scythe in one hand and an hour-glass in the other. Thus he has remained to the present day.

Closer analysis of the role of Saturn as the planet of time indicates that he wears borrowed clothing. The Roman Saturn was an agricultural deity whose principal feast, the Saturnalia, was held around 25 December at a time when Orion rises at sunset and is visible throughout the night. Moreover, the staff Orion carries in his left hand can easily be interpreted as a scythe while his right, reaching out towards the ecliptic, does in a very real way hold the sands of time. For these reasons it seems much more likely that the original Saturn or Chronos, 'Lord of Time' as opposed to planet of adversity, was indeed Orion. The real reaper in the sky is not Saturn but Orion, whose appearances at dawn, sunset and midnight have for aeons marked out the agricultural seasons.

It is easy to see how the attributes of Orion as Lord of Time passed to the planet Saturn. In the Hebrew Kabbalah the Sephirah or sphere associated with Saturn is Binah or 'Understanding'. This stands at the top of the Pillar of Severity and is followed by Hochma or 'Wisdom', which stands on top of the Pillar of Mercy and represents the zodiac or sphere of the fixed stars (see colour illustration no. 25). Here too, then, Saturn was seen as the last station in the 'Lower Heavens' which the soul had to pass before crossing to the zone of the fixed stars: the 'Higher Heavens'. Yet the portal to this sphere above the planets was not Saturn itself, but rather the position on the celestial sphere where the ecliptic (the path followed by the sun in its annual course) crossed the Milky Way.

The idea of a 'stargate' above Orion was something I had first come across in a completely different context while I was researching *The Mayan Prophecies*. Giorgio de Santillana and Hertha von Dechend had drawn my attention to this point by a short passage on the subject in *Hamlet's Mill*. In the course of a chapter called 'The Galaxy' they explored the ancient idea, to be found most clearly expressed in Macrobius' *Commentaries on the Dream of Scipio*, that between lives men's souls dwell in the Milky Way. The gateways through which these souls pass in and out of life were, they said, at the two points in the sky where the ecliptic crosses the Milky Way. One of these gateways is in the constellation of Gemini – actually above Orion – and the other between Scorpio and Sagittarius.

In the Book of Genesis the connection between the Kabbalistic Tree of Life and the soul's journey to the gate of heaven is illustrated in an earlier dream of Jacob's when he sees a ladder with angels climbing up and down it:

> And he [Jacob] dreamt that there was a ladder set up on the earth, and the top of it reached to heaven; and behold the angels of God were ascending and descending on it! . . .
> Then Jacob awoke from his sleep and said, 'Surely the Lord is in this place; and I did not know it.' And he was afraid, and said, 'How awesome is this place! This is none other than the house of God, and this is the gate of heaven.' (Gen. 28: 12, 16–17)

If we equate Jacob with Orion and his ladder with the Milky Way, then it would appear that this 'gate of heaven' is the same stargate that Macrobius describes as being at the crossroads of the latter with the ecliptic. We have, therefore, the image of Jacob seeing the angels passing through the stargate which lies at the top of the ladder of the Milky Way.

My bus to Tiberias, the most important town on the shores of the Sea of Galilee, was now reaching its destination. For the last hour or so we had followed a route through lush orchards and vegetable fields, the handiwork of local kibbutzim. Occasionally the bus would stop to pick up a kibbutznik or soldier, but we stopped for slightly longer at Beit She'an. As is so often the case in Israel, there was little about this rapidly growing town to indicate its importance historically. Originally an Egyptian stronghold, it gained everlasting fame in Jewish eyes as the place where King Saul's body had been hung up by the Philistines after his defeat and death at the Battle of Mount Gilboa. There was nothing to see of these events today but Beit She'an's site, at the junction of the fertile Valley of Jezreel and the great declivity of the Jordan, means that it is still as strategically important as it was in the time of Saul.

Soon we arrived at Tiberias, which was named after the emperor who reigned at the time of the Crucifixion. In the twenty-five years since I had last paid it a visit it had changed beyond all recognition. I remembered it as a sleepy little town, not much larger than a village, with a few old ruins and some riverside cafés. Today it is anything but quiet, having been transformed into a holiday centre. Instead of fishing boats calmly plying their trade, there are floating disco-bars, lit up at night by a thousand electric bulbs and blaring out popular music over the previously tranquil Sea of Galilee. It seemed to me the very opposite of progress.

The following day I teamed up with a couple of Australians, an American and another Briton to take a trip to Upper Galilee and the Golan Heights. Unlike the

Dead Sea canyon, which is fringed with cliffs made from sedimentary rocks, this area of Israel is largely volcanic in origin. As our minibus hauled itself up the precipitous road leading out of Tiberias, I could see that the northern edge of the gorge in which the Sea of Galilee sits was almost entirely made out of black basalt. This was something that I had either forgotten, or perhaps never noticed back in 1972, but the change in rock form was very obvious and spoke volumes about a violent geological past quite at odds with today's tranquil scene. The forces which had produced this landscape were clearly still at work deep down in the earth's mantle, for in the vicinity of Tiberias were the hot springs which had so delighted the Romans and caused them to build the city in the first place.

We continued further north, up into the Golan Heights, and there I had another stark reminder of the region's volcanic past when, 2 kilometres south of the Druze village of Majdal Shams, we stopped at Birket Ram – the almost perfectly round crater of an extinct volcano which today contains a lake. Though there were no plumes, fumeroles or other evidence of volcanic activity, the place still had a somewhat menacing quality about it that was hard to define. In part, no doubt, this was due to the sheer starkness of the surrounding landscape with the almost vertical rise of the Mount Hermon range to the rear. But there was something more to it than this that inspired fear in the pit of my stomach, an almost palpable sense that there lurked here a brooding force that was merely sleeping. This feeling of incipient panic was not allayed by the friendliness of the local Druze people nor the delicious pancakes served by a girl dressed in their national costume at the little kiosk on the rim of the lake. I was glad when we left.

Leaving Birket Ram we followed the road through Majdal Shams, whose name means 'The Tower of the Sun'. We then skirted around the lower slopes of Mount Hermon until we reached our next destination: Banyas, where the River Jordan has its principal source. Originally this place was named after the god Pan, who was supposed to inhabit the forest glades, and for this reason the town was more generally known as Paneas, from which is derived the modern Arabic name. It was easy to see why the ancients felt this place to have been special. Now enclosed within a national park, the springs at Banyas spew forth the most precious liquid in the Middle East: not oil but water. Though we visited it at the end of one of the worst droughts in living memory, the waters of the Jordan still erupted from the belly of Mount Hermon to swirl down a small canyon before cascading over a magnificent waterfall. The whole area has a magical feeling of vitality, emphasized greatly by the fact that were it not for the river, the Jordan valley would be utterly arid.

In classical mythology Pan, the presiding deity, was primarily a god of shepherds. With the upper body of a man but the legs and horns of a goat, he was a great musician and was famed for his ability to enchant with the music of his pipes. Lustful and exuberant, he spent much of his time pursuing the nymphs of the forest and, as his festivals tended to be orgiastic, he became associated with debauchery. However, Pan was also a god of terror who could inspire 'panic'. In Roman times his sanctuary of Paneas was a place of merriment where the rulers and those wealthy enough to join them propitiated with sacrifices the fearful side of his character so that they could enjoy the good things in life: wine, women and song. This must have been anathema to the orthodox Jews of the time for, as we have seen, the Mount Hermon area was the place where the fallen angels or Nephilim were supposed to have come to earth.[10] As far as the Jews were concerned, Pan was another name for the Devil, and to set up a shrine in his honour was an open invitation to further interference from the Nephilim.

Pan's sanctuary was built around a cave and the spring from which the Jordan gushes. Though the spring is still active, today all that remains of the Roman buildings are the foundations of the Temple of Augustus, some fallen columns and a few empty niches in the cliff face which would once have contained statues of Pan and other pagan idols. Close to the ruins of what may once have been a palace or even a brothel, I came across a lone fig-tree. It brought to mind the one cursed by Jesus, which must have looked very similar, for this one too, though wild and rampant in its growth, was also without fruits. It seemed fitting that, perhaps because of the drought, it too looked stricken and close to death.

In Jesus' time Paneas was better known as Caesarea Philippi, by which name it is referred to in the Bible. Near the entrance to the archaeological complex there was a strange contraption whose function took us a while to work out. It consisted of a large and heavy metallic cone on the face of which was engraved a reversed inscription. Beneath the cone was fine sandy clay, so that when the cone was rolled around it made an impression, spelling out the text as though on a cylinder seal. The text was, of course, from the New Testament and told the story of what had happened when Jesus and his followers had visited what may well have been this exact spot.

> Now when Jesus came into the district of Caesarea Philippi, he asked his disciples, 'Who do men say that the Son of man is?' And they said, 'Some say John the Baptist, others say Elijah and others Jeremiah or one of the prophets.' He said to them, 'But who do you say I am?' Simon Peter replied, 'You are the Christ, the Son of the living God.' And Jesus answered him, 'Blessed are you, Simon Bar-Jona! For flesh and blood has not revealed this to you, but my Father who is in heaven. And I tell you, you are Peter, and on this rock I will build my church, and the gates of Hades shall not prevail against it. I will give you the keys of the king-dom of heaven, and whatsoever you shall bind on earth

shall be bound in heaven, and whatsoever you shall loose on earth shall be loosed in heaven.' Then he strictly charged the disciples to tell no one that he was the Christ. (Matt. 16: 13–20)

The name 'Peter' is derived from the Greek word Πετροσ, meaning 'Rock'. Why Simon should be given this strange name is not explained, except to say that he is to be the rock on which Christ's church is to be built. Yet at that time there was no 'church' as such, certainly not in the sense of a fixed building. The Greek word used for church is εκκλεσια, *ecclesia* (from which we derive the adjective 'ecclesiastical'), meaning literally 'that which is called out'. Thus a literal reading of Jesus' statement implies that 'Simon the Stone' was destined to be 'the rock on which that which was called out would be built'. Using a different but related metaphor, Peter also was to become the door-keeper of heaven, as he was to be given the keys to the gates of Hades. In church art and statues of St Peter he is usually shown holding the keys: one gold and the other silver, suggesting two different gates. What these are, or where the gates of Hades are to be found, is not explained. This passage is generally considered to be figurative only; yet on it hangs much of the authority of the pope, who claims that as the successor of Peter he today is the custodian of these self-same keys. This may or may not be true in a figurative sense; but I had come to the conclusion that there was more to this passage than meets the eye. I also suspected an Egyptian connection to all of this: that the rock referred to as the foundation stone was none other than the Great Pyramid, itself a giant replica of the Benben stone of Heliopolis, and that the 'keys' Peter held were in some way connected with this building.

As far as we know, the language Jesus and his apostles spoke was Aramaic, the vernacular of Palestine at that time. The New Testament was written in Greek in order to transmit the new faith to a wider audience beyond

Palestine. Thus it is that we find in John's Gospel that Peter's real given name was not Πετροσ (Petros) but rather Κηφασ (Cephas) – an Aramaic word with the same meaning of 'rock' or 'stone'. It appears that Jesus had already called Simon by this name on the occasion of their first meeting. This is described in the first chapter of John's Gospel:

> One of the two who heard John speak, and followed him, was Andrew, Simon Peter's brother. He first found his brother Simon, and said to him, 'We have found the Messiah' (which means Christ). He brought him to Jesus. Jesus looked at him, and said, 'So you are Simon the son of John? You shall be called Cephas' (which means Peter). (John 1: 40–2)

The bracketed interpolations explaining the meanings of the words 'messiah' and 'Cephas' would appear to be glosses inserted for Greek readers of the text, either by John himself or by some later scribe. Closer examination of the name 'Cephas', however, suggests another and older derivation than this.

In Greek mythology there was a King Cepheus, whose daughter Andromeda was very beautiful. Unfortunately her mother, Cassiopeia, boasted that her daughter was fairer than the Nereids, the nymphs of the sea. As a result their father Poseidon, god of the oceans, sent a sea monster to devastate the coastlands of Cepheus' kingdom. In order to avert disaster, Cepheus was instructed by the oracle of Zeus Ammon to make a gift to the monster of Andromeda, and she was accordingly tied to a rock at the sea's edge. Fortunately for Andromeda, she was spotted in her plight by the young Perseus, who was flying that way on the back of Pegasus, his heavenly steed, after beheading the Gorgon Medusa, whose hair was a nest of snakes and who could turn men to stone with a single glance. He slew the sea monster terrorizing Cepheus' kingdom in return for the promise of

Andromeda's hand. However, before he could marry the girl the king's brother, Phineus, to whom she had previously been betrothed, intervened to stop the wedding. Undaunted, Perseus exposed the grisly Gorgon's head to Phineus and his men, turning them all to stone. He and Andromeda returned to his home on the island of Seriphos. After they had died, Perseus, Andromeda, Cepheus, Cassiopeia and the sea monster were all turned into constellations of the northern sky.

While the story of Perseus and Andromeda is mythical, it is undoubtedly founded on older traditions connected with astronomy. The Greeks were avid collectors of myths from all over the known world, adapting them as they saw fit. The location of the kingdom of Cepheus varies in the telling but is usually said to be either Ethiopia or Jaffa (Joppa), the old Philistine port to the south of modern-day Tel Aviv. However, details of the Andromeda myth suggest that its origins are really to be found not in Palestine or Ethiopia but rather in Egypt, which lies between the two. (For example, the oracle consulted by Cepheus was at the Siwa oasis in the western desert between Egypt and Libya.) Greeks visiting the pyramids of Giza would have been told, had they asked, that these buildings were named after kings and were thought in some way to embody their souls after death. It seems likely, therefore, that the story of Perseus turning the uninvited wedding guests to stone refers to a deeper understanding of how people in ancient times had been 'turned into' pyramids.

The name Cepheus is sufficiently close to the Greek rendering of the Aramaic word Cephas to suggest a common origin. It seems likely that both are derived from the Egyptian 'Khufu', the name of the most memorable of all Old Kingdom pharaohs and the builder of the Great Pyramid. His 'brother', Phineus, is probably to be identified with the pharaoh Khafre, while the other wedding guests who were turned to stone can be identified with the subsidiary pyramids and tombs nestling around these two giants. Given this tentative connection we may therefore suspect that the name 'Khufu' in the ancient Egyptian lexicon meant 'rock' – the same as its Aramaic equivalent 'Cephas'.

Astronomy would seem to confirm that the Perseus–Andromeda myth is connected with the appearance of the stars over the pyramids. At around 330 BC, when Egypt was conquered by Alexander the Great, the constellation of Perseus used to pass directly overhead just as Leo was rising in the east. Seen from Giza, the star Beta-Perseus or Algol, which is one of the brightest stars in the constellation and is in the head of Medusa the Gorgon, would actually be aligned on a vertical axis from the pyramids. Each night as the Gorgon glared down from her zenith point over Egypt, so King Phineus and his wedding guests were turned into stone pyramids below her. Amazingly, this would have happened just before dawn on the day of the Regulus conjunction, something which would not have occurred 2,200 years earlier when the pyramids were built. In this way we can see that the Greek myth of Perseus, or at least that part of it relating to his turning Phineus and the wedding guests to stone, probably comes from Egypt. Here, at the time of Alexander, the alignment of Algol, recognized by the Greeks as the principal star of Medusa's head, must have been used as an indicator of the Regulus conjunction. The Khufu pyramid we know to have been built in such a way as to mark this conjunction at the time it occurred near to the solstice. Even though by Alexander's time the date of the Regulus conjunction was much later, its connection with Khufu or 'Cepheus' must not have been entirely forgotten. At the time Jesus was born (7 BC), Algol was no longer crossing the zenith at Giza. It was, however, doing so at Bethlehem and would in fact have done so just fifteen minutes before sunrise on Jesus' birthday on 29 July, when the sun was conjunct with Regulus in Leo. Thus the crossing of the zenith by Algol at dawn can be seen as conferring some other special power, in this case to turn evil back on itself as Perseus did with the Gorgon's head.

There are other connections linking Peter with Jaffa, the centre of the Perseus legend. After the Crucifixion he spent some time in this city. It was here that he had a dream which signified to him that he should open the Christian mission to non-Jews (Acts 11) and it was from here that he was called to see to Paul after the latter's conversion on the road to Damascus. Most significantly of all, it was in Jaffa that Peter carried out the miracle of raising a woman from the dead (Acts 9: 36–42), something which had previously been done only by Jesus himself. This miracle, more than anything else, seems to signify that Peter had indeed had special powers bestowed on him. The choice of Jaffa for the location of this miracle is also significant, for it was a home city of the tribe of Dan and therefore closely linked with the region of Caesarea Philippi in the north. Moreover, at that time (c.AD 30) Algol would be regularly crossing the zenith at Jaffa, which was also identified with the Perseus legend.

As noted in Chapter 2, there was a large Jewish community in Egypt at the time of Jesus. We know that as a baby he was taken to Heliopolis and it is very likely that he spent more time there during his teens and twenties, the period of his life that remains a blank in the Bible. If so he would have seen the pyramids, perhaps even spent time studying them. If we understand Cephas as being the Aramaic equivalent of Khufu, and accept that this (not Petros) is the name by which Jesus originally called Simon, we get a very different understanding of their conversation in Matthew 16. It would seem then that what Jesus was really saying to Simon was: 'You are Khufu [in Greek, Petros], and on this rock [i.e. the Great Pyramid of Khufu], I will build my church and the Gates of Hades shall not prevail against it.'

At first sight this would seem to be an extraordinarily unlikely rendition of this text. Why on earth, one might wonder, should Jesus call one of his disciples after the pharaoh Khufu? And why, even if this were so, should Jesus say that he was going to build his church on the foundation stone of the Great Pyramid? Yet further investigation reveals that this is not as far-fetched as it seems. One line of reasoning might suggest that in calling Peter 'Cephas' Jesus was implying that the apostle was the reincarnation of Khufu and therefore a fit man to take on such a difficult undertaking as building a church. Unchristian as this may seem in the light of later dogmas refuting the doctrine of reincarnation, it is not at all impossible. Many, perhaps even most, early Christians believed in reincarnation. Certainly the Gnostics, the early Christians of Egypt, did. It was only after the church fathers, including Clemens and Origen of Alexandria, Augustine of Hippo and Irenaeus of Lyon, attacked the teachings of the Gnostic schools that the doctrine of reincarnation was treated as a heresy.[11] Even if we dismiss the possibility of Simon Peter being identified as the physical reincarnation of Khufu, there is still a strange connection between the pyramids, Orion and a key to the gate of heaven. To understand what this is we have to return to Giza.

In *The Orion Mystery* we presented graphic as well as written evidence showing how important the Egyptians considered the constellation of Orion to be. We published an illustration based on a drawing from the ceiling of the tomb of Senmut, companion and vizier to Queen Hatshepsut. In this picture Sahu/Orion is shown standing in a small boat with three prominent stars (representing Orion's belt) over his head. This figure carries in his left hand a staff of office, while in his right he holds an *ankh* – the Egyptian hieroglyph usually translated as 'life'. Behind him, following in her own boat, is a goddess identifiable as representing the star Sothis or Sirius. Another diagram showed part of the ceiling painting from the mausoleum of Seti I, one of the greatest of the

New Kingdom pharaohs and father of Ramses II. In this drawing Orion is again shown in his boat with the staff in one hand and an *ankh* in the other, above which is a five-pointed star. A third illustration of Orion came from the Cairo Museum, custodian of the pyramidion which once capped the pyramid of Amenemhet III at Dashur. Being from the Middle Kingdom, this pyramidion is older than the ceilings of the tombs of Senmut and Seti but it carries a very similar representation of Orion. Again he is shown as a walking man holding a staff in one hand, but this time he is cupping a star with the other.

In *The Orion Mystery* we sought to identify this star, and concluded that it had to have been intended to indicate Aldebaran, 'the eye of the bull', which stands near to Orion in the constellation of Taurus. A powerful reason for reaching this conclusion is that on the ceiling of Senmut's tomb there is a glyph that seems to represent Aldebaran in the register next to the one depicting Orion. This is not surprising as Aldebaran rises shortly before Orion and these registers seem to represent a sort of stellar almanac recording times of rising. It therefore seemed likely that in the glyph on the pyramidion Orion would be shown reaching out to this star. We accordingly included in *The Orion Mystery* a picture, based on this hieroglyph, showing Orion in the sky with a staff in his right hand and cupping Aldebaran in his left.[12] Looking again at this picture, I could now see that we were probably mistaken in identifying this star as Aldebaran. For one thing the constellation of Orion, as actually seen in the sky, holds what can be interpreted as a staff in his left, not his right hand. His right hand, the one which should be cupping the star, reaches upwards towards the ecliptic and away from Aldebaran.[13]

The positioning of a star above the outstretched hand of Orion has another important meaning which would not have been lost on the Egyptians. The hieroglyph of a five-pointed star is transliterated as *s'ba*, literally meaning 'star'. However, *s'ba* has a secondary meaning, which is 'door'. It is used in this way in Wallis Budge's monumental edition of the *Egyptian Book of the Dead*, where he translates a particular sentence as 'I open the door in heaven'. The hieroglyphs for 'door', which he transliterates as *s'ba*, are a five-pointed star with an Egyptian vulture symbol next to it.[14] Thus the star held out in the hand of the Sahu figure on the *benben* stone of Amenemhet III conveys in shorthand the exact meaning of 'stargate'. (As we know from many examples, the Egyptians were fond of punning as a way of concealing hidden meanings. In fact, in the *Hermetica* it is stated openly that it would be impossible properly to translate their texts into Greek for the very reason that secondary meanings based on puns and similarities of words would be lost.) We can see from this that the placing of a star in the hand of Orion was entirely appropriate. It indicated that the point where the Milky Way intersected with the ecliptic above the hand of Orion was the location of one of the gates of heaven.

This I found very interesting, and it got me thinking about the symbol of the *ankh*, which on the ceiling of Seti I is similarly held out by a Sahu figure, this time underneath the star representing the stargate. It is well known that the literal translation of the symbol *ankh* had the meaning of 'life'; yet the derivation of the symbol is a matter of great debate. This association of the *ankh* with the concept of life or the life-force is very curious and seems to have been something of a mystery even to the Egyptians. All the later Egyptians seem to have known is that it was an ancient symbol and somehow represented good fortune – and indeed, it retains that connotation today. In ancient Egyptian art, both painted and sculpted, the gods are frequently shown holding *ankhs*, to indicate either that they are alive themselves or that they give life. Why the gift of life should have been associated with this curious, cross-like symbol is not explained. According to orthodox Egyptology the *ankh* symbol is derived from the strap of a sandal. Yet in the Cairo Museum and in

SAHU (ORION) HOLDING AN *ANKH*
OR KEY TO THE STARGATE

other places large numbers of *ankhs* are to be seen made
from metal or ceramic, and not at all like sandal-straps.
Nor is it explained why the gods of the Egyptians should
be shown holding sandal-straps, other than to say there
is a phonic similarity in the Egyptian words for 'life' and
'sandal-strap'. Yet the choice of this symbol was clearly
no accident. To me it seems entirely obvious, regardless
of any similarity to sandals, real or imagined, that the
ankh represents a key. In the context of what we have
noted about the stargate above the hand of Orion, this
seems hugely significant.

In our solar system the support of all life is the sun.
Without its precious rays there would be no life on earth.
The sun reaches its greatest power at the summer solstice
and this, I believe, is an important clue to the derivation
of the *ankh* symbol. At the solstice, the sun stands on the
principal celestial meridian. This meridian, which is at

90° to the one running through its equinoctial positions, was clearly regarded by the Egyptians themselves as the celestial equivalent of an imaginary line drawn on the earth's surface: the geographical prime meridian. Today, by convention, we think of the prime meridian as being the line of longitude running through Greenwich in the suburbs of London. Though arbitrarily chosen, this is by common consensus the zero point for all time measurements on earth. As a consequence, all other lines of longitude are defined as being so many degrees east or west of Greenwich. In ancient Egypt, though for different reasons, the equivalent zero meridian, if we may call it such, seems to have been the line running north–south through the Khafre pyramid. This pyramid, as we have seen, has a slope of 53° 10' and was therefore designed to be illuminated all over exactly as the sun crossed the east–west axis on the day of the summer solstice. The meridian running through it, like that through its neighbour the Great Pyramid, neatly bisects the delta of Egypt and roughly corresponds to the direction of flow of the Nile from south to north. This corresponds closely with the idea expressed in the *Kore Kosmu* that Egypt lay at the heart of the earth. It would seem that the importance of Egypt's location had not been entirely forgotten even in the early centuries of the Christian era.

Given the Egyptians' preoccupation with the Hermetic dictum 'as above, so below', they probably saw an equivalence between their prime meridian on earth, the axis of Egypt, and its celestial counterpart, the solsticial meridian. Thus the summer solstice, the day when the sun crossed the prime meridian in the sky, was of great importance to them. It both symbolized the sun at its greatest power (which in the time of the Old Kingdom occurred when it was in its most favoured sign of Leo) and it also represented the sun god Re's special regard for Egypt, through whose lands the earthly meridian passed, made manifest each year at this very time by the flooding of the Nile when symbolically Re opened the flood-gates in the southern lands and thereby enabled life to prosper in Egypt. Without those waters there would be no more life in Egypt than there is in the deserts surrounding the country. Thus in a roundabout way the gift of the sun is water, the element of life itself, and this could be symbolized by the *ankh* or key by means of which the flood-gate was secured.

Yet it would seem that the flood-gate of the solstice, if such we may call it, is not the only one that can be opened with this key. As we have seen, because of precession the position in the zodiac that is occupied by the sun at its summer solstice shifts slightly year by year. Over short periods of time this is barely perceptible, but over a period of roughly 2,160 years it will move by an entire zodiacal sign. At the time the pyramids were built (*c*.2500 BC) the sun at its solstice was in Leo. By the time Jesus was walking the earth it had moved backwards through the zodiac to the cusp of Cancer and Gemini. It has been in the latter sign ever since. Yet, as we have seen, beyond Gemini lies a metaphorical 'stargate' directly over the outstretched hand of Orion, at the point where the ecliptic intersects with the Milky Way. This gateway is really an abstraction based on time rather than space. However, by analogy it would seem that when the *ankh* or solsticial key of the sun reaches this position, this is the signal for the 'stargate' to be unlocked. Curiously, this is also indicated by alignments taken from the Khafre pyramid. Strange as it may seem, the implication is that the ancient Egyptians anticipated our own time, the end of the Age of Man. For today the constellation of Orion extends its hand, with its metaphorical key (the sun at the solstice) to the stargate of Hades, and does so as the sun sits over the Khafre pyramid in the east and the west.

This, to me, is what the symbol of the *ankh* is really all about. It is the key to the gate of heaven, that is to say to eternal life in the world beyond this world. Jesus, who was obviously highly initiated and knew about these matters, was representing these ideas for a new age: the

Christian Age of Pisces. By entrusting the key to Peter, whose Aramaic name 'Cephas' is probably derived from the same root as the Egyptian 'Khufu', he was making him the new custodian of the Orion tradition. As I was now to discover, the choice of Caesarea Philippi for elevation to this role was also connected with the secret astrology to which Jesus was here alluding.

In 1994 a Hollywood blockbuster called *Stargate* hit the big screen. The story-line of this sci-fi movie, which was very much in the 'Indiana Jones' genre, concerned the imaginary discovery, close to the Giza pyramids, of an ancient machine that pre-dated the Egyptian civilization by many millennia. This machine turned out to be a 'stargate', enabling interdimensional space travel between the earth and another, similar planet in a distant constellation. Scientists and engineers were baffled by this discovery until a young scholar with an open mind deciphered the hieroglyphs that surrounded the stone casing in which the machine was wrapped. Significantly, the clue that led to the decipherment and, subsequently, the reactivation of the 'stargate', was his identification of one of the symbols as representing the constellation of Orion.

I was astounded when I saw this; for the movie was released only a few months after the publication of *The Orion Mystery* and must therefore have been in production during the time we were preparing the book. It seemed an uncanny piece of synchronicity that the writers of this movie should have chosen Orion of all constellations to provide the clue to the location of the earth's twin.

For me this coincidence was all the stranger as I was by this time working on my next book, *The Mayan Prophecies*, and I had become interested in the idea of stargates as raised by de Santillana and von Dechend in *Hamlet's Mill*. It had become clear that the position of one of these gateways was right over the outstretched hand of Orion, which seemed further confirmation for the theory contained in *The Orion Mystery* that this constellation had a very special meaning in the stellar religion of the Egyptians as the physical location of their heaven. However, at that time I had no reason to pay very much attention to the other traditional gateway, the one between Sagittarius and Scorpio. Now, following my trip to Banyas, I came to see that there was a connection between this area and the sign of Scorpio, the location of this second gateway.

At Dan, a few kilometres from Paneas, is the other main spring feeding the Jordan. Long before the building of Caesarea Philippi the city of Dan, called Laish or Leshem prior to its conquest by the Israelites, had been the principal town in the region. The sign of the zodiac associated with the tribe of Dan was Scorpio and, according to William Drummond, author of *Oedipus Judaicus*, the name Leshem derives from the Hebrew word *lesha*, meaning 'destruction'. By a process of astrological correspondences, he links this earlier name for Dan with Lesath, one of the stars in the tail of Scorpio. Reading this, I reasoned that if Dan can be equated with Lesath, then it seems likely that Paneas or Caesarea Philippi was viewed as corresponding to its close neighbour in the sky, a brighter star called Shaula. This name could be related to the Hebrew word *shaul*, meaning 'asked'. In the Book of Enoch, the prophet is said to have met with Samyaza, Azaziel and the other Nephilim and to have received supplications from them to intervene with God on their behalf. According to Enoch, they 'asked' him to do this somewhere in the region of 'Danbadan'. It seems likely that the place where they held this meeting was in fact Paneas, which may then have been called Shaul or Shaula – 'asked'. If so, then by a similar process of analogy Mount Hermon itself, where the Nephilim are said to have come to earth, is connected symbolically with the gateway above the sting of Scorpio at the place where the ecliptic intersects with the Milky Way.

From these considerations alone it becomes obvious

that the ancient Israelites, and maybe those who occupied the land before them, looked upon the River Jordan as symbolizing the Milky Way in just the same way as the Egyptians viewed their own River Nile. The 'stargate' in the region of Sagittarius/Scorpio lies on the Milky Way which subsequently 'flows' through the sky to the opposite gateway above the outstretched hand of Orion. Similarly the Mount Hermon area, where the Nephilim were supposed to have come to earth, would have been linked to one gate, while the other end of the Jordan, on the Dead Sea, would have been connected with the other gate (see colour illustration no. 26). The region ruled over by Orion would have been just to the north of this gate in the vicinity of Jericho. It is notable that it was here, close to the present-day Allenby Bridge, that John (himself in some senses an Orion figure) was said to have baptized Jesus, an act which, as we have seen, was laden with symbolic meaning. Jesus, meanwhile, elevated Peter to the position of 'keeper of the keys of Hades' at Caesarea Philippi, close by the cave of Pan which would then have been thought of as the entrance to the underworld of Hades. All this indicated that Jesus, and maybe other Jews of his day, knew about the ancient gnosis that saw the Jordan river system as a terrestrial counterpart of the Milky Way. I was now to discover further evidence that Orion figured strongly in Jewish as well as Egyptian thought.

CHAPTER 15

THE SIGN OF THE SON OF ADAM

The day after we visited Banyas I took a bus from Tiberias to Safad, to the Jews one of the four holy cities of Israel. The journey was not long but it was slow, as again there was a steep climb: from the depths of the Valley of Galilee, 212 metres below sea level, to the hill-top town, some 800 metres above. Unlike the day before it was raining, a blessing for the local farmers who had been suffering from the effects of a prolonged drought but a wretched nuisance for travellers such as myself. The old town of Safad, which is what I had come to see, is arranged in concentric circles going down the hillside around what was the citadel but is now a pleasant park. From the top of the hill, where there is now a memorial celebrating the capture of Safad from the Palestinian Arabs in 1948, there were magnificent views towards the Sea of Galilee in one direction and the Golan Heights in another. Not a particularly old town by Holy Land standards, Safad is famous as a centre of the Kabbalah, the most mystical form of Judaism. It was my intention to visit the Ha'Ari Ashkenazi synagogue in the hope that I might find some further clues linking the Kabbalah with my own quest.

As I looked over towards the Golan I remembered how, twenty-six years earlier, I had sat at sunset on the hill above Kefar Szold reading chapter 24 of Matthew's Gospel. Then I had wondered what the writer could possibly have been referring to when he wrote of 'the

Sign of the Son of man in heaven'; now I was beginning to have more of an idea. The whole of chapter 24 is redolent with foreboding as St Matthew describes the tribulations the world must go through prior to the start of the new age. To me the most telling passage concerned lightning:

> For as the lightning cometh out of the east, and shineth unto the west; so shall also the coming of the Son of man be.
>
> For wheresoever the carcass is, there will the eagles be gathered together.
>
> Immediately after the tribulation of those days shall the sun be darkened, and the moon shall not give her light, and the stars shall fall from heaven, and the powers of the heavens shall be shaken;
>
> And then shall appear the sign of the Son of man in heaven: and then shall all the tribes of the earth mourn, and they shall see the Son of man coming in the clouds of heaven with power and great glory.
>
> And he shall send his angels with a great sound of a trumpet, and they shall gather together the elect from the four winds, from one end of heaven to the other. (Matt. 24: 27–8)

I wanted very much to understand this prophecy, but couldn't fathom its meaning from so cryptic a text. Nevertheless, the prophetic passages of chapter 24 were quite direct and were obviously meant to be taken very seriously. I knew that there were likely to be further clues to the mystery which only made sense in the original Greek, while all I had to hand was the English translation of the King James version. So later, back in England, I purchased an interlinear translation of the New Testament, which provided a word-by-word English translation with the original Greek text written above it.[1]

The title 'Son of man' is one that Jesus frequently used to describe himself, so that my first instinct on reading

295

the above passage was that the 'sign of the Son of man' must be a cross or some such Christian symbol. There is a story told by Eusebius of Caesarea that Constantine the Great saw in the sky at noon a flaming cross accompanied by the words 'by this conquer'. Other accounts say that he saw this image in a dream; at all events, he adopted the chi-rho symbol of Christianity as his device and went on to defeat Maxentius at the Battle of the Milvian Bridge on 8 October 312, thereby becoming undisputed master of the Western Roman Empire. With this account in mind, it seemed likely that St Matthew was warning us to look for some similar apparition – perhaps a flaming cross, like lightning, in the sky – that would announce to us the end of the age.

Yet on examining the text more closely I became less sure that this was what the original author (who may or may not have been the apostle Matthew) had in mind. For one thing the title 'Son of man' is not used in the Bible exclusively for Jesus. The prophet Ezekiel is always so addressed whenever the 'word of the Lord' comes to him. So also was Daniel when he was spoken to by the angel Gabriel on the banks of the River Ulai. In the Book of Isaiah the term 'son of man' or its plural 'sons of men' seems to mean no more than human, or simply 'son of Adam' – the word 'Adam' meaning 'man' in Hebrew. Taking into account these Old Testament references, I became convinced that the 'sign of the Son of man' which we are told to look out for was not a cross, or some other symbol relating specifically to Jesus Christ; rather, it was something more universal that would relate to humanity in general, in that we are all 'sons of Adam'. What, then, could this universal symbol be?

The Greek text translated as 'For as the lightning cometh out of the east, and shineth unto the west; so shall also the coming of the Son of man be' is ὥσπερ γαρ ἡ ἀστραπη ἔξερχεται ἀπο ἀνατολων και φαινεται ἕωσ δυσμων, οὕτωσ ἐσται ἡ παρουσια του υἱου του ἀνθρωπου. The Greek word ἔξερχεται (*exerchetai*), which is translated as 'cometh out', is related to the Latin verb 'exeo, -ire' from which is derived the English word 'exit'. All these words in all three languages convey the sense of passing through a doorway from one area or chamber to another. In the ancient world, in addition to the idea of stargates, there was a generalized belief that there were doorways on the horizon, to the east and the west, through which celestial bodies, most especially the sun, would pass when they rose and set. Thus William Lethaby writes in his *Architecture, Mysticism and Myth*: 'The general early view ... was that there were two openings – the Gates of the East, and the Gates of the West. Through the one the sun enters in the morning the mundane temple, to pass out at the other in the evening, and thence pursue its way back by the dark path of the underworld.'[2] This was all very well; but still the idea of lightning rising in the east and shining to the west didn't make sense. It is obviously nonsensical to talk about lightning in this way. As anyone who has watched a storm knows, it flashes momentarily in the sky and does not 'come forth' or 'exit', like the sun, through hypothetical doorways in the east and west of the sky. If anything it travels vertically, from the sky to the earth. Why, then, use the word *exerchetai*, a verb that would be more applicable to the sun or some other luminous body which rises and sets, when talking about lightning?

I thought that a possible clue to the real meaning of this passage might be found in the secret teachings of the Jewish Kabbalah, as taught and studied at Safad. According to the Kabbalists, God created the universe through the mediation of ten 'lights', called 'Sephirot' (translatable as 'spheres'), arranged in a figure known as the Tree of Life, with twenty-two pathways linking the spheres. The creation manifested itself as a lightning flash, going from one Sephirah to another, as it passed down the tree from heaven to earth. The lightning flash represented the course of creation. This doctrine is expressed most succinctly in an early rabbinical book called the *Sepher Yetzirah*, believed by some to have been written by Abraham himself but probably dating back to around the third century AD.

> Section 1.
> Yah, the Lord of hosts, the living God, King of the Universe, Omnipotent, All-Kind and Merciful, Supreme and Extolled, who is Sublime and Most-Holy, ordained and created the Universe in thirty-two mysterious paths of wisdom by three Sepharim, namely: 1) S'for; 2) Sippur; and 3) Sapher which are in Him one and the same. They consist of a decade out of nothing and of twenty-two fundamental letters . . .
> Section 5.
> The appearance of the ten spheres out of nothing is like a flash of lightning, being without an end, His word is in them, when they go and return; they run by His order like a whirlwind and humble themselves before His throne.[3]

Matthew was clearly an initiate and probably knew a great deal about the Kabbalah, though it may not have been called by this name in his day. From the above quotations we might be prompted to conclude that the sign in the heavens that Matthew tells us to look for could be a metaphor for the creative lightning flash as it cascades through the crystal spheres and sets them in motion. Unfortunately, tempting as this is, further reflection shows that it does not seem to have been what the Gospel writer had in mind. Rather, the prophecy seems to be talking about some definite event involving 'lightning' rising in the east and setting in the west. To understand this we have to look further into the teachings of the Kabbalah.

The arrangement of the spheres on the Tree of Life diagram was probably modelled on the form of the lampstand or 'candlestick' that once stood in the sanctuary of the Temple of Solomon in Jerusalem. How this was to be made is described in the Book of Exodus:

> And thou shalt make a candlestick of pure gold: of
> beaten work shall the candlestick be made: his shaft and
> his branches, his bowls, his knops and his flowers, shall
> be of the same.
>
> And six branches shall come out of the sides of it;
> three branches of the candlestick out of one side, and
> three branches of the candlestick out of the other
> side:
>
> Three bowls made like unto almonds, with a knop
> and a flower in one branch, and three bowls made like
> almonds in the other branch, with a knop and a
> flower: so in the six branches that come out of the
> candlestick. And in the candlestick shall be four bowls
> made like unto almonds, with their knops and their
> flowers.
>
> And there shall be a knop under two branches of the
> same, and a knop under two branches of the same, and
> a knop under two branches of the same, according to
> the six branches that proceed out of the candlestick.
>
> Their knops and their branches shall be of the same:
> all it shall be one beaten work of pure gold.
>
> And thou shalt make the seven lamps thereof: and
> they shall light the lamps thereof, that they may give
> light over against it. (Exod. 25: 31–7)

When finished the candlestick, or lamp-stand, must
have looked a bit like a golden Christmas tree, with its
almond-shaped bowls and flowers like decorative
baubles and its hanging lamps like tree-lights or clip-on
candles. Its design, however, was not arbitrary: it was
intended to represent the world-tree, whose 'trunk' is the
axis of the earth and whose 'lights' are the seven planets.
This symbol would have been well understood in the
ancient world, as indeed it was to Lethaby when he wrote
the following:

MENORAH OR JEWISH SEVEN-BRANCHED
CANDLESTICK REPRESENTING THE SEVEN
LIGHTS OR PLANETS

It is thus as a light-bearer, a candelabrum, that the
artificial tree would best fulfil a symbolic function in
the representation of the great mysterious tree whose
canopy forms the firmament and bears the light-giving
stars as its fruit – a symbolism which we appear to
perpetuate, as year by year at the winter solstice we
light the candles on the Christmas tree . . .

Nor can we forget the seven-branched candlestick in
the Temple, of gold, ornamented with 'knops and
flowers'; the seven lamps symbolizing to Josephus the
seven planets.[4]

The reference to Josephus is apt. As a first-century AD
Jewish leader and later as a historian of the Jews, he too
would have known about such things. Describing the
sanctuary of Herod's Temple shortly after its destruction
by the Romans, he writes:

Passing through the gate one entered the ground-floor chamber of the Sanctuary, 90 feet high, 90 long, and 30 wide. But the length was again divided. In the first part, partitioned off at 60 feet, were three most wonderful, world-famous works of art, a lamp stand, a table and an altar of incense. The seven lamps branching off from the lamp stand symbolized the planets; the twelve loaves on the table the Zodiac circle and the year. The altar of incense, by the thirteen spices of the sea and land, inhabited and uninhabited, with which it was kept supplied, signified that all things are from God and for God.

The innermost chamber measures 30 feet and was similarly separated by a curtain from the outer part. Nothing at all was kept in it; it was unapproachable, inviolable, and invisible to all, and was called the Holy of Holies.[5]

Stripped down to its basic elements, the lamp-stand later became the archetype of the menorah or seven-branched candlestick to be seen in every Jewish home. In the artists' quarter of Safad I bought a copy of a fourteenth-century depiction of a menorah taken from an illuminated manuscript in the British Museum. However, this symbol is much older than that – as evidenced by a sculpted menorah that I saw in the archaeological museum at Katzrin, a new town in the Golan Heights. Esoterically, the seven candles of the menorah still represent the seven lights, or planets of the ancients: the sun, moon, Mercury, Venus, Mars, Jupiter and Saturn.[6] As we have seen, in the pre-Copernican model of the solar system, these planets were thought each to inhabit a 'crystal sphere'. These spheres, the original Sephirot of the *Sepher Yetzirah,* were arranged like the layers of an onion around the earth with the lowest-moving planet, Saturn, on the outermost sphere and the fastest, the moon, on that closest to the earth.

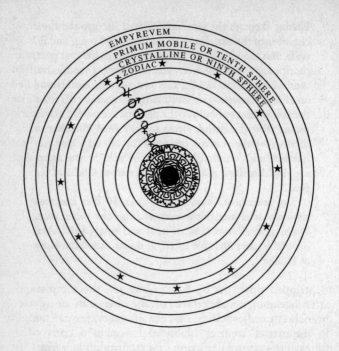

THE CRYSTAL SPHERES ACCORDING TO
HERMETIC PHILOSOPHY

In the secret traditions of the Kabbalah the Sephirot
were expanded from seven to ten in number and were considered to be emanations of God. The twenty-two
pathways that linked them on the Tree of Life diagram
each represented one letter of the Hebrew alphabet. In this
arrangement the lowest Sephirah represented the earth
itself, that is to say physical matter. Arranged around the
earth, like concentric glass spheres, were the seven
planetary Sephirot, beginning with the moon and ending at
Saturn, thereby bringing the number up to eight. Beyond
these was the sphere of the fixed stars, and above this the
'Primum Mobile' or 'first mover', the abode of God.

Counting the earth itself as the lowest Sephirah, this gave ten in all (see colour illustration no. 25).

As a further elaboration, the ten Sephirot were sometimes placed around an archetypal figure, 'Adam Kadmon', the 'First Man' or man made in the image of his creator. The meaning behind this image of Adam, or the universal man, is still the subject of much Kabbalistic speculation. How it may have come about is explained by Warren Kenton, a modern Kabbalist who writes under the pen-name of Z'ev ben Shimon Halevi, in his finest work, *Adam and the Kabbalistic Tree*:

> Adam and the Tree of Life are conceived in the same design. This idea originates in the statement in the first chapter of Genesis: God created man in His own image.
>
> According to Kabbalist tradition God generates, out of the Void of Non Existence, wherein He is All and Nothing, the first state of Unmanifest Existence. From this World without End, crystallizes a realm of Limitless Light, in the midst of which, there emerges a point of no dimensions, called the First Crown. These three states of Unmanifest Existence become the negative background to the positive universe that streams through the primal point of the First Crown to evolve into the archetypal world of Emanations. This manifestation on its completion is known as Adam Kadmon, that is, the Primeval and Universal Man. Although composed of the ten aspects of the Creator, Adam is the symbol of a unified working whole, the first man being a living image of the relative universe . . .
>
> Adam Kadmon is the Universe made after a likeness to God, the allegorical figure abstracted by Kabbalists into the diagram called the Tree of Life. This metaphysical presentation is a comprehensive formulation of universal principles and processes . . .
>
> As a miniature copy of the Universe man has within him not only the characteristics of Creation but also the attributes of the Creator. Through the inherent nature

of his composition, an individual, therefore, has access to cosmic resources, and should he wish, the possibility, while still earthbound, of contact with the Divine within himself. Such a consciousness of the Presence of the Creator allows him to know and be known by God.[7]

Clearly it is the goal of the Kabbalist, by means of his practice of Kabbalah, to gain contact with the divine while still in the body. As the passage quoted above shows, the Kabbalah can become extremely cerebral and complex when studied at depth. Reading this, I felt sure that there was something missing; that Halevi, assuming he understood the deeper meaning of the symbol himself, was concealing something important. Later I began to suspect that the clues to what this might be lay not in the teachings of the Kabbalah but in the Hermetic traditions of Egypt and Mesopotamia, from which they were clearly drawn. How, then, did the Adam Kadmon figure come about?

According to the doctrines of Hermetic astrology, from which I now believe these Kabbalistic doctrines ultimately derive, the planets and their spheres were the rulers or lesser gods (angels of a sort) who meted out fate to incarnating humans. From an astral or cosmic point of view, birth was seen as a process by which the soul passed from the higher heaven of the fixed stars, down through the crystal spheres of the planets, to enter a physical body. En route the entity would be lent something of the essence of each planet, in varying proportions according to the position of that planet at birth. The amount of 'astral stuff' or energy received from each planet would determine the fate of the individual. It would also determine the talents he would bring into life, which it was down to him to use and develop. On dying he would have to return to the rulers these planetary energies, which had only been loaned. However, used wisely during life, his talents would have been multiplied and he could retain the 'interest' he had made on the original 'capital' invested in him.[8]

The first part of this doctrine is beautifully expressed

in *Libellus I*, the first 'pamphlet' of the *Corpus Hermeticum*, where the descent of man – the *anthropos* – is described in detail.

> But Mind the Father of all, he who is Life and Light, gave birth to Man, a Being like Himself. And he took delight in Man, as being His own offspring; for Man was very goodly to look on, bearing the likeness of the Father. With good reason then did God take delight in Man; for it was God's own form that God took delight in. And God delivered over to Man all things that had been made.
>
> And Man took station in the Maker's sphere,[9] and observed the things made by his brother,[10] who was set over the region of fire [i.e. the solar system]; and having observed the Maker's creation in the region of fire, he willed to make things for his own part also; and his Father gave permission . . . having in himself all the working of the Administrators [rulers or planets]; and the Administrators took delight in him, and each of them gave him a share of his own nature.
>
> And having learnt to know the being of the Administrators, and received a share of their nature, he willed to break through the bounding circle of their orbits [i.e. the eighth sphere of the fixed stars]; and he looked down through the structure of the heavens, having broken through the sphere, and showed to downward-tending Nature the beautiful form of God. And Nature, seeing the beauty of the form of God, smiled with insatiate love of Man, showing the reflection of that most beautiful form in the water, and its shadow on the earth. And he, seeing this form, a form like to his own, in earth and water, loved it, and willed to dwell there. And the deed followed close on the design; and he took up his abode in matter devoid of reason. And Nature, when she had got him with whom she was in love, wrapped him in her clasp, and they were mingled in one; for they were in love with one another.[11]

The same text, having discussed the creation and the birth of man on earth, goes on to explain the situation of humankind today and the possibility of re-ascending to the higher heaven after death.

At the dissolution of your material body, you first yield up the body itself to be changed, and the visible form you bore is no longer seen. And your vital spirit you yield up to the atmosphere so that it no longer works in you; and the bodily senses go back to their own sources, becoming parts of the universe, and entering into fresh combinations to do other work. And thereupon the man mounts upward through the structure of the heavens. And to the first zone of heaven [sphere of the moon] he gives up the force which works increase and that which works decrease; to the second zone [Mercury], the machinations of evil cunning; to the third zone [Venus], the lust whereby men are deceived; to the fourth zone [Sun], domineering arrogance; to the fifth zone [Mars], unholy daring and rash audacity; to the sixth zone [Jupiter], evil strivings after wealth; and to the seventh zone [Saturn], the falsehood which lies in wait to work harm. And thereupon, having been stripped of all that was wrought upon him by the structure of the heavens, he ascends to the substance of the eighth sphere, being now possessed of his own proper power; and he sings, together with those who dwell there, hymning the Father; and they that are there rejoice with him at his coming. And being made like to those with whom he dwells, he hears the Powers, who are above the substance of the eighth sphere, singing praise to God with a voice that is theirs alone. And thereafter, each in his turn, they mount upward to the Father; they give themselves up to the Powers, and become Powers themselves, they enter into God. This is the Good; this is the consummation, for those who have got Gnosis.[12]

It is clear from this text that even in Roman times, when these *Libelli* were probably written, the Egyptians of Alexandria believed in the possibility of the soul's ascent to a place in the heavens above the spheres of our local solar system. The ninth sphere above the earth, that of God, corresponds to the Crown Sephirah or Keter on the Kabbalistic Tree of Life diagram and represents the point of reunion between the individual soul and God. However, before reaching this point of final union, the soul has to take up its position once more in the eighth sphere, the sphere of the fixed stars or zodiac, which according to this scheme stands beyond the sphere of Saturn.[13] It was from this sphere, above the solar system but below the level of the Primum Mobile, that man had first looked down on the creations of his 'brother', the Solar Logos. Reading this, it occurred to me that for Adam Kadmon, the archetypal man, we should have in mind not a philosophical abstraction based on the Kabbalistic spheres, but an image of him looking down on the world of the planets from the stars. For the Egyptians at least, this seems to have had a real meaning.

We know from Egyptian texts that there was a common belief that Osiris ruled over a kingdom in the sky to which Egyptians hoped to go after death. In *The Orion Mystery* Robert Bauval and I argued that this kingdom, laved by the Nile's counterpart, the Milky Way, was believed to be in the constellation of Orion. For this reason the pyramids of Giza were laid out as Orion's Belt. There was also a narrow shaft from the King's Chamber of the Great Pyramid which pointed towards the southern meridian, at the culmination point of Alnitak, the southernmost star of the belt. This shaft, we argued, had been incorporated into the plan to provide the pharaoh's soul with a symbolic channel along which it could travel to this star. In this sense the pharaoh was going straight to the eighth sphere, for Orion, like all the constellations, was above the planets and on this sphere. It does not take a great leap of imagination to see that

307

where the *Libellus I* says that man, the *anthropos*, had looked down from heaven towards the created worlds of the demiurge (the planets), he could have been thought to do this from Orion. This constellation the Egyptians called Sahu and identified with the form of a walking man. In *The Orion Mystery* we linked it with the star form of the god Osiris, but it is clear that in Egypt Orion was originally the embodiment of Osiris' grandfather, the god Shu, who was the first-born son of Atum, the father of the gods. It would seem that the Egyptian version of this first son of God was not an intellectual abstraction of the principles of nature but was indeed composed of 'lights' – the very stars which made up his body.

Shu is a somewhat shadowy figure in Egyptian mythology whose principal function seems to have been to separate heaven from earth. As the god of the air or atmosphere he obviously does this in a very physical way, but he was also thought of as the custodian of the pillars which metaphorically held up the sky. Often he was depicted as himself holding aloft the sky, like the Titan Atlas of the Greeks. In Egyptian art Shu is most often represented holding apart the two lovers, his daughter Nut, the sky goddess, and his priapic son Geb, the earth. This symbolism is clearly drawn directly from what the Egyptians saw happening most nights in the sky itself. They identified the body of Nut with the Milky Way. When Orion is visible above the horizon, the Milky Way arches high across the sky and hence Nut is separated from the earth. However, as Orion passes the meridian, so the Milky Way twists around and slides lower and lower in the sky. As Orion sets, so she 'lies down' and forms a band of bright stars that encircles the entire horizon. Mythologically speaking, Nut, now free from the ever-vigilant eyes of her father, is able to renew her embrace with Geb. Understood astronomically, Shu does not permanently separate the lovers but only regulates their intercourse, a cosmic interaction between heaven and earth on which the whole of life depends.

Thus it is that the sky goddess Nut becomes pregnant by the earth god Geb and gives birth not only to the planets but also to anthropomorphic gods.

According to Egyptian cosmology Osiris, along with his brother and sisters, was a child of Nut. He was sent to earth by the great god Atum-Re himself in order that the fundamentals of civilization should be taught to men. The emblem of Shu was two ostrich feathers, which were incorporated into the headdress of Osiris known as the Atef crown. The ostrich feather also symbolized Maat, a goddess or principle of justice. Osiris, then, governed on earth in the name of his grandfather Shu, whose 'just kingdom' in heaven was identifiable as the constellation of Orion. After Osiris died and was resurrected, Sahu, his stellar form, ascended back to Orion. Thenceforward Orion, the man in heaven who looks down on the earth, was identified with Osiris rather than with his grandfather Shu.

The Egyptians, or at least those who could afford to pay for the elaborate rituals entailed, wanted to follow in the footsteps of Osiris, to join him in heaven; thus it was to Orion or Sahu, the archetype of all men, that they hoped they would return after death. To do this they needed first to crystallize their own stellar, Sahu body and be in a fit condition to meet with God. Concerning this Wallis Budge writes:

> The word *sahu*, though at times written with the determinative of a mummy lying on a bier, like *khat*, 'body', indicates a body which has obtained a degree of knowledge and power and glory whereby it becomes henceforth lasting and incorruptible. The body which has become a *sahu* has the power of ascending with the soul and holding converse with it. In this form it can ascend into heaven and dwell with the gods, and with the *sahu* of the gods, and with the souls of the righteous . . . In the late edition of the *Book of the Dead* published by Lepsius the deceased is said to 'look upon his body

and rest upon his *sahu*', and souls are said 'to enter into their *sahu*'; and a passage extant both in this and in the older Theban edition makes the deceased to receive the *sahu* of the God Osiris.[14]

It is not hard to see the parallels between these Egyptian ideas concerning the afterlife possibilities of the *sahu* or resurrected body and Christian beliefs. The personal *sahu* body of the deceased can be likened to the wedding garment described in the parable of Matthew's Gospel chapter 22, as indispensable for attending the mystical, heavenly marriage: 'But when the king came in to look at the guests, he saw there a man who had no wedding garment; and he said to him, "Friend, how did you get in here without a wedding garment?" And he was speechless. Then the king said to the attendants, "Bind him hand and foot, and cast him into the outer darkness; there men will weep and gnash their teeth." For many are called but few are chosen.'

There are further parallels to be made between Christian and Egyptian ideas of personal salvation. For just as the Egyptians believed they needed to be linked to and thereby drawn up to heaven by the *sahu* of Osiris, so resurrection 'in Christ', i.e. linked to the resurrected body of Christ, is a central doctrine of the Christian Church.

Further investigation along these lines reveals that the identification of Orion as the goal for ascending masters was also a central feature of esoteric Judaism. The first man was called Adam, meaning 'of the ground' as well as 'man', but the constellation of Orion would seem to be what the Kabbalists had in mind when they called the cosmic symbol of man Adam Kadmon. A comparison of the stars of Orion with the diagram of the Sephirot disposed according to the Kabbalistic Tree of Life shows that there is more than a passing resemblance between the two. The major stars of Orion fit uncannily well with the positions designated to almost all of the Sephirot (see colour illustration no. 25). Seeing this, it became clear to me that it was the bright stars of Orion, not some intellectual extrapolation of the planetary spheres, that constituted the real Adam Kadmon, the stellar archetype from which the Kabbalists believed the pattern of all mankind was derived.

This seems to have been a very old doctrine of the Israelites, and to have been part of their inheritance from Egypt from the time of Moses. For the Egyptians, Orion was the star form first of Shu and then, by association, of Osiris. Jacob/Israel had a vision of angels ascending and descending a ladder that stretched up to heaven. According to tradition, Orion's belt was emblematic of his 'staff', by which was meant his phallus. Jacob's ladder, another important symbol for Kabbalists, is also connected with the Tree of Life and therefore Orion. All this makes sense when it is realized that Orion is the star form of Adam, the symbol of the archetypal man in heaven, the first father of all humanity, as he was before the Fall. Further investigation reveals that this must have been one of the Israelites' most secret teachings, handed down by word of mouth from the ancient schools of the prophets. Jesus too must have known about this connection, for, as we have seen, at Caesarea Philippi he promoted Peter to the role of prophet of Orion. It would seem that the connection between Orion and the prophets of Israel goes right back to the very origins of the Israelite religion and even to the time of Abraham.

That the figure of Orion fitted so closely with the concept of the cosmic Adam came as no great surprise. Orion features prominently in the mythologies of the world, which give us further clues to the real meaning of this figure. In the course of researching my book *Magi*, I had discovered the existence of a secret brotherhood in northern Mesopotamia that had a keen interest in this same constellation. One of the centres for this brotherhood was the city of Edessa (modern Urfa), which was famous as a very early centre of Christianity. Visiting this city in 1994 I discovered, as related in Chapter 6 above, that there is still a strong local belief that it was here, in a cave under the citadel, that Abraham was born; and that there are legends of Abraham current here which, while probably untrue in a literal sense, are certainly intriguing for the light they throw on the star lore of northern Mesopotamia. Nor did the link between the patriarchs and northern Mesopotamia end with Abraham: a large part of his family remained behind in the region of Aram, the biblical name for the province of Harran, long after his own migration. Later a wife, Rebecca, was found here for his son Isaac. Jacob, too, is said to have dwelt here, in the household of his uncle Laban, for fourteen years, eventually marrying the latter's two daughters: Leah and Rachel.

Working as a shepherd for his uncle and with few distractions, Jacob would have had plenty of time to acquaint himself with the stars as he sat at night under the clear skies of Aram. According to William Drummond in *Oedipus Judaicus*, the 'three great stars of Orion' (presumably the stars of Orion's Belt) are still referred to as 'Jacob's staff' and the Milky Way as 'Jacob's ladder'.[15] Perhaps Jacob was privy to the same secret Mesopotamian teachings concerning Orion discussed earlier and thereby had his name associated with this constellation. Without the glare of modern lighting the Milky Way would have been visible as a great arching band across the sky; and who is to say that he never fantasized about Orion climbing it like a ladder? This would seem to be the message underlying the story of Jacob's vision of the angels and the ladder described in Genesis chapter 20. The later Kabbalists also associated an extended form of the 'Tree of Life' diagram, one that spans the non-physical as well as the physical world, with Jacob's ladder. It thus seems reasonable to assume that originally the ladder was the Milky Way, Orion the climber; later, the ladder became thought of as a symbolic connection with ethereal worlds rather than the very visible Milky Way, and the connection between Jacob and Orion was all but lost.

In *Magi* I argued that the theological college known as the School of the Persians which at one time was based in Edessa, near the 'Pools of Abraham', may very well have been connected with the Magi, or 'three wise men', of the Nativity story, who were themselves members of a secret brotherhood called the Sarmoung. This college, I was sure, was also connected with another ancient order of prophets, once operative in Israel itself, whose initiates had included such biblical figures as Samson, Elijah and John the Baptist. These prophets all conformed to the archetype of 'wild man of God' and were distinctively dressed in rough garb with a belt. The belt, mentioned in the descriptions of the clothing of both Elijah and John the Baptist, seems to have been a covert indication of a link with Orion. I was beginning to see that the secret brotherhood, to which I believed many of the major prophets belonged, was a 'School of Orion', and that it was from this brotherhood that the later School of the Persians was descended.

After its expulsion from Edessa in AD 489 the School of the Persians moved eastwards to the city of Nisibis (modern Nusaybin). This city also has biblical connections, as it lies on the headwaters of the River Khabour or Chebar, and in this region many of the captive Israelites of the ten lost tribes were settled by the Assyrians. It also has connections with the biblical prophets, for it was near here that Ezekiel had some of his most important visions. The highly esoteric Book of Ezekiel begins with the story of how the prophet saw strange visions of angelic beings and what appear to have been machines of some sort. These machines have been interpreted by some people (notably Erich von Däniken, the Swiss author of *Chariots of the Gods*) as UFOs or spaceships. Ezekiel's vision culminates in a light-form image of the 'glory of God', described as being like a seated man, who addresses him by the title 'Son of man'.

Taking these deliberations together, it became obvious to me that the biblical school of the prophets, among whose numbers we must count Ezekiel and Daniel as well as Samson, Elijah and John the Baptist, should perhaps be called the 'School of the Son of man' rather than the 'School of Orion'. The celestial image of man is the constellation of Orion, and it would seem from the evidence in Edessa and elsewhere that this school secretly used this symbol of Orion in their instruction, masking his identity under the name of Adam. When the school of the Safad Kabbalists, which was probably also descended from the same school of the prophets, set this previously oral tradition down in writing, the Orion figure became Adam Kadmon; however, the full esoteric significance of this figure was disguised and concealed from the uninitiated. They were not to know of the connection between the Tree of Life symbol, Adam Kadmon and the constellation of Orion – still less that this constellation was considered by the ancient Egyptians, and probably also by the Chaldeans, who inhabited northern Mesopotamia and from whom Abraham was descended, to be the place in heaven from which the souls of men had come and to which they would one day return prior to their full reunion with God.

The ancient Egyptians, we know, believed Osiris, Isis and Thoth (Hermes Trismegistus) to have been demigods 'sent from above' to educate mankind, and it is clear that the Hebrews had similar ideas concerning such figures as Enoch, Moses and Elijah. Taking all of the above arguments into consideration, it became clear to me that the address 'Son of man' was a coded title for any prophet believed to have been connected with the School of Orion. Peter, who had formerly been a senior student of John the Baptist, was promoted to this role by Jesus in succession to John after his execution. With these thoughts in mind, I was now ready to return to Jerusalem.

314

CHAPTER 16

ORION RISING

Leaving Tiberias, I retraced my route back to Jerusalem. I checked into the Christ Church Hospice, a little more expensive than the Petra but agreeably cleaner. Refreshed and unpacked, I steeled myself and plunged back down into the busy bazaar which is David Street. This time, my destination was not the Dome of the Rock but the most important of all Christian shrines: the Church of the Holy Sepulchre. Although this is a quite massive edifice, it is surprisingly difficult to find, tucked away as it is amid the back streets and alleyways that make up the Christian quarter. Asking directions is also a problem, as almost invariably any interaction with the local populace results in persistent invitations to do a little shopping. To stop and look at a street map is even worse, as it is an open invitation for someone to volunteer to act as your guide – only to bring you to a shop, his own or belonging to a member of his family, before leading you on to your final destination. Such are the perils that beset the modern pilgrim; but they are probably no different from when the present Church of the Holy Sepulchre was built shortly before the First Crusade.

I recognized the church immediately when I came to it from the time of my last visit in 1972. It is a very sad place for any devout Christian, not because of the presence of what is believed by many to have been Christ's tomb in which he was laid prior to his resurrection, nor for its being the supposed site of

315

Calvary where he was crucified, but rather for the way in which it highlights the animosities and divisions between the different branches of the present-day church. Though it is a large building, not all of it is open to the public and even those parts which one may enter are the subject of territorial disputes between the monks and priests who live there that at times end up in fist-fights. Indeed, so intense is the rivalry among the different denominations responsible for the church's upkeep that the keys to the main doors are kept in the custody not of Christians but of two Muslim families whose responsibility it is to open them in the morning and to lock up every night. In this way all the Christian denominations with shares in the church are satisfied in the knowledge that even if they don't have the privilege of owning the keys, at least their rivals don't either.

The church itself is built on the site identified by the Empress Helen, mother of Constantine the Great, as the place where Jesus was crucified and later buried. She had a round, domed structure built over what was believed to be the tomb of Joseph of Arimathea in which Jesus was buried. A separate rectangular building was built over the site of the Crucifixion, which was believed to have taken place a little to the east. The buildings were dedicated in AD 335 but not finished until 348. Thus built, Helen's church was to remain more or less the same until the year 1009 when, Jerusalem having long since become a Muslim city, it was destroyed by Caliph Hakim. In the middle of the eleventh century it was rebuilt, the necessary money being supplied by the Byzantine emperor Constantine Monomachus. However, it was not fully restored until after the knights of the First Crusade seized Jerusalem in 1099. They completed the reconstruction, roofing over the courtyard which had previously separated the round from the rectangular building. This, with some alterations, is the church as we see it today.

Entering the building brought back memories of my

last pilgrimage to the Holy Land in 1972. On that occasion I had been quite scandalized when I had been pounced upon by a little Coptic priest who urged me to come and 'touch the tombstone of Christ'. He had then led me into a tiny chapel at the back of the main shrine and, after thrusting a lit candle into my right hand, had pulled my left towards a small, smooth stone protruding from the floor. I touched the stone but recoiled in horror when I saw scattered next to it high-denomination dollar bills and other banknotes. It became clear at once that the purpose of my being brought to his chapel was that I should make a similar donation to its upkeep. Now, while I didn't object to this in principle – for after all, we all of us have to earn our living and his chapel was providing a service of sorts – I found this juxtaposition of the tokens of Mammon with what he apparently believed to be the very tombstone of Christ an affront. My negative feelings about the place were only heightened when a girl I knew from the kibbutz, almost in tears, told me of how one of the other monks had put his hand up her skirt while she was trying to pray. I considered that if this sort of thing was allowed to go on then these 'men of God' were a disgrace to the religion they were supposed to serve; and I had vowed never to return. These, however, were the feelings of a young man; and, the passage of years having given me a little more understanding of human nature and of the temptations which drive people to act contrary to their principles, I was ready to go back on my vow and pay the church a second visit. Inside I found it much as I remembered, still rather dark and untidy. I made my way to the round church, dominated by the large shrine covering the tomb itself; round the back was the same Coptic chapel that I remembered – but this time there were no dollar bills in evidence.

As I left the church the sun was setting and the muezzins' summons to prayer, broadcast from a dozen loudspeakers, echoed over the rapidly emptying city. The Muslims, however, did not have a monopoly on calls to the faithful; as I approached the Jaffa Gate, intermingled with their cries of 'God is Great' was the sonorous clanging of church bells from the nearby Armenian Cathedral of St James. This church, I knew from a previous visit, was one of the wonders of Jerusalem and so I decided to go along and join in their service. My experiences here were to be in complete contrast to those of the Holy Sepulchre, for whereas that church has rightly been described as looking like a 'cross between a builders' site and a furniture depot', St James's turned out to be quite the opposite, with an intensely spiritual atmosphere.

Entering the church was like going through a time warp, for whereas the outside was nondescript, the interior was beautifully ornate. There were no fixed seats and most people were standing; however, the floor was carpeted and there were a few fold-up chairs for those who needed them. Hanging above the altar were dozens of oil lamps; but, as the walls and ceiling were so stained with soot from candles, incense and indeed the oil lamps themselves, the church was still very dark and womb-like. On the north side of the cathedral were several small chapels featuring carved lattice and mother-of-pearl doors executed in what might loosely be called Islamic designs. It was the most beautiful workmanship I had yet seen in Israel and reminded me greatly of the Baghdad Kiosk at the Topkapi Palace of Istanbul. The pillars supporting the dome over the centre of the church were covered with ornate tiles, imported from Turkey in the eighteenth century, and the walls adorned with icons of the saints. My careful study of the church's interior was interrupted when an Armenian priest with his entourage entered from a side door. Over his robes he wore a simple black cloak with cowl. This rose above his head to a sharp point, giving him the appearance of a Merlin. The Armenian mass which followed, with clouds of incense and a well-trained choir chanting in resonantly deep tones, was pervaded through and through with a sense of magic that was totally missing from the Holy Sepulchre.

I was enraptured and felt surges of religious emotion that I had not experienced for very many years.

Uplifted and refreshed by the experience of the Armenian mass, I walked back to the Jaffa Gate. Although I was staying at the Christ Church Hospice, my destination now was the Petra, where I had been invited by the staff to a barbecue party on the roof. Being December, it was quite a cold night, even though temperatures had been fairly high during the day. We were therefore glad to huddle round a blazing fire, despite getting smoked like kippers in the process. From the rooftop we had, as before, a perfect view right across the old city, this time of the nocturnal prospect. The main draw was, of course, the Dome of the Rock, which is eye-catching in daylight and even more stunning seen dramatically flood-lit against the horizon. Then, as we watched, the full moon rose over the Mount of Olives, which acted as a backdrop to the golden dome. It was a truly magical moment, made all the more spectacular by the fact that the moon was being held firmly in the grasp of Orion as that now most familiar of constellations hung in the sky before us. Excitedly, with the Great Hunter laid out before me, I gave an impromptu lecture on the subject of Orion to all and any who would listen, explaining its connections with the pyramids and with Christmas. Then, all too soon, he ducked behind a cloud and the party was over. This, however, had been enough to get me thinking again about the Matthew prophecies, for now I had seen with my own eyes that, at Jerusalem, Orion rose over the Mount of Olives. This I had not realized before, but it confirmed certain ideas I had been working on before leaving England.

I knew that the Mount of Olives features prominently in the Gospel story. For one thing, it seems to have been a favourite meeting place for Jesus and his apostles whenever they were in the vicinity of Jerusalem. Indeed, it was during one of these meetings, while sitting looking towards Jerusalem, that Jesus had given his 'Matthew prophecies' for the end of the age. Because of its major role in the Christian epic, I had long suspected that the Mount of Olives might have some unknown importance connected with my own quest for the meaning of these prophecies. Could the rising of Orion and Jesus' own ascension to the stars be linked events? As I returned to my hotel, there was much to think about.

The next day, refreshed by a good night's sleep, I set off to take a look at the Mount of Olives for myself. Walking back through the Armenian quarter, past the entrance to St James's Cathedral, I made my way to Zion Gate. This lies on the south side of the city and leads out to Mount Zion, the believed location of the Coenaculum, the room where Jesus and the apostles are reported to have eaten the Last Supper. It is also the location of what by Jewish tradition is believed to be the tomb of King David. I paid a visit to both before moving on to the nearby Church of the Dormition. This is built on the site where the Virgin Mary is traditionally believed to have died and been 'assumed into heaven', body and soul. Though modern, the church was certainly impressive and, like the Armenian Cathedral of St James, had far more atmosphere than the Holy Sepulchre. Then, leaving Mount Zion, I walked on around the outside of the city walls, past the unattractively named Dung Gate and the sealed Golden Gate,[1] down to the road bridge which spans the part of the valley formed by the dried-up Kidron Brook known as the Valley of Jehoshaphat ('God will judge'). This is only a narrow gorge and not very deep, but it is sufficient to separate Jerusalem from the Mount of Olives. I walked over the bridge, which was jam-packed with cars and buses, and made my way to the Church of All Nations, which stands at the foot of the Mount. This too is a modern structure, built in 1924, but was raised on the site of an earlier church, also founded by the Empress Helen, and stands next to the traditional site of the Garden of Gethsemane. The most noticeable feature of this church was the large golden mosaic filling the

16 The citadel or 'Throne of Nimrod' with the pillars of Edessa, where Abraham was bound.

17 The pools of Abraham which broke his fall when he was cast down from the citadel.

18 Orion as St Christopher carrying the infant Jesus (the sun) over the Milky Way river.

19 Jesus dancing over the Rock of Temptation in the monastery of the same name above Jericho.

The Temple of Solomon

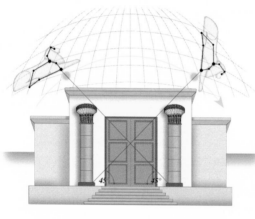

*The Sun sits symbolically over the
pillars before the Temple of Solomon.
When built, it cast shadows –
giving the perfect angle of 45°
on the day of the Regulus conjunction.*

21 Curtains before the Ark protecting the Torah scrolls: Ha'Ari Ashkenazi synagogue in Safad. Twin lions surmount symbolic pillars.

22 The Western or Wailing Wall: all that remains of Herod's temple.

23 The Dome of the Rock, covering the *kibleh* or foundation stone of Abraham.

24 The valley of Jehoshaphat with the pyramid tomb of Zechariah in the foreground.

Orion and the Kabbalistic Tree of Life

In Kabbalah, the 'Tree of Life' is compared to linked spheres or 'sephirot', arranged symbolically on the Pillars of Solomon's Temple

Primum Mobile
(Keter)

Saturn
(Binah)

Stars
(Hokhmah)

Mars
(Gevurah)

Jupiter
(Hesed)

Sun
(Tiferet)

Mercury
(Hod)

Venus
(Nezah)

Moon
(Yesod)

Pillar of Severity

Pillar of Mercy

Earth
(Malkhut)

Kether

Binah

Hochma

Hesed

Gevura

Tepheret

Yesod

Hod

Netzah

Orion as 'Adam Kadmon' or 'First Man' can also stand between pillars. The stars of Orion, not the planetary spheres, are the probable origin of the 'Tree of Life'

The Milky Way and the River Jordan

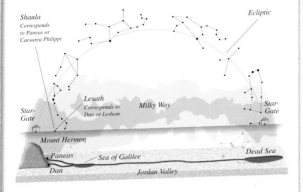

Shaula
Corresponds
to Paneas or
Caesarea Philippi

Ecliptic

Lesath
Corresponds to
Dan or Leshem

Milky Way

Star-
Gate

Star-
Gate

Mount Hermon

Paneas

Sea of Galilee

Dead Sea

Dan

Jordan Valley

*Symbolically, there are two 'star-gates' in the sky:
one above the tail of Scorpio and the other above
the raised hand of Orion. Geographically, they correspond
to Mount Hermon and the Dead Sea, the source
and terminator of the River Jordan.*

27 Orion rising over the Mount of Olives to the East of Jerusalem.

28 Pediment of the Church of All Nations with the cosmic Christ, the Alpha and the Omega, above the figure of Jesus praying in the Garden of Gethsemane.

29 The sun over the Pyramid of Khafre, summer solstice 2000.

30 Opening the stargate, summer solstice 2000.

31 The Dome of the Ascension, Mount of Olives.

32 The rock from which Jesus is said to have ascended, Dome of the Ascension.

33 Painting by Bengt Alfredson, 'Opening the Stargate: 29th June AD 2000'. The spirit of Orion as the Alpha and Omega instructs St John as he writes the Book of Revelation.

pediment above the main entrance, which could be seen clearly from the other side of the valley. At the centre of this mosaic was the figure of an anguished-looking Jesus praying while by his side figures representing several apostles slept soundly. This was, of course, a reference to the story told in Matthew chapter 26, where, following his Last Supper, Jesus prayed through most of the night in the Garden of Gethsemane. His apostles, whom he had asked to watch out for him, were unable to control their tiredness and kept falling asleep. Above this all-too-human looking Jesus was a more nebulous figure of the risen or cosmic Christ, shown in all his glory holding the letters A (Alpha) and Ω (Omega), the first and last letters of the Greek alphabet. This was a reference to the Book of Revelation, where 'one like the Son of man' appears to John and calls himself by this title. Leaving the church I went into the adjoining Garden of Gethsemane itself. It looked rather small, but it did contain some very ancient-looking olive trees, and who is to say that it is not part of what was once a much larger garden or olive grove that probably then covered most of the hillside? In the story of the Passion and Crucifixion Jesus and his apostles are said to have come to this garden immediately after the Last Supper. If so, they would have followed the same route around the outside of the city walls which I had taken myself.

While still in the garden, Jesus was betrayed by Judas Iscariot who identified him to the authorities by kissing him on the cheek. I had long been fascinated by this story, which seems to suggest a very interesting but contradictory relationship between master and pupil. For though Judas is universally reviled as the traitor who brought about or at any rate facilitated Jesus' arrest and crucifixion, in reality he seems to have been performing a role over which he had little control. One could even go so far as to say that he was a puppet whose job it was to act as the vehicle for the forces of darkness.

Psychologically speaking, Judas was clearly a complex

character who seems to have both feared and been attracted by the challenge to orthodoxy posed by the teachings of Jesus. Throughout the New Testament he is presented as the carping critic, the apostle who calls into question profligacy, and we can imagine him becoming more and more concerned about the unorthodox direction being taken by the esoteric group of which he now found himself a member. This concern seems to have reached its height following Jesus' anointing with oil, probably by Mary Magdalene, shortly before the Last Supper (Matt. 26: 6–13). The apostles, probably in this instance led by Judas, accused Jesus of wastage, saying the oil could have been sold and the money given to the poor. Jesus rebukes his apostles for their meanness towards Mary, saying, 'Why do you trouble the woman? For she has done a beautiful thing to me. For you always have the poor with you, but you will not always have me.' This admonishment seems to have been the final straw as far as Judas was concerned. Feeling humiliated and probably in a state of high emotion, he went to the authorities and made a deal with them that he would betray Jesus into their hands in exchange for thirty pieces of silver. However, Judas, though himself now an apostate, does not seem to have realized that Jesus would be put to death by the authorities; he seems to have thought his master would merely be brought to trial and admonished for his messianic claims. When he realized the enormity of his betrayal, he repented and tried to buy back Jesus' freedom:

When Judas, his betrayer, saw that he was condemned, he repented and brought back the thirty pieces of silver to the chief priests and the elders, saying, 'I have sinned in betraying innocent blood.' They said, 'What is that to us? See to it yourself.' And throwing down the pieces of silver in the temple, he departed; and he went and hanged himself. But the chief priests, taking the pieces of silver, said, 'It is not lawful to put them into the treasury, since they are blood money.' So they took counsel, and bought with them the potter's field, to bury strangers in. Therefore that field has been called the Field of Blood to this day. Then was fulfilled what had been spoken by the prophet Jeremiah, saying, 'And they took the thirty pieces of silver, the price of him on whom a price had been set by some of the sons of Israel, and they gave them for the potter's field, as the Lord directed me.' (Matt. 27: 3–10)

It is clear from all this that Judas was playing a pre-ordained role which began with the anointing with oil and was confirmed at the Last Supper. This is described most clearly in John's Gospel.

When Jesus had thus spoken, he was troubled in spirit, and testified, 'Truly, truly, I say to you, one of you will betray me.' The disciples looked at one another, uncertain of whom he spoke. One of his disciples, whom Jesus loved, was lying close to the breast of Jesus; so Simon Peter beckoned to him and said, 'Tell us who it is of whom he speaks.' So lying thus close to the breast of Jesus, he said to him, 'Lord, who is it?' Jesus answered, 'It is he to whom I shall give this morsel when I have dipped it.' So when he had dipped the morsel, he gave it to Judas, the son of Simon Iscariot. Then after the morsel, Satan entered into him. Jesus said to him, 'What you are going to do, do quickly.' Now no one at the table knew why he said this to him. Some thought that, because Judas had the money box, Jesus was telling him, 'Buy what we need for the feast'; or that he should give something to the poor. So, after receiving the morsel, he immediately went out; and it was night. (John 13: 21–30)

The importance of Judas as one of the principal actors in what is to follow is clearly emphasized here. It is almost as if Jesus himself had hand-picked Judas for this role and has been preparing him for it all along. Indeed, by implication it is the very morsel handed to him by Jesus that enables him to be taken over by Satan. What this seems to mean is that Judas was overshadowed by the influence of Saturn, the planet of chastisement, which in traditional astrology tests people with misfortune to see if they are up to the mark. It is, of course, in this context that Satan/Saturn is met with in the Book of Job, where he is allowed to rob Job of family, wealth, reputation and even his health in order to test the strength of his faith in God. Similarly, as we have seen, in the New Testament Satan was allowed to tempt Jesus in the wilderness after his baptism to see if he really was up to the job of taking on his mission of redemption. Now, using Judas as his agent, Saturn was going to test Jesus' faith again – this time to the point of death itself. The connection between Satan and Saturn is made clear by the thirty pieces of silver, which were subsequently used after Judas' suicide to buy a field in which strangers could be buried. Thirty is the number of Saturn (its orbital period being roughly twenty-nine and a half years); and Saturn is the planet which is said to rule over bones and graveyards.

Large graveyards are painfully in evidence all over the southern end of the western slopes of the Mount of Olives. This is because from time immemorial it is here that Jews have wanted to be buried. Today there are serried ranks of whitened sepulchres facing towards the Temple Mount on the other side of the Valley of Jehoshaphat. Their occupants await the day of judgement when God, sitting on his throne at the Temple Mount, will awaken the dead. It is then, so many believe, that those sleeping in their graves on the Mount of Olives will be the first to be awakened and that two bridges will appear across the valley, one of them of iron and the other of paper. The iron one will collapse under the weight of those attempting to cross and they will fall to their damnation. The elect will choose the seemingly flimsier paper bridge and they will be the first to be saved.

Seeing the graveyards and the Valley of Jehoshaphat, just to the right of the Garden of Gethsemane, set me thinking once more about the resurrection of Jesus. Having discovered meaningful star patterns appropriate to his birth in Bethlehem, I had been anxious to see if his crucifixion, resurrection and ascension were similarly indicated. These were ideas I had been thinking about for some time before leaving England and, perhaps not surprisingly in view of the importance of the subject, I had discovered that there were indeed 'signs in the sky' for all these important events. In order to work out the astrology behind the culminating events of Jesus' life it was first necessary to know when these actually took place. This has, of course, been a matter of great debate for many centuries, both within and without the church. Not trusting to my own judgement on such an important matter, I went first to the *Encyclopaedia Britannica* to see what their experts had to say on the subject. In an exhaustive article, covering historical and astronomical evidence as well as internal evidence from the Gospels, they arrived at the years 7–6 BC for the birth, AD 26–7 for the baptism and AD 29 for the Crucifixion, Resurrection and Ascension:

> To sum up: the various dates and intervals, to the approximate determination of which this article has been devoted, do not claim separately more than a tentative and probable value. Perhaps their harmony and convergence give some additional claim to acceptance, and at any rate do something to secure each one of them singly – the Nativity in 7–6 bc, the Baptism in ad 26–27, the Crucifixion in ad 29 – from being to any wide extent in error.[2]

The range of dates given for the Nativity included that at which I had arrived independently from astronomical consideration: 29 July, 7 BC. Similarly, as we have seen, 6 January AD 26 is a likely date for the baptism. We have already examined the implications of this date in terms of

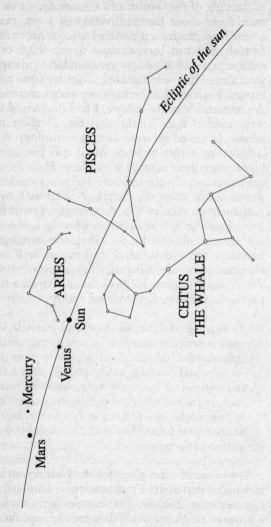

STELLAR SIGNATURE OF THE CRUCIFIXION,
15 APRIL AD 29

astronomical symbolism. It remained only to be seen if the events of Christ's death, resurrection and ascension would be equally revealing, astronomically speaking.

Jesus is generally believed to have had a three-year ministry from the time of his baptism to his crucifixion, which by this reckoning would have taken place in AD 29.[3] The correct year having been identified, it is not difficult to arrive at exact dates for the climactic events in his life. The so-called Last Supper was in reality the Jewish feast of the Passover. This meal was always celebrated on the evening between the fourteenth and fifteenth days of the Hebrew month of Nisan, which means on the day of the first full moon following the spring equinox. In AD 29 there was a full moon just before the equinox, which means that the Passover full moon would have been the one after this. Consequently the feast of the Passover would have been celebrated very late that year. According to our Gregorian calendar, the Passover meal would have been eaten on the evening of 14 April. At 8.25 p.m. on that day Saturn, the Judas star, would have been seen to set in the western sky. This can be seen as symbolizing Judas' departure from the table. The Crucifixion would have taken place the next day, the 15th, and would have had to be over before the start of the Sabbath at sunset. The Sabbath ended at sunset on the 16th, so the Resurrection would have to have occurred before dawn on the 17th. The Ascension, according to the Bible, took place forty days later. I now had a chronology for the death, resurrection and ascension of Jesus. It remained to be seen if any or all of these were astrologically significant.

Feeding the data into my computer, I was once more in for a shock. It quickly became clear that just as Jesus' baptism was connected with the sign of Capricorn, the 'scapegoat', so the Crucifixion was linked to Aries, the 'sacrificial lamb'. On 15 April AD 29 the sun was, in fact, directly under Delta-Aries, the last star of that constellation. Now of course, the idea of Jesus as the sacrificial lamb who takes away the sins of the world is familiar to

Christians everywhere. But here was a clear astronomical reference to that same event. It was also significant that in the sky at the time of the Crucifixion, which we are told lasted for three hours, from 12 noon until 3 p.m., all of the planets, with the exception of the moon, were present above the horizon and therefore in some sense bearing witness to the tragic event. Interestingly, just before noon, at 11.23 to be precise, the star Algol in the head of Medusa the Gorgon would have passed directly over the zenith point. Algol is the principal star on the forehead of the skull of the dead gorgon; this would seem to be linked with Jesus' arrival for execution at Golgotha, which the Gospel writers tell us means 'the place of the skull'. Fifteen minutes later, as Jesus was being prepared for his crucifixion, the royal star Regulus in the sign of Leo would have been rising in the east. At this very moment the Roman soldiers were probably nailing to the cross the piece of paper reading 'Jesus of Nazareth, King of the Jews'. All this seems to be more than coincidental and to illustrate again how the doctrine of signatures, 'as above, so below', dominated Jesus' short life.

Moving on two days brings us to 17 April AD 29 with the stars not much changed. However, I discovered another sign in the sky that was very important symbolically and which would have been seen just before the dawn on that first Easter Sunday. A very important Christian image, one symbolizing the idea of Jesus as a victorious rather than a sacrificial figure, is the Agnus Dei or 'Lamb of God', shown as a lamb holding in one hoof a staff or flagpole from which flies a banner carrying the Christian emblem of the red cross on a white background. I had long wondered about the esoteric significance of this symbol; now I found that it too was astrological. For on 17 April AD 29, which I had calculated to be the day of the first Easter, the constellation of Aries would have been seen rising over the eastern horizon just before the dawn. Jerusalem stands at latitude 31° 47' north. SKYGLOBE revealed that at this latitude and at that time, at the precise

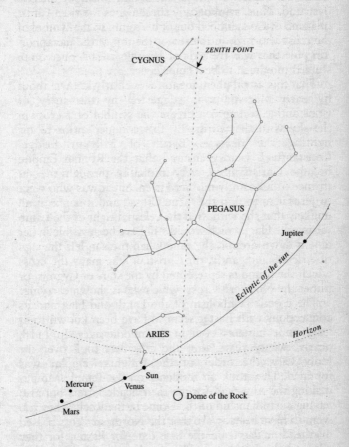

CYGNUS

ZENITH POINT

PEGASUS

Jupiter

Ecliptic of the sun

ARIES

Horizon

Sun

Mercury

Venus

○ Dome of the Rock

Mars

moment Aries crossed over the horizon, the constellation of Cygnus the swan, also known as the Northern Cross, would have been visible in the zenith position, directly overhead. Thus, symbolically speaking, as the risen Christ or Lamb of God climbed out of his tomb, so the symbol of the cross was high in the sky at the top of the metaphorical pole that was the axis of Jerusalem. This once more seemed too much to be a coincidence.

That this astral phenomenon was clearly known about by early Christians is suggested by the story of Constantine seeing in a dream the symbol of a cross in the sky with the words 'By this conquer' prior to his fighting the decisive Battle of Milvian Bridge. Constantine's victory ensured that the Roman Empire became Christianized, very probably through the influence of his saintly mother Helen. She it was who went to Jerusalem to find the 'True Cross', and it is not at all unlikely that she witnessed the celestial sight of the Lamb raising the Flag, which would still have been visible in her day at dawn around the time when the sun left the sign of Aries. Significantly, on Christian star maps the cross which she found is represented by the stars of Cygnus, or rather the Northern Cross, which she is shown carrying.

The cosmic symbolism of the Lamb and Flag and its connections with Easter seem to have been known to at least some initiates even in the middle ages. In 1118, nearly twenty years after the crusaders took over the Holy City, the order of the Knights Templar was founded. They took up residence on the Temple Mount, making the Al Aqsa Mosque their headquarters but also having custodianship of the Dome of the Rock. They too seem to have been aware that the Northern Cross passed overhead at dawn on the true date for Easter, for they adopted the Lamb and Flag as their totem. That they were interested in this sort of astrology is indicated by their other totem of two knights riding a horse. The horse represents the constellation of Pegasus, which at that time made its dawn rising at exactly the spring equinox, with the sun nearby in the double constellation of Pisces, the Christian fish, which crosses the eastern horizon at the same time. From their vantage point on the Temple Mount, the Templars would have seen these configurations of Easter stars every year rising over the Mount of Olives. With these ideas in mind I carried on up the hill.

The Agony in the Garden, the betrayal by Judas and the Resurrection itself all seemed to be connected with the lower slopes of the Mount of Olives; but it was from the crown of the hill that Jesus, according to the Gospels, left the earth altogether as he ascended into heaven. Long prior to this he and his disciples would have walked up and down the Mount to and from the village of Bethany, where his friends Mary, Martha and Lazarus lived. Following now in their footsteps, I walked up a long stairway leading from near the back of the Garden of Gethsemane to the top of the hill. This, as it turned out, was not such a good idea, as on either side the stairway is flanked by high walls. Alone and out of sight I was an easy target for the muggers for whom the Mount of Olives is today sadly famous. Walking alone up this back route was a risk I should not have taken. Fortunately, nothing untoward happened and presently I found myself by the nearby Church of the Ascension, whose 45 metre high tower was clearly visible from the roof of the Petra. Unfortunately, it was closed, but I was able to look at the much older Mosque of the Ascension, which lies at the heart of the village and is in fact a crusader building raised on the ruins of another of Helen's churches. Like the Dome of the Rock, though in a much poorer condition, it is octagonal in design. If anywhere in the area was the site of the Ascension – whatever mysterious event this might have been – this, I felt, was it.

Jesus' ascent to heaven is reminiscent of that of Elijah and of Enoch before him. The story is not contained in the Matthew Gospel, which ends with an entreaty by the risen Jesus to his eleven remaining disciples that they should go forth and teach all nations, 'baptizing them in the name of

331

the Father, and the Son and the Holy Ghost'. For the story of the Ascension we have to turn to the other Gospels. Mark takes the Jesus story beyond the exhortation to teach and tells us: 'So then after the Lord had spoken unto them, he was received into heaven, and sat on the right hand of God' (Mark 16: 19). Luke gives slightly more detail to the story, telling us that it took place at Bethany:

And he led them out as far as Bethany, and he lifted up his hands and blessed them.

And it came to pass that while he blessed them, he was parted from them, and carried from them.

And they worshipped him, and returned to Jerusalem with great joy:

And were continually in the temple, praising and blessing God. Amen. (Luke 24: 50–3)

The fullest account of all, and the one on which the traditional image of the Ascension is based, is to be found in the Acts of the Apostles:

To them [the Apostles] he presented himself alive after his passion by many proofs, appearing to them during forty days, and speaking of the kingdom of God . . .

So when they had come together, they asked him, 'Lord, will you at this time restore the kingdom to Israel?' He said to them, 'It is not for you to know the time or the seasons which the Father has fixed by His own authority. But you shall receive power when the Holy Spirit has come down on you; and you shall be my witnesses in all Judea and Samaria and to the end of the earth.' And when he had said this, as they looked on, he was lifted up, and a cloud took him out of their sight. And while they were gazing into heaven as he went, behold, two men stood by them in white robes, and said, 'Men of Galilee, why do you stand looking into heaven? This Jesus, who was taken up from you into heaven, will come in the same way as you saw him going into heaven.' (Acts 1: 3–11)

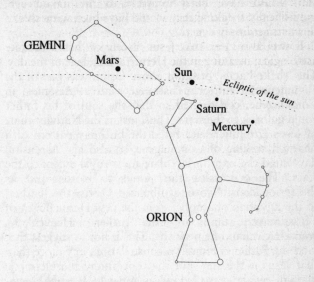

I felt sure that this major event, itself of cosmic significance, would, like the ascent of Elijah, have astronomical parallels; so once again I consulted SKYGLOBE. We are told in the above passage – and this, as far as I am aware, has always been the tradition of the church – that the Ascension took place forty days after the Resurrection. So if the first Easter took place on 17 April AD 29, then the Ascension would have been on 27 May. I fed this date into my computer. To my utter amazement the program showed me that on this day the sun would have been in the 'shake-hands' position, that is to say directly above the outstretched right arm of Orion. In Jerusalem, during the morning of that day (from around 6 a.m. to 11 a.m.), all seven planets of the ancients – that is, the sun, moon, Mercury, Venus, Mars, Jupiter and Saturn – were above the horizon. Although all bar the sun would have been invisible to the naked eye, symbolically speaking they would have been witnesses to this extraordinary event.

It was also clear that Jesus' ascension has a definite astrological meaning in the Hermetic language of the day. The 'shake-hands' position above Orion was one of the alignments of Antiochus' strange shaft at Arsameia in Commagene, constructed so that the soul of his father could go back to the stars. Thus, just as the Nativity chart of Jesus (29 July, 7 BC) fitted the birthday pattern of a pharaoh or king of Commagene, so also his 'Ascension day' fitted the appropriate date for a royal ascent to the stars. The conclusion this points to is that just as the Orion constellation symbolized Osiris, the 'Father' of the Egyptian pharaohs, so in the new Hermeticism of Christianity it stands for Jesus' 'Father in Heaven', by whose right hand he now sits. This is not to suggest that God the Father is himself a constellation, any more than that Jesus is the sun, but that once more the Hermetic dictum, 'as above, so below', is apposite. It would seem, therefore, that, symbolically at least, Jesus' ascension into heaven was intricately linked with the idea that the 'shake-hands' position above Orion represented some sort of gateway into heaven.

However, there was even more to it than this. Jesus had told his disciples that he would return in the same way that he had left. Assuming that he was telling the truth, then as he had apparently ascended from the Mount of Olives, it was logical that this was where he should come back to. What this could mean physically – whether we should expect the sudden appearance of a man with holes in his hands and a spear wound in his side floating down from the clouds – is matter for conjecture. What I was now to discover is that there are further signs in the sky indicating that this or some other perhaps more symbolic event is scheduled for our own times.

CHAPTER 17

BIRTH OF A NEW AGE

In 1972, shortly after returning from Israel, I paid a visit to one of the most remarkable Englishmen of his generation: John Godolphin Bennett. A veteran of the First World War, an accomplished linguist and a former student of Gurdjieff and Ouspensky, he was by then in his seventies. Still highly active, physically and mentally, he was at that time running an esoteric school of his own at Sherborne House near Cheltenham. I went to visit him partly out of curiosity but also with the possibility in mind of enrolling at his school. I didn't join as it turned out, feeling that it was not for me – at least, not at that time; and as he died two years later the opportunity did not re-present itself. However, the visit did enable us to have a long talk.

During the course of our conversation he returned again and again to the importance of our own times and how people of my generation needed to grasp certain opportunities that were being offered. He explained that we were living at the end not just of the short Age of Pisces but of a whole epoch of roughly twelve or thirteen thousand years. Shortly, after a period of chaos, there would be the birth of a new world. We were going to witness the events of the Apocalypse as foretold in the Bible. At the end of the epoch we were going to be awoken from the deep sleep in which humanity has lain entranced for millennia. At that time the evolution of our species, which was currently stalled, was going to take a giant leap. Our spiritual faculties would be awakened and we would at last see ourselves for what we really are: children of God with great possibilities for self-development.

These ideas must have been in his mind a great deal at the time I met him, for they formed the basis of a lecture he gave around then which was afterwards published. In this he talks about the impending change in the world as being comparable with that which took place at the time of the last Ice Age in c.10,000 BC.

> If the last great change happened ten thousand years before Christ – that is, twelve thousand years ago, the time of the ending of the Ice Ages and the beginning of the great movements towards our modern languages, cultures and religions – then maybe we are due for another change equally as great in the way in which man lives on this earth. Or, possibly, we may be due for something that is even greater: really the arriving of a new race of people. We should take this seriously. We should take it seriously because it not only comes from the evidence of tradition, and from the evidence that comes from the study of cycles, but simply from what our eyes see as we look about us.[1]

At the time I met Bennett I had just returned from Israel, where the 'Jerusalem Syndrome' was already in evidence among some of the Christian pilgrims that I met. (This term is used to describe a propensity for the city emotionally to overwhelm certain visitors. Perhaps already overly religious before they arrive, once in Jerusalem they lose all sense of reality, identifying themselves as the reincarnation of Jesus, Moses, Elijah or one or another of the prophets. Fortunately, it is usually a passing phase.) In these circles in Jerusalem there was already a feeling abroad that we were living at the end of an epoch, but I was surprised to hear the same thing from a rational philosopher such as Bennett. However, what made his words of special interest was that his forecast changes to the world and to humankind related to long-period cycles, going back to the last Ice Age, and not just the ending of the Age of Pisces and beginning of an Age of Aquarius. As I was later to discover, what he was really talking about was the present Age of Orion, which seems to have begun, as he suggested, during or near the end of the last Ice Age *c.*11,000–10,000 BC. It would end with the Second Coming, which should happen at the end of the age and also be connected in some way with the movement of Orion. Logic dictated that the re-appearance of Jesus on the Mount of Olives, an event longed for by many fundamentalist Christians, ought also to be connected with Orion, the constellation of the heavenly Adam.

The discovery that the ascension of Jesus from the Mount of Olives was signified by the appearance of the sun over the outstretched hand of Orion, in the 'St Christopher' position, inevitably posed the question of whether or not the promised Second Coming was simply this. As I had seen for myself, one very good reason for this association of the Mount of Olives with the ascension of Jesus is that, being east of Jerusalem, it is the place of sunrise as viewed from the city and in particular from the Temple Mount. At sunrise on the equinox, around the time when the feast of the Passover was celebrated, the sun would have risen directly in the east and in line with the Golden Gate through which, according to tradition, Jesus entered Jerusalem on a donkey with palm-leaves strewn beneath his feet. The Mount of Olives therefore symbolizes, astrologically speaking, birth, rebirth and the direction from which the expected Messiah will come. There is something else, however, that is unique to our time: today the Belt of Orion itself, if viewed from the Temple Mount, can be seen to appear over the horizon directly above the Church and Mosque of the Ascension. This sign in the sky seems to be yet another harbinger indicating that we are rapidly approaching the end of an age, something hinted at, albeit for different reasons, in *The Orion Mystery*.

In that book we were much indebted to the work of our illustrator, Robin John Cook. His illustrations, carefully conceived and well executed, brought to life many of the difficult concepts we were putting forward. His skill in this respect was invaluable; yet Robin was no ordinary illustrator. He was himself a pyramid researcher of many years' standing who had written extensively on the subject. His particular focus of interest was pyramid geometry, and he had made some interesting discoveries of his own. These he summarized in a small book called simply *The Pyramids of Giza*, which he had self-published, and also in an unpublished manuscript entitled 'The Giza Pyramids: A Design Study'. In these works Cook presented some insights concerning the positioning of the subsidiaries, the so-called 'Queens' pyramids'. Three of these, named G1a, G1b and G1c for convenience, lie to the east of the Great Pyramid of Khufu, which is often referred to as G1 (i.e. 'Giza 1') by Egyptologists. Three more, G111a, G111b and G111c, stand to the south of the Menkaure pyramid, which is known as G111. Robin had analysed the alignment of these satellite pyramids in relation to the central construction of the Giza complex, the Pyramid of Khafre or G11. In doing so he had made some startling discoveries, about which he writes:

> Three parallel lines leave G111a, b and c at 30° azimuth to meet the north-east corner, the centre, and the south-west corner of G11. Similarly, three parallel lines leave these points at 26.5° (the angle of the double square) to pass through the centres of G1a, b and c. It was from this observation that the 'master diagram' was discovered.[2]

In an appendix to *The Orion Mystery* Cook presented a more elaborate version of his 'master diagram' with these alignments shown. Robert Bauval proposed that the 26.5° angle was probably chosen to indicate the point of sunrise at the time of the heliacal rising of the lowest star of Orion's Belt as it would have appeared *c.*2450 BC.[3] Once more, it would seem, the ancient Egyptians had combined geometry – the 26.5° angle is important as it gives the diagonal of a double square and is the same as the angle of slope of the descending passage of the Great Pyramid – and astronomy. Yet even this was only part of the story; the appendix did not explain the purpose of the 30° alignment through the subsidiaries of the Menkaure pyramid. Robert and I discussed this, but as it did not seem particularly relevant to our central theme at that time, we left out any explanation of this important alignment from the book.

The major theme of *The Orion Mystery*, that the three major pyramids of Giza were laid out to represent the stars of Orion's Belt, stands independently of when and in which order they were built. It is, however, generally accepted that the order of building of the pyramids was first Khufu's, then Khafre's and finally Menkaure's. This would seem to imply that the satellite pyramids to the east of G1 were built long before and independently of those south of G111. Yet for the subsidiary pyramids to be aligned with the centre of the Khafre pyramid in the way Cook indicates this layout would have to have been designed *before* the building of the Great Pyramid. There has to have been an overall design plan for all the pyramids, taking as its centre G11, the Khafre pyramid. Yet how could this be if, as the archaeology indicates, the Great Pyramid pre-dates the Khafre pyramid? The only possible answer to this is that all were built in accordance with an overall Giza master plan. The question then is, how was this plan marked out in practice?

One possible answer to this question, which we tentatively suggested in *The Orion Mystery*, would be that the pyramids were placed on top of earlier structures. These earlier structures, which may not even have been pyramidal in shape, could have been built long before the time of Khufu, Khafre and Menkaure; indeed, before Egypt was desertified. Their purported existence could even be what excited Gurdjieff so much when he first saw the map of 'pre-sand Egypt'. The pyramids we see today could then have been built in any order so long as they were placed on top of or as replacements for these earlier buildings. The Giza alignments would still have been retained.

We can, alas, only guess at what structures may lie concealed within the present-day pyramids, for nobody is going to tear them apart to see what earlier buildings they may or may not contain. However, these putative earlier structures could have been the handiwork of the generation of Thoth/Hermes. If their existence could be proven beyond doubt, then we would have an explanation for how it is that the pyramids are said to have been designed by Thoth and also by Imhotep (Asclepius), the vizier of Zoser, who lived thousands of years later and only a generation or two before Khufu. As the Khafre pyramid is the central unit in the whole plan of the Giza necropolis, it seems likely that it was placed either on top of or in place of the central temple, the remains of which may still be entombed underneath the present pyramid. The alignments from this structure towards the summer solstice position (now marked by the lines between the Khafre pyramid and the G1 subsidiaries) could have predated the building of the current pyramids in c.2450 BC in just the same way that the summer solstice alignment over the Heelstone at Stonehenge pre-dates the later building of the sarsen and blue stone circles on that site. If this is so, then the question comes back to: when might these earlier structures, which pre-dated today's pyramids, have been built and towards what might the other, 30°, alignment towards the subsidiaries of G111 have been directed?

The answer to this is very simple, once one follows the logic of time and precession. In *The Orion Mystery* we presented the theory that the Egyptian *Tep Zepi* or 'first Time' corresponded with the epoch represented in Plato's dialogues as seeing the destruction of Atlantis. Following the line of the famous American clairvoyant Edgar Cayce, we suggested that this was *c.*10,500 BC. This was the time when the Belt of Orion would have been at its lowest in the sky. As the Belt stars set to the south-west of Giza, so they would have formed an angle of approximately 27° west of the southern meridian drawn from G2, the Khafre pyramid. This is close to, but not precisely in alignment with, the Cook line; but if we go back a further 330 years to *c.*10,880, then the alignment is exact. This, I now discovered, indicated something else of enormous importance. For whereas in *c.*10,500 the Belt of Orion was at the lowest part of its cycle, in *c.*10,880 BC the winter solstice would have occurred when the sun was right over the hand of Orion. Thus, by marking the position of the Belt stars with the 30° angle at this epoch, the pyramid builders were indeed indicating the 'First Time'. However, this was not so much the beginning of Egyptian civilization but rather of the 'Age of Orion'; or, to put it in biblical terms, the 'Age of the Son of man'. This, I now realized, must have been what was at the forefront of Egyptian esoteric thinking.

With this last part of the jigsaw puzzle of the pyramids in place, it was possible to see what Giza was really all about. It was a map of time, or rather of our present Age of Adam. The Menkaure satellite pyramids indicated the beginning of the age when the Orion stargate was in its most southerly position and the Scorpio one in its most northerly. Then, as the earth precessed about its axis, so these gateways began to exchange positions, like two cosmic elevators moving in opposite directions. By the time the pyramids were built they were well over half-way through their journey.

In *c.*2450 BC, the date that Robert and I proposed for the building of the Great Pyramid, the sun when conjunct with Regulus would have risen at exactly 27.5° north of

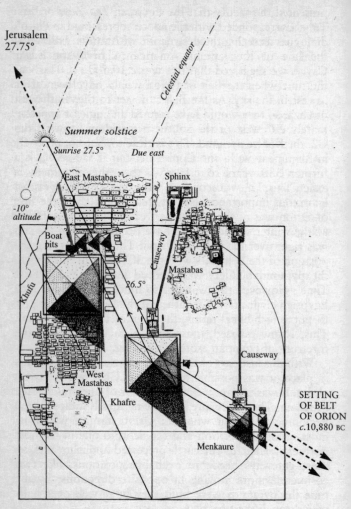

Jerusalem
27.75°

Celestial equator

Summer solstice

Sunrise 27.5° Due east

East Mastabas Sphinx

-10°
altitude

Boat
pits

Khufu Causeway

Mastabas

26.5°

West
Mastabas Causeway

Khafre

SETTING
OF BELT
OF ORION
c.10,880 BC

Menkaure

THE 'COOK' DIAGRAM SHOWING THE AGE OF ORION FROM
THE FIRST TIME TO THE END OF DAYS

east as seen from Giza. This would still have been true a few days later at the summer solstice. The sun would have reached the angle of 26.5° within five minutes of rising, when it was visible as a great red ball. At that time it would have been perfectly aligned with the 'Cook lines' drawn through the satellite pyramids G1a, G1b and G1c. At the time the Egyptians built their pyramids this would have been an exciting sight, which they no doubt linked with their own age of Leo, but today it marks something even more remarkable. Now, when the sun is in the solstice position, it stands over the hand of Orion. It is in fact in line with the stargate itself, which is now to be found in its most northerly position. To use the metaphor of the elevator once more, it has reached the top of the building and it is now time for the doors to open and the passengers to disembark. This, then, seems to be the message of Giza: that it marks out the period of the grand cycle of Orion, that is to say the 'Age of Adam', from its beginnings c.10,880 BC to its end c.AD 2000. Even today the Egyptians have a saying: 'Man fears Time but Time fears the Pyramids.' Well time might, for they have its measure.

As if this were not enough, the Cook lines have one more message for us. The alignment of 27.5° turned out to be very curious, for it can be shown by spherical geometry that a line drawn from the Khafre pyramid with an angle of 27.75° points towards Jerusalem. The sun has an overall diameter of 0.5°, which means that as it rises on the solstice so its left-most edge, i.e. the part of it that is furthest north, points directly towards Jerusalem. At the time the pyramids were built and for long afterwards the summer solstice occurred in the constellation of Leo. This, I thought at the time, was a remarkable coincidence and could be an explanation for the prophetic name of Jerusalem as Ariel or 'Lion of God'. However, as we have seen, today the solstice occurs when the sun is in the shake-hands position above the outstretched hand of Orion. Thus, whereas at the time the pyramids were built the summer solstice rising pointed towards Jerusalem as the future lion city, today it can be said that it points to it as the city of the ascended Jesus. How this tied in with the Matthew prophecies was the subject of the next stage of my quest.

The text which still interested me most was chapter 24 of Matthew's Gospel, which describes the signs that people are to look out for as heralding the end of the age. One of these signs was the branch of a fig tree putting forth new leaves. This, as the old man in Tel Aviv had explained to me, signified the rebirth of the state of Israel in 1948 following the return of the Jews after nearly 2,000 years of exile. I understood from this that there would be a period of some seventy years, notionally one lifetime, during which all the other prophecies were to be accomplished. This gave a date of 2018 by which time the Second Coming, whatever we mean by this term, would have happened. There were, however, other more specific prophecies concerning other signs in the sky that would be seen prior to this date. These were contained in verses 27 and 28:

> For as the lighning cometh out of the east, and shineth unto the west; so shall also the coming of the Son of man be. For wheresoever the carcass is, there will the eagles be gathered together.
>
> Immediately after the tribulation of those days shall the sun be darkened, and the moon shall not give her light, and the stars shall fall from heaven, and the powers of the heavens shall be shaken:
>
> And then shall appear the sign of the Son of man in heaven: and then shall all the tribes of the earth mourn, and they shall see the Son of man coming in the clouds of heaven with power and great glory.

Properly to understand the prophecies in the Bible it is best, where possible, to go back to the original language in which they were written. That way one has a better chance of not being misled by mistranslations of important words or even misunderstandings of subtle nuances. Turning now to the Greek version of Matthew's Gospel, I discovered that the word used here for 'lightning' is ἀστραπη (*astrape*) which is remarkably similar to ἀστερεσ (*asteres*), a word which means 'stars'. Could it be, I wondered, that either deliberately by Matthew to obscure the meaning of his text, or accidentally by some later copyist who had no idea what the prophecy could relate to, the Greek word for 'lightning' had been substituted for 'stars'? Given that the Greek letter rho (ρ) looks like a 'p' in Latin, this seemed entirely possible. It could be that a pi (π) had first been inserted by mistake and ἀστερεσ miswritten as ἀστρεπεσ. A later copyist, realizing that this was wrong, could have changed the word to αστραπη, thinking that he was correcting the error but actually introducing another. This seems to me entirely likely, given that all ancient manuscripts were handwritten and subject to errors of this sort. If this is so, then in English the passage in question should really read: 'For as the *stars* cometh out of the east, and shineth unto the west; so shall also the coming of the Son of man be.' Even if this were not the case, both ἀστραπη and ἀστερεσ come from the same root word ἀστρο, which though translated as 'star' really means a light. Even in English there remains this duality in meaning for the word 'lightning', which literally means something that 'lightens' the sky. I therefore concluded that this passage was talking about stars and not electrical flashes.

As we have seen, the 'Son of man' is a term used to describe prophets in some way associated with the constellation of Orion. It seemed obvious, therefore, that the prophesied return of the Son of man would in some way be connected with this constellation. This began to make sense of the passage above. Because of the precession of the equinoxes, the stars of Orion's Belt have been moving steadily northwards for the past 13,000 years. While over this time they have remained more or less constant in relation to one another and indeed to the ecliptic, the path of the sun, they have moved relative to the celestial equator. At the time the pyramids were built (c.2500 BC) they would have been seen to reach a maximum height of 45° from the Cairo area, but today the northernmost star of the belt, Mintaka, is poised just under the celestial equator. This, I discovered, is the end of its cycle, for it will never actually cross the equator into the northern hemisphere before it starts to retreat back south.

The fact that Mintaka now sits close to the celestial equator means that when viewed from Heliopolis it crosses the southern meridian with an angle of 60°. This is the same angle as that cast by the equinoctial sun and means that when in the south Mintaka will, for a few minutes, literally stand on top of the great obelisk of Senusert III and generate the *vesica piscis*. This seemed to have some symbolic significance, as both the obelisk and the Belt of Orion were in some way viewed by the Egyptians as being symbolic of the phallus of God. The coincidence of these two images therefore seemed to link the fertilizing power of Osiris in the sky with the obelisk. This position of Orion's Belt could therefore symbolize the idea of the returning phoenix at the end of one age and the beginning of another. I was soon to discover, however, that there is far more to it than this, with striking implications for Jerusalem.

At the beginning of chapter 24 of Matthew's Gospel the writer had talked about looking for the signs of the end of the 'world' – but this word too had been mistranslated: in the original Greek it was αἰωνοσ, meaning aeon or age. Returning to the Matthew prophecy, which was delivered in a sermon given on the Mount of Olives, I remembered that it was over this hilltop that I had seen Orion rising while standing on the roof of the Petra Hotel. The prophecy speaks of 'lightning', a word I now interpreted as meaning stars, rising in the east and setting in the west. Now, only stars which are on, or at least very close to, the celestial equator can be said to rise exactly in the east and set in the west. Today, uniquely in human history, the Belt of Orion – or, more properly speaking, its most northerly star, Mintaka – performs this feat. As the Belt stars, sometimes referred to as 'Jacob's staff', form the central part of the constellation associated with the symbol known as the 'Son of man', this was of enormous significance. As the rising of the Belt of Orion to its most northerly position represents the culmination of a long period or age that lasted for nearly 13,000 years it seemed to me that this, and not hypothetical lightning, was the sign which we had been told to look out for as heralding the end of the aeon; and the aeon in question was not the Age of Pisces but rather the much longer Age of Adam, as charted by the movements of Orion.

The identification of Orion as the primary symbol for the 'Son of man in heaven' I now found to be the key to understanding many other strange prophecies contained in the Book of Revelation. This, the last book of the Bible, is prophetically linked with the earlier Book of Daniel.[4] Though there are some doubts about its authorship, it is generally believed to have been written by St John of Patmos, who was probably the same person as the apostle of that name.

The Book of Revelation is an extraordinary work that has perplexed even the most erudite scholars. It presents a deeply disturbing account of St John's visions concerning judgement day at the end of the present age. In these visions he is guided by an angelic being, who initially calls himself, rather mysteriously, 'Alpha and Omega, the first and the last'. John falls into a trance in the company of this vast being, who has much in common with the entity Ποιμανδρεσ (Poimandres), 'the Shepherd of Men', who in similar circumstances appears to Hermes Trismegistus in *Libellus I* of the *Corpus Hermeticum*. In his Revelation, John is very specific in his description of this being:

I was in the spirit on the Lord's day, and heard behind me a great voice, as of a trumpet, Saying, I am Alpha and Omega, the first and the last: and, What thou seest, write in a book, and send it unto the seven churches which are in Asia unto Ephesus, and unto Smyrna, and unto Pergamos, and unto Thyatira, and unto Sardis, and unto Philadelphia, and unto Laodicea.

And I turned to see the voice that spake with me. And being turned I saw seven golden candlesticks; And in the midst of the seven candlesticks one like unto a Son of man, clothed with a garment down to the foot, and girt about the paps with a golden girdle.

His head and his hairs were white like wool, as white as snow; and his eyes were as a flame of fire; and his feet like unto fine brass, as if they burned in a furnace; and his voice as the sound of many waters.

And he had in his right hand seven stars: and out of his mouth went a sharp two-edged sword: and his countenance was as the sun shineth in his strength.

And when I saw him, I fell at his feet as dead. And he laid his right hand upon me, saying unto me, Fear not; I am the first and the last: I am he that liveth, and was dead; and behold, I am alive for evermore, Amen; and have the keys of hell and death.

Write the things which thou hast seen, and the things which are, and the things which shall be hereafter;

The mystery of the seven stars which thou sawest in my right hand, and the seven golden candlesticks. The seven stars are the angels of the seven churches: and the seven golden candlesticks which thou sawest are the seven churches. (Rev. 1: 10–20)

Reading the above, it became evident to me that the angelic figure calling itself 'the Alpha and Omega, the first and last' and likened to a 'Son of man' was clearly Orion. Confirmation of this was the reference to the golden girdle, the connection with the seven candlesticks and finally the idea that the seven stars (actually the planets or governors) could be contained in his hand. Orion is the only constellation which is like a man in its shape, which has a belt and which at times holds the planets, the seven stars, in its outstretched hand. Jesus had supposedly risen into heaven forty days after his resurrection on the very day when the sun was in its 'St Christopher' or 'shake-hands' position. Thus Orion now also symbolized the ascended Jesus. He was the second Adam who had redeemed the first and consequently the symbol of Adam Kadmon, the man in the sky, was now to be understood as Jesus' 'star form' as it had been that of the ascended Osiris in the days of ancient Egypt.

I was in no doubt that Orion symbolized the ascended Jesus Christ as the 'Son of man'. However, in the Book of Revelation he is depicted neither as the archetypal hero nor as a prophet but rather as the Lord of Time. It was therefore clear that we are expected to see Orion as a marker of the ages: the letter A (alpha), the beginning or first letter of the Greek alphabet, signified the beginning of the Age of Adam, while the last letter Ω (omega) represented its end. Now, as we have seen, *Tep Zepi* or the 'First Time' symbolized to the Egyptians the beginning of their civilization. To them this was the period when the gods had walked the earth bringing knowledge and civilization to a waiting world. This time seemed to correspond roughly with the ending of Plato's civilization of Atlantis (*c.*9500 BC) and linked in astronomically speaking with when the shake-hands position was at its lowest latitude. This I could now see represented the A position, the time when the stargate was symbolically closed at the beginning of the Age of Adam. This is not an arbitrary date; it corresponds very closely with what is believed by geologists to have been the end of the last Ice Age and the beginning of the Palaeolithic period when modern man emerged. According to the religious philosopher J. G. Bennett it was also the time when evolving mankind went through a major change of consciousness. Ever since then, because of the precessional cycle, the constellation of Orion has been moving steadily northwards. This being the case, the Ω position had, by inference, to symbolize the 'Last Time' or 'End of Days'. Then, for a short time, the doors of heaven would be re-opened. This would be the time of judgement spoken of in the Book of Revelation. As the shake-hands position is now at its zenith and is occupied by the sun when he 'shineth in his strength' at the summer solstice, I realized with some trepidation that this had to be about now. Accordingly I went back to the computer to see if there were any more clues as to exactly when the doors might be opened and the judgement begin.

The SKYGLOBE program showed that the Belt of Orion will reach its most northerly position in *c.* AD 2380, which seems quite a long way off. However, because the 'shake-hands' position on the ecliptic is not in line with the belt but some 6° further round the celestial globe, it peaks earlier. In fact the shake-hands position has already reached the top of its cycle, around 1938. However, because the space over Orion's hand occupies about 2° on the ecliptic, and the precessional cycle moves about 1° every seventy years, the solstice position will stay over Orion's hand until approximately the end of the next century. It is now in the middle of the hand. This seemed to mean that it would be during this time, and probably within the first twenty years of the twenty-first century, while the solstice would occur with the sun above the centre of Orion's outstretched hand, that the stargate would be symbolically open, the 'Age of Man' having been declared at its end. With Orion at the Ω position, this would also be the time when the prophecies of St John in the Book of Revelation would be fulfilled. This was all still rather vague; but I was now to find further confirmation for this as well as what I now believe to be details of the exact date on which the stargate will be formally opened.

In chapter 24 of Matthew's Gospel, just after the verse

mentioning lightning, there is a further cryptic comment: 'Wheresoever the carcass is, there will the eagles [or vultures, according to some translations] be gathered together.' I had first taken note of this prophecy while reading in the Golan in 1972. Now, pondering it again, its meaning became clear. As any number of wildlife documentaries will testify, out in the savannah carrion birds (eagles or vultures) fly round and round in circles waiting and anticipating the death of an animal, such as a sheep, so that they can feast on its body. Clearly the sign we were to see related to something similar. We were to look out for something that symbolically resembles eagles or vultures, flying round in circles waiting for death to supply them with a carcass. Given the context of the prophecy, towards the end of the Gospel, and the subsequent climax of the book with the death and resurrection of Jesus himself, the 'carcass' in question had to be his own dead body; the likelihood was that the circling vultures had something to do with his crucifixion on Calvary.

As discussed earlier, the most likely year for Jesus' crucifixion is AD 29 and the date was almost certainly 15 April. Jesus is often referred to as the Agnus Dei or 'Lamb of God', and it is well understood by those who have studied the meaning behind Christian symbols that there is a connection between the death of Jesus and the sacrifice of the Paschal lamb in commemoration of the Exodus from Egypt. The point is well made by John Baldock: 'In the establishment of the New Covenant the Crucifixion is the once-and-for-all living human sacrifice of the Son, the Lamb of God, which abolishes the animal sacrifice of the Passover lamb.'[4] Using SKYGLOBE I had been able to show that the sun would, at midday on 15 April AD 29, have been positioned directly under Delta-Aries, the last star in that constellation and the appropriate place for the death of a man who is often referred to mystically as the sacrificial Lamb of God. However, there was something else noteworthy on this day and that is the position of the planets. With the exception of the moon, which being below the horizon was not present at the Crucifixion, they were all in the same vicinity in the sky. Thus when Jesus was crucified, in the sky above him, like so many circling eagles, were Saturn, Mars, Mercury and Venus in Taurus, the sun in Aries and Jupiter rather lower in the sky in Pisces. Without going into the significance of what this horoscope may or may not have meant, it seems to me that these circling planets were what Jesus refers to as the 'eagles' gathering over his carcass. In this sense they were signs in the sky indicative of his imminent death. He was, however, not just prophesying his own death, which has little significance in the context of the end of the age; he was talking about something else relating to our own times, for, as I now discovered, we are shortly to see, nearly 2,000 years later, a repetition of this configuration – only expressed in a far more powerful way.

Taking the computer forwards to a date of AD 2000 I found that something very significant would happen when the sun was in the constellation of Aries. On 8 May there would be a very unusual, multiple conjunction between the sun and the planets Mercury, Saturn and Jupiter: the 'three kings' of Jesus' Nativity horoscope. To make this an even more spectacular event, the planet Venus would also be in Aries, roughly 8° behind the sun, while Mars would be in the neighbouring sign of Taurus, but still only about 16° ahead. Thus six of the seven planets of the ancients (once more minus the moon) would all be clustered very tightly together. This close grouping of the planets is a very rare occurrence and it was, I could see, scheduled to happen directly over the head of Cetus the Whale. Could this, I wondered, be the sign of Jonah and the whale which we had been told to look out for?

Going back to Matthew's Gospel, I once more found the text in question where Jesus castigates the Pharisees for not recognizing him, and read it in full:

> Then some of the scribes and Pharisees said to him,
> 'Teacher, we wish to see a sign from you,' But he
> answered them, 'An evil and adulterous generation
> seeks a sign; but no sign shall be given to it except the
> sign of the prophet Jonah. For as Jonah was three days
> and three nights in the belly of the whale, so will the Son
> of man be three days and nights in the heart of the
> earth. The men of Nineveh will arise at the judgement
> with this generation and condemn it; for they repented
> at the preaching of Jonah, and behold, something
> greater than Jonah is here. The queen of the South will
> arise at the judgement with this generation and con-
> demn it; for she came from the ends of the earth to hear
> the wisdom of Solomon, and, behold, something greater
> than Solomon is here.' (Matt. 12: 38–42)

While this passage seemed at first to refer to the burial
of Jesus in the tomb prior to his resurrection, it was
clearly erroneous in saying he would be underground for
three days and nights. From sunset on Good Friday to
sunrise on Easter Sunday was only thirty-six hours, or a
day and a half. Not only that, but if the Gospels are to be
believed the claim that Jesus would give no 'signs' to his
own generation was also factually wrong. He performed
hundreds of miraculous healings, walked on water,
turned water into wine, multiplied loaves and fishes and
even raised people from the dead. Surely, then, there was
no shortage of signs for his own generation. I was therefore by now fully convinced that he was really addressing
himself to another 'evil and adulterous generation' that
would be alive later, at the end of the age.

This tied in with something else I could see in the stars
for spring 2000. Three days and three nights after the
amazing conjunction in Aries, on 11 May 2000 the sun
would be positioned under the star Delta-Aries, and
therefore in the same position it had been in at the time

of the Crucifixion. On this day, though the conjunction of the sun with Mercury and Jupiter would not be as tight, the sun would still be aligned with Saturn. It would also be much closer to Mars and Venus. We would therefore be witness to the scenario of the same six planets circling close to the sun as they had done on the day of the Crucifixion in AD 29. Could this, I wondered, be the sign we are told to watch out for of 'eagles' gathering over the carcass?

Once more, reference to the original Greek text indicated that this was probably so. The word for eagles is αετοι (*aetoi*), which is very similar to αστερι (*asteri*), meaning 'star'. This seems to me to be a means of concealing the real meaning of the prophecy until such time as it is applicable. The gathering of the planets in this manner in the immediate vicinity of Delta-Aries is a far from common event. It is unlikely to have happened before in the two millennia since the time of Jesus' crucifixion, and it has certainly not previously occurred over this period with Orion, the sign of the Son of man, reaching its most northerly position.

This gathering of the planets in Aries is, I now believe, only the harbinger of even more significant events scheduled around the solstice in the year 2000. On 21–2 June the sun will rise at Giza in alignment with the direction of Jerusalem. It will, as it has always done at the summer solstice, shine upon the east and west of the Khafre pyramid without casting any shadow. On this day Orion will hold in his hand the *ankh* (symbolized by the sun) and place it in the lock which seals the northern stargate. This ties in with St John's Revelation, where it is said that the First and Last, the cosmic form of Christ, holds the 'keys to Death and Hades'. He clearly uses these keys at the start of the book, for shortly after meeting this great being St John says: 'After this I looked, and lo, in heaven an open door! And the first voice, which I had heard speaking to me like a trumpet, said, "Come up hither, and I will show you what

354

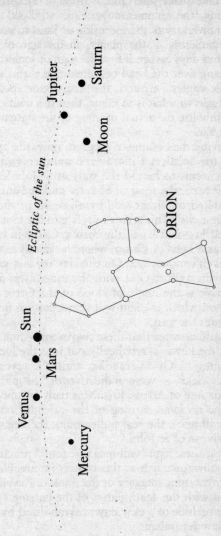

STELLAR SIGNATURE OF ORION (ALPHA AND OMEGA) STANDING AMID THE 'SEVEN CANDLESTICKS', 29 JUNE AD 2000

Saturn

Jupiter

Moon

Ecliptic of the sun

Sun

Mars

Venus

Mercury

ORION

must take place after this"' (Rev. 4: 1). Astronomically speaking, the summer solstice of AD 2000 will be the first anniversary of the ascension of Jesus to occur after the great gathering of the planets in the sign of Aries some forty-five days earlier. If first the 'sign of Jonah' (the planets gathering over the head of Cetus) and then the 'gathering of the eagles' around the crucifixion position were harbingers of what is to come, then this configuration had to symbolize the actual opening of the stargate at the end of the age.

Moving the computer program onwards by eight days from the solstice, I discovered another sign in the sky which seems to herald the start of St John's Revelation. On 29 June, the feast of St Peter and St Paul, Orion will be flanked on either side by all seven of the planets or 'candlesticks'. This seems to relate to the first appearance of the 'First and Last', the cosmic Christ in his risen star form as a Lord or Orion, where he stands in the midst of the seven candlesticks. On this day the sun will cross the east–west axis at Giza with the magical pi angle of 51° 51'. This is the angle of slope of the Great Pyramid of Giza, on which the sun will shine, casting no shadow as it crosses the axis.

I could now see that these two events – first the solstice, when the key is symbolically put into the lock, and then the figure of Orion standing amid the seven planets or 'candlesticks' – were indicative of the passing of the present Age of Adam. It is these truly cosmic events, and not the notional turning of the calendar on 1 January, that will mark the real millennium: the beginning of the apocalypse of St John.

What these signs will mean in actual practice for those of us alive on earth at this time is impossible to predict. The frightening imagery of the Book of Revelation is concerned with the death pangs of the passing age, but only as the prelude to a new dawn, symbolized by the birth of the New Jerusalem:

356

And I saw the holy city, new Jerusalem, coming down out of heaven from God, prepared as a bride adorned for her husband; and I heard a great voice from the throne saying, 'Behold, the dwelling of God is with men. He will dwell with them, and they shall be his people, and God himself will be with them; . . .'

And he who sat upon the throne said, 'Behold, I will make all things new.' Also he said, 'Write this, for these words are trustworthy and true.' And he said to me, 'It is done! I am the Alpha and the Omega, the beginning and the end. To the thirsty I will give water without price from the fountain of the water of life. He who conquers shall have this heritage, and I will be his God and he will be my son.' (Rev. 21: 1–7)

These are comforting words that indiate that the birth of the new age is not really to be dreaded but rather looked forward to. It could be, as Bennett evidently believed, a time when a new race of humankind will appear, one as different from us as we are from the Cro-Magnons and Neanderthals who preceded us. As I pondered these momentous possibilities my attention turned once more towards the Mount of Olives, where the prophets have said certain other major events are to unfold.

CHAPTER 18

THE TRIBULATION OF ISRAEL

When I returned to Jerusalem in 1998, I was surprised at how much the city had changed – not least the area of the Kidron valley. I remembered this from my first visit, more than twenty-five years earlier, as an untidy scrap of land, filled with garbage and with a reputation for banditry. My guidebook still warned travellers to beware of pickpockets and muggers when visiting this area, and women were definitely discouraged from walking there alone; but it was now much tidier than I remembered, laid out with viewing points almost like an ornamental garden. However, the true significance of the Mount of Olives really only struck me after I returned home and reviewed the rising of Orion which I had seen in person from the rooftop of the Petra Hotel.

Jesus, we know, visited the Mount of Olives on more than one occasion. Indeed, it was on a previous visit, a few days before his betrayal, that he made his strange prophecies concerning the fig tree and eagles circling round a carcass. At the same time as he made these predictions, he also made certain prophecies concerning the fate of Jerusalem and the judgement of the world:

> And as he sat upon the Mount of Olives, the disciples came unto him privately, saying, 'Tell us, when shall these things be? And what shall be the sign of thy coming, and of the end of the world?'
>
> And Jesus answered them and said unto them, 'Take

heed that no man deceive you. For many shall come in my name, saying, I am Christ; and shall deceive many. And ye shall hear of wars and rumours of wars: see that ye be not troubled: for all these things must come to pass, but the end is not yet. For nation shall rise against nation, and kingdom against kingdom: and there shall be famines, and pestilences and earthquakes, in divers places. All these are the beginning of sorrows. And then shall they deliver you up to be afflicted, and shall kill you: and ye shall be hated of all nations for my name's sake. And then shall many be offended, and shall betray one another, and shall hate one another. And many false prophets shall rise, and shall deceive many. And because iniquity shall abound, the love of many shall wax cold. But he that shall endure unto the end, the same shall be saved. And this gospel of the kingdom shall be preached in all the world for a witness unto all nations; and then shall the end come.

When ye therefore shall see the abomination of desolation, spoken of by Daniel the prophet, stand in the holy place (whoso readeth, let him understand): Then let them which be in Judaea flee into the mountains: Let him which is on the housetop not come down to take anything out of his house: Neither let him which is in the field return back to take his clothes. And woe to them that are with child, and to them that give suck in those days! But pray ye that your flight be not in the winter, neither on the sabbath day: For then shall be great tribulation, such as was not since the beginning of the world to this time, no, nor ever shall be. And except that those days be shortened, there should be no flesh saved: but for the elect's sake those days shall be shortened . . . Immediately after the tribulation of those days shall the sun be darkened and the moon shall not give her light, and the stars shall fall from heaven, and the powers of the heavens shall be shaken. (Matt. 24: 3–29)

This whole speech, which these days is rarely

mentioned by the mainstream church, is the source of much of the millennial expectation currently engulfing Jerusalem. For, in terms unfashionable among liberal Christians, it speaks unequivocally of a day of judgement and a time of great upheavals at the end of the current age. At the eye of this storm will stand the Holy City of Jerusalem, the scene of many major conflicts in the past as well as the present; and the focus of attention will be the Mount of Olives.

There has been much debate over the centuries regarding what is to be understood by the 'abomination of desolation' standing in the holy place. The words come directly from the prophecy at the end of the Book of Daniel, where it is written:

And at the time shall arise Michael, the great prince, who has charge of your people. And there shall be a time of trouble, such as never has been since there was a nation till that time; but at that time your people shall be delivered, every one whose name shall be found written in the book. And many of those who sleep in the dust of the earth shall awake, some to everlasting life, and some to shame and everlasting contempt. And those who are wise shall shine like the brightness of the firmament; and those who turn many to righteousness, like the stars for ever and ever. But you, Daniel, shut up the words, and seal the book, until the time of the end: many shall run to and fro, and knowledge shall increase.

Then I, Daniel looked, and, behold, two others stood, one on this bank of the stream and one on that bank of the stream. And I said to the man clothed in linen, who was above the waters of the river, 'How long shall it be till the end of these wonders?' The man clothed in linen, which was upon the waters of the river, raised his right hand and his left hand toward heaven, and I heard him swear by him who lives for ever that it would be for a time, two times and half a time; and that when the shattering of the power of the holy people comes to an end all these things would be accomplished. I heard, but I did not understand. Then I said, 'O my lord, what shall be the issue of these things?' He said, 'Go your way, Daniel, for the words are shut up and sealed until the time of the end. Many shall purify themselves, and make themselves white, and be refined; but the wicked shall do wickedly; and none of the wicked shall understand; but those who are wise shall understand. And from the time that the daily offering is taken away, and the abomination that makes desolate is set up, there shall be a thousand two hundred and ninety days. Blessed is he who waits and comes to the thousand three hundred and thirty-five days. But go your way till the end; for you shall rest, and shall stand in your allotted place at the end of the days.' (Dan. 12: 1–13)

This passage has always puzzled commentators, not least in its cryptic numerology. What is clear is that the period of 1,290 days is very close to the three and a half years (or 'time, two times and half a time') mentioned by Daniel earlier in the same passage and also by John in the Book of Revelation (12: 14). Nor is it in doubt that the 'holy place' from which the daily sacrifice is to be removed is the sanctuary of the Temple of Jerusalem. The question is: when will these events occur? The reference in Daniel to the 'abomination that makes desolate' is thought to be a prophecy referring to some future event comparable to the takeover of Jerusalem by Antiochus IV Epiphanes of Syria (r.175–164 BC) in 168 BC.[1] He, having been driven out of Egypt, fell upon Jerusalem and sought to Hellenize the Jews. He is said to have sacrificed a pig on the high altar, thereby desecrating it with the blood of this and other animals considered unclean by the Jews. He also turned the Temple over to the worship of Zeus Olympius and set up an idol described as the 'abomination that makes desolate' in the first Book of Maccabees.

These irreligious acts led to the revolt of the Maccabees, who, exactly three years later, having defeated Antiochus' armies and retaken Jerusalem, rededicated the Temple.

Jesus' speech on the Mount of Olives was made some 200 years after the desecration of the Temple by Antiochus, so he could not have been prophesying this event even if this is indeed what Daniel was referring to. However, his surviving disciples could have been forgiven for thinking that they were witnesses to the end of the world. For in AD 66, during the reign of the mad emperor Nero, the Jews revolted and strove to break free from the yoke of Rome. Their uprising was brutally suppressed by Vespasian and in AD 70, as a punishment for their daring to oppose the might of Rome, the Temple at Jerusalem, which had been built by King Herod barely a hundred years earlier, was demolished. Forty-five years later, in AD 115, the Jews rose again. This revolt was put down by Hadrian, then still only a general. A third revolt, led by Simon Bar Kochba in 132–5, was also suppressed and the surviving Jews were expelled from Judea altogether. Hadrian, by now emperor, commissioned a new Roman city called Aelia Capitolina, and a Temple of Venus was built over the old sanctuary. Jews were not allowed to enter this city, which forms the core of the present Old City; but that did not stop them from lamenting the loss of their former capital. This destruction of Jerusalem, and still more the raising of the temple to Venus, could be considered an 'abomination that makes desolate'. Yet it is clear that even this catastrophe was not the end of the world as we know it. It would seem that we have yet to see the true fulfilment of Jesus' prophecies for the 'tribulation'.

Today, once again, the Temple Mount in Jerusalem is a focus of tension. In 1967 the Israelis captured the Old City and brought it under Jewish jurisdiction for the first time since the reign of King Herod nearly 2,000 years earlier. Since then the Jews have been able to pray and celebrate in the space next to the Western or 'Wailing'

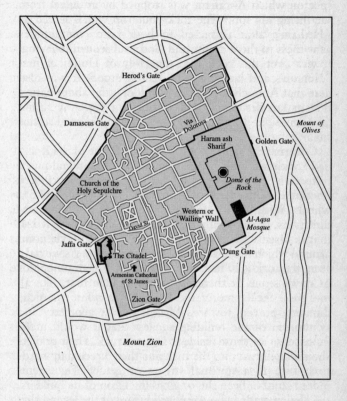

Herod's Gate

Damascus Gate

Via Dolorosa

Mount of Olives

Haram ash Sharif

Golden Gate

Church of the Holy Sepulchre

Dome of the Rock

Western or 'Wailing' Wall

Al-Aqsa Mosque

David St.

Jaffa Gate

The Citadel

Dung Gate

Armenian Cathedral of St James

Zion Gate

Mount Zion

OLD JERUSALEM

Wall, which is all that remains visible of Herod's Temple. Still, however, a question mark hangs over the precincts of the Temple itself, which most Orthodox Jews wish to see rebuilt. At the epicentre of all these events is Mount Moriah, believed by Jews and Muslims alike to be the spot on which Abraham was stopped by an angel from sacrificing his son.[2] The rocky outcrop which served as Abraham's altar is sacred to both faith communities as witness to these events and God's subsequent blessing. It was over this rock that the Holy of Holies of first Solomon's and later Herod's Temple stood. It was also here that Antiochus IV placed an idol – the abomination that makes desolate – and sacrificed a pig. Any future 'abomination' must surely in some way be related to this site.

Covering the same spot today is the Dome of the Rock, or El Sakhrah, built by the Muslims in AD 688 and much restored since. As is befitting for the covering of a *kibleh* (in this case the rock of Abraham), it is shaped like a wheel. With doors facing in each of the cardinal directions, north, south, east and west, it is eight-sided so that in a sense the rock at its centre is like an axle point around which the heavens are seen to revolve. As we have seen, the rock is in fact, in a classical sense, an omphalos or navel stone. It therefore seems strange that, like all mosques, the Dome of the Rock has a *mirab* or niche directing prayers towards Mecca; for the geometry and symbolism of the building suggest that it would make more sense for those inside to face the rock. Their prayers should be drawn into the rock and then directed upwards to heaven in a spiritual stream or geyser. This seems indeed to have been the original intention of its builders, the Ummayyads, who were well aware of the legend that it was from here that Mohammed is supposed to have ascended to heaven on his night journey. For them at least, the rock of Jerusalem was the more important *kibleh* and it seems doubtful if in their time the Dome contained a *mirab* directed towards Mecca.

The journey of Mohammed, as well as the role of the rock in the legend of Abraham and Isaac, implies that Jerusalem is to be thought of as yet another door to heaven. To emphasize this connection the rock has a cave beneath it, which I entered on my first visit to Jerusalem in 1972. It was through a vertical 'well shaft' cut through the rock, which symbolically linked this cave with the heavens above, that Mohammed is said to have commenced his journey. At that time there would have been no dome over the rock, so that the shaft pointed straight up into the sky. By the time of Mohammed the star Algol no longer passed over this zenith position. However, Mohammed is said to have made his night journey carried aloft on the back of a fabulous flying creature. It is therefore not without significance that, as we have seen, at the latitude of Jerusalem the constellation of Cygnus, the Swan, would daily still have been seen directly overhead. This bright northern constellation, which in Christian iconography signifies the cross raised by the Agnus Dei, 'flies' along the Milky Way towards Sagittarius and Scorpio. Alternatively, it can be seen that as Orion rises in the east, so the constellation of Andromeda, riding on the back of Pegasus the flying horse, passes directly over the well shaft. The myth of Mohammed's flight to heaven from Jerusalem would therefore seem to be an allusion to one or other of these astronomical facts.

In all of these ways the rock of Jerusalem can be seen to have had a similar symbolic function to the Great Pyramid of Egypt. For like that building, it was a place of ascension to the stars, its well shaft having a similar spiritual function to the air shafts of the pyramid. There is, however, a further link between Jerusalem, the Pyramids of Giza and Orion. As we have seen, the direction of sunrise at Giza on the summer solstice points directly towards the Jerusalem area. If continued eastwards, this line linking the pyramids with Jerusalem would cut the Jordan river near to where John was baptizing and Elijah made his own flight to heaven. Thus, by a process of transference, Jerusalem would seem to have been regarded by the ancients as in some way connected with the Orion stargate even though it does not lie inside the Jordan valley.

For Orthodox Jews the presence of a mosque over the site of the Holy of Holies is itself an 'abomination', while the larger area of the Temple Mount, once occupied by first Solomon's and later Herod's Temple and called the Haram ash-Sharif or 'Noble Sanctuary' by the Arabs, remains a 'desolate' open space. Logically, if the Jews are ever to rebuild their temple it must stand there, with its Holy of Holies over the rock, even if this means demolishing, or at least moving, the Dome. This is the thorny issue that sours all talk of peace between Arabs and Israelis, made even more complicated by the belief among Muslims that during his night journey Mohammed himself flew to heaven from this self-same rock. For this reason alone the status of the Dome of the Rock, after Mecca and Medina the third most holy shrine of Islam, is non-negotiable as far as Muslims are concerned. If the Dome of the Rock were demolished and a new Jewish temple built on the crest of Mount Moriah, this would undoubtedly lead to a holy war of unprecedented scale between Israel and the entire Muslim world. As the United States would come to the aid of Israel, this would have devastating consequences for all concerned. Given that we are currently living at the end of the age as marked by the movements of Orion, it is tempting to think that this is exactly what is going to happen and that what Jesus and Daniel really had in mind when making their prophecies concerning the 'abomination that makes desolate' at the end of time is the destruction of the Dome of the Rock.

The idea of a 'tribulation' (literally, a 'threshing') marked by a great earthquake and the darkening of the sky also has its origins in the Old Testament. According to the prophet Zechariah, whose tomb at the edge of the

Valley of Jehoshaphat is, by tradition, the one capped by a small pyramid, the Mount of Olives is to be split in two by an earthquake and a mighty river will flow from springs under Jerusalem.

> Behold a day of the Lord is coming, when the spoil taken from you will be divided in the midst of you . . .
> On that day his [the Lord's] feet shall stand on the Mount of Olives which lies before Jerusalem on the east; and the Mount of Olives shall be split in two from east to west by a very wide valley; so that one half of the Mount shall withdraw northward, and the other half southward. And the valley of my mountains shall be stopped up, for the valley of the mountains shall touch the side of it; and you shall flee as you fled from the earthquake in the days of Uzziah king of Judah. Then the Lord your God will come, and all the holy ones with him.
> On that day there shall be neither cold nor frost. And there shall be continuous day (it is known to the Lord), not day and not night, for at evening time there shall be light.
> On that day living waters shall flow out of Jerusalem, half of them to the eastern sea [Dead Sea] and half of them to the western sea [Mediterranean Sea]; it shall continue in summer as in winter. (Zech. 14: 1–8)

The idea of springs flowing from Jerusalem connects with certain widespread beliefs concerning the role of a *kibleh*. Such stones seem to have been regarded as blocks or plugs holding back the waters of the Great Flood of Noah, which had drained into the centre of the earth through a channel concealed under the stones. The rock of Abraham at Jerusalem is one such stone; there seems to have been another near Mount Hermon and yet another at Olympia in Greece. Lethaby quotes several interesting sources presenting this idea:

Of [Mount] Hermon Miss Beaufort wrote: 'It is remarkable that Hermon was anciently encompassed by a circle of temples facing the summit. Can it be that this mountain was the great sanctuary of Baal, and that it was to the old Syrians what Jerusalem was to the Jews, and what Mecca is to the Moslems?' . . . Another Syrian temple, that of Mabog (Hierapolis), seems to have been a world centre and well of the abyss; this city occupied the site of Carchemish, the capital of the Hittites, and it is probably their rites and legends which are continued here. The temple stood at the very centre of the 'Holy City' and it was built (so went the legend) by their Noah directly over the chasm where the waters of the Deluge had been swallowed up (Sayce, *Hittites*). 'At Jerusalem also there was a cleft in which the waters of the flood disappeared' (Robertson Smith, *Semites*).[3]

Today the Belt of Orion is to be seen rising in the east over the Mount of Olives, this constellation seeming to symbolize 'the Alpha and the Omega, the First and the Last'. On the pediment of the Church of All Nations, by the Garden of Gethsemane, there is a large representation of the cosmic Christ holding the signs of the Alpha and Omega standing above the mortal figure of Jesus as he prays next to his sleeping disciples. Once we understand that the 'First and Last' is really Orion, which looms over the Mount of Olives as it rises, this image makes a great deal of sense. As we have seen, the Belt of Orion is also sometimes called 'Jacob's staff'; so is Orion's rising in the east what is meant by the 'Lord's feet standing on the Mount of Olives'? Orion is the great timekeeper of the Age of Adam and symbolizes the 'Son of man' or Lord. With the sun now rising in the 'shake-hands' position at the summer solstice, we seem to be at the time when the bolts are to be drawn back and the gates of heaven opened. In this context further prophecies concerning the Mount of Olives need to be considered.

Given the apocalyptic nature of all these writings, I

was anxious to see how things looked on the ground. This is why, when I went to Israel in 1998, I journeyed along the entire length of the country, from Eilat in the south to the 'Good Fence' at Metula on the Lebanese border in the north. What, I asked myself, was the likelihood of major seismic changes in the Holy Land and what could be the possible outcome of a really powerful earthquake in the region? To my surprise I came to see that the prophecies of the Bible make sense when you consider the terrain. Geologically the land of Israel is part of an ancient plateau, embracing also the Kingdom of Jordan and parts of Saudi Arabia, which rises steadily from east to west. This plateau has been severely fractured by earthquakes and is now barely recognizable as the hills of Judea, Samaria and Galilee. What struck me most while travelling through Israel was that although we think of it as a mainly desert country, much of it is very vulnerable to catastrophic flooding.

To understand this we need to look at the land as a whole and consider its position between the continents of Africa and Asia. In the fifty years or so that have elapsed since the end of the Second World War major discoveries have been made concerning the way continents move over the surface of the earth. Most earthquakes occur at the boundaries between the tectonic plates which carry the continents. To the south of Israel is the Red Sea, which is an extension of the Great Rift Valley of eastern Africa. It was formed because the plate which carries Arabia is moving away from Africa. The Gulf of Aqaba, the finger of the Red Sea which separates the east of the Sinai peninsula from Arabia, terminates on the southern border of Israel at Eilat (next to the Jordanian city of Aqaba). North of here there are salt marshes on either side of which rise mountains. Here, in places where the land is fertile and they have been able to bring in fresh water, the Israelis have set up kibbutzim. The plain terminates in some low hills before the land again drops to form another plain called the Araba, which gradually sinks below sea level. This plain is mostly desert which eventually, near Sodom, drops steeply into the deep canyon of the Dead Sea. This is the lowest point on earth, and in only a few places on its banks is there enough land and fresh water to support human occupation. North of the Dead Sea there is the wide valley of the River Jordan, which is among the most fertile land in Israel. This valley, including Lake Tiberias (the Sea of Galilee) at its northernmost end, is all still well below sea level. In fact, the Jordan/Dead Sea valley is the principal rift or fracture in the plateau which makes up Israel and Jordan; if it were not there, then the highlands of Israel would be contiguous with the highlands of the Hashemite Kingdom of Jordan. This valley exists because the land has been torn apart by the same geological processes which created the Red Sea and the Great Rift Valley in Africa. Geologically Israel owes its special character to the same forces of nature that caused these massive features.

North of the Jordan valley lies Mount Hermon. This, as we have seen, is the highest peak in the Levant and today forms a natural cornerstone between Israel, Syria and Lebanon. That this area has been volcanic in the fairly recent past is shown by the presence of basaltic stones all over the region north of the Sea of Galilee. Around that lake there are a number of thermal baths, and in Upper Galilee there is further evidence of ancient volcanoes such as Birket Ram, now a water-filled crater. These volcanoes may now be extinct, but earthquakes of a strength to demolish churches and other structures are by no means unheard-of in Israel. Indeed, the sudden fall of the walls of Jericho in the time of Joshua was more likely to have been due to a timely earthquake than to the sound of the Israelites' horns. Jericho, after all, lies inside the Jordan valley close to the Dead Sea.

Travelling north from Eilat, it was not hard to see that Israel is especially vulnerable to any further quakes that might occur along the axis line running from Eilat to Metula. While it is certainly feasible that the Mount of

ISRAEL

showing areas most at risk of
flooding should the prophecies
come true

Area most at risk
of flooding through
earthquake

Olives could be split by an earthquake and new springs spurt forth into the Kidron valley, it seemed to me that the land below sea level was much more vulnerable. Should the fault line between the continents of Africa and Asia open wider and the land here split further south, then a channel could be opened linking the Dead Sea to the Red Sea. There would then be nothing to stop water from the Red Sea from flooding the entire Jordan valley. Thus a relatively small earthquake in the plains above Eilat could result in massive flooding. In effect, the Gulf of Eilat would come as far north as the Sea of Galilee, thereby separating Israel from Jordan by an inland body of water much larger than the Dead Sea. Jerusalem would then be a seaport, its centre no more than five or ten miles from this inland sea.

Future geological changes could be even more extensive than this. Splintering off from the major fault line running up the Jordan/Dead Sea valley are a number of sub-faults, mainly running in a south-east to north-west direction. It is not inconceivable that a major earthquake in the Jerusalem area could split the Mount of Olives so that a wide valley was formed cutting east–west across the Judean hills and, as prophesied by Zechariah, forcing shut the present Kidron valley. Springs rising in the hills of Jerusalem would then pour into this new valley, and it is conceivable that some of this water could flow eastwards towards the Dead Sea and some westwards to the Mediterranean. Of course, it can be argued that this prophecy is to be understood figuratively rather than literally and that no such earth changes are likely. However, it is clearly not impossible that such a fracture could occur as there are others of a similar nature already in existence.

The largest of these east–west fractures has given rise to the Jezreel valley, which runs from Beit She'an, just south of the Sea of Galilee, to the Bay of Haifa. Like the Araba plain or the plain above Eilat, the Jezreel valley is not much above sea level. A major earthquake along the

Jordan valley axis, such as might produce a Dead Sea–Red Sea link, could easily result in sub-quakes along this zone. Should the land here split further, then the Jezreel valley could also end up below sea level and form a connection between the new gulf in the Jordan valley and the Mediterranean Sea to the west. The land bridge broken, the continent of Africa would then be totally separate from Asia. Israel would be split in two, with the bulk of the country joined to Africa and only the Galilee and Golan regions still in Asia. In this way a natural alternative to the Suez Canal would have been created. In years to come, Haifa and Jersualem would be in a position to become major ports on the new channel now linking the Mediterranean world with the Red Sea and hence the Indian Ocean.

All this may seem fanciful; but again, major events are prophesied for the Jezreel valley, for overlooking it is the hill of Megiddo, or Armageddon as it is called in the Book of Revelation. Here a great battle is foretold, when the enemies of Israel are drawn there for their final destruction:

> The sixth angel poured his bowl on the great river Euphrates, and its water was dried up, to prepare the way for the kings from the east. And I saw, issuing from the mouth of the dragon and the mouth of the beast and from the mouth of the false prophet, three foul spirits like frogs; for they are demonic spirits, performing signs, who go abroad to the kings of the whole world, to assemble them for battle on the great day of God the Almighty. ('Lo, I am coming like a thief! Blessed is he who is awake, keeping his garments that he may not go naked and be seen exposed!') And they assembled them at the place which is called in Hebrew Armageddon.
>
> Then the seventh angel poured his bowl into the air, and a great voice came out of the temple, from the throne, saying, 'It is·done!' And there were flashes of lightning, loud noises, peals of thunder, and a great

earthquake such as had never been since men were on the earth, so great was that earthquake. (Rev. 16: 12–18)

In the Old Testament similar prophecies are made concerning the destruction of the forces of Gog of Magog in a final battle.

And the word of the Lord came unto me, saying Son of man, set thy face against Gog, of the land of Magog, the chief prince of Meshech and Tubal, and prophesy against him, and say, Thus saith the Lord God; Behold I am against thee, O Gog, the chief prince of Meshech and Tubal:

And I will turn thee back, and put hooks into thy jaws, and I will bring thee forth, and all thine army, horses and horsemen, all of them clothed with all sorts of armour, even a great company with bucklers and shields, all of them handling swords:

Persia, Cush and Put with them; all of them with shield and helmet. Gomer and all his bands; the house of Togomah of the north quarters, and all his bands: and many people with thee . . .

After many days thou shalt be visited: in the latter years thou shalt come into the land that is brought back from the sword, and is gathered out of many people, against the mountains of Israel, which have been always waste: but it is brought forth out of the nations, and they shall dwell safely all of them . . .

Therefore, son of man, prophesy and say unto Gog, Thus saith the Lord God; in that Day when my people Israel dwelleth safely, shalt thou not know it?

And thou shalt come up against my people of Israel, as a cloud to cover the land; it shall be in the latter days, and I will bring thee against my land, and the heathen may know me, when I shall be sanctified in thee, O Gog, before their eyes.

Thus saith the Lord God; Art thou he of whom I have

spoken in old time by my servants the prophets of Israel, which prophesied in those days many years that I would bring thee against them?

And thus it shall come to pass at the same time when Gog shall come against the land of Israel, saith the Lord God, that my fury shall come up in my face.

For in my jealousy and in the fire of my wrath have I spoken, Surely in that day there shall be a great shaking in the land of Israel; so that the fishes of the sea, the fowls of the heaven, and the beasts of the field, and all creeping things that creep upon the earth, and all the men that are on the face of the earth, shall shake at my presence, and the mountains shall be thrown down, and the steep places shall fall and every wall shall fall to the ground.

And I will call for a sword against him throughout all my mountains, saith the Lord God: every man's sword shall be against his brother.

And I will plead against him with pestilence and with blood; and I will rain upon him, and upon his bands, and upon the many people that are with him, an overflowing rain, and great hailstones, fire and brimstone . . .

And it shall come to pass in that day, that I will give unto Gog a place there of graves in Israel, the valley of passengers on the east of the sea: and it shall stop the noses of the passengers: and there shall they bury Gog and all his multitude: and they shall call it the valley of Hamon-Gog. (Ezek. 38: 1–22; 39:11)

It is, of course, difficult and even dangerous to try to interpret in the politics of today such inflammatory prophecies as these. In a famous book, *The Late Great Planet Earth*, published in the 1970s, Hal Linsey identified Gog with the Soviet Union and forecast that there would be a massive invasion of Israel by Russia and its allies, precipitating a third world war and a nuclear holocaust. Today, with the Soviet Empire in ruins and

Russia barely able to feed itself this seems much less plausible than it did at the height of the Cold War. The identity of Gog remains obscure, but the land of Magog, then in the Soviet Empire, is normally identified with the region south of the Caucasus and west of the Caspian Sea. This today roughly corresponds with the Republic of Azerbaijan. Gomer is an old name for Cappodocia, Togomah is Pontus; Meshech is Cilicia, with Tubal slightly to its east. All of these regions are in what we would today call Turkey. Cush is Nubia, now part of the Sudan, while Put is Libya. These last-named states, along with Persia (modern-day Iran), are governed by revolutionary Islamic regimes that are implacably hostile to the state of Israel. At present Turkey, a secular state, is friendly towards Israel, but this could change now that it no longer has so much to fear from Russia to its north and is experiencing a swelling tide of Islamic fundamentalism within its borders. Having had its application for membership of the European Union rejected, Turkey is currently courting the various Islamic republics to its east, including Azerbaijan. These republics, many of whose peoples still speak Turkish, were once part of the Ottoman (Turkish) Empire. Indeed, the Turks came from this region (still known as Turkestan) prior to their successful invasion of Anatolia after the Battle of Manzikert in AD 1071. In the Bible Gog is described as chief prince, that is to say overlord, of Meshech and Tubal. It is possible, therefore – but by no means certain – that by 'Gog' we are meant to understand the state of Turkey, whose people came originally from 'Magog' or Turkestan.

Turkey is currently in political crisis as its poorer people, like many others in the Middle East and to the consternation of the governing classes, are increasingly turning towards Islamic fundamentalism for the solution to their problems. As Turkey has one of the largest and best-equipped armies in the world, it does not take much imagination to see that should it undergo the sort of

376

Islamic revolution which has already swept Libya, Sudan, Iran and Afghanistan, it would pose a very real threat to the future of Israel.

These prophecies may, of course, be entirely wrong or misunderstood. But should we see a great army led by a revolutionary Turkey and allied to forces from Iran, Libya, Sudan and Turkestan gathering on the borders of Israel this should surely be sign enough for us that the time of Armageddon is at hand. In the current political climate, with the United States the world's sole remaining superpower and a staunch ally of Israel, such an adventure may seem improbable. Yet the modern world is full of surprises – how many people foresaw the fall of the Berlin Wall?

At the first sign of trouble, anyone in Israel would be wise to get out of the Jordan/Dead Sea valley and, as Jesus said, to take to the hills. As the explosion of the Mount St Helens volcano in America showed, geological processes are not always gradual. Changes can be very sudden and very quick. The next earthquake in the Dead Sea/Jordan area could be a big one that opens the crack and floods the entire valley. We can but wait and see. In the meantime, and even if this does not happen in our lifetimes, we have enough to consider with the signs in the sky indicating the imminence of the 'Day of the Lord' and the dawning of a new age.

CHAPTER 19

AT THE END OF AGES

With the return journey to Israel in 1998 my quest had come full circle. I now had the final pieces of the puzzle in my hand and a much clearer understanding both of the prophecies which had puzzled me so many years ago and of the significance of the symbol of the pyramid that I had seen as an image from the collective unconscious when in trance in Oregon. The process of getting to this point, which has been the subject of the present book, is a complicated business involving many different avenues of investigation. I would therefore like to bring matters to a close by presenting a summary of the major theses.

I began with a re-evaluation of the pyramids of Giza. These, it is clear to me, were, like many other grand monuments, built by the ancients not only for their own glory but as a means of preserving knowledge for future generations. The Egyptians of the Old Kingdom knew about the ravages of time and foresaw the threat posed to civilization by future periods of barbarism. They built their pyramids massively in the hope that enough of their structures would remain to enable us, living at the end of the age, to read their message. The pyramidologists of the nineteenth century guessed at this and tried to work out a prophetic sequence based on the measurements of the passageways and chambers of the Great Pyramid. Though with the benefit of hindsight it is clear that their methodology was wrong, in that there is no logical connection between the measurements of the tunnels and the unfolding sequence of history, their intuitions about the pyramid's significance as indicating the end of the present age were correct. The pyramids of Giza, and in particular the Great Pyramid, do contain the measures of time; it is just that this was not done in the way the pyramidologists thought.

The pyramids of the Fourth Dynasty are empty of hieroglyphic inscriptions but not of meaning. They are themselves a message carved in stone and written in the languages of mathematics and astronomy. They are laid out to represent most of the brightest stars making up the constellation of Orion. They also tell us of the beliefs of their makers, of how the present epoch, the Age of Adam or Orion, started in c.10,880 BC and will end in c.AD 2000. They speak eloquently of the beliefs of the Egyptians, of how in their own time the dominant sign of the zodiac was Leo and of how they received their units of measure directly from the 'phallus of God', the original column of Atum-Re at the centre of the Temple of the Phoenix at Heliopolis. This pillar, surmounted by its Benben stone, was the archetype of all the later obelisks. Its noonday shadow at the equinoxes gave the proportions of the *vesica piscis*, the 'dish of fish', from which the *ad triangulum* system of proportions is derived. Later in the year, just before the summer solstice, on the day the sun was conjunct with the star Regulus in Leo, the pillar would cast shadows in the morning and afternoon with an angle of 51° 51'. This gave the pi relationship of height to length of shadow of 14:11. In this way the most important measures used in Egypt were taken directly from the sun, so that in effect they were God-given. Moreover, these proportions were, I believe, the so-called magic numbers of the chamber of Thoth: the *'ipwt* of the *wnt* which the Westcar Papyrus tells us were sought by King Khufu and subsequently incorporated in the design of the Great Pyramid.

The later Khafre pyramid, the central monument of the Giza group, had a different angle of slope from the Great

Pyramid: 53° 10'. Unlike the Great Pyramid, it was designed so that it would light up as the sun crossed the east–west axis on the day of the summer solstice itself. At the time the pyramids were built this occurred with the sun in Leo; today the solstice happens when the sun is in the 'shake-hands' position over Orion. Orion, or Sahu as this constellation was called by the Egyptians, was often depicted either cupping a star or holding an *ankh* in his right hand. The Egyptian for 'star' was *s'ba*, but this word had a second meaning: 'gateway'. Orion's hand reaches up to the gate of heaven, a point in the sky marked by the intersection of the ecliptic with the Milky Way. I therefore see the star cupped in Orion's hand as symbolizing this gateway and the *ankh* as representing the key to the door of which he is the keeper.

The placing of the *ankh*, or key of life, into the lock is connected with the movements of the sun and the precession of the equinoxes. For the last 13,000 years or so the constellation of Orion, and in particular his 'hand', has been drifting steadily north. Today it is in its most northerly position before it begins to move south again in a rhythmic cycle that takes 26,000 years to complete. As a result the sun now occupies the 'shake-hands' position over the outstretched hand of Orion exactly at the summer solstice. I see this as indicating that the opening of the stargate with the *ankh* will occur around this time.

The Great Sphinx, which some researchers believe to have been carved many thousands of years before the pyramids were built, I believe to symbolize the passage of the age. Possibly originally carved as a lion, its head may have been re-carved in the form of a pharaoh much later. It faces east towards where Leo would have risen at the beginning of the epoch in 10,880 BC. The re-carving of the head probably took place during the Middle Kingdom, at a time when the Sphinx was aligned with the rising of the head of Orion. In any case the riddle of the Sphinx, which has the body of a lion and the head of a man, seems to be linked with the secret of

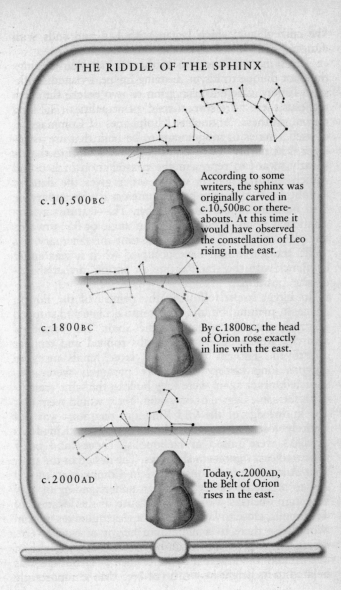

THE RIDDLE OF THE SPHINX

c.10,500BC

According to some writers, the sphinx was originally carved in c.10,500BC or thereabouts. At this time it would have observed the constellation of Leo rising in the east.

c.1800BC

By c.1800BC, the head of Orion rose exactly in line with the east.

c.2000AD

Today, c.2000AD, the Belt of Orion rises in the east.

the current age which began with Leo and ends with Orion.

The symbol of the lion as the constellation of kings was not unique to Egypt. Leaving Egypt, I visited southeast Turkey, where a generation or two before the birth of Jesus there were several small principalities. The king of one of these, Antiochus I Epiphanes of Commagene, caused a series of monuments to be built that are astrological in nature. Here there is a lion sculpture that is clearly meant to represent the constellation of Leo and which features planets whose order gives the date of 6 July, 62 BC. Of even greater interest is a sanctuary he had built in honour of his father. This features a long shaft that points westwards at an angle of 35° towards the place in the sky which, at the time the sanctuary was built, the sun would have occupied when it was either conjunct with the star Regulus or sitting in the 'shakehands' position.

In Egypt itself, following the demise of the Fourth Dynasty, pyramid building went into decline and stopped abruptly with the ending of the Sixth. The period of anarchy which ensued saw tombs robbed and temples destroyed. Though there were later renaissances in Egypt's long history and more pyramids were constructed, never again were they built to the same scale or with the same degree of precision. Yet it would seem that the knowledge of the Old Kingdom pharaohs was not entirely lost. During the Middle and New Kingdoms obelisks were raised at Heliopolis, Thebes and other places to cast significant shadows. The design of the shaft that Antiochus had constructed in Commagene turned out to be the necessary key to an understanding of how Egyptian obelisks were used. Because of the location of Heliopolis, close to latitude 30°, at the equinoxes the sun would rise there to a maximum height of exactly 60°. Using simple geometry it can be shown that the length of the midday shadow cast by an obelisk at Heliopolis was related to its height by a ratio of 1:√3. More importantly

382

still, it would give an angle in the east and west of approximately 51° 51' on the day the sun was conjunct with Regulus. This is the so-called π angle and is the same as the slope of the Great Pyramid. Knowledge of this angle and of how it was generated seems to have been one of the secrets kept by the priesthood of Heliopolis. This knowledge, and how it was revealed to King Khufu, seems to have been what was behind the story of Djedi the magician in the Westcar Papyrus.

Long after the demise of the Old Kingdom, the Egyptians continued to be famed for their knowledge of geometry, and indeed in New Kingdom times this seems to have been one of the subjects taught to Moses as a prince of the royal house. He incorporated much of his knowledge about divine proportions in the design of the Ark of the Covenant and the Tabernacle in which it was to be housed wherever the Israelites were to be camped. The dimensions of the Tabernacle were to be the basis for the design of King Solomon's Temple at Jerusalem when this was eventually built in c.900 BC. The choice of Jerusalem as the Davidian capital of Israel has great significance astrologically. For, just as at Heliopolis in c.3100 BC, at the start of Dynastic Egypt, the sun would cast, to the east and west, a shadow giving the special angle of 51° 51' on the day of the Regulus conjunction, so at the time of Solomon's Temple this same conjunction would give an angle of 45° at Jerusalem (see colour illustration no. 20). It was therefore, like Heliopolis before it, a 'city of the lion', and this accounts for its name of Ariel, meaning 'Lion of God', as recorded by the prophet Isaiah.

The site on Mount Moriah chosen by Solomon for his Temple has further symbolic significance. The rock over which it stood is, by tradition, the very place where Abraham, in obedience to the will of God, was about to sacrifice his son Isaac (Ishmael according to the Muslims) when his hand was stayed by an angel. In place of his beloved son, Abraham was given a sheep, its horns caught in a thicket, to offer up on his sacrificial pyre. Nobody knows the exact date of these events but they are likely to have taken place in *c*.1800–1700 BC and are therefore emblematic of the start of the age of Aries which began around that time.

More sheep were sacrificed by the Israelites on the night of the tenth and final plague of Egypt. Again there is a connection with first-born sons, but this time it was the turn of the Egyptians to suffer. The Israelites daubed their own doorways with sheep's blood and consequently were spared by the destroying angel who 'passed over' their houses. Thus originated the feast of the Passover. According to my calculations this event would have taken place in 1363 BC. On this day the sun would have been positioned under Delta-Aries, the first star of the constellation of Aries at the time of the full moon. In commemoration of their miraculous deliverance, every year the Jews held a ritual meal on the night of the first full moon of spring.

While opinions vary concerning the chronology of the mission of Jesus, the general consensus as expressed by the *Encyclopaedia Britannica* is that he was born in 7–6 BC, baptized in AD 26 and probably crucified in AD 29. This fits very well with observed star patterns for the days in question. In *Magi* I showed how the most likely date for Jesus' birth, explaining both the symbolism concerning the visit and gifts of the Magi as well as contemporary thinking concerning the birth of a 'lion king', was 29 July, 7 BC. His baptism would have taken place on 6 January AD 26. On this day the sun was in Capricorn underneath the 'baptizing' hand of Aquarius, the water bearer, and in conjunction with Venus, the planet symbolized by a dove. The implication of this baptismal symbolism seems to have been linked to the idea of a 'scapegoat' as described in Leviticus. In being baptized by John, Jesus was symbolically taking on to his shoulders the sins of Israel. Then, like the scapegoats of old, he went out into the desert to meet with the devil.

Here he was tempted three times to misuse his powers but he did not succumb. Having passed this test, he began his mission in earnest.

By my analysis the Crucifixion of Jesus probably took place just after the Passover full moon on 14–15 April AD 29. On that day the sun was again, as at the time of the Exodus, positioned directly under the star Delta-Aries. The recurrent theme linking the Passover lamb with the death of Jesus is obvious. So too is the connection between the spilling of Jesus' blood on the cross as a recompense for sins and the proposed sacrifice, many centuries earlier, of Abraham's son Isaac, both events having taken place at Jerusalem. As he died on the cross Jesus quoted the first verse of Psalm 22: 'My God, my God, why hast thou forsaken me?' This psalm, written by King David, exactly describes the Crucifixion which was to take place a thousand years later. Given this evidence it is difficult to escape the conclusion that the death of Jesus was a pre-ordained event. Indeed, it seems to have been planned from even before the building of King Solomon's Temple.

Using the date of the Crucifixion as a base we can easily work out when the Resurrection and Ascension are supposed to have taken place. The first would have been at dawn on 17 April and the second forty days later, on 27 May. The Resurrection is symbolized by the *Agnus Dei*: at dawn, as Aries rose, so Cygnus, the Northern Cross, passed directly overhead. On the day of Jesus' ascension from the Mount of Olives forty days later, the sun was directly over the outstretched right hand of Orion. This was one of the positions pointed at by the shaft built by Antiochus I Epiphanes of Commagene in his funerary monument for his father at Arsameia. It is also one of the two places in the sky (at the crossing points of the Milky Way with the ecliptic) where the ancients believed there to have been a stargate. Given these coincidences, it seemed more than likely to me that the choice of this day for Jesus' ascension was deliberate, as it implied his departure from this world through the stargate.

In the Acts of the Apostles, where Jesus' ascension is described, it is said that he will return in a similar manner as he was seen departing into heaven. Since these events are described as taking place on the Mount of Olives, it is here that many Christians expect him to return, appearing out of a cloud in the same way that he left. What this means in a practical sense is open to conjecture; but what is not open to doubt is that now, at the dawning of the new millennium, the Mount of Olives itself is witness to some strange signs in the sky.

In one of his final lectures to his apostles, also given on the Mount of Olives and recorded in chapter 24 of Matthew's Gospel, Jesus had described certain signs that would imply the end of the current age or aeon. One of these was the appearance of 'lightning', going from the east to the west. This description has little meaning if taken literally, but the similarity in Greek between the words for 'lightning' and 'stars' suggested he was speaking esoterically about the rising and setting of heavenly bodies. Even in English the word 'lightning' means literally 'that which lightens', which need not be an electrical flash but could be a heavenly body such as the sun, the moon or a star. The fact that the stars of the Belt of Orion are now in their most northerly position, with Mintaka almost exactly on the celestial equator, is very telling in this respect. The Mount of Olives is directly east of Mount Moriah or the Temple Mount, so that anyone standing in the vicinity of the Dome of the Rock would today see the stars of Orion's Belt rising in the eastern sky and setting in the west: a phenomenon that is unique to our time. Moreover, because Mintaka is so close to the equator, it can be seen from any point on earth with the exception of a very small area at the North Pole. The positioning of this star is therefore very significant as a global indicator of the end of the current age.

In the New Testament Jesus often refers to himself as

the 'Son of man', a title which was used of some of the earlier prophets such as Ezekiel. This title at first seems obscure, especially for Christians who are taught by the church that he was the son of God and not of any mortal man. Yet the meaning behind these words becomes clear once it is realized that the 'man' in question is Adam, who is symbolized by Orion. For the Egyptians this constellation represented the stellar form of Osiris and marked out the place in the sky where their heaven was to be found. Within the Jewish Kabbalistic tradition Orion would seem to have been the original archetype for Adam Kadmon, the divine prototype after which all men are fashioned. The constellation of Orion is also identifiable as the archetype behind such patriarchs, judges and prophets as Abraham, Jacob, Samson, Elijah and even John the Baptist. It therefore seems to be intimately connected with the whole idea and process of the redemption of mankind. We may justifiably talk of a 'School of Orion' of which all of the above-named individuals were initiates.

The Revelation to John, the last book in the Bible, opens with St John meeting an angelic being called 'the first and the last, the Alpha and the Omega'. It is made clear later in this book that this being is the heavenly Christ or celestial dimension of the man who lived on earth as Jesus. The 'first and the last' is described as the guardian of time itself and holds the keys of Hades. He stands amid seven candlesticks, symbolic of the seven stars (the planets), which he also holds in his hands. This being too is to be identified with Orion; in confirmation of this, like so many other Orion prophets, he is described as wearing a belt.

Today, seen from Jerusalem, Orion rises over the Mount of Olives. It is a large constellation and though the Belt rises more or less directly in the east, his right hand rises some 24° north of east and his 'right foot', marked by the star Saiph, about 21° to the south of east, in the vicinity of the present Jewish graveyard that flanks the Mount of Olives over the Valley of Jehoshaphat. In its rising, therefore, the constellation of Orion straddles more or less the entire mount as viewed from Jerusalem. Even more significant is that, as we have seen, today Orion reaches out towards the sun when it is at the summer solstice and therefore in its most extreme northerly position. This seems to be what the Book of Revelation means when it describes the Alpha and the Omega as having a countenance like the 'sun shining in his strength', i.e. when it is at the solstice.

In the year AD 2000 the planets come together in a very rare configuration. On 4 May all of the seven planets of the ancients, which include the sun and moon, are to be found close together, with six of them in the sign of Aries. The seventh, Mars, is nearby in the neighbouring sign of Taurus. On 8 May the sun is in exact conjunction with Mercury, Jupiter and Saturn. Three days later, on 11 May, the sun will have moved to a position under the first star of Aries, as it was at the time of the Crucifixion. As these conjunctions take place over the head of Cetus, the Whale, I take this to symbolize the sign of Jonah spoken of in Matthew chapter 12. Throughout the period of May most of the other planets are in close attendance on the sun. This seems to symbolize the gathering of the eagles over the corpse, another of the signs recorded in Matthew chapter 24.

The Apocalypse of John implies that the opening of the Orion stargate around the solstice of AD 2000 is to be the start of some powerful earth changes. This does not mean the immediate end of the world as we know it, but rather that, with the gate open, changes will be possible. We therefore need to prepare ourselves for what is to come: initially perhaps a time of chaos but afterwards a great awakening to the real intention and purpose of human life that goes beyond our current materialistic civilization.

We should not forget Egypt in all of this. On the day of the summer solstice AD 2000 the sun will illuminate the

PASSAGE OF THE AGE SHOWN BY THE POSITION OF THE SUN AT THE SUMMER SOLSTICE *c.*2400 BC–AD 2000

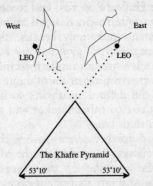

The slope angle of the pyramid (53°10') is such that it
casts no shadow on the day of the summer solstice between
the time the sun crosses the east axis in the morning and the time
it crosses the west axis in the afternoon.

At the time it was built (*c.*2400 BC) the solstice took place in the
sign of Leo. Today (*c.*2000 AD) it occurs in Gemini with the sun
sitting in the 'shake-hands' position over Orion.

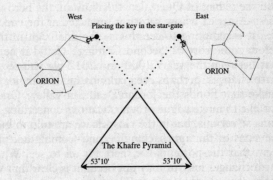

Khafre pyramid as, viewed from the west, it symbolically sits over its *benben*. For some twenty or more years now researchers have been actively seeking the secret chamber of Thoth, the Hall of Records, said to be concealed in the vicinity of the Sphinx. To date all attempts at finding it have been thwarted, mainly because the academic and political atmosphere in Egypt has not been conducive to a serious search using all modern technologies. It could be that with the opening of the stargate this will change, and that the old dictum 'as above, so below' will apply. Perhaps the door to this chamber will also be opened – sooner rather than later.

Twelve years further down the line there is a possible connection between the ending of the Mayan calendar in 2012 and the opening of the stargate. The Mayan calendar, or at any rate its present cycle, is due to end on 22 December 2012. A few months earlier in that year, in August, Venus, symbolically the planet of the 'Bride of Heaven', who along with Sirius was linked with Isis in Egypt and Ishtar in Babylonia but which also signifies Mary in Christianity, will be stationary within the hand of Orion. This is an extremely rare event and can be read as symbolizing the mystic marriage in heaven between Orion as the 'Christ' and the 'bride' who holds his hand. As this occurs at the ending of the Mayan calendar and Venus is also the planet of Quetzalcoatl/Kukulcan, the hero-god of Meso-America whose return is predicted at the end of the age, it is tempting to see this as the final sign in the sky before some sort of 'Second Coming'. Could it be, then, that between the years 2000 and 2012 we will see many earth changes, perhaps even culminating in a major earthquake that floods the Jordan/Dead Sea valley? One does not like to make vague prognostications concerning something so serious, but in the Gospels we are told to look for the signs of the approaching Second Coming and it does seem that the portents are there for all to see. Whatever earth changes may or may not occur, it is clear that we are living at the birth of a new age of man.

EPILOGUE

In the course of this book I have attempted to demonstrate the lines of enquiry and the logic that led me to the conclusion that 21 June AD 2000, (i.e. the summer solstice) was the time of the opening of a stargate. I do not believe that there is a physical gateway somewhere in the sky. This book is not a work of science fiction. I am not suggesting for one minute that there is indeed a material portal over the hand of Orion nor that it could be opened and shut like a door. However, like the ancients, I do believe that time is not merely a linear progression from past to future: it is governed by cycles, large and small. We live in a world and a universe of repetition and because of this there is a certain predictability about events in the future. Time can be measured by the movements of the heavens and because of its cyclical nature we have some foreknowledge of what is to come.

The half-precessional cycle of some 13,000 years has a beginning and an end, points which are as immovable as the numbers 6 and 12 on a clock face. The precessional movement of the summer solstice represents the turning of the small hand on this cosmic clock. The fact that the sun now stands at the Orion stargate at the precise time of the summer solstice signifies that the small hand is pointing towards 12. This in itself is an exciting concept but as we have seen there is a further twist in this story. My work with the SKYGLOBE computer program indicated that in the Giza area, on the day of the summer solstice, at the precise moment that the sun would cross the east–west axis of the sky, it would have an angle of elevation above the horizon of 53° 10'. This angle was clearly considered to be important by the ancient Egyptians as they used this angle of slope for the sides of the Khafre Pyramid. From the SKYGLOBE predictions I realized that on 21 June, an observer standing at the foot of the pyramid and looking up its slope, at two precise moments (at 10.11 a.m. and 3.49 p.m., when the sun crosses the axis in the east in the morning and when it crosses back in the west in the afternoon), would see the sun sitting on the capstone. Unfortunately, though I could imagine what this would be like and I had little doubt that the computer was telling the truth, I had no proof that reality would match theory. It was therefore essential that I should try to go to Egypt for the summer solstice to see it for myself. This millennial year was, of course, all the more significant because of the positioning of the planets on either side of Orion that would occur a week or so later on 29 June. On that day the sunrise over the Mount of Olives in Jerusalem, even though Orion itself would be invisible, would be especially significant and I wanted to be there too.

Thus it was that I decided to organize a tour to the Middle East that would take in both Egypt and Israel. In the course of this tour I would take a party of guests to a number of different sites described in this book and explain their cosmic significance on the spot. Foremost among these would, of course, be the Pyramids of Giza, which I planned to visit on the day of the summer solstice but I also wanted us to be on the Mount of Olives in Jerusalem on 29 June.

The Opening of the Stargate Tour, which took place between 16 June and 1 July, was a great success. In Egypt we visited various pyramids and tombs at Giza, Dashur and Saqqara as well as what remains of the sanctuary of the Phoenix at Obelisk of Senusert III at Heliopolis. However, the undoubted highlight of this part of our trip was to be our visit to the Pyramid of Khafre. In preparation for what was to come we gathered together close by the Sphinx, in good time for when the Giza Necropolis would be opened for visitors. Walking up the Khafre Causeway, we made our way to the foot of the Pyramid, just as the ancient Egyptian priests would have done at the time it was built in *c*.2400 BC. Half-way up the causeway we stopped by the so-called water-shaft or 'Tomb of Osiris', which has been the cause of some controversy in recent years. The access to it was caged off and its entrance filled with litter, we didn't tarry long but made our way round to the Khafre Pyramid. By around 9.30 a.m. we were inside the little courtyard, if such one may call this rather desolate area, close to its western face. To our surprise we found that we had the place to ourselves, except for one Egyptian boy who had followed us up the causeway while trying to sell postcards, and a camel-mounted Bedouin, as ever hopeful of persuading at least one of us to go for a ride. Though it had been a hot walk up from the Sphinx and for all of this way we had been bathed in brilliant sunlight, the western face of the pyramid was still in shadows. However, by standing further back in our little plaza we were already able to see the sun hovering just above the pyramid. Looking at my watch I knew that we had only a few more minutes to wait until the real event and so we went back to the foot of the pyramid itself.

To put ourselves in the right mood we gathered in a circle and closed our eyes for a few minutes of meditation. Almost immediately I felt what was like an electric shock, which entered through my head, went down through my body and passed out through my feet. This was not what I was expecting as I have always been sceptical about 'pyramid power'. I don't believe that pyramids are of themselves capable of sharpening razor blades, or causing seedlings to grow at an accelerated rate. Yet this shock of energy, which I felt through my whole being, was something that I could not deny. Was a transformation of solar energy the real pyramid power, I wondered? If so, what was it for?

These questions were still floating freely in my mind as we broke up the circle and moved even closer to the base of the pyramid. I handed out miniature *ankhs*, symbolic of 'life' and therefore the power of the sun, to each member of the group. As I had an extra one of these I gave it to the boy, Mustafa, explaining to him through our guide, Soheila, what he was witnessing and that long after we were all dead, when he was an old man, he would be able to tell his grandchildren that he had been there on that fateful day. In my own hand I had a much larger *ankh*, which I had bought in the Cairo Bazaar the day before. I now pointed this towards the tip of the pyramid, in the direction of the Orion stargate. Was this what the Egyptian priest had done over 4,000 years ago, I wondered? Would they have known or even guessed that in some far off year, when the summer solstice sun would be placed exactly over the Orion stargate as it crossed over the crest of the pyramid, a group of pilgrims from overseas would gather to witness the event? I doubt it but certainly it seems that they did know about the stargate. In the Egyptian Museum the previous day we had ourselves seen how the Benben stone of Amenemhet III carries the glyph of Orion holding in his hand a star. 'As above, so below', the Hermetic dictum, was once more in my mind as like Orion I pointed an *ankh* towards the stargate. Would this appearance of the sun at the stargate now mean that a gateway to the legendary 'Hall of Records', which many believe to be buried near the Khafre Pyramid, might now soon be opened? Who knows; until it is found there is no proof that such a chamber even exists. However, I did have a feeling that in some esoteric way the two events might be linked: that no 'hermetically sealed' gateway on earth would be discovered until such time as the gate of heaven had been symbolically opened.

Already the sun was beginning to move into position

and at exactly 10.11 a.m., the time predicted for the event by the SKYGLOBE computer program, it could be seen sitting precisely on top. What a thrill it was for us to look up the side of the Khafre Pyramid and see the awesome disc of the sun blazing over the few remaining facing stones close to its peak. It brought to mind certain words of the Pyramid Texts: 'O Atum! When you came into being you rose up as a High Hill, you shone as the Benben Stone in the Temple of the Phoenix at Heliopolis'.[1]

As the sun climbed higher in the sky, so the shadows departed altogether. Standing back a little we could see its reflection on the casing stones at the apex of the pyramid. It was a sobering thought to think that we were probably the first people to consciously see and register this event in at least a thousand years and probably much longer.

We regrouped at the Khafre Pyramid the following afternoon. This time we wanted to view the sun from its eastern face and watch its transit over the apex in the west. At around 3.30 p.m., as we sat huddled in the sweltering heat below the enormous mountain of stone, things did not seem all that encouraging. The sun was still high in the sky and over to the left of the pyramid's cap. It therefore seemed unlikely that it would sit on top of the pyramid at 3.49 p.m. as the computer predicted. However, all such negative fears were to prove unfounded, for from this time onwards the sun fell like a stone, its movement of 1° every 4 minutes of time being almost vertical. At precisely 3.49 p.m. it was positioned directly over the capstone of the pyramid, which as in the morning shimmered in reflected sunlight. Further confirming the accuracy of the workmanship of the ancient Egyptians, the few remaining angled facing stones at the foot of the pyramid cast no shadow.

Once more we raised a great cheer as we raised aloft the *ankh* and presented it to the sun and stargate. This afternoon crowning of the pyramid was in some ways more noticeable than in the morning for it only lasted for a few minutes before the sun, continuing on its progress, was gradually eclipsed by the pyramid. As one of our party had brought eclipse glasses with him, I was able to watch this; the disc of the sun being steadily cut by the pyramid until it was visible no more. With the sun behind the crown of the pyramid the latter appeared to give off a dazzling radiance, not too dissimilar to the aura I had seen around the sun at the time of the total eclipse of August 1999. Though I took many pictures of the day's events, these barely do justice to the extraordinary nature of what we witnessed. To see the sun rise and set behind the capstone of a pyramid is a remarkable sight and one I shall never forget.

The next day we left Egypt for Israel and a few days of sightseeing before the next major event: sunrise over the Mount of Olives. On 29 June we once more gathered together, this time at dawn outside the walls of the Old City. Behind us was the bricked-up Golden Gate, through which the long-promised messiah is supposed to make his entrance into Jerusalem prior to the judgement of mankind. Behind that, but invisible to us, was the Haram ash-Sharif and the Dome of the Rock. In front of us but still shrouded in the morning twilight was the Mount of Olives. Hanging above it like a silver sickle was a narrow, crescent moon and next to this we could see the lights of two planets: Jupiter and Saturn. This was all as it should be, for the SKYGLOBE program showed that these three celestial bodies were positioned in the sign of Taurus and would therefore herald the sunrise. I knew that we would be unable to see Orion itself as the sun was still too close for its stars to be visible before the dawn. However, seeing these three 'lamps' was better than nothing and somehow made the events of that day all the more real.

Half an hour or so later the sun rose over the Mount of Olives, and almost immediately the temperature, which had till then been pleasantly cool, began to rise uncomfortably. From our vantage point we could see the shadow cast by the Mount of Olives opposite slink its way down over the city walls so that the Golden Gate, which had a solar disc sculpted above it, was once more illuminated in the dawn sunlight. In the ancient world it was normal practice to open the great gates of a temple to greet the sun at dawn and allow his rays to penetrate into the inner sanctum. William Lethaby writes about the winged, solar disc in respect to Egyptian temples in *Architecture, Mysticism and Myth*, here he describes the Temple of Denderah:

> The winged globe depicted upon a gigantic scale on the curve of the cornice seems to hover above the central doorway.
>
> On certain mornings in the year, in the very heart of the mountain, as the sun comes up above the eastern hill-tops, one long, level beam strikes through the door-way, pierces the inner darkness like an arrow, penetrates to the sanctuary, and falls like fire from Heaven upon the altar at the feet of the gods. No-one who has watched for the coming of that shaft of sunlight can doubt that it was a calculated effect, and that the excavation was directed at one especial angle in order to produce it.[2]

It is clear that the Golden Gate, which faces east towards the Mount of Olives, must once have had a similar function to that of an Egyptian temple; it too was probably opened at dawn and closed at sunset. But there is a fine line to be drawn in religious terms between saluting the sun as symbolic of the life-giving power of an invisible though omnipotent God and idolatry. That the connection between the great gate of the sun and sun-worship was all too apparent to be entirely acceptable to the Jews is shown by Ezekiel's description of an 'abomination' involving men turning their backs on the temple as they worshipped the rising sun:

And he brought me into the inner court of the house of

the Lord; and behold, at the door of the temple of the Lord, between the porch and the altar, were about twenty-five men, with their backs to the temple of the Lord, and their faces toward the east, worshipping the sun towards the east.[3]

Josiah, who ruled over the Kingdom of Judah shortly after the Assyrians took the lost tribes of Israel into captivity, receives praise from the ancient chroniclers of the Bible for removing idols and other abominable images from Jerusalem and the surrounding countryside. Among the things he took away and had burnt are listed the chariot and horses of the sun which stood at the entrance to the house of the Lord. These were presumably large, wooden carvings similar in style to the chariot and horses of the sun shown on the Parthenon frieze.

It is probably out of a similar sense of outrage at sun-worship that the Arabs eventually had the gateway bricked up, not so much to prevent the entrance of a Jewish messiah but rather to signify that in their eyes salutations to the sun-god was inappropriate behaviour for Muslims too. Yet that the Golden Gateway was really intended to honour Yahweh, the God of Moses, is indicated by its shape. Unlike the other gateways to the city, which are purely functional, it is a double doorway shaped like the twin tablets of the law brought down from Mount Sinai by Moses. This is clearly not a co-incidence and indicates a further connection between solar astronomy and the Mosaic covenant.

Leaving the Golden Gate we went back to our hotel for breakfast before heading on down the Kidron valley to our second destination: the, probably misnamed, tomb of Zechariah. This tomb, which is capped by a small pyramid lies below the Jewish graveyards, which cover the south-eastern flank of the Mount of Olives and more or less opposite the Al Aqsa Mosque. On a previous visit to Jerusalem the December before I had photographed the pyramid from a vantage point exactly level with it on the other side of the valley. From this photograph I had been able to ascertain that the angle of slope was exactly 60°. Now astronomically speaking this angle doesn't make any sense. Seen from Jerusalem the sun will never reach this elevation in the sky as it crosses the east–west axis. It would do so as it crossed the southern meridian about five days after the spring equinox but this doesn't seem to be particularly relevant. It would seem, therefore, that the selection of an angle of 60° for the slope of the pyramid was done for aesthetic and symbolic (as opposed to astronomical) reasons. As the angle of 60° would have been entirely appropriate for a pyramid raised in the Heliopolis/Giza area to mark the equinox, I had to suppose that the reason the master mason had built this one in Jerusalem with such an angle was that he wanted to draw attention to an Egyptian connection. In a symbolic sense this pyramid pointed the mind towards the Cairo area just as surely as the alignments through the Khufu satellite pyramids pointed towards Jerusalem. There was, therefore, an invisible line linking this little pyramid with the Khafre Pyramid at Giza.

Standing below the pyramid at around 9.30 a.m. we were able to see the sun sitting on its apex as it crossed the east–west axis. However, this was not quite the same thing as we had witnessed in Egypt as the altitude of the sun was ony 49°, whereas the angle of slope was 60°. The sun only appeared to sit on the apex because we were standing back from the building and not looking directly up the sloping roof as we had with the Khafre Pyramid. These details aside it was, nevertheless, an impressive sight to once more see the sun crowning a pyramid, albeit that this one was so much smaller than the last.

Leaving the pyramid we made our way to the Church of All Nations, which stands next to the Garden of Gethsemane at the foot of the Mount of Olives. Here we were able to inspect the pediment of the risen Christ, the Alpha and Omega, and meditate on the fact that at that very moment, though unseen in the morning sunshine,

Orion was hanging over the Mount of Olives. After spending an hour or so in the church and garden we made our way back up the hill to our final destination: the Dome of the Ascension. This is a small, octagonal chapel built in the early Gothic style and placed inside a courtyard with an eight-sided boundary wall. The chapel was originally built on the instructions of the Empress Helen, mother of Constantine, to mark the believed site of Jesus' ascension into heaven. In the sixth century it was one of the many churches to be destroyed by the Persians immediately prior to the advent of Islam. When Jerusalem was retaken by the crusaders in 1099, it was one of the churches they rebuilt. After they in turn were driven out of Jerusalem by Saladin, the chapel, which continued to be a holy place for Muslims as well as Christians, was incorporated into a mosque. Today it is open to all visitors, who are free to light a candle and pay their own respects to the rock on which Jesus is believed to have stood prior to his ascent into heaven.

Entering the little courtyard we made our way inside the venerable structure. It was now close to midday and, as it was a very hot day, there were no other pilgrims or tourists in the vicinity. We therefore had the place to ourselves and were able to light candles and prepare ourselves for the climax of our trip: the moment at noon when Orion would be standing exactly erect, with the sun like a blazing torch in his hand, crossing the southern meridian. Without any prompting the members of the tour group sat down in a circle and began meditating under the enclosing dome. As we sat there in perfect silence the atmosphere, which was already strong, began to build in intensity.

We sat like that for what must have been an hour with nobody saying a word when suddenly in through the open doorway flew a pigeon. It fluttered back and forth between the windows high above us below the dome, settling for a short time to coo before flying off again. Soon it was joined by a mate and then the two of them repeated the performance of this strange, flying ballet. I remembered the story of how a dove, the symbol of peace, landed on Jesus at the time of the baptism and how this was seen as signifying the descent of the Holy Spirit. Truly we too felt blessed by an unseen spirit as we prayed together for peace, there at the place of ascension, at the very moment when Orion was standing amidst the seven candlesticks.

The identification of the 'Son of man' with the constellation of Orion, whose precessional movement over the past 13,000 years has marked out the 'Age of Man', was the climax of a long quest. The identification of the great being, called by St John in his Revelation 'the first and the last, the Alpha and the Omega', seemed now to be beyond doubt. It was Orion, who keeps the keys to the gates of heaven, St Peter being in a sense his steward. As part of my own celebration for the forthcoming millennium, I commissioned another painting from my old friend Bengt Alfredson. He had previously painted the magnificent 'Star-correct Adoration of the Magi', which I reproduced in my earlier book *Magi*. I knew, therefore, that he would understand immediately the significance of these discoveries and be capable of expressing them artistically.

I had visited Bengt in Sweden in the autumn of 1998 and we had discussed in detail how best to summarize symbolically the opening of the stargate by Orion. The painting he had brought over to England the following spring exceeded my wildest expectations. It shows St John in the act of receiving the message he is to record in his Apocalypse. The Christ-like figure of the 'first and last' stands by the now open Omega doorway and shows John the signs in the sky indicating what is to come. He has white hair and round his head is a radiant glow, as of the sun shining in his strength. He wears a cummerbund which carries, like jewels, the three stars of Orion's Belt. In his left hand he holds a shepherd's crook while his right cups the seven brightest stars of Orion. Above these, hover the seven planets of the ancients: Saturn, Jupiter, Mars, Sun, Venus, Mercury and Moon. They are shown accompanied by eagles, as this is how they are described in Matthew 24. The positions of the planets are exactly as they were to be on 29 June AD 2000. For on that day Orion stands in their midst. To emphasize this last point, the 'first and last' is shown surrounded by seven candlesticks, which St John tells us are emblematic of the seven planets. As on this day the sun would shine over the Great Pyramid of Giza and generate the perfect pi angle as it crossed the east–west axis, so the sun is shown generating a pyramid shape in the sky, one ray from it passing to the lips of the giant figure before St John. Below the sky are pyramids by a meandering river, symbolizing the way these mighty edifices were prepared for just this moment: the opening of the stargate at the end of the Age of Adam.

For those of us who were gathered in the Chapel of the Ascension on the Mount of Olives, 12 noon on 29 June AD 2000 was an unforgettable moment of great consequence. What it might mean in the context of the wider world we have yet to discern. It does seem that despite the best efforts of the world's statesmen, peace between Israel and its Arab neighbours is not yet to be a reality. Whether the world is anyway on its way to Armageddon is yet to be seen but it is just possible that our silent prayers in that little chapel might make a difference and what seems like an inevitable disaster be averted. If so then our pilgrimage through these ancient lands to witness the opening of the stargate would not have been in vain.

Bengt's picture, which I shall always treasure, was prophetic of this journey and contains many hidden symbols. So that others may see it and, should they wish, use it as a focus for their own meditations, we have reproduced it in the colour section. I hope that readers will find it as moving as I do. It has the title 'Opening the Stargate: 29 June 2000 AD'. Once more I thank Bengt for his fine work.

APPENDIX 1

The Architectural Gnosis

The basis of all serious architecture in the ancient world was proportionate geometry. There seem to have been two main systems employed. The first was based upon the dimensions and proportions of the rhombus or *vesica piscis*. This system makes use of equilateral triangles and their division. The *vesica* is most easily constructed by drawing two interlocking circles of the same diameter, such that the circumference of each passes through the centre of the other (see diagram on p. 168). If the centre of one circle is O and the other is O', then the *vesica* shape is given by the figure AOBO'. By joining the points OO' and AB, we quadrasect the *vesica* into four equal triangles. These are 30°, 60°, 90° triangles and carry within them the harmonic proportion of $1:\sqrt{3}$. This means that OX:AX = $1:\sqrt{3}$. OO':AB is also $1:\sqrt{3}$.

Furthermore, if the length AB is used as the radius of two other circles with their origins at A and B, then a new *vesica* can be constructed: ACBD. In this case AB:CD has the relationship of $1:\sqrt{3}$. However, as AB = $\sqrt{3} \times$ OO', it follows that CD = $\sqrt{3} \times \sqrt{3} \times$ OO' = $3 \times$ OO'.

At Heliopolis it would have been easy to devise a system based on these proportions by observing the shadows cast by the sun at the equinox. As the sun culminated in the south, so it would cast a shadow of length $1 \div \sqrt{3}$ of the height of the obelisk. Budge tells us that the surviving obelisk of Usertsen (Senusert I) at Heliopolis is 'about 66 feet high'. If we divide this by $\sqrt{3}$

403

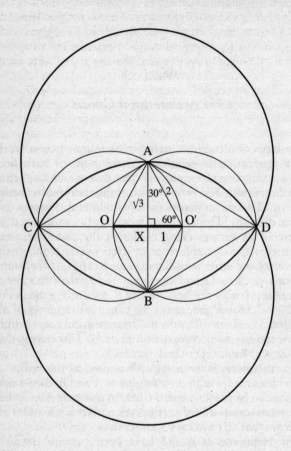

If OA = 2 units, then OX = 1 and AX = √3
By the same proportions, CX = √3 x AX
Therefore CX = √3 x √3 = 3.

This is the basis of ad-Triangulam proportions.

it gives 38.1 feet. This would seem to be correct, for if we imagine a shadow of length 25 ordinary cubits – each cubit being 18 inches in length – then it is $25 \times 18 \div 12 = 37.5$ feet in length. If we multiply this by $\sqrt{3}$ it gives 64.95 feet. This is close enough to the rough height of 66 feet given by Budge to suggest that the Egyptians were working to a shadow length of 25 cubits.

The camp of the Israelites, as described in the Book of Numbers, is designed to be such a cosmic reflection. The fact that it features a module which is three times as long as it is broad suggests a connection with *vesica piscis* geometry. The twelve tribes of Israel reflect, of course, the twelve signs of the zodiac and these are set around a tabernacle, or tent, containing the Ark of the Covenant. The design of Solomon's Temple was based on the earlier Tabernacle of the Israelites except that it was larger by a factor of 2 in all dimensions.

Egyptian temples, too, were modelled on what must have been earlier tent-like structures. Often they were arranged as 'tents within tents', the stonework imitating what must have been an original construction consisting of cloth stretched over poles. They, too, enclosed a 'Holy of Holies' accessible only to higher levels of the priesthood. This would contain a portable image of a god (or goddess) which, like the Ark of the Covenant of the Hebrews, could be brought out of the temple on special occasions and carried around in procession.

The later Temple of Solomon, as described and measured by Ezekiel, is designed as a heavenly enclosure, its measurements reflective of a geometric gnosis. So too the heavenly city of the 'New Jerusalem' described by St John at the end of the Book of Revelation. The plan of this city is a cosmic representation of the heavens. The twelve gates of the city are symbolic of the signs of the zodiac, while the Tree of Life standing at its centre seems to symbolize the axis of the ecliptic. This axis points towards the still-point in the sky around which the ages precess, in succession one after the other. That such a symbol should be included at the end of the New Testament indicates that the disciples of Jesus, or at least some of them, were also initiates into the ancient gnosis.

A Chronology in the Stars

*c.*10,880 BC. The stargate above the hand of Orion was in its most southerly position. As the cosmic Adam is represented in the stars by Orion, so this seems to refer to the beginning of the 'Age of Adam', i.e. of humankind as we know ourselves today. Esoterically it would correspond roughly to the destruction of Atlantis and the placing of records in Egypt by Thoth/Hermes/Enoch. Calendrically this date also ties in closely with the end of the last Ice Age. We can suppose that our remote forebears at this time went through some sort of evolutionary change of consciousness that made civilization possible. At this time the sign of Leo was rising in the east. The spring equinox was then at the cusp of Virgo and Leo.

*c.*8700 BC. The sun rises exactly in the east when it is conjunct with the star Regulus. It is possible, according to West and Schoch's erosion theories, that this could be when the Sphinx was first carved. It would then have had the head of a lion.

*c.*3100 BC. This period seems to mark the beginning of many ancient civilizations. In America, 3114 was the start of the 'Age of the Jaguar' and the beginning of the first *baktun* of the present Mayan calendar. In Europe it was the beginning of the Neolithic or New Stone Age. In Egypt, although Taurus the Bull was now the sign for the spring equinox, it was the climactic of Leo as this was the sign ruling midsummer. For this reason the father-god Atum was especially revered in the form of a lion. It was also the beginning of Dynastic Egypt when there was a sudden upsurge in civilized activity. Almost overnight, it would seem, the Egyptians developed skills in building with stone. Esoterically this seems to be the time when Isis and Osiris were on earth. According to the *Hermetica*, they were destined to find some of the buried records of Thoth. The Temple of the Phoenix at Heliopolis is built with a pillar and *benben* stone casting a shadow giving the important pi relationship on the day of the Regulus conjunction.

*c.*2700–2200 BC. The Old Kingdom Pyramid Age. A massive building programme gets under way on the banks of the Nile by Memphis. On the one hand, this seems to have been nothing less than the construction of a huge stone map of the stars of 'heaven', i.e. the Orion constellation, on earth. On the other, the Egyptians seem to have been setting into stone certain knowledge concerning the age of Orion from the 'First Time' (*c.*10,880 BC) to the 'End of Days' (c. AD 2000). The Great Pyramid was constructed at this time as a scaled-up version of the Temple of the Phoenix at Heliopolis. It was given a slope of 51° 51' – the pi angle. The Khafre Pyramid was constructed later with a slope of 53° 10'; this is appropriate for the east–west shadows at the summer solstice. At *c.*2280 BC the Regulus conjunction would have occurred exactly at the summer solstice.

*c.*1800 BC. The 'head' of Orion rises directly in the east. This is the most likely time for when the head of the Sphinx was recarved to look like a pharaoh instead of a lion. This would be during the period of the Middle Kingdom (Twelfth to Thirteenth Dynasties). Around this time the pharaoh Senusert I erected the first of the great obelisks at Heliopolis. This would have cast meaningful shadows at the equinoxes. Because the constellation of

Leo was now back in retreat, the Regulus conjunction would once more have given the pi angle of 51° 51'. This is also the start of the 'Age of Aries' as the spring equinox moved backwards out of Taurus into the sign of Aries.

*c.*1750–1560 BC. Egypt is ruled over by the Hyksos or 'Shepherd Kings'. During this time the Israelites migrate to Egypt.

*c.*1363 BC. Moses leads the Israelites out of Egypt, perhaps during the rule of Pharaoh Ramses II. Standing on Mount Sinai, Moses is able to measure out the pi angle with the shadow from a staff when the sun is conjunct with Rho-Leonis.

*c.*900–800 BC. King Solomon's Temple is built. At this time the conjunction of the sun with Regulus gives a 45° angle at Jerusalem. As a result it becomes the new lion capital, prophetically named 'Ariel'.

6 July, 62 BC. Date of the Lion horoscope from Commagene. Seen from Arsameia, the winter capital, the sun is at exactly 75° as it crosses the southern meridian. At around this time a shaft was dug giving alignments with the sun–Regulus conjuction; this was the royal birthday, 28 July. The shaft also pointed to the 'ascension' position, as understood by the Commagene kings. This was when the sun was placed above the outstretched hand of Orion. The ancients believed that in this position there was a stargate leading to the kingdom of heaven.

29 July, 7 BC. The birth of Jesus. During the summer of this year the planets Jupiter and Saturn were in conjunction for much of the time, symbolized by the 'star of the Magi'. At least some of the Magi probably came from Commagene and neighbouring principalities. On this day the sun was conjunct with the star Regulus, the

'lion's-heart'. This corresponded with the birth of a king or pharaoh according to traditional ideas that were widespread throughout the Middle East.

6 January AD 26. The baptism of Jesus. In the early church the baptism of Jesus was a most important feast and it was celebrated on 6 January. The actual baptism would have taken place on 6 January AD 26. At this time Jesus was thirty-one years of age, which fits with St Luke writing that he was 'about thirty' at the time.

When Jesus was baptized the sun was in the sign of Capricorn, the sea-goat, but placed under the outstretched hand of Aquarius, the water-bearer. Conjunct with the sun on this day was the planet Venus, whose symbolic bird, according to traditional astrology, is the dove. The role of water-bearer is taken by St John the Baptist. Jesus is once more symbolized by the sun which is taking on the garb of the goat. It was customary for the Israelites, going back to the time of Moses and Aaron, to put the sins of the nation on the back of a goat and send this out into the desert to meet with the devil or Azaziel.

15–17 April AD 29. The Last Supper, Crucifixion and Resurrection. The Passover meal was celebrated annually by the Jews at the time of the first full moon after the spring equinox. The Passover in question took place in AD 29. As a full moon had only just taken place before the equinox, there was a long gap of nearly a month between it and the Passover Feast which probably took place on Thursday 14 April AD 29. On this day the sun was placed under the first star of Aries, symbolizing the role of the sacrificial lamb. The following day, Good Friday, would have seen the sun still close to the same place in Aries.

The date of 15 April AD 29 for the Crucifixion seems to echo the events surrounding the Exodus, when the first Passover took place and the Israelites daubed their doorways with the blood of sheep. We cannot be certain when

410

this happened, but a likely date is 6 April, 1363 BC. On this day the sun was in the same place as on Good Friday at the time of the first full moon after the spring equinox.

The Resurrection would have taken place on the first Easter Sunday, 17 April AD 29. Symbolically the sun had by this time moved out of the sign of Aries, the sacrificial Sheep, into Taurus, the Bull. Seen from Jerusalem, at dawn on this day, the constellation of Aries would be seen rising in the east while the 'Northern Cross' was directly overhead. This gives the symbol of the Agnus Dei or 'Lamb and Flag'.

27 May AD 29. The Ascension of Jesus from the Mount of Olives, This event is said to have taken place forty days after the Resurrection. On this day the sun was close by the 'shake-hands' position over Orion. This makes sense of Jesus' statement that he was going to the right hand of his father in heaven. The right hand of Orion symbolized in the starry world his spiritual transition back through the 'stargate'.

c.1938. Since this date the summer solstice has been taking place when the sun is over the outstretched hand of Orion. It will continue to do so for about 200 years.

14 May 1948. The new Jewish state of Israel is proclaimed. Fulfilment of the prophecy of Jesus telling his disciples to observe when the fig-tree (symbolic of the Jewish nation) puts on new growth, for then the time is nigh. A generation (seventy years) will not pass away until all the prophecies are fulfilled.

AD 2000. The start of the Tribulation? At this epoch the Belt of Orion rises directly in the east with the star Mintaka just below the celestial equator. From Jerusalem the Belt is seen rising over the Mount of Olives.

4 May: Gathering of the sun, moon, Mercury, Venus,

Jupiter and Saturn in the sign of Aries and over the head of Cetus the Whale. Could this be the sign of Jonah?

8 May: Grand conjunction of the sun, Mercury and Jupiter still in Aries.

11 May: The sun under the first star of Aries, as it had been at the Crucifixion. Close by are Jupiter, Saturn and Mercury with Venus slightly further away. Is this the eagles gathering over the carcass as prophesied by Matthew?

21 June: The summer solstice with the sun standing over the hand of Orion. Close by, in Gemini, are Venus and Mars in conjunction. Saturn and Jupiter are further behind in Taurus. Is this the symbol of Orion (Peter?) putting the key in the lock? On this day, as always on the solstice, the sun will shine directly down the west face of the Khafre Pyramid as it crosses the east–west meridian. It will rise with an alignment from Giza pointing in the direction of Jerusalem and the Mount of Olives.

29 June: Orion stands flanked by the seven planets of the ancients, which in Revelation are called lamps or candles. As Orion rises, so it stands upon the Mount of Olives. It is the symbol of the Alpha and the Omega, the ultimate sign of the end of the age.

22 December 2012: End of the thirteenth *baktun* of the Mayan 'Age of the Jaguar'. According to Mayan prophecies, the age will close with a cataclysm.

May 2018: End of the seventy-year period that began with the declaration of the new State of Israel. The Tribulation should be over by this time.

The Lion of God

Throughout this book references have been made to the constellation of Leo and in particular the conjunction of the sun with the star Regulus as signifying the birth of kings. In ancient Egypt the living pharaoh was regarded as an incarnation of Horus, the son of Osiris. Osiris was the god of the dead but Horus was very much identified with the living and in some way personified the power of the sun as it was manifest in human society. The prime task of the pharaoh was the maintenance of the rule of law. It was his obligation to heaven to make sure that justice was maintained. He was the servant of the sun, his divine father, and his task was to make sure that the will of the father was done on earth as it was in heaven.

At the time of the Egyptian Old Kingdom the period of midsummer occurred while the sun was in the sign of Leo. For some of this time (*c.*2300–2100 BC) the conjunction with Regulus would have actually occurred on midsummer's day. As this was the day when the sun reached its greatest height in the northern skies, it was natural to associate Regulus with the power of God in his fullest majesty and glory.

The Egyptians were not the only race to venerate the sign of Leo as representing the power of the ruler. At the time of the patriarchs it is evident that this idea was accepted in Israel as well. Thus in the blessings of Jacob given to his twelve sons, rulership is bestowed upon

413

Judah. To him, it is prophesied, the sceptre will belong:

> Judah, your brothers shall praise you; your hands shall be on the neck of your enemies; your father's sons shall bow down before you.
>
> Judah is a lion's whelp; from the prey, my son, you have gone up.
>
> He stooped down, he couched as a lion, and as a lioness, who dares rouse him up?
>
> The sceptre shall not depart from Judah, nor the ruler's staff from between his feet, until he comes to whom it belongs; and to him shall be the obedience of the peoples.
>
> Binding his foal to the vine and his ass's colt to the choice vine, he washes his garments in wine and his vesture in the blood of grapes; his eyes shall be red with wine and his teeth white as milk. (Gen. 49: 10–12)

The kings, first of the united kingdom of Israel and then later of Judah only, were from the tribe of Judah. The greatest of them, David and Solomon, were lion-kings *par excellence* and it was they who established Jerusalem as the capital city of the Israelites. This city is called prophetically Ariel by Isaiah (ch. 29), meaning 'Lion of God'. It is probably no coincidence that during the period when the Temple of Solomon stood on Mount Moriah, the sun crossed the east–west axis with an elevation of 45° above the horizon. In doing so it would have produced shadows of the same height as the pillars placed in front of the Temple. Forty-five degrees is the angle of a diagonal drawn across a square, so that these pillars and shadows invite one to think of the geometry of squares. The profile of the Temple was a square and the dimensions of the Holy of Holies formed a cube. This again was surely no accident.

Few pharaohs of Egypt or kings of Jerusalem were up to the heavy responsibility of being God's *Regulus* or 'regent'. The idea, however, persisted right up until fairly recently that kings and emperors were chosen before they were born to govern over the nations which they served. Thus it was that the king was considered to rule by 'divine right'. He was in some sense a demi-god, imbued with royal majesty and healing power.

This seems to be how the apostles at first viewed Jesus, who was initially expected to assert his messiah-ship by leading a revolt against Rome. As a 'lion of the tribe of Judah' it was expected that he would be crowned as king in place of both the hated Romans and the usurping Herodians. His divine glory was apparently made manifest to the apostles Peter, James and John at the time of the transfiguration. During this event, which probably took place on Mount Hermon, 'his face shone like the sun, and his garments became white as light' (Matt. 17: 2). We don't know when this event actually took place, but the Feast of the Transfiguration is today celebrated by the church on 6 August.

The reasons for this are interesting and once more seem to hark back to the association of the messiah-ship of Jesus with the royal sign of Leo. According to the St Andrew's Daily Missal – a book no longer in use since the Catholic Church gave up celebrating the mass in Latin – it was Pope Callistus III who in 1456 established 6 August as the Feast of the Transfiguration (also known as the Feast of St Saviour) throughout the western church. This day was chosen in celebration of a military victory near Belgrade that year over the forces of Islam. However, according to the Missal 6 August had 'long' been solemnized as the Feast of the Transfiguration in different churches of east and west before this. How long is 'long' it doesn't say, and perhaps nobody knows. What is of interest, though, is that in 1456, and for some time before this, the sun was each year in conjunction with Regulus on 6 August. This would suggest that someone in the church, perhaps even the pope himself, recognized that the Transfiguration event as described in the Bible was connected with the belief that Jesus was a 'lion of

God', a messiah who would in due course take up residence in Jerusalem to become a King of Judah. Interestingly, at the time when these events occurred, perhaps AD 27 or 28, the Regulus conjunction would have taken place on 29 July, which would seem to have been his birthday.

Today there is another sign in the sky to be seen at Jerusalem. For whereas at the time of Solomon's Temple the angle made by the sun as it crossed the east–west axis on Regulus day was 45°, today it is exactly half this: 22.5°. Symbolically it would seem to herald the return of kingship to Israel and possibly the rebuilding of the Temple of Solomon in the next 'octave'. What this means practically remains to be seen, but it is certainly an interesting observation.

The true date for Easter and the Fatima letters

On 13 May 2000, Pope John Paul II went on pilgrimage to Fatima in Portugal, where in 1917 three shepherd children saw apparitions of the Virgin Mary. At first the children, Jacinta and Francisco Marto and Lucia dos Santos were not believed and indeed for a short time the church authorities had them imprisoned whilst they were interrogated. Today all this has changed and the Pope himself went to Fatima to celebrate the beatification of the brother and sister, Jacinta and Francisco, who died whilst still children (Lucia, a Carmelite nun, is still alive at the ripe old age of ninety-three).

What makes the Fatima apparitions interesting, over and beyond their spiritual significance for Catholics, is that when the children saw their apparition of the Virgin Mary she apparently made certain prophecies to them. Lucia later wrote these down in the form of three letters. The first of these prophesied that Russia would become communist and spread this evil throughout the world. The second said that although the First World War would end (in 1917 it was still raging) a Second World War would follow. The contents of the third letter is still a mystery. It was opened by Pope Pius XII in 1960 and what it says has been kept secret from all, except for his successors as popes and their closest advisers.

Needless to say the secrecy surrounding the third Fatima letter has only served to fuel curiosity concerning its contents. Rumour has it that it contains prophecies relating to the end of the present age and possibly even to the Second Coming of Jesus Christ. On 13 May the Pope's representative revealed that amongst other things it contained, as many other people have suspected for some time, a prophecy relating to the attempt to assassinate John Paul II in 1981. This took place on 13 May – the anniversary of the first appearance of the Virgin at Fatima. As he collapsed to the ground, a bullet lodged in his stomach, the Pope is said to have glimpsed a poster of 'Our Lady of Fatima'. This in part explains why he has chosen 13 May 2000 (nineteen years after his near-death at the hands of an assassin and eighty-three years after the first apparitions) to make his pilgrimage to Fatima but is there more to it than this? In particular is there something special about 13 May? Surprising as it may seem, I believe this to be so and that it is directly connected with the real date for the Resurrection of Jesus Christ and the 'opening of the stargate' on 21 June 2000.

To explain all this we need to consider what we know about the timing of the first Easter. Now as we have seen, the Crucifixion almost certainly took place on 15 April AD 29. The sun was then positioned under the last star of Aries. The Resurrection is said to have taken place two days later, on 17 April, with the sun having moved along the ecliptic by two degrees. Jesus Christ is supposed to have ascended to heaven on the fortieth day, at the time when the sun was at the 'St Christopher' or 'stargate' position.

Now all these events, true or mythical, took place a long time ago. Even so the Christian church continues to celebrate the Ascension as well as Easter as a very important feast. Finding the right day to celebrate Easter has in the past been a matter of serious debate. However, it is normally determined by the lunar calendar. There is a complex formula for fixing the date but it corresponds to the first Sunday after the first full moon after the spring equinox. This means that the calendar date of Easter

Sunday changes year by year and in the year AD 2000 it was celebrated on 23 April.

This was a very late Easter and as a consequence the sun was in the sign of Aries instead of Pisces as it usually is. Even so the sun was only at the beginning of Aries and not in the same place along the zodiac that it was at the time of the Resurrection in AD 29. This is because of the precession of the equinoxes, the slow, cyclical motion caused by the 'wobble' of the earth. The period of this cycle is roughly 26,000 years and its effect is to move the first day of spring (the vernal equinox) back through the zodiac at a rate of one sign every 2,160 years. At the time Jesus was alive the vernal equinox took place with the sun near the end of the sign of Pisces, today it is close to its beginning and it will soon move into Aquarius. This means that today the first Sunday after the equinox can never occur with the sun in the same position relative to the stars that it was on the day of the first resurrection. Thus looked at from a stellar, or sidereal, point of view, Easter never corresponds with the true anniversary of the Resurrection. This may not seem very important but in terms of the 'signs in the sky' it has enormous repercussions.

To take this argument further, we have to ask ourselves what, from a stellar point of view, should be the correct date for celebrating the Resurrection? The answer to this is when the sun is at the same position in the zodiac that it occupied on the day of the Resurrection. This, as we have seen, is 2° on from its 'crucifixion' position under the star Delta-Aries. Now amazing as it may seem, this is precisely the place that these days the sun occupies on 13 May, the anniversary of the first apparition of the Virgin Mary at Fatima and of the failed assassination attempt on the Pope in 1981 (apparently prophesied in the third Fatima letter). It is also the day chosen by the Pope to make his latest pilgrimage to Fatima and to announce the beatification of the two children: Jacinto and Francisco Marto.

419

Now all this may just be a coincidence but if so it is still quite an extraordinary piece of synchronicity for it means that the day especially revered by this Pope, 13 May, is the real anniversary of the Resurrection of Jesus Christ. However, there is even more to it than this. As we have seen, Jesus is supposed to have appeared to his apostles during the forty days following his resurrection. On the fortieth he is said to have ascended to heaven. Counting forty days from Easter this year (23 April) brings us to Ascension Day (1 June). Astronomically this has no meaning but if we take 13 May (the real Easter) as the first day and count to forty we come to 21 June. This is the correct day for the Ascension when the sun is by the stargate over the hand of Orion. However, as we have seen, these days the sun comes over Orion's hand at exactly the summer solstice. In other words the solstice today occurs when the sun is at the stargate position over the hand of Orion. Moreover, because of the special gathering of the planets that has been occurring this year, this year they are tightly grouped around the sun. This to me symbolizes the 'Opening of the Stargate' and I believe it to mark the true beginning of the Age of Aquarius and the start of some very important changes on earth. What these might be I would not like to speculate but perhaps the second part of the Fatima letter, which the Pope will not reveal until the faithful have been properly prepared, concerns what is shortly to happen.

Feeling that the Pope ought to be informed of the connection between the Fatima date, Easter and the opening of the stargate, I wrote to Cardinal Sodano, his right-hand man and head of the Vatican Secretary of State. As it was he who had made the pronouncements concerning the Fatima letter on 13 May, I felt it was appropriate to ask him to pass on the information to the Pope. At the same time I sent the letter, I also sent a parcel containing copies of *The Orion Mystery* and *Magi* in Italian and Polish as well as the hardback, English edition of *Signs in the Sky*. Whether either Cardinal Sodano or the Pope has read any of this material, I don't know. However, I did receive back a friendly letter from Monsignor Pedro Lopez Quintana saying that His Eminence appreciated the sentiments which prompted me to write and that he invokes upon me God's abundant blessings. Whether I was right in linking the Fatima letter with signs in the sky he did not say. It remains to be seen if there really is a connection between the opening of the stargate and the expected return of Jesus Christ. It may be that both we and the Catholic Church will not have long to wait in order to find out!

NOTES

CHAPTER 1

1 Mount Tabor, the alternative site favoured by the church, is in the vicinity of Nazareth. However, as according to Matthew the Transfiguration took place immediately after the visit to Caesarea Philippi and there is no mention of a return to Nazareth in the interim, Mount Hermon seems the more likely location.

2 In Greek X (Chi) and P (Rho) are the first two letters for the word 'Christos' (ΧΡΙΣΤΟΣ), meaning Christ. Superimposed one on the other they give the chi-rho monogram (℞), a shorthand for 'Christos'. Constantine the Great is said to have either seen or dreamt of this symbol appearing in the noonday sky along with the legend 'By this conquer' shortly before the Battle of Milvian Bridge.

3 The division was actually slightly more complicated than that, for the tribe of Levi was elevated to become a priestly caste, their land rights passing to Ephraim and Mannasseh, the sons of Joseph, who thereby received a double portion.

4 The black, Ethiopian Jews or Falashas claim to be descended from the lost tribes and have already, in recent years, been resettled in Israel.

CHAPTER 2

1 If he was born, as I believe, on 29 July, 7 BC and baptized by John on 6 January AD 26, he would have been thirty-one at the time. This is because there is no year AD 0 – the calendar goes straight from 1 BC to AD 1 – and his last birthday before his baptism, his thirty-first, would have been 29 July AD 25.

2 Quoted in Mead, *Thrice Greatest Hermes*, vol. 1, p. 142. Mead has much to say about Philo in this interesting work.

3 Ibid., pp. 142–3.

4 By Gymnosophists Philo clearly means practitioners of yoga.

5 Mead, *Thrice Greatest Hermes*, vol. 1, pp. 143–4.

6 Ibid.

7 Details of these comparisons can be found in Mead, *Thrice Greatest Hermes*, vol. 1, see e.g. pp. 145–58.

CHAPTER 3

1 Extracted from *The Great Pyramid*, documentary first shown in the UK on BBC2 Television in February 1994.

2 Ibid.

3 Ouspensky, *A New Model of the Universe*, pp. 360–1.

4 Mead, *Thrice Greatest Hermes*, vol. 3, pp. 148–9.

5 Ibid., p. 74.

6 There is also a Serbian Book of Enoch, which is an entirely different work.

7 Imhotep or Imuthes was called Asclepius by the Greeks. In the *Corpus Hermeticum* Asclepius is presented as one of the students of Hermes Trismegistus.

8 The length of Noah's Ark is given as 300 cubits, its breadth as 50 cubits and its height as 30 cubits (Gen. 6: 15). It was therefore a narrow, coffin-like box, one-sixth as broad as it was long and only a tenth as high. The dimensions of the Ark of the Covenant were to be two and a half cubits in length, one and a half in breadth and

one and a half in height (Exod. 25: 10). Ezekiel is given a reed of six cubits in length by means of which he is to measure various dimensions of the temple, its porches and gates (Ezek. 40–2). In the Book of Revelation the Holy City, the New Jerusalem, lies four-square, with its length equal to its breadth and a wall of 144 cubits (Rev. 21).

9 The Egyptians also employed a common cubit of 18 of their inches or 6 'hands', a 'hand' being equal to 3 Egyptian inches. The royal cubit was therefore longer than this ordinary cubit by one hand.

10 For this reason the US dollar bill still carries a picture of a Hermetic symbol: a truncated pyramid surmounted by the all-seeing eye of God.

11 Scott (trans.), *Hermetica*, p. 195.

CHAPTER 4

1 This is considerably later than is generally believed by Egyptology, which gives a date of construction of around 2550 BC. Basing our assessment on the astronomical evidence of the air-shaft alignments, Robert Bauval and I gave a date of *c*.2450 BC in *The Orion Mystery.*

2 Piazzi-Smyth, *The Great Pyramid*, p. 38.

3 Formerly Reader in the History of the Renaissance at the University of London, Fellow of the British Academy, Fellow of the Royal Society of Literature and Honorary Fellow of the Warburg Institute. Her books on the Renaissance and the Hermetic tradition, most especially *Giordano Bruno and the Hermetic Tradition*, are core works for anyone interested in this field. She died in 1981.

4 Intelligent spirits or angels, not the demons of Christian belief.

5 Scott (trans.), *Hermetica*, pp. 191–2.

6 Some accounts say 42 pieces, one for each of the *nomes* or counties of Egypt.

7 There are different versions of the *Book of the Dead*

dating from different periods of Egyptian history. The earliest version, a collection of spells and prayers dating from the Old Kingdom, is the so-called 'Pyramid Texts'. The 'Coffin Texts' date from the Middle Kingdom and are similar though with more elaboration. The illustrated papyrus versions of the *Book of the Dead* date from the New Kingdom. By the time they were written, the Egyptian religion had become baroque in the extreme, so that they are very much more complex in structure and content than the earlier Pyramid and Coffin Texts.

8 The word 'alchemy' is derived from Al-Chemia, Khem or Chem being the ancient name for Lower Egypt. Al-Chemia is literally the science of Egypt, where alchemy was widely practised. This alchemy though, as the Leiden Papyrus attests, was not necessarily the manufacture of gold from base metal; rather it was the practical chemistry of refining metals from their ores and blending copper or silver with gold in order to increase its bulk.

9 Scott (trans.), *Hermetica*, p. 136.

10 Ibid., pp. 105–6.

11 The Pyramid Texts, which are inscribed in some of the later pyramids of the Fifth and Sixth Dynasties, are the oldest known corpus of religious writings in the world. Written in hieroglyphs, they are collections of prayers, hymns and spells relating to the religious rituals performed on behalf of the dead pharaoh and his successor.

12 Mead, *Thrice Greatest Hermes*, pp. 139–41.

CHAPTER 5

1 The Pyramid Texts are numbered according to 'Utterances' and subdivided by verses. They were first grouped in this way in the German translation published by Sethe in 1910. He numbered the 'Spruche', a word translated as 'Utterances'. This way of dividing up the Pyramid Texts has been retained by later translators such as Faulkner. Each Utterance makes up a complete prayer,

hymn or other discrete recitation.

2 Mead, *Thrice Greatest Hermes*, vol. 3, p. 97.

3 Ibid., vol.1, p. 49.

4 Both Rostau and the Memphite necropolis were linked with the mysterious god Sokar (after whom is named Saqqara in all its spellings).

5 Edwards, *The Pyramids of Egypt*, p. 10.

6 Neugebauer and Parker, *Egyptian Astronomical Tests*, vol. 1, pp. 24–5.

7 This discovery was made by an American astronomer, now a professor at Maryland University, Victoria Trimble.

8 Unfortunately, whatever the merits of the scheme in theory, as the fan is generally left switched off by those in charge, the pyramid remains as humid as ever.

9 Schwaller de Lubicz, a writer from the 1930s who had a substantial influence on West's ideas.

10 This, the oldest saga in the world, comes from Sumeria. Its many versions have been found written on clay tablets by archaeologists in Mesopotamia and Assyria. It includes the story of Utnapishtim, who, like the Noah of the Bible, is instructed by a god (Ea) to make an ark so that he and his family may escape the consequences of a flood that is to be sent by the other gods to destroy mankind.

CHAPTER 6

1 Ouspensky, *In Search of the Miraculous*, p. 302.

2 As the reasons for thinking this are fully documented in my book *Magi*, I refer the reader to this work for more detail concerning this story.

3 'Diophysitism' means believing in the dual nature of Jesus Christ as a man who became imbued with the spirit of God, as opposed to 'monophysitism', a belief in the singular nature of Jesus as Son of God 'one in substance with the Father'.

4 The Nestorian church owed its foundation to

Nestorius, who became patriarch of Constantinople in AD 428. He was later deposed and banished to Upper Egypt where he died.

5 Throughout the Near East high places, especially those with archaic ruins, are often associated with Nimrod. He is the biblical son of Cush, great-grandson of Noah, who is listed in Genesis (10: 8–14) as founder of many cities in Assyria and Mesopotamia, including Babylon, Erech, Nineveh and Calah. He is also described as 'the first on earth to be a mighty man. He was a mighty hunter before the Lord.'

6 De Santillana and von Dechend, *Hamlet's Mill*.

7 On the site where the School of the Persians had once stood the Edessans later built the church, one tower of which still stands. It is tempting to think that this might have been such a watch tower, though it isn't exactly on the north–south axis between the pillars.

8 Segal, *Edessa*, p. 57.

CHAPTER 7

1 The ecliptic is the path travelled by the sun through the zodiac. In one year the sun makes a complete cycle of the ecliptic.

2 See Bauval and Gilbert, *The Orion Mystery*, for more details concerning this aspect of Egyptian astrology.

3 J. G. Bennett, one of Gurdjieff's students and whom I met in the 1970s, writes that the word 'Sarmoun' or 'Sarman' appears in some Pahlawi or Persian texts to designate those who preserved the doctrines of Zoroaster. See Bennett, *Gurdjieff: Making a New World*, pp. 56–7.

4 This discovery formed the main focus of the book *Magi*, which I completed on returning home from Commagene.

CHAPTER 8

1 In other versions of the myth, this egg was laid not by a goose but an ibis: the bird sacred to Thoth/Hermes. The city of Wnw in Upper Egypt was the most important cult centre of Thoth, i.e. Hermes Trismegistus. It was renamed Hermopolis by the Greeks after they took control of Egypt in 331 BC.

2 This axis mysteriously changes direction by a few degrees half-way along its route.

3 According to E. A. Wallis Budge, a former Keeper of Egyptian antiquities at the British Museum and a prolific writer, one (the obelisk now in Paris) was roughly 75 feet high and weighed 222 tons. The other (that which remains at Luxor) was larger, 82 feet in height and 253.5 tons in weight.

4 Budge, *Cleopatra's Needles*, p. 200.

5 The top part of its companion, which has long since fallen down and broken, is now a curious tourist attraction. As we saw there, guides demonstrate the sonic properties of granite by striking the stone with their fists and inviting tourists to listen to the resonant tones it emits. For this reason if for no other, it is believed by some esotericists that the main purpose of the obelisks was to act as some sort of sound transmitters; that the rays of the sun would cause the stone to vibrate and thereby emit sound waves of a particular frequency. Whether or not this is true, there is nothing in the inscriptions on the standing obelisk of Queen Hatshepsut to either affirm or deny it.

6 Budge, *Cleopatra's Needles,* p. 103.

7 Some Egyptologists attribute this obelisk to his grandson, Tuthmosis III. Certainly the latter had his name carved upon it, but this may have been appropriation on his part.

8 Budge, *Cleopatra's Needles*, p. 95.

9 Ibid.

10 Ibid., p. 92.

11 According to other accounts the event took place every 1,461 years or on an even longer cycle.

12 The tip of an obelisk is called a *benben't*: the extra 't' makes it of the feminine gender, which is strange given the obviously masculine nature of obelisks.

13 Budge, *Cleopatra's Needles*, pp. 81–2.

14 Because of precession the date had shifted by one day from 28 to 29 July.

15 Faulkner (trans.), *The Ancient Egyptian Pyramid Texts*, p. 246.

16 Rundle Clark, *Myth and Symbol in Ancient Egypt*, p. 37.

17 By the time of the New Kingdom (*c*.1670 BC) the spring equinox was in the sign of Aries, the ram. This seems to be why the Temple of Karnac features ram-headed sphinxes and also why during the New Kingdom the ram-headed god Khnum grew in importance.

18 As the sun itself occupies an angle in the sky of roughly half a degree, the small variation of 6' of arc between the exact 30° line of latitude and the actual latitude of Heliopolis is within allowable limits of observation.

19 The triple-six or 666, given as the 'Number of the Beast' in the Book of Revelation, is also solar in character and symbolizes authoritarianism. For an interesting analysis of the meaning behind this and other numbers the reader is referred to John Michell's *City of Revelation* (now called *Dimensions of Paradise*).

CHAPTER 9

1 Sokar of Rostau is a very ancient god associated with Memphis. The name Saqqara for the Memphite necropolis is derived from Sokar.

2 Scott (trans.), *Hermetica*, p. 191.

3 Alan H. Gardiner, 'The Secret Chambers of the Sanctuary of Thoth', *Journal of Egyptian Antiquities*,

vol. 11, 1925.

4 Bauval and Gilbert, *The Orion Mystery*, p. 252.

5 Edwards, *The Pyramids of Egypt*, p. 282.

6 Faulkner (trans.), *The Ancient Egyptian Coffin Texts*, vol. 3, spell 992.

7 Rundle Clark, *Myth and Symbol in Ancient Egypt*, p. 96

8 Budge, *The Egyptian Book of the Dead*, p. cvii.

9 As the subject of Sothic cycles and Egyptian chronology goes well outside the subject matter of this book, the reader is referred to *Centuries of Darkness* by Peter James et al., Jonathan Cape, London, pp. 225–8; *A Test of Time* by David Rohl, pp. 128–31; and the now classic but still highly controversial *Ages in Chaos* by Immanuel Velikowsky, pp. 70–1. Primarily these books provide a critique of the way Sothic cycles have been misused by Egyptology to shore up an extremely suspect system of datings but they also explain in detail how the Sothic calendar is thought to have worked.

CHAPTER 10

1 'Rudolf Gantenbrink on the Great Pyramid', *Quest for Knowledge*, no. 10; Chester, 1998.

2 It can easily be calculated that the perimeter of the circle being roughly $2 \times 280 \times 22/7$ cubits it equals 4×440 cubits.

3 Lehner, *The Complete Pyramids*.

4 Rundle Clark, *Myth and Symbol in Ancient Egypt*, p. 57.

5 This statue is only one of twenty-three similar ones which have been found, the others having been more severely damaged. It was found by Mariette in the vestibule of the Valley Temple associated with the Khafre Pyramid.

CHAPTER 11

1 *Symbol and the Symbolic*, first published in French in 1949 as *Symbol et Symbolique*, has been translated into English by Robert and Deborah Lawlor. It is a good introduction to his work.
2 Scott (trans.), *Hermetica*, pp. 135–6.
3 Breasted, *Ancient Records of Egypt*, part II, pp. 320–4.
4 In *Keeper of Genesis* Bauval and Hancock give several quotes from eminent Egyptologists to this effect; interested readers are therefore directed to that work.
5 This was the subject of a lecture given by the young Egyptologist Bassam El Shammaa at the 'Gizagate' debate held in London in March 1998.
6 See Budge, *The Egyptian Book of the Dead*, p. cxii.

CHAPTER 12

1 How I arrived at these figures is explained in my book *Magi*, p. 94.

CHAPTER 13

1 Robert Temple, *The Sirius Mystery*.
2 While in northern Mesopotamia researching *Magi*, I was shown a small statue which I take to have been an ancient votive lamp. This was shaped like a crescent moon and cleverly modelled in such a way that one end was the bearded head of a man, the middle part consisted of branches with leaves, and the 'tail' end consisted of the head of a fish. At the time I thought this curious sculpture represented the moon god, Sin, but in retrospect I now think it may have been symbolic of the Annedotus Oannes.
3 Laurence (trans.), *Book of Enoch*, VIII: 1–2.
4 Ibid., IX: 4–11.
5 An area of the Negev just south and east of the Dead Sea, near to the antediluvian city of Sodom.

6 Lawrence (trans.), *Book of Enoch*, X: 1–12.

CHAPTER 14

1 Lethaby, *Architecture, Mysticism and Myth*, pp. 77–8.

2 Ibid., pp. 79–80.

3 For a fuller account of this story see Gilbert, *Magi*, pp. 210–12.

4 Halman and And, *Mevlana Celaleddin Rumi and the Whirling Dervishes*.

5 Boyce, *Zoroastrians*.

6 Drummond was a prominent politician as well as a first-rate scholar of ancient languages including Hebrew, Sanskrit, Greek and Latin. His priceless book *Oedipus Judaicus*, originally published privately for the benefit of his friends and subtitled 'Allegory in the Old Testament', presents a profound analysis of the astronomical and astrological ideas underpinning the Book of Genesis.

7 *Praeparatio Evangelica*, book 4, ch. 16.

8 Drummond, *Oedipus Judaicus*, p. 4.

9 Greene, *Saturn: A New Look at an Old Devil*.

10 It may be of interest that the Sidonians called the mountain Sirion, a possible connection with the star Sirius from where, according to Robert Temple in his *The Sirius Mystery*, a strange race of extra-terrestrials descended on to the earth.

11 This is not the place to go into such debates but the interested reader is referred to the works of G. R. S. Mead, especially his *Fragments of a Faith Forgotten*.

12 Plate 16 in Bauval and Gilbert, *The Orion Mystery*.

13 I now realize that what had misled us were the depictions of Sahu/Orion on the *benben* of Amenemhet III and on the ceiling of Seti I, which are in fact reversed. The way Orion is shown in these pictures represents how he would look if you were to stand outside the celestial sphere and look down upon it. It is a 'God's-eye' view of Orion, as he appears on a celestial globe. However, standing on the earth, theoretically at the centre of the

celestial sphere, and looking up at the night sky, this is not what we see. For us everything is the other way round, and we see Orion holding a staff in his left hand and raising his right towards the ecliptic. It is this hand which either holds an *ankh* or cups a star.

14 Budge, *The Egyptian Book of the Dead*, p. 219.

CHAPTER 15

1 This was the interlinear Greek–English translation of the New Testament, translated by Reverend Dr Alfred Marshall and published by Samuel Bagster & Sons in 1958 (repr. 1975). It uses the Nestle Greek text, which was compiled from a number of different sources and is believed to be as near as possible to the original documents. All future Greek references in the present work are drawn from this edition.

2 Lethaby, *Architecture, Mysticism and Myth*, pp. 146–7.

3 Anon., *Sepher Yetzirah*.

4 Lethaby, *Architecture Mysticism and Myth*, pp. 101–2.

5 Williamson (trans.), Josephus, *The Jewish War*. Josephus is describing the sanctuary of Herod's Temple, which was built long after the Ark of the Covenant had disappeared. In Solomon's Temple the Holy of Holies was not empty as it contained the Ark.

6 Within the ancient scheme of things, the sun and moon counted as planets, called 'wanderers' as they moved through the zodiac.

7 Halevi, *Adam and the Kabbalistic Tree*, pp. 17–18.

8 This doctrine is also clearly related to the esoteric meaning behind Jesus' parable of the talents in Matthew 25.

9 The highest sphere or Sephirah, above the planets and even the fixed stars of the zodiac.

10 Man's 'brother' is the demiurgic intelligence, or 'Solar Logos', deemed responsible for creating the solar system. Its creations, admired by man, are the sun itself and the planetary system.

11 Scott (trans.), *Hermetica*, pp. 49–50.

12 Ibid., pp. 52–3.

13 The ancients did not know about the outer planets of our solar system – Uranus, Neptune and Pluto – which cannot be seen with the naked eye and whose orbits are beyond that of Saturn.

14 Budge, *The Egyptian Book of the Dead*, pp. lx–lxi.

15 Drummond, *Oedipus Judaicus*, p. 4.

CHAPTER 16

1 The Golden Gate is the eastern entrance to the Temple Mount or Haram ash-Sharif. By Christian tradition this is the gate through which Jesus entered Jerusalem on Palm Sunday. It is also, according to Jewish tradition, the point of entry that will be used by the Messiah when he comes to judge humankind at the end of the age. It was sealed up in the seventh century to stop non-Muslims from entering the precincts of the Haram; some say this was also done to make sure that the Jewish prophecy concerning the Messiah would not be fulfilled.

2 *Encyclopaedia Britannica*, vol. 3, p. 527.

3 This chronology is not universally acknowledged. Mark's Gospel implies a ministry of at least two years, and this is backed up by John's Gospel. Luke's Gospel, however, could be fitted into a briefer ministry of a single year. Careful examination of evidence from other sources, e.g. the dates for the governorship of Pontius Pilate and for Caiaphas' tenure as high priest, point towards AD 29 as the most likely year for the Crucifixion.

CHAPTER 17

1 Bennett, *Intimations*.

2 Robin Cook, 'The Giza Pyramids: A Design Study', 1988, p. 5–9.

3 The heliacal rising of a star is when it makes its first appearance at dawn after a period of invisibility. For

further details see Bauval and Gilbert, *The Orion Mystery*.
4 Baldock, *The Elements of Christian Symbolism*, p. 69.

CHAPTER 18

1 This Antiochus is not to be confused with Antiochus I Epiphanes of Commagene. It is now generally believed that the Book of Daniel was not written during the Babylonian captivity but rather centuries later – after the reign of Antiochus IV of Syria, during the era of the Maccabees.
2 The Bible teaches that this son was Isaac, but Muslims believe him to have been Ishmael, Abraham's elder son by his Egyptian bondwoman, Hagar. According to the Bible, Ishmael and his mother were cast out into the desert. Ishmael subsequently married an Egyptian and is regarded as the patriarch of the Arab nation.
3 Lethaby, *Architecture, Mysticism and Myth*, p. 80.

EPILOGUE

1 Rundle Clark, *Myth and Symbol in Ancient Egypt*, p.37.
2 Lethaby, *Architecture, Mysticism and Myth*, p. 149.
3 Ezekiel 8:16.

BIBLIOGRAPHY

Anon, *Sepher Yetzirah*, New York, L. H. Frank & Co., 1877.

Baldock, J., *The Elements of Christian Symbolism*, Shaftesbury, Element Books, 1990.

Bauval, R. and Gilbert, A. G., *The Orion Mystery*, London, Heinemann, 1994.

Bauval, R. and Hancock, G., *Keeper of Genesis*, London, Heinemann, 1996.

Bennett, J. G., *Gurdjieff: Making a New World*, London, Turnstone, 1973.

Bennett, J. G., *Intimations*, Aldsworth, Beshara, 1975.

Bligh Bond, F. and Lea, T. S., *Gematria: A Preliminary Investigation of the Cabala*, London, Research into Lost Knowledge Organization, 1977.

Boyce, Mary, *Zoroastrians*, London, Routledge & Kegan Paul, 1987.

Breasted, J. H., *Ancient Records of Egypt*, London, Histories and Mysteries of Man, 1988.

Budge, E. A. Wallis, *Cleopatra's Needles and other Egyptian Obelisks*, New York, Dover, 1990.

Budge, E. A. Wallis, *The Egyptian Book of the Dead*, New York, Dover, 1967.

Campbell, J., *The Masks of God: Occidental Mythology*, London, Souvenir Press, 1964.

Cook, R. J., *The Pyramids of Giza*, Glastonbury, Seven Islands, 1992.

de Lubicz, S., *Symbol and the Symbolic* (trans. Robert and Deborah Lawlor), Brookline, Mass., Autumn Press, 1978. (First publ. as *Symbol et Symbolique*, 1949.)

de Santillana, G. and von Dechend, H., *Hamlet's Mill*, Boston, Gambit Inc., 1969.

Drummond, William, *Oedipus Judaicus*, London, Bracken Books, 1996.

Edwards, I. E. S., *The Pyramids of Egypt*, London, Penguin, 1992 (first publ. 1947).

Faulkner, R. O. (trans.), *The Ancient Egyptian Coffin Texts*, 3 vols, Warminster, Aris & Phillips, 1996.

Faulkner, R. O. (trans.), *The Ancient Egyptian Pyramid Texts*, London, Oxford University Press, 1969.

Gardner, J. and Maier, J., *Gilgamesh*, New York, Random House, 1984.

Ghyka, M., *Geometrical Composition and Design*, London, Alec Tiranti, 1956.

Gilbert, A., *Magi: The Quest for a Secret Tradition*, London, Bloomsbury, 1996.

Greene, Liz, *Saturn: A New Look at an Old Devil*, York Beach, ME, Samuel Weiser, 1976.

Gurdjieff, G. I., *Meetings with Remarkable Men*, London, Picador, 1978.

Halevi, Z'ev ben S., *A Kabbalisic Universe*, London, Rider & Co., 1977.

Halevi, Z'ev ben S., *Adam and the Kabbalistic Tree*, London, Rider & Co., 1974.

Halevi, Z'ev ben S., *Tree of Life*, London, Rider & Co., 1972.

Halman, T. S. and And, M., *Mevlana Celaleddin Rumi and the Whirling Dervishes*, Istanbul, Dost, 1983.

Hone, W. (trans.), *The Lost Books of the Bible*, New York, Gramercy Books, 1979.

Iversen, E., *Canon and Proportions in Egyptian Art*, Warminster, Aris & Phillips, 1975.

Kingsland, W., *The Gnosis in the Christian Scriptures*, Shaftesbury, Solos Press, 1993.

Krupp, E. C., *Echoes of the Ancient Skies*, Oxford, Oxford University Press, 1983.

Laurence, R. (trans.), *Book of Enoch*, Kegan Paul, Trench & Co., 1883 (facs. repr. San Diego, Wizards Bookshelf, 1983).

Lehner, M., *The Complete Pyramids*, London, Thames & Hudson, 1997.

Lemesurier, P., *The Great Pyramid Decoded*, Shaftesbury, Element Books, 1977.

Lethaby, W., *Architecture, Mysticism and Myth*, Shaftesbury, Solos Press, 1993.

Mead, G. R. S., *Fragments of a Faith Forgotten*, New York, University Books, 1960.

Mead, G. R. S., *Thrice Greatest Hermes*, 3 vols, London, John M. Watkins, 1964.

Michell J., *City of Revelation*, London, Garnstone Press, 1972; repub. as *Dimensions of Paradise*, London, Thames & Hudson.

Mills, H. R., *Positional Astronomy and Astro-Navigation Made Easy*, Cheltenham, Stanley Thornes, 1978.

Neugebauer, O. and Parker, R., *Egyptian Astronomical Tests*, 3 vols, London, Brown University Press/Lund Humphries, 1964.

Nicoll, M., *The New Man*, London, Robinson & Watkins, 1972.

Ouspensky, P. D., *A New Model of the Universe*, 3rd edn, London, Routledge & Kegan Paul, 1967.

Ouspensky, P. D., *In Search of the Miraculous*, London, Routledge & Kegan Paul, 1950.

Pennick, N., *Sacred Geometry*, London, Turnstone Press, 1980.

Piazzi-Smyth, C., *The Great Pyramid*, New York, Gramercy Books, 1978.

Rundle Clark, R. T., *Myth and Symbol in Ancient Egypt*, London, Thames & Hudson, 1978.

Scott, W. (trans.), *Hermetica*, Shaftesbury, Solos Press, 1992.

Segal, J. B., *Edessa: 'The Blessed City'*, Oxford, Clarendon Press, 1970.

Stahl, W. H. (trans.), *Commentary on the Dream of Scipio by Macrobius*, New York, Columbia University Press, 1990.

Stirling, W., *The Canon: An Exposition of the Pagan Mystery Perpetuated in the Cabala as the Rule of all the Arts*, London, Garnstone Press, 1974.

Temple, Robert, *The Sirius Mystery*, London, Sidgwick & Jackson, 1978.

Thurston, H., *Early Astronomy*, New York, Springer, 1994.

Tompkins, P., *Secrets of the Great Pyramid*, London, Penguin, 1973.

Ulansey, D., *The Origins of the Mithraic Mysteries*, Oxford, Oxford University Press, 1991.

Velikowsky, I., *Ages in Chaos,* London, Sidgwick & Jackson, 1953.

Williamson G. A. (trans.), Josephus, *The Jewish War*, London,

Penguin, 1969.

Yates, F. A., *Giordano Bruno and the Hermetic Tradition*, London, Routledge & Kegan Paul, 1964.

Yates, F. A., *The Occult Philosophy*, London, Routledge & Kegan Paul, 1979.

Yates, F. A., *The Rosicrucian Enlightenment*, London, Routledge & Kegan Paul, 1972.

Young, R., *Analytical Concordance to the Bible*, Guildford, Lutterworth, 1975.

INDEX

Note: this index covers pages 1–402. Page numbers in italics refer to illustrations or diagrams.

441

443

451

THE HOLY KINGDOM
by Adrian Gilbert
Alan Wilson and Baram Blackett

In this explosive book the authors, using ancient historical records, show that Britain was never fully conquered by the Romans but retained its culture, its royal families intermarrying with the Caesars. With the coming of Joseph of Arimathea in AD 37, its kings became converts to Christianity and the island the secret home of many of Jesus's followers.

Two of those kings were named Arthur – one, Arthur I of Warwickshire, the fourth-century son of the emperor Magnus Maximus, the other his sixth-century descendant and a king of Glamorgan – their careers rolled into one and elaborated upon by the medieval poets, they became the single King Arthur of myth and legend.

As a result of research going back over forty years, the authors are able to reveal the location of the graves of both Arthurs, the location of Camelot, the burial place of the 'true cross of Christ' and uncover a secret historical current that links our own times with the mysteries of Arthur and the Holy Grail. In doing so, they challenge many orthodox beliefs perpetuated by a Church which long ago lost touch with its roots.

0 552 14489 4

THE DEAD SEA SCROLLS DECEPTION
by Michael Baigent and Richard Leigh

The sensational story behind the religious scandal of the century.

The Dead Sea Scrolls were found in caves 20 miles east of Jerusalem in 1947 and 1956. Now Michael Baigent and Richard Leigh, co-authors of *The Holy Blood and The Holy Grail*, have succeeded in uncovering what has been described as 'the academic scandal par excellence of the twentieth century': the story of how and why up to 75 per cent of the eight hundred ancient Hebrew and Aramaic manuscripts, hidden for some nineteen centuries, have, until very recently, remained concealed from the world.

Through interviews, historical analysis and a close study of both published and unpublished scroll material, the authors are able to reveal the true cause of the bitter struggle between scholars, for these documents disclose nothing less than a new account of the origins of Christianity and an alternative and highly significant version of much of the New Testament.

'A sensational story . . . this scandal has gone on far too long'
The Times

'It is enough to make anyone curious about the early days of Christianity weep with frustration'
Mail on Sunday

'If it succeeds in advancing the publication of material from Qumran, it will have achieved genuine good'
The Times Literary Supplement

0 552 13878 9

TURIN SHROUD: IN WHOSE IMAGE?
How Leonardo da Vinci fooled history
by Lynn Picknett and Clive Prince

FULLY REVISED AND UPDATED

In 1988, carbon dating of the world's most famous Christian relic revealed that it was a medieval or Renaissance forgery. Therefore it could not be Christ's burial cloth, miraculously imprinted with his image, as millions believed.

Yet many questions remained. How could a hoaxer of 500 or more years ago have created an image that appears so astonishingly lifelike when seen in photographic negative? How was such an inexplicable image formed? Who was the genius behind it? And who would have dared to fake the Holy Shroud of Jesus?

Setting out to answer these questions, Lynn Picknett and Clive Prince discovered that the faker was none other than Leonardo da Vinci, the Renaissance artist, scientist, inventor – and hoaxer – whose innovations are acknowledged to have been centuries ahead of his time. They also reconstructed Leonardo's secret technique – becoming the first ever to recreate the Shroud image.

Turin Shroud – In Whose Image? also uncovers the dark secret that lay behind Leonardo's great fake, and asks: is the face of the man on the Shroud not that of Jesus at all?

'Astonishing, gruesome, shocking, and sensational . . . An impressively argued book'
Washington Times

0 552 14782 6

A SELECTED LIST OF NON-FICTION TITLES AVAILABLE FROM CORGI AND BLACK SWAN

13878 9	THE DEAD SEA SCROLLS DECEPTION	Michael Baigent &Richard Leigh	£6.99
14750 8	BLACK HAWK DOWN	Mark Bowden	£5.99
14493 2	THE JIGSAW MAN	Paul Britton	£6.99
09828 0	THE PROPHECIES OF NOSTRADAMUS	Erika Cheetham	£5.99
14465 7	CLOSE QUARTER BATTLE	Mike Curtis	£5.99
13582 8	THE GOD SQUAD	Paddy Doyle Farmaian	£7.99
99482 0	MILLENNIUM	Felipe Fernández-Armesto	£14.99
14489 4	THE HOLY KINGDOM	Adrian Gilbert, Alan Wilson, Baram Blackett	£6.99
99545 2	ISRAEL: A HISTORY	Martin Gilbert	£14.99
12555 5	IN SEARCH OF SCHRÖDINGER'S CAT	John Gribbin	£7.99
14760 5	THE CUSTOM OF THE SEA	Neil Hanson	£5.99
14288 3	BRIDGE ACROSS MY SORROWS	Christina Noble	£5.99
14607 2	THE INFORMER	Sean O'Callaghan	£6.99
14330 8	THE TEMPLAR REVELATION	Lynn Picknett & Clive Prince	£6.99
14782 6	TURIN SHROUD	Lynn Picknett & Clive Prince	£6.99
14550 5	PURPLE SECRET	John Röhl, Martin Warren, David Hunt	£7.99
14709 5	THE YAMATO DYNASTY	Sterling and Peggy Seagrave	£7.99
13950 5	JESUS THE MAN	Barbara Thiering	£7.99
14665 X	THE BOOK THAT JESUS WROTE	Barbara Thiering	£6.99
13288 8	IN GOD'S NAME	David Yallop	£6.99